Victorian Delights

Robert Wood

Robert Wood

Evans Brothers Limited, London.

Designed by Brian Denyer ARCA MSIA

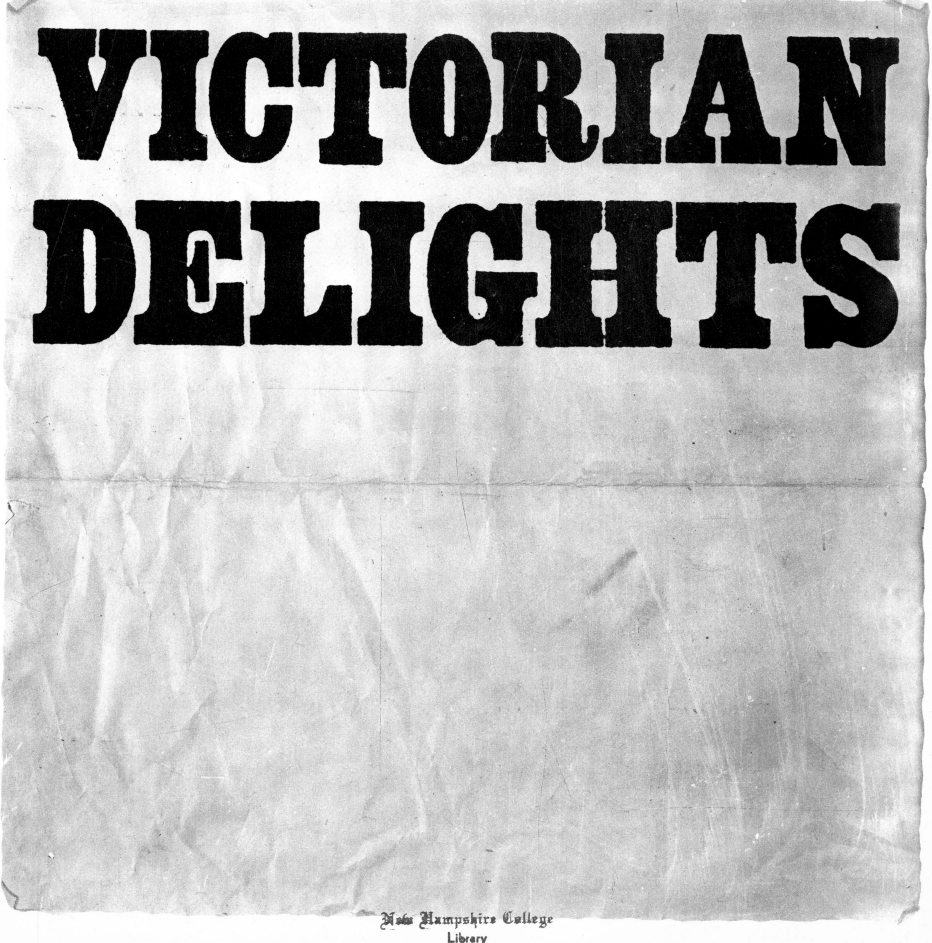

VICTORIAN DELIGHTS

TAKE NOTICE ALL,

THAT NOVELTY IS
NOW THE GO,
THE ORDER AND, THE
FASHION!

WHERE'ER YOU GO,
SO MERRILY
YOU DASH ON!!!

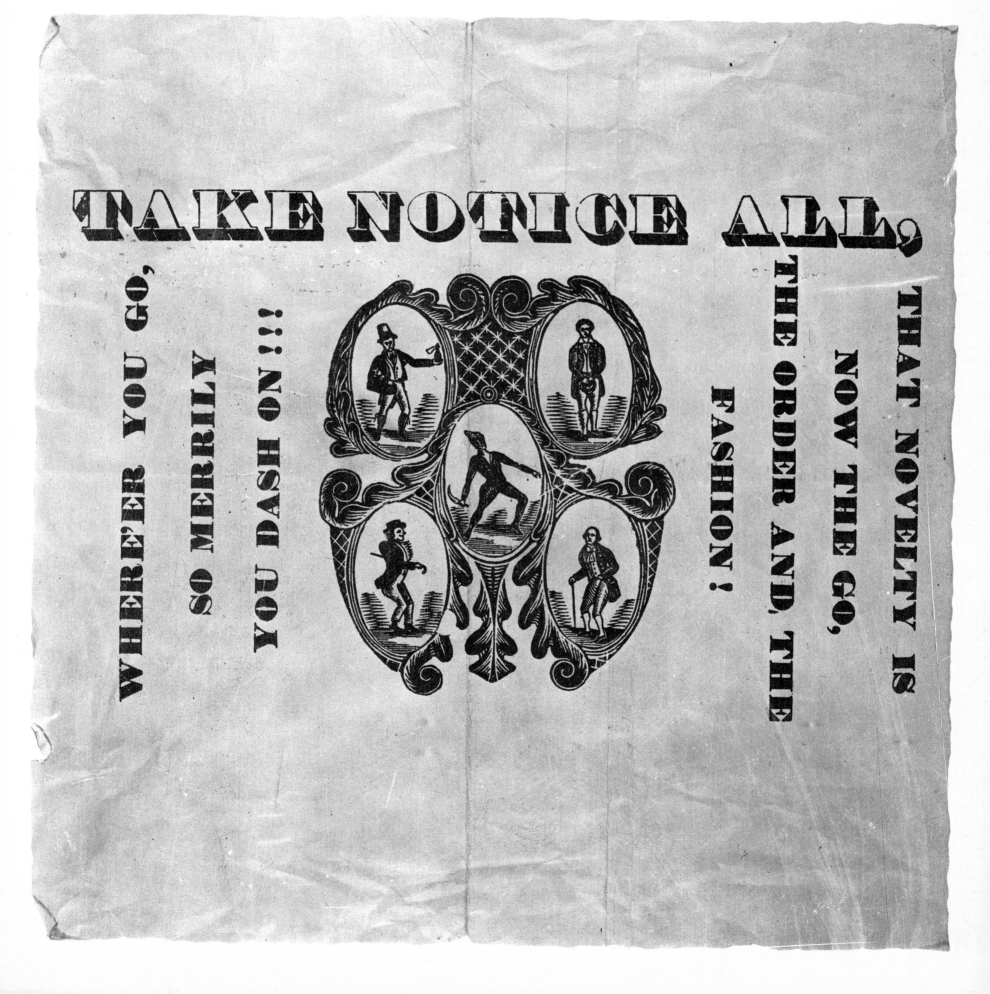

Introduction

The word Victorian implies a way of life very different from our own. But unfortunately it also seduces us into believing that everything and everybody within that period was much the same.

To many the Victorians appear as industrious and rather unimaginative people who built ugly factories and uglier civic buildings, churches and chapels, and worshipped wealth and respectability. Their factory workers, building workers and others of similar status were crowded in slums of indescribable squalor, and their paupers existed miserably in workhouses amid upper classes who employed their spare time in doing 'good works' and 'improving' themselves. On Sundays they went to their places of worship to sing with all sincerity

'The rich man in his castle,
The poor man at his gate,
God made them, high and lowly,
And ordered their estate.'

Probably the most appropriate way of thinking afresh about this period is to consider whether this general opinion applies to those living in 1837 or those in 1901, for they were all Victorians.

A few moments thought will make most of us realise that our picture of the period is largely made up from impressions of the end of the longest reign in British history, and that our knowledge of its beginnings is rather vague.

Although the England of the young Princess Victoria may appear stifling and squalid, to those of its inhabitants moving from village to town and from one part of the country to another in order to secure a higher standard of living, it was a land of promise.

Prior to the Poor Law Amendment Act of 1834, any ambitious worker travelling around in search of higher wages had the constant threat of the Law of Settlement hanging over his head. The constables of the parish in which he was temporarily out of work were permitted by such legislation to remove him to his parish of origin to prevent him becoming chargeable to the local Poor Law authorities. After 1834, if he had the money or the energy to travel, he was free to move as he pleased. In 1843 2,000 miles of railway track were operational and used annually by some 23,000,000 passengers. By 1850 there were 6,621 miles of track carrying 73,000,000 passengers a year. Since a typical journey of fifty miles cost only 6 shillings third class a man, and his family, could move cheaply wherever his work took him.

The old order had changed completely. In 1790 there had been two labourers working in villages for each unskilled worker in the towns, yet by 1840 the situation had reversed for there were two town labourers for each farm-hand left in the villages.

The period from 1832 to 1850 was one of very rapid capitalist expansion. British exports increased in value from £36,000,000 to £71,000,000; shipping increased by 50 per cent, as did the number of seamen employed. The production of pig-iron was trebled and the output of coal more than doubled. Twice as much cotton was used and the revenue obtained for the goods manufactured from cotton increased by 50 per cent. The number of hands employed in British textile mills rose from 340,000 in 1835 to 570,000 in 1850.

In the twenty years between 1831 and 1851 the population of Great Britain increased from 16,261,000 to 20,816,000. Of these, about half a million were Irish who fled to Britain between 1841 and 1851 to escape the great Potato Famine.

The populations of our industrial towns increased at astonishing rates. For instance, in 1801 Manchester had 90,000 inhabitants; in 1831, 231,000; and in 1851, 400,000. The equivalent figures for Leeds were 53,000, 123,000, and 172,000. Sheffield showed similar increases from 46,000 to 92,000 and then to 135,000, and Oldham's population rose from 23,000 to 51,000 and then to 72,000.

The great majority of these newcomers had been born and bred in agricultural communities and inevitably they brought with them into the towns their rural way of life. Such people could not be expected to understand that habits which were harmless, or even commendable in a rural environment, were not merely anti-social but positively dangerous in congested urban surroundings.

The manure heap outside the country cottage door was a source of wealth. Every countryman knew the old saying 'Where there's muck, there's money.' But the earth closet in the town street was a very real hazard unless emptied regularly. The pig rooting in the back-garden of the cottage provided a welcome addition to the menu, but that kept in the back-yard of back-to-back terraced houses in the town, as it frequently was, helped to spread cholera.

Little was done to guide or restrain the anti-social habits of these newcomers. Towns grew and spread without planning. There was little or no street cleaning, no proper water supply, and no drainage system. Sewage soaked into the soil and polluted the wells from which most of the families drew their water. This resulted in the re-appearance of contagious diseases, principally cholera and typhus, followed by hasty legislation designed to prevent and remedy the conditions in which they flourished. But much that had been done could not be undone. Many town authorities in their greed had sold, or otherwise disposed of, common land to provide more building sites, and the open spaces which had provided past generations with a place for recreation and enjoyment disappeared at the time when they had become most necessary to the town dweller.

It may seem strange that people should continue to flock to the towns to endure such conditions for the working classes cannot be said to have been attracted by remarkably high wages in which there was no material increase between 1830 and 1850. The hands in the cotton mills averaged about 10 shillings per week, the male weavers of Huddersfield received 20 shillings, and so did the carpenters of Newcastle.

However, in those days, before the spread of trades unions, the rates of pay throughout the country were far from uniform. A builder's labourer in Glasgow could expect to receive 12 shillings per week; a man in the same trade in London received 20 shillings. Scottish cotton workers were paid 7 shillings and 6 pence per week compared with 10 shillings in Lancashire. There was ample reason, therefore, for families to move around in search of higher earnings.

The new skills and occupations paid well. Those employed in engineering works, for instance, received 27 shillings and 6 pence per week and engine drivers from 24 shillings to 30 shillings. Plate layers earned from 18 shillings to 20 shillings a week.

But although the wages of the community as a whole did not increase this was amply compensated by a 17 per cent fall in the cost of living by 1850. Falling prices had substantially increased the purchasing power of the working man's wages so that compared with his parents he was better fed and clothed.

But the members of the industrial working classes were less fortunate in other respects. The sports and recreations of rural life were largely denied them. There were few open spaces available in the larger industrial towns and no one considered it desirable to provide them. Indeed, when the opportunity arose in Leeds, for instance, for the Town Council to acquire some Botanical Gardens which could be opened to the working classes on Sundays, it was bitterly opposed by the local newspapers. They stated

'it would be a wretched exchange to draw the poor of England out of their Churches, Chapels, Sunday-schools and quiet homes into public exhibitions and places of amusement on the Lord's Day.'

Leeds did not get its Botanical Gardens but its citizens were no worse off than those of Liverpool where all the public walks, cemeteries, and zoological and botanical gardens were closed on Sundays.

There had been little time in earlier days for recreation but the working hours of adults in textile factories had been progressively reduced since the passing of Lord Althorp's Factory Act of 1833, which set legal limits to the working hours of children and young persons. Various processes in the manufacture of textiles had been carried out by them, and when they stopped work it was virtually impossible for grown men to carry on alone.

When, in 1847, the Ten Hours Bill limited the daily work of women and youths in the textile factories to ten hours, it meant, in effect, a ten hour day for all the adult employees, too. Agitation by workers in other industries for a similar relaxation in the number of working hours led to this principle being extended by a series of Acts to other manufacturers also.

Living in crowded and uncomfortable surroundings with only a little leisure time and so few places in which to enjoy it, is there any wonder that most of the adult population thronged the few avenues of relaxation open to them? The bibulous crowded the public houses in the same way that the religious filled the churches and chapels. Although the Methodists were scarcely likely to be found in the theatres of the towns, they thronged the improving dioramas and educational exhibitions.

The Puritanical spirit still present among the evangelical clergy, and the snobbery of the squires and High Church Divines who thought that theatres were not suitable for the working classes, prevented the opening of proper theatres in the new towns.

Charles Dickens wrote:
'The narrow-minded fanatics who decry the theatre and defame its artists are absolutely the advocates of depraved and barbarous amusements. For, wherever a good drama and well regulated theatre decline, some distorted form of theatrical entertainment will inevitably arise in their place.'

Those with ambition attempted to better themselves by attending classes held in Mechanics Institutes, but these were not very successful, much to the surprise of the high-minded and well-meaning persons who had raised money for them and benevolently guided their destinies. The lack of enthusiasm was not due to apathy but to the working man's instinctive distrust of any institution governed and supported by patronage. There was remarkable eagerness to learn but successful societies for education and mutual improvement arose from below and were not imposed from above.

Men would congregate for discussions and teach each other. Those qualified and willing to come to lecture to them for a small fee were much in demand. One well-known in this field was Mr. Richardson, a self-educated teacher whose poster is to be found on page 00. By 1850 he had been travelling from one northern village to another as a peripatetic teacher for fifteen years.

It was said of his lectures that

'The toiling mining populations of Northumberland and Durham proceed over the hills in rain, sleet, and frost that they may learn the great truths that civilisation has made manifest.'

The Industrial Revolution which had involved the North of England and the Midlands in particular came late to Northumberland and Durham in the North-east. The canals and rivers of the North and Midlands had been the throbbing arteries of trade there but the hilly and rocky North-east was not suitable for this method of commercial exploitation. The net result was that the most developed coalfields of England had to wait for the railway age before they could be linked up with the rest of the country by routes other than road or sea.

Work started on the building of a railway to serve the coalfields of the North-east in 1823, and the first public railway in the world, the Stockton and Darlington Railway, was opened in 1825. The great demand for cheap coal which ensued led to the rapid utilisation of coal seams not yet exploited. Improved mining techniques and the development of superior machinery, especially more efficient pumps, made it possible for mines to be sunk successfully to the south-east of Durham City.

Shrewd business men, eager to participate in the profitable exportation of coal, founded the Hartlepool Dock and Railway Company with the object of reviving the long dead port of Hartlepool and excavating docks where ships could be loaded with coal brought down from the collieries by their railway.

There was similar development in many other regions of Britain and the associated growth of the railways already mentioned was one of the most striking and far-reaching effects of the continuing Industrial Revolution. The roads were appalling, and like the extensive canal system, grossly overloaded. The railways provided the much needed facilities for carrying goods from one part of the country to another, and by 1844 most major cities were linked. There were lines from London to Bristol, London to Birmingham and Liverpool to Manchester.

The construction of docks and railways required large numbers of labourers, for the docks had to be excavated and railway cuttings and embankments made. Little wonder that business should boom in such a productive atmosphere. Houses were built at an astonishing rate, new shops opened, and other commercial enterprises prospered.

The field of printing was no exception, and any enterprising printer in one of the new towns could expect to have a full order book.

During the reign of William IV a young man named John Procter had completed his seven year apprenticeship with Thomas Jennett, printer and bookseller, of Stockton on Tees. Within three years he had married and decided to set up in business on his own. At the age of twenty-four he opened his office in Hartlepool, County Durham, and on October 15th, 1834, paid a man 13 shillings to paint his sign,

---

'J. Procter, late assistant to Mr. Jennett, Stockton.
Printer, Bookbinder, Bookseller and Stationer.'

Six months after John Procter had settled in Hartlepool the first ships were being loaded in the revitalised docks, and from that time onwards he saw the town grow and prosper. At first business came his way because he had no rivals, but when other printers eventually came into the town he had established such a reputation for industry and good service that his pre-eminence was never disputed.

In addition to the usual notices that a provincial printer is expected to produce, he provided all the stationery, time-tables, and tickets for the Hartlepool Railway, and later, for the Stockton and Hartlepool Railway. Collieries needed coal certificates and rule-books, and shipping companies required documents of all kinds; John printed them all.

There was another aspect of his business which probably took up a greater proportion of his time than other more profitable undertakings. In this period of working-class emancipation, when men worked fewer hours than their fathers and enjoyed a higher standard of living, the railways made it much easier for itinerant performers to move around the country. The inhabitants of drab industrial towns welcomed the rich and varied assortment of entertainments these touring performers offered them.

Circuses and menageries, theatrical companies and bands of instrumentalists, the proprietors and managers of waxworks, dioramas and panoramas; all were eager to present themselves to the citizens, and John Procter did a great deal of their printing.

He was a most methodical man. He kept all his correspondence, and the survival of these tattered and grimy spike-files, some a hundred and thirty years old, enables us to fill in the background to those bills he printed which are of more general interest to us. A printer in a small town was a key-man in the cultural life of the community. When players and lecturers paid a visit he not only printed their bills but often acted as impresario, agent, and general factotum for the numerous people who wished to educate, entertain, or elevate the inhabitants for an evening or two.

A 'boom' town, with its unsettled, floating population of navvies and labourers with money burning a hole in their pockets, always attracted more than its fair share of entertainers, singers, and lecturers, and Hartlepool was visited by as diverse and picturesque a crew as ever stepped out of Dickens. Like Micawber, they were always optimistic about their future prospects, and inevitably 'circumstances beyond their control' made it necessary for many of them to leave the town owing money.

The singers and musicians very often cloaked themselves in a pretended gentility, and had to be carefully watched lest they vanished without paying their bills. Printers in other towns who had been deceived passed on friendly warnings to their colleagues. A message from Kendal dated Nov. 16th, 1850 runs:

Sir,
I beg to caution you against two fellows of the name of Childe and Walker who are travelling together with astronomical apparatus and dissolving views. They have left this town without paying for the room, advertising in the newspapers, etc. etc. Pray caution the traders in your place by sending this round to the Shops.

Yours,
J. Hudson,
Printer.

Old Harrison Penney, the celebrated Quaker printer of Darlington, made his warning more forthright.

Darlington 8 mo. 31 1853

N. B. Wethrell,
If Von Hartman calls upon thee, don't trust him ½d nor believe his promises to pay.

Please to inform others in the trade,
Thine truly,
Harrison Penney

These kind warnings were very gratefully received, for the local printer was often much more deeply involved in these enterprises than appears at first sight, as the following letter shows.

Newcastle,
Brunswick Place,
Dec. 20th

Sir,
I shall feel truly obliged by you informing me whether any astronomical lectures have been recently given in your Town. Also the charge for the hire of the most eligible room, and your own terms for printing the usual number of bills for the town.

If you are disposed to speculate I beg to submit the following proposition, viz:– that you print and circulate the bills, pay for the hire of the room–in fact be at all the expense–and that we divide the cash received for the admission of the Public to the lecture equally.

If the matter was well-worked I think it would prove mutually advantageous,

Your obdt. servant,
T. L. Simpson.

Such a proposition was far from unusual, and how often John Procter 'speculated' and found it profitable I do not know. I have evidence that on at least one occasion he regretted entering into show business. The following letter from his files presents the familiar pattern.

Mrs. Masons,
10 Terrace Place,
Newcastle on Tyne

Mr. Procter,
Sir,
Will you have the goodness to inform me by return of Post whether you think your town will support a concert such as the enclosed, and if so, whether you are willing

to undertake it for us on the following terms—you to be at the expense of Bills, room, and piano, and share the half of the receipts. The concert to be given some night next week or the week following.

By answering speedily you will most oblige,
Yours truly,
J. A. Fairbairn.

for the Misses Bennett. We are lately from Scotland.

Attached to it is another document which throws some light on the unseen, but necessary, expenses incidental to affairs of this sort which must have bewildered unfortunate printers in their efforts to make an honest living.

Coming to Hartlepool, Mrs. Bennett to make the arrangements	4–6
Michael, for distributing the bills, attending the doors, etc.	5–0
The Cryer	4–6
The Boy for walking with the boards	1–0
For beds, two nights	4–0
3 of us corning in the train	4–6
3 of us for provisions, two days	7–0
Returning in train to Sunderland, 3 of us	4–6
	£2–3–0
Receipts of the first concert	£1–10–0
Do of the second	12–6
	£2– 2–6

For what purpose was this Balance Sheet concocted? Was it an appeal for his sympathy? Perhaps he came to the conclusion that he was dealing with some wily customer for at first sight it would appear from the letter that he is entitled to half of £2–2–6 but that isn't quite what it says. It proposes that he 'share the half of the receipts'.

Isn't it possible that they attempted to fob him off with one half of half the receipts as one reading of the terms of the letter would allow and that he became annoyed and demanded a Balance Sheet and this was presented to gain his sympathy?

There were others following the same profession who gave him more work and less anxiety. We are accustomed to associate strolling players with Elizabethan times, but in the more remote parts of England and Scotland they were still to be found amusing the rustics in the early years of the present century. At the beginning of Queen Victoria's reign they were very numerous in the industrial areas of the North. They followed faithfully in the footsteps of their forebears in many respects. They begged the free use of the Town Hall from the Mayor, if it was available, but they would make do with the local inn if it became necessary. They were housed in its Long Room, not in the inn-yard, possibly because the old inns with their spacious galleried courtyards were not so common in the North of England, or the climate was too rigorous for out-door entertainment.

The more prosperous and longer established companies carried a canvas booth which served as a portable theatre when the weather was not too stormy. Their announcements styled it as a 'Magnificent Pavilion' but these hardened professionals knew how fragile their theatre really was. Mr. Adam's company, for instance, lost their 'Sans Pareil' in an October gale in 1838 and took shelter in the hospitable 'George nearby for the rest of their stay in Hartlepool.

Mr. Campbell's 'Large and Commodious Portable Theatre' lost its best canvas in a gale at Middlesbrough and had to make do with a second-hand tilt, which put the owner in the humiliating position of having to insert in his bills a notice requesting his patrons to bring umbrellas with them in case the weather proved inclement!

Billy Purvis from Newcastle, who travelled the North of England and part of Scotland for nearly forty years, would never allow his company to give a performance of the popular farce 'Raising the Wind' in his booth. He declared it was tempting Providence!

These companies were made up of honest families of professional players who ran their theatres in much the same way that a travelling circus of today is organised. They followed an old tradition but they kept themselves up-to-date. At Hartlepool they boasted that they used gas for illumination. The Corporation hired them a piece of land on which to erect their booth for a rent of 6 shillings per week, and as that site was very close to the Gas House, as gasworks were then called, they had no difficulty in having a supply laid on.

The same companies travelled the district year after year, making their appearances coincide with the local Race Week, or Regatta, or Village Feast. From Easter to October they were on the move, and in winter they laid up in some snug billet in a town large enough to give them sufficient weekly patrons to pay their way.

At first their bills were true posters – just small enough to be displayed on a gate-post yet large enough to be read at first glance by a casual passer-by. Their programme followed the old recipe – a drama, followed by an interlude, which consisted of a song and dance, followed by a farce—and their repertoire was immense. They could rise to the heights of Shakespeare and Schiller, but were not too proud to delight their audiences with a dramatised version of the local legend of 'The Lambton Worm'. They gained a firm hold on their local audiences because theirs was essentially a folk drama, and no matter what classical pieces appeared in any of their performances there is no doubt that they would be 'adapted' to suit the circumstances.

By the middle of the century the increasing prosperity and steady rise in the population of the industrial towns had encouraged the strolling players to settle down and invest in permanent buildings where they could hope to make a living all the year round.

At first in wooden halls, and later in more ornate buildings of brick and stucco, the new theatres of the working classes became centres for the drama and the music hall. Permanent buildings encouraged ingenious stage managers to invent and perfect apparatus which enabled more realistic scenes to be played on the stage. Horse races, railway engines, and shipwrecks on the stage were advertised on the playbills which themselves had blossomed into extravagant types and multicoloured inks far removed from the simple posters of the strolling players.

In the 1840's, alongside and running parallel with the more modest posters of the strollers, there appeared the exuberantly large and typographically stunning bills of the casinos and saloons. In the public houses of London in the 1830's it became the practice to give sing-songs and concerts, with stepdancing and other 'turns' for variety.

In a port thronged with seamen such attractions inevitably drew more customers, and there came a time when the patron was asked to pay a nominal sum for his entertainment, in addition to buying his drinks. When the financial success of such an arrangement induced landlords to build special rooms to cater for this new side-line to their business, the music hall was born. In these posters printed by John Procter the emergence of the Victorian music hall in England can be clearly seen.

The more respectable citizens, the tradesmen and the artisans, could not be expected to permit their families to enter the wicked world of the music hall. There were some who questioned the propriety of patronising the drama, and when drama and drink were linked together their doubts were resolved — that way led to certain damnation.

But they and their families did not forego other pleasures. There were gifted singers and speakers who would entertain them for an evening for a modest price before passing on to the next town. Here entertainment was coupled with culture. Local folk songs were raised to respectability and popularity by musicians such as Robert Topliff, the blind organist who collected, sang, and published the ballads of Durham and Northumberland twenty years before Cecil Sharp, who became nationally famous for preserving folk songs and country dances, was born.

There were more exciting occasions when all work was stopped for the day and the Mayor ordered all shops to be closed so that every citizen could see the circus come to town. Van Amburgh and his lions were the toast of the early Victorians. The young Queen was fascinated by them and the great Duke of Wellington himself could never see them often enough; he even prevailed upon Landseer to paint the lion tamer and his pets.

Cooke's were the oldest circus-owning family in the British Isles and they were especially popular in Scotland and the North of England. It was unfortunate that the advertising gimmick of the clown drawn in his tub by four geese led to a national calamity at Yarmouth in 1846, when the weight of the dense crowd assembled on the suspension bridge over the River Yare caused it to collapse and many were drowned.

Bostock and Wombwell's toured the country until well within living memory, having a long and honourable history, for George Wombwell first put his show on the road in 1807.

Waxworks were more unusual in the provinces. Such delicate figures were risky things to venture on the road. Procter's bills provide only two examples in sixty years.

In addition, there were the regular seasonal events hallowed by time and custom, the Races, Regattas, and Feasts. In the early days of the Industrial Revolution the majority of townsmen in the new centres of population were country labourers who had migrated from their villages in search of a better livelihood. Although they had left their fields behind them they still delighted in rustic pastimes. Every town, village, and hamlet seems to have held its own races with the accompanying crude competitions which raised a laugh, and which were followed, according to the bills, by 'The usual plays and assemblies in the evening'.

A typical example is the Middleton June Meeting of 1840 which was held on the sands near Hartlepool. There were four races. A Purse of Gold, not exceeding £10 nor less than £3, was added to a sweepstake of 5 shillings each for horses not thoroughbred. The second race was a sweepstake of 2 shillings and 6 pence to which was added a prize of One Sovereign. A double-reined bridle or 10 shillings was the prize for ponies whose entrance fee was 1 shilling. A cart saddle and trapping could be won by draught horses whose fee was 3 shillings. The same condition applied to all the races, 'Three to enter and start or no race.'

Among the other competitions offered was a prize of 5 shillings for the winner of a race in sacks, in which four had to start, and a New Hat was offered to whoever succeeded in climbing the greasy pole. If no one was successful then it was to be run for in a foot-race. 5 shillings could be won in a blindfold race with wheelbarrows. In all cases the entrance fee was 6 pence.

Other amusements promised during the day were Quoit playing, Grinning through collars for tobacco, Supping hot Hasty Puddings, Swallowing Treacle Rolls, etc, and whoever could catch the pig by the tail, which was greased for the occasion, could have it. It was also announced that a band of music would play all day and that all dogs found on the course would most assuredly be destroyed. Anyone was at liberty to set up a booth on payment of a fee to the Committee.

A seaport town such as Hartlepool had the best of both worlds for it also enjoyed the delights of a regatta which was well-organised, liberally supported, and of a more than local fame. The events had a greater variety than we should expect in an age devoid of speedboats and water skiing. Coal trimmers used their shovels to propel boats in the same way that Africans paddle canoes, whilst fisher lasses displayed the first manifestations of female emancipation.

But when the winter storms and dark nights made out-of-door pursuits impossible, and evangelical consciences eschewed light entertainment, the educational lecturer came into his own. He might demonstrate the wonders of electricity with mysterious apparatus and many coils of wire, or the marvels of modern chemistry with the aid of laughing gas and a few willing victims, or the sinister and baffling power of mesmerism. He might carry with him a combination of microscope and magic lantern to project on a white sheet fleas as large as elephants, or he might surround himself with plaster heads and impressive charts to prove that phrenology was a science and not common fortune-telling. The flow of enthusiastic lecturers seemed never-ending.

Another exciting and educational delight was to be experienced by visiting the Panorama or Diorama. They were the Victorian equivalent of our news-reels and travelogues, and had the additional advantage of being, in part at least, three dimensional, most decidedly educational, and absolutely and without doubt, strictly moral. To be precise, no diorama was ever likely to be seen outside the largest towns, for it involved a large amount of capital and considerable and complicated mechanical arrangements. The audience sat in a circular room facing a window, as we sit facing a television set. Through this they could look into an outer well-lit room furnished with models and scenery depicting a famous battle or some calamity, an Arctic expedition, or a romantic foreign landscape. Some of the figures were fitted with ingenious machinery which enabled them to perform certain lifelike actions; a favourite was that of a gamekeeper shooting a rabbit.

When the audience sitting in darkness had gazed its fill, the room revolved through a semi-circle and a different landscape was viewed through another window. In this way the assistants behind the scenes always had a room which they could set out ready for the next viewing. Hence the title of diorama.

Naturally the travelling showman could not arrange so complicated a contraption. He kept the original title of diorama and even invented others of greater perplexity to mystify and astound his audience. There were Franklin's 'Eidouranion' and Professor Groves' 'Eidophusikon', but the 'Professor' left with our printer an illustration of what purported to be the interior of his show which reveals that it was nothing more nor less than a common panorama.

The backcloth or canvas before which all the models and animated figures were placed was rather like a cinema screen. On it was painted the particular scene or episode that the audience had come to see. The canvas moved horizontally, for it was wound off one vertical roller in the wings at one side of the stage on to a similar roller in the wings on the other side. Thus the landscape or the progress of the battle rolled silently before the eyes of the audience whilst the commentator, standing at the side with a long pointer, filled in the details or drew their attention to particular episodes in such historical scenes as the Battle of Trafalgar or Waterloo, or last minute news from such scenes of warfare as the Siege of Sebastopol. Local calamities were not neglected. The harrowing occurrences at the Hartley Pit disaster, and the Wreck of the 'Forfarshire' coupled with the heroism of Grace Darling, were popular pieces.

Moral and religious episodes included tours of Jerusalem and the Holy Land, with the Prince of Wales thrown in for good measure. Parents and guardians had no grounds for alarm. They were assured that the mechanical figures were chaste!

An interest in other peoples and foreign countries displayed itself in the popularity of Tyrolean Singers in national costume, German Bands, Swiss Bells, and a never-ending procession of artistes billed 'Herr This' and 'Von That'. This interest was often coupled with a curiosity concerning peculiar musical instruments. Tunes were extracted from musical glasses and steel bands, planks of wood, rock harmonicons, and other strange devices.

But undoubtedly the most popular form of musical entertainment was the Nigger Minstrels. The vogue for these shows lasted for forty years, from 1836 until after 1870; and we still have them today. It was a young white actor, Thomas D. Rice, who first conceived the idea after a summer season in Louisville, Kentucky, in 1828. He invented the 'Jump, Jim Crow' song and dance, and after a successful career in the United States he came to London in 1836. Within a couple of years or so, as this collection of posters testifies, he had imitators in the provinces.

E. P. Christy first originated the style which became the standard routine among negro minstrels, namely, that of sitting round in a semi-circle, singing ballads with harmonised choruses, and cracking jokes between the centre and end-men. There were three parts to the show, the first consisted of jokes, songs, and the grand walk-around, the second was the olio, or mixture of items, and the third contained sketches and after-pieces.

The original Christy Minstrels appeared in New York in 1846 and that same year the 'Ethiopian Serenaders' sailed from Boston to London. Five in number, they took the Metropolis by storm and crowned their success by appearing before Queen Victoria herself at Windsor Castle.

In the days of the American Civil War and 'Uncle Tom's Cabin', when the theatres produced such melodramas as 'Dred, or the Dismal Swamp', with slavery as their theme, the plight of the negro slave was of much public concern. At Athenaeums and Mechanics' Institutes up and down the country negroes made a good living recounting their alleged experiences as slaves and the perils of their daring escapes to freedom.

Victorian workers, who would have been surprised to hear themselves designated as wage-slaves, escaped from the scene of their labours in a variety of fashions. There were excursions by railway but the most popular mode of travel on a summer's day was by sea. Steamboats took passengers on board at the unearthly hours of 7 or 8 a.m. for trips to such places as Scarborough and Whitby, although there were evening excursions on the Tees and a regular Sunday service to Middlesbrough. Their popularity lasted beyond the span of Queen Victoria's reign. In 1841 the John and William took people from Hartlepool to Middlesbrough, about 8 miles, for 6 pence. In 1908 the return fare on the Conqueror was 1 shilling. In 1841 the Middlesbro steamboat took Hartlepudlians 40 miles to Whitby for 2 shillings return. In 1908 the Conqueror left Hartlepool at 7 a.m. for the 60 mile voyage to Scarborough and returned her passengers at 9 p.m. for the modest sum of half-a-crown.

This mode of transport had been popular long before the days of steamboats but was certainly not so reliable. Sailing ships were at the mercy of wind and weather, and it was in connection with the late appearance of a theatrical company at South Shields that James Cawdell, a favourite Northern actor of about 1800, wrote his prologue, 'The Royal Cargo.' It was spoken on the stage when the players appeared, a fortnight late, after sailing from Scarborough!

'Now we are met, with expectation big
I'll tell you all I saw in Cock'ril's brig;
Kings wrapt in blankets—Queens ty'd up in sacks,
Bishops in baskets—Princesses in packs.
Becalm'd they lie, expos'd i' the open sea
Tossing and tumbling, sick as sick can be.

The ordinary tradesman travelling to London from the North of England used the weekly service of schooners or steamboats and had his goods delivered in the same fashion. There were only two occasions I know of when John Procter sustained a loss. One was when the weekly trader was cast ashore on the Norfolk coast by a 'Most tremendious hurricane', and the other occurred when sparks from the railway engine set fire to some parcels in an open truck. John's philosophical comment was that next time he would see that his goods were carried in the engine-driver's hip-pocket!

Emigrants could sail from Hartlepool direct to Boston or New York, or even to Australia on occasion, and there were regular passenger services to most of the leading ports on the other side of the North Sea, including the Baltic countries. The return deck passage to Hamburg in 1853 cost 15 shillings!'

Such ease of transport sometimes caused difficulties. A harbour crowded with ships lay at the back of the printing office, and on warm Spring nights many a lad must have found it difficult to restrain his desire for adventure.

The price-lists and sale bills John Procter printed are of considerable interest to the social historian but their attraction for the ordinary reader lies in their unfamiliar terms. In 1837 Lutestrings, Ducapes, and Gros de Naples were sold by the yard; there were Tuscan, Dunstable, and Tissue Bonnets; and Harlaquen, Filled Silk, and Norwich Shawls. All Blonds were advertised as 4–4. Gunpowder, Hyson and Ouchain, were green teas, and Congou, Pekoe, and Lapsang Souchong, black. We are shopping in a different world.

The first newspaper printed in the North of England was the Newcastle Courant published in 1711, the fourth English provincial paper. In 1814 the Durham County Advertiser appeared. The boom in the northern ports subsequent to the advent of the railway was reflected in the appearance of the Sunderland Herald, and the Shields and Stockton Observer in 1831. This was followed by a spate of local, and in most cases short-lived, papers.

It was not until 1855 that the Stockton and Hartlepool Mercury and Middlesbrough News began to appear. It was printed and published at Chare-Head Field in Hartlepool which was very near the office of John Procter, who printed their placards; and very detailed they were! In fact it could almost be said that the newspaper appeared in two parts, the solid reporting in the paper itself, and the headlines on the placards.

Elections in those days were great events! The Eatanswill Election in Pickwick Papers is no exaggeration dreamed up by Dickens. The familiar portrait of the staid and respectable Victorian has a very different picture on the other side, and this is it. Parliamentary elections caused plenty of excitement and gave the local printers a great deal of business, but the choicest invective and the most telling allusions were reserved for Municipal contests. It was then that the contents of the bills posted on the fences ranged from friendly badinage to bitter recrimination. There were abuses and everyone knew it, but if some candidate managed to 'pull a fast one' his fellow citizens soon forgave him if he had given them something to talk about and chuckle over. Like Mr. Perker, they could admire a smart agent.

The public casting votes at the hustings could lead to manoeuvres and tactics designed to favour some unscrupulous candidate. The regular publication of the State of the Poll at intervals during the day made it possible for candidates to lull their opponents into a false feeling of security by reserving their supporters until the last possible moment and then swamping the issue with a solid block of voters.

People like a little excitement and the even tenor of Victorian days was most likely to be upset by local alarms which are prominently headlined in a number of posters of a sensational nature. There was the threat of cholera, of which they had every reason to be terrified, and the nightmare of mad dogs. Wrecks on the coast were too frequent in the days of sailing ships to do more than punctuate the monotonous succession of the months. The more sensational served as a picturesque form of local chronology — a year was remembered as that in which the 'Rising Sun' was wrecked, or when the 'Francais' broke up before the horrified eyes of most of the citizens. Such episodes provided material for local versifiers and the traditional function of the 18th century broadside was continued until the end of the 19th century.

Every Victorian life was likely to end in verse, for mourning cards were a form of folk art which flourished then and has since been forgotten by all except museum curators. We are often reminded of the gloom and panoply of the Victorian funeral with its mutes and black ostrich plumes, black-edged notepaper and an interminable period of mourning. All this is true enough, for Death was never very far away from the Victorian mind. Large families and insufficient medical knowledge, coupled with bad sanitation, made a death in a town house a frequent occurrence. Victorians were more demonstrative in their expression of grief than we appear to be, and, if this indulgence in what we like to consider morbid and sentimental manifestations of sorrow helped to relieve their feelings, who are we to criticise? We tolerate the rank commercialism of the modern Christmas Card in comparison with which these mourning cards are infinitely superior both in execution and in taste.

So ends this selection of the material on the files of John Procter, Printer, of Hartlepool. The bills illustrated are chosen from thousands available, and if the reader is disappointed in not finding some particular aspect of Victorian life in which he is interested included, the fault is more likely to rest with the author and editor than with John Procter.

Plays and Players

It is well known that in Elizabethan times companies of strolling players tramped the roads of England performing their dramas in barns and inn-yards. Similar companies were still to be found touring in the eighteenth century, but whilst such barnstormers contrived a precarious living in the more remote regions, portable theatres had been developed in the fairs of the more prosperous farming communities during the seventeenth century. By the end of the eighteenth century these theatrical booths had become quite elaborate and could present really ambitious productions. They achieved considerable popularity at the great London fairs and during the celebration of Bartholomew Fair, the London theatres were temporarily closed down whilst their audiences deserted them for their fairground rivals.

The rapid growth of the towns of the Industrial Revolution in the middle of the nineteenth century and the building of permanent theatres led to the disappearance of most portable 'fit-ups'. Some survived to fall victim to the cinema, and one or two still flit mysteriously like ghosts from one country town to another.

The earliest playbills shown here are of the portable theatres of the industrial North. The best known and most popular was the Victoria Theatre of Billy Purvis. A stage-struck Newcastle carpenter he imagined himself as a great dramatic actor, but the turning point of his career came when he managed to persuade a theatrical manager to let him play the part of Young Norval in the melodrama 'Douglas'. When he appeared in an overlarge helmet, armed with sword and shield, and declaimed: 'My name is Norval, on the Grampian Hills My father feeds his flock.' a broad Tyneside voice bawled out from the gallery, 'Ye're a greet leer. Yor father and mither sells apples an' peers in Denton Chare!' Not unexpectedly the performance became a farce and Billy discovered his true métier as a comedian and spent another dozen years learning to make the most of his talents whilst travelling the country. It was not until 1826 that Purvis really established himself and made enough money to equip himself with a better booth and attract a faithful band of actors.

In 1835 a new 'Splendid Theatrical Pavilion' was built at Newcastle for him. It was 90 ft long and 30 ft wide and made of timber at a cost of £202. The roof was of canvas and the decoration and scenery copied from the Theatre Royal. This booth was destroyed by a gale during a tour of Scotland in 1842, yet he continued, using barns, weaving lofts, and smithies as theatres. Despite losing money, he still had sufficent capital to pay for a new theatre which is reported to have been designed by George Stephenson the noted locomotive engineer.

In 1837 when Purvis visited Hartlepool he worked extremely hard. Between the first performance of May 18th and the last on June 10th he managed to present thirteen separate and distinct 'double feature' programmes. The usual programme began with the melodrama, followed by an interlude of songs and dances, and concluding with a 'laughable farce'. 'The Vampire' was coupled with 'Mischief Making', 'Luke the Labourer', with 'William Tell', and 'Douglas' could share the programme with 'The Lambton Worm', The Mock Doctor', or 'Don Juan'.

Of course Mr. Purvis had many rivals who also found Hartlepool a profitable port of call. Blanchard's company first came in March 1838. His repertoire was of an entirely different sort – the 'Edgware Road Murder', 'The Fire Raiser', 'The Golden Farmer', and 'Jane Shore' were accompanied by farces with titles such as 'The Honeymoon', 'The Married Rake', 'The Innkeeper's Daughter' and 'The Married Bachelor'. In July of that same year Mr. Wynne's company of the Theatre Royal, Perth, appeared on the boards in Mr. Manner's Long Room in the George Inn. The only plays they presented which had not been performed previously that year were 'Rob Roy', 'Barnwell, or the London Merchant', and 'The Spectre Bridegroom'.

In October Mr. Adams appeared with his booth, the 'Sans Pareil'. If he was the Mr. Adams who had been Billy Purvis's stage manager during his 1837 visit it would appear that he was stealing a leaf out of his former employer's book. But he was less fortunate, although he had the imagination to announce the disaster in terms which would appeal to a sea-faring community.

'Owing to the wreck of Mr. Adams' brig the 'Sans Pareil' on Monday, many passengers were disappointed, therefore Mr. Adams wishes to impress upon the minds of his friends and patrons that he has made arrangements with Mr. Manners and intends to sail this evening at 7 o'clock in the George at Hartlepool'.

Campbell's 'Large and Commodious Portable Theatre' was a regular annual visitor in the 1840s. Although his letters suggest that he was badly educated he played sophisticated stuff – 'The Pitman's Strike', 'The Mutiny at the Nore', 'A Gambler's Life' and favourites such as 'Tom Cringles Log', 'Esmeralda', 'She Stoops to Conquer', and 'The Merchant of Venice'. The farces still continued, however.

As the towns grew in size and the audiences began to provide regular patronage throughout the year so the portable theatres were either abandoned for permanent structures or squeezed out to continue their rounds in the villages. Parallel with this changeover from the temporary to the permanent building came the publicans' bid to attract customers by providing entertainment. The first indications of the trend are to be seen in Purvis's Merry Night at Middlesbrough (poster 4), and the process can be seen very clearly when members of Purvis's Company provide a night of entertainment at the George (30) and one of the actors, Mr. Billings, is later to be found in sole charge of Smith's Royal Music Saloon at the same inn (35).

The rival town of West Hartlepool appeared in 1847 and by the 1850s each of the Hartlepools had permanent theatres. They were both called the 'Theatre Royal' and very often the sole distinguishing feature in their playbills is whether the description includes Northgate, which is in Hartlepool, or Whitby Street in West Hartlepool. As the new town prospered an ambitious plan for a magnificent new theatre was carried through and the new Theatre Royal was built. Here appeared all the well known acts of the legendary Victorian music hall.

Show business lives in the glare of publicity and perhaps this short sketch of the development of the drama in a provincial town can be brought to a pleasant end with the story of the feud between the managers of the two Theatres Royal of the Hartlepools in 1864. They expressed their opinion of each other on their playbills – 'Toothless Imbecile', 'Poisonous Worm', 'Venomous Animal' – and designated the rival theatres as the Old Shed or the County Asylum.

1
Our Victorian ancestors in provincial towns were somewhat unsophisticated and this sort of proclamation would certainly attract much more attention than it would get today. In the days before newspapers it was only by means of official bills couched in this style that the populace was kept informed of vital information. Nowadays such blatant imitations would be likely to be forbidden by the authorities.

1

V. R.

PROCLAMATION

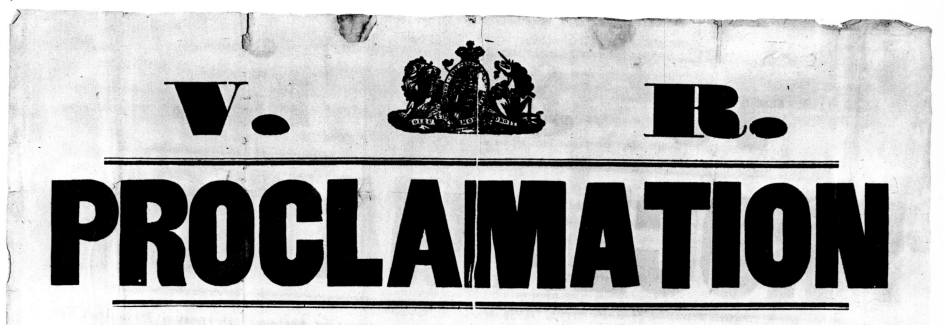

Whereas, it has come to our Royal Ears in our capacity of "King of Jesters," Perpetual President of the "Funny Club," and Vice-President of the "Laugh-and-Grow-Fat Society," that there are in this town divers and numerous persons afflicted with the Dumps, Mumps, Blues, Sighs, Never-Smiles, Melancholy, Long Faces, and various other Maladies too numerous to mention, all of which are curable by the application of our Sovereign Balsam, GOOD HUMOUR!

Now this is, therefore, to summon all such persons to be and appear in the COURT OF MOMUS, to be holden in our Palace of Mirth, at the Prince of Wales Music Hall, North Street, Scarborough, on the Evening of FRIDAY, FEBRUARY 11th, 1870, at a Quarter to Eight o'clock prompt.

And this is also to summon before us all Politicians—Whig, Tory, and Conservative—in order that we may lay before them the Provisions of our proposed NEW REFORM BILL!

And this is also severally to admonish our dear friends, the Ladies, with their Pork Pie Hats, Small Bonnets, and Pretty Faces, to appear before us, and to bring their Husbands and sweethearts with them, so that we may fully possess them of our project for the establishment of a "Strong-minded Females and Woman's-rights Parliament," in which the Women (bless 'em) shall all talk at once.

And this is also humbly to request the Blessed Angels who wear Crinolines to narrow them into the smallest possible space, so as to make room for the crowds expected to be present on this auspicious occasion.

Given under our Hand and Seal, this 8th, day of February, 1870.

FRED STANLEY.

G. Martin, Printer, Stationer, &c., Queen Street Scarboro'.

2
The players are prepared for their summer tour of the mining villages and country towns of the northern counties and the lowlands of Scotland. The theatre would be newly painted in 'bonny red an' yeller' and all the accessories and scenery lovingly and skilfully refurbished during the dark days of the winter months ready for the hectic excitement of the many changes of the overnight stops of the tour.

3
This farce is said to have been produced originally as 'Did you ever send your wife to Camberwell?' As this was (and still is) part of London, most provincials would not have heard of the place and a local substitute was always found. The Hartlepool theatre used the name of the nearby village of Stranton. Later, when this grew into West Hartlepool, the theatre there used the little seaside resort of Seaton as their substitute.

4
History is said to repeat itself. Nowadays when many stars of the entertainment world are more likely to be found performing in Working Men's Clubs than in the few legitimate theatres or music halls that remain in Britain, we need not be surprised to see a veteran trouper like Billy Purvis taking the opportunity of making a few shillings in the same manner. The programme shows his infinite variety.

2

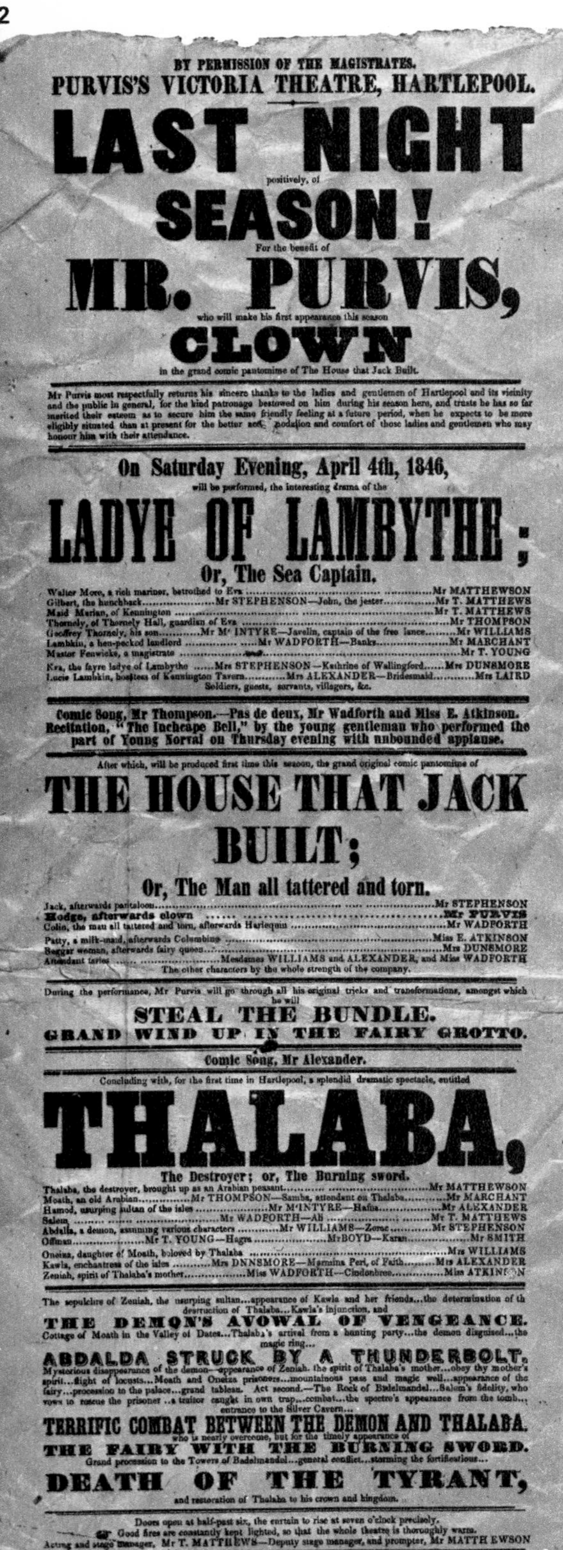
BY PERMISSION OF THE MAGISTRATES.
PURVIS'S VICTORIA THEATRE, HARTLEPOOL.
LAST NIGHT
positively, of
SEASON!
For the benefit of
MR. PURVIS,
who will make his first appearance this season
CLOWN
in the grand comic pantomime of The House that Jack Built.

Mr Purvis most respectfully returns his sincere thanks to the ladies and gentlemen of Hartlepool and its vicinity and the public in general, for the kind patronage bestowed on him during his season here, and trusts he has so far merited their esteem as to secure him the same friendly feeling at a future period, when he expects to be more eligibly situated than at present for the better acc[om]modation and comfort of those ladies and gentlemen who may honour him with their attendance.

On Saturday Evening, April 4th, 1846,
will be performed, the interesting drama of the
LADYE OF LAMBYTHE;
Or, The Sea Captain.
Walter More, a rich mariner, betrothed to Eva ... Mr MATTHEWSON
Gilbert, the hunchback ... Mr STEPHENSON—John, the jester ... Mr T. MATTHEWS
Maid Marian, of Kennington ... Mr T. MATTHEWS
Thornely, of Thornely Hall, guardian of Eva ... Mr THOMPSON
Geoffrey Thornely, his son ... Mr M'INTYRE—Javelin, captain of the free lance ... Mr WILLIAMS
Lambkin, a hen-pecked landlord ... Mr WADFORTH—Banks ... Mr MARCHANT
Master Fenwicke, a magistrate ... Mr T. YOUNG
Eva, the fayre ladye of Lambythe ... Mrs STEPHENSON—Kathrine of Wallingford ... Mrs DUNSMORE
Lucie Lambkin, hostess of Kennington Tavern ... Mrs ALEXANDER—Bridesmaid ... Mrs LAIRD
Soldiers, guests, servants, villagers, &c.

Comic Song, Mr Thompson.—Pas de deux, Mr Wadforth and Miss E. Atkinson. Recitation, "The Inchcape Bell," by the young gentleman who performed the part of Young Norval on Thursday evening with unbounded applause.

After which, will be produced first time this season, the grand original comic pantomime of
THE HOUSE THAT JACK BUILT;
Or, The Man all tattered and torn.
Jack, afterwards pantaloon ... Mr STEPHENSON
Hodge, afterwards clown ... Mr PURVIS
Colin, the man all tattered and torn, afterwards Harlequin ... Mr WADFORTH
Patty, a milk-maid, afterwards Columbine ... Miss E. ATKINSON
Beggar woman, afterwards fairy queen ... Mrs DUNSMORE
Attendant faries ... Mesdames WILLIAMS and ALEXANDER, and Miss WADFORTH
The other characters by the whole strength of the company.

During the performance, Mr Purvis will go through all his original tricks and transformations, amongst which he will
STEAL THE BUNDLE.
GRAND WIND UP IN THE FAIRY GROTTO.

Comic Song, Mr Alexander.

Concluding with, for the first time in Hartlepool, a splendid dramatic spectacle, entitled
THALABA,
The Destroyer; or, The Burning sword.
Thalaba, the destroyer, brought up as an Arabian peasant ... Mr MATTHEWSON
Moath, an old Arabian ... Mr THOMPSON—Samba, attendant on Thalaba ... Mr MARCHANT
Hamod, usurping sultan of the isles ... Mr M'INTYRE—Hafna ... Mr ALEXANDER
Salem ... Mr WADFORTH—Ali ... Mr T. MATTHEWS
Abdalla, a demon, assuming various characters ... Mr WILLIAMS—Zerac ... Mr STEPHENSON
Offman ... Mr T. YOUNG—Hagra ... Mr BOYD—Karan ... Mr SMITH
Oneiza, daughter of Moath, beloved by Thalaba ... Mrs WILLIAMS
Kawla, enchantress of the isles ... Mrs DNNSMORE—Mamina Peri, of Faith ... Mrs ALEXANDER
Zeniah, spirit of Thalaba's mother ... Miss WADFORTH—Cindonbree ... Miss ATKINSON

The sepulchre of Zeniah, the usurping sultan...appearance of Kawla and her friends...the determination of th[e] destruction of Thalaba...Kawla's injunction, and
THE DEMON'S AVOWAL OF VENGEANCE.
Cottage of Moath in the Valley of Dates...Thalaba's arrival from a hunting party...the demon disguised...the magic ring...
ABDALDA STRUCK BY A THUNDERBOLT.
Mysterious disappearance of the demon—appearance of Zeniah, the spirit of Thalaba's mother...obey thy mother's spirit...flight of locusts...Moath and Oneiza prisoners...mountainous pass and magic well...appearance of the fairy...procession to the palace...grand tableau. Act second.—The Rock of Badelmandel...Salem's fidelity, who vows to rescue the prisoner...a traitor caught in own trap...combat...the spectre's appearance from the tomb...entrance to the Silver Cavern...
TERRIFIC COMBAT BETWEEN THE DEMON AND THALABA,
who is nearly overcome, but for the timely appearance of
THE FAIRY WITH THE BURNING SWORD.
Grand procession to the Towers of Badelmandel...general conflict...storming the fortifications...
DEATH OF THE TYRANT,
and restoration of Thalaba to his crown and kingdom.

Doors open at half-past six, the curtain to rise at seven o'clock precisely.
Good fires are constantly kept lighted, so that the whole theatre is thoroughly warm.
Acting and stage manager, Mr T. MATTHEWS—Deputy stage manager, and prompter, Mr MATTHEWSON

Printed by J. PROCTER, Hartlepool.

3

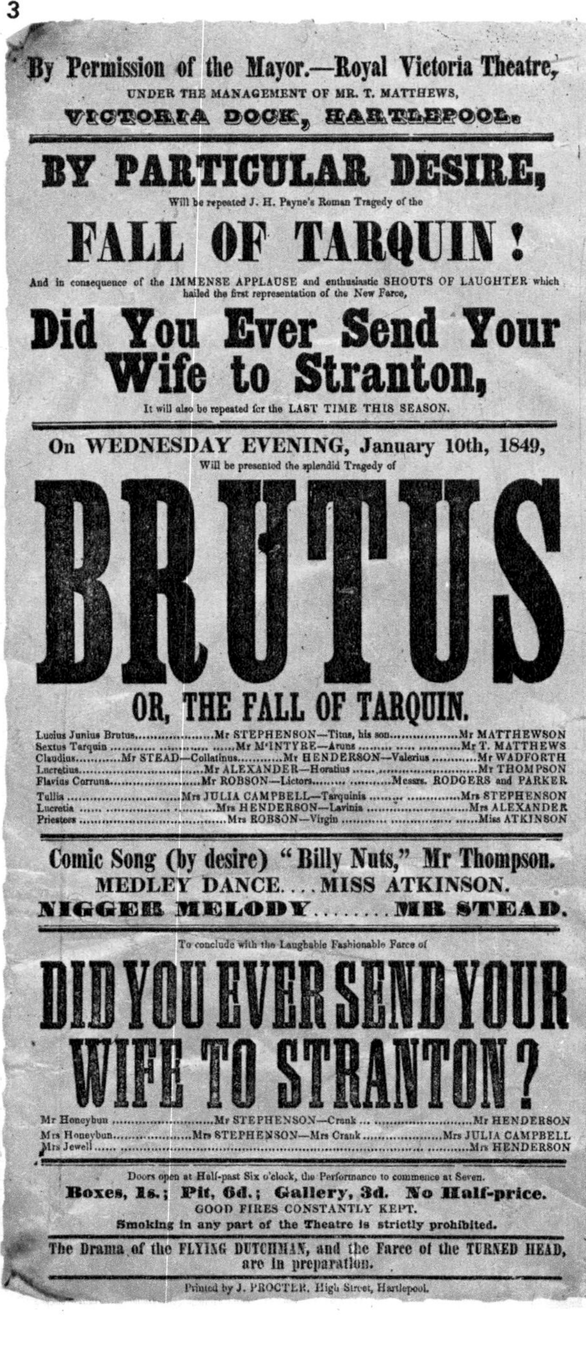
By Permission of the Mayor.—Royal Victoria Theatre,
UNDER THE MANAGEMENT OF MR. T. MATTHEWS,
VICTORIA DOCK, HARTLEPOOL.

BY PARTICULAR DESIRE,
Will be repeated J. H. Payne's Roman Tragedy of the
FALL OF TARQUIN!
And in consequence of the IMMENSE APPLAUSE and enthusiastic SHOUTS OF LAUGHTER which hailed the first representation of the New Farce,
Did You Ever Send Your Wife to Stranton,
It will also be repeated for the LAST TIME THIS SEASON.

On WEDNESDAY EVENING, January 10th, 1849,
Will be presented the splendid Tragedy of
BRUTUS
OR, THE FALL OF TARQUIN.
Lucius Junius Brutus ... Mr STEPHENSON—Titus, his son ... Mr MATTHEWSON
Sextus Tarquin ... Mr M'INTYRE—Aruns ... Mr T. MATTHEWS
Claudius ... Mr STEAD—Collatinus ... Mr HENDERSON—Valerius ... Mr WADFORTH
Lucretius ... Mr ALEXANDER—Horatius ... Mr THOMPSON
Flavius Corruna ... Mr ROBSON—Lictors ... Messrs. RODGERS and PARKER
Tullia ... Mrs JULIA CAMPBELL—Tarquinia ... Mrs STEPHENSON
Lucretia ... Mrs HENDERSON—Lavinia ... Mrs ALEXANDER
Priestess ... Mrs ROBSON—Virgin ... Miss ATKINSON

Comic Song (by desire) "Billy Nuts," Mr Thompson.
MEDLEY DANCE....MISS ATKINSON.
NIGGER MELODY........MR STEAD.

To conclude with the Laughable Fashionable Farce of
DID YOU EVER SEND YOUR WIFE TO STRANTON?
Mr Honeybun ... Mr STEPHENSON—Crank ... Mr HENDERSON
Mrs Honeybun ... Mrs STEPHENSON—Mrs Crank ... Mrs JULIA CAMPBELL
Mrs Jewell ... Mrs HENDERSON

Doors open at Half-past Six o'clock, the Performance to commence at Seven.
Boxes, 1s.; Pit, 6d.; Gallery, 3d. No Half-price.
GOOD FIRES CONSTANTLY KEPT.
Smoking in any part of the Theatre is strictly prohibited.

The Drama of the FLYING DUTCHMAN, and the Farce of the TURNED HEAD, are in preparation.

Printed by J. PROCTER, High Street, Hartlepool.

4

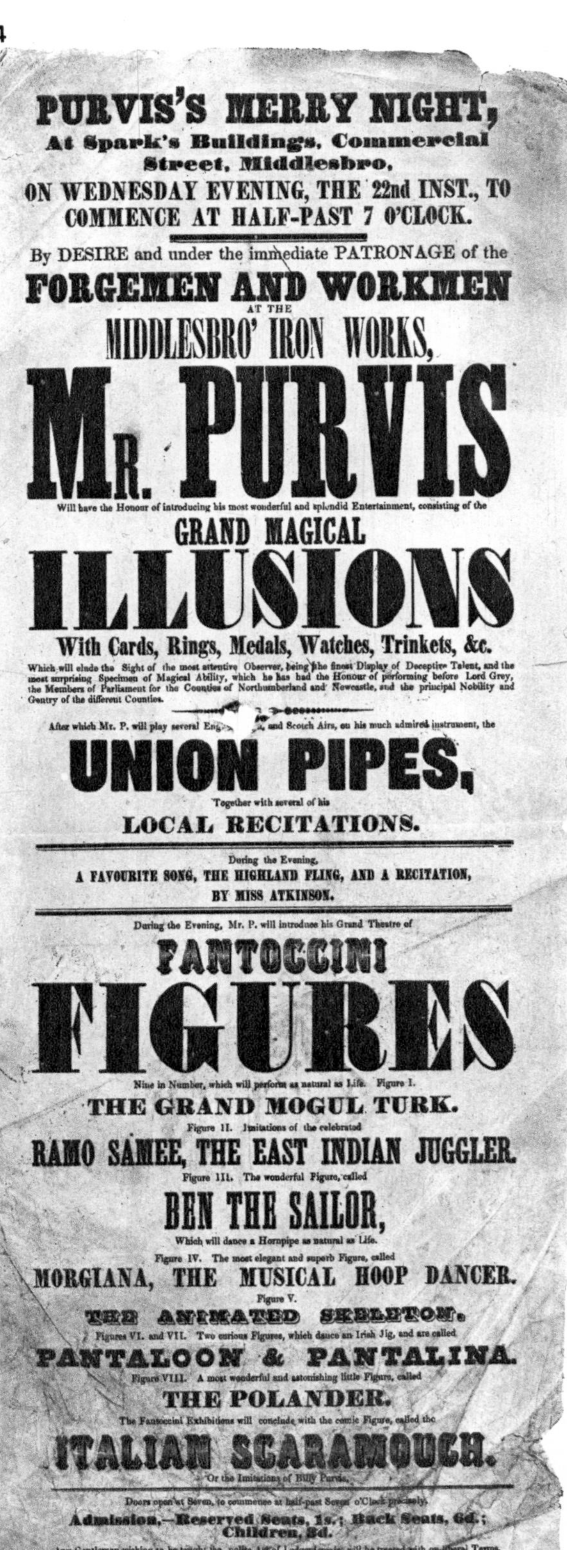
PURVIS'S MERRY NIGHT,
At Spark's Buildings, Commercial Street, Middlesbro,
ON WEDNESDAY EVENING, THE 22nd INST., TO COMMENCE AT HALF-PAST 7 O'CLOCK.

By DESIRE and under the immediate PATRONAGE of the
FORGEMEN AND WORKMEN
AT THE
MIDDLESBRO' IRON WORKS,
MR. PURVIS
Will have the Honour of introducing his most wonderful and splendid Entertainment, consisting of the
GRAND MAGICAL
ILLUSIONS
With Cards, Rings, Medals, Watches, Trinkets, &c.
Which will elude the Sight of the most attentive Observer, being the finest Display of Deceptive Talent, and the most surprising Specimen of Magical Ability, which he has had the Honour of performing before Lord Grey, the Members of Parliament for the Counties of Northumberland and Newcastle, and the principal Nobility and Gentry of the different Counties.

After which Mr. P. will play several Eng[lish] ... and Scotch Airs, on his much admired instrument, the
UNION PIPES,
Together with several of his
LOCAL RECITATIONS.

During the Evening,
A FAVOURITE SONG, THE HIGHLAND FLING, AND A RECITATION,
BY MISS ATKINSON.

During the Evening, Mr. P. will introduce his Grand Theatre of
FANTOCCINI
FIGURES
Nine in Number, which will perform as natural as Life. Figure I.
THE GRAND MOGUL TURK.
Figure II. Imitations of the celebrated
RAMO SAMEE, THE EAST INDIAN JUGGLER.
Figure III. The wonderful Figure, called
BEN THE SAILOR,
Which will dance a Hornpipe as natural as Life.
Figure IV. The most elegant and superb Figure, called
MORGIANA, THE MUSICAL HOOP DANCER.
Figure V.
THE ANIMATED SKELETON.
Figures VI. and VII. Two curious Figures, which dance an Irish Jig, and are called
PANTALOON & PANTALINA.
Figure VIII. A most wonderful and astonishing little Figure, called
THE POLANDER.
The Fantoccini Exhibitions will conclude with the comic Figure, called the
ITALIAN SCARAMOUCH.
Or the Imitations of Billy Purvis.

Doors open at Seven, to commence at half-past Seven o'Clock precisely.
Admission,—Reserved Seats, 1s.; Back Seats, 6d.; Children, 3d.
Any Gentleman wishing to be taught the polite Art of Ledgerdemain, will be treated with on liberal Terms.

Printed by J. PROCTER, High Street, Hartlepool.

5
We can scarcely do better than allow Mr. Campbell to make his own announcement. This he does with dignity and clarity and without making himself as sickeningly obsequious as Mr. Scott.

6
Your Very Humble Servant! What better example could we have of the worst sort of early Victorian announcement than Mr. Scott's preamble to his playbill?
All the vocabulary and polite phraseology of shabby gentility is brought into use. 'Deference and Consideration', 'begs leave', 'condescend', 'Countenance and Support', 'it will ever be his ardent wish' are all echoes of the Victorian genteel beggar. The details of the properties and scenery given on the bill are worthy of study.

5

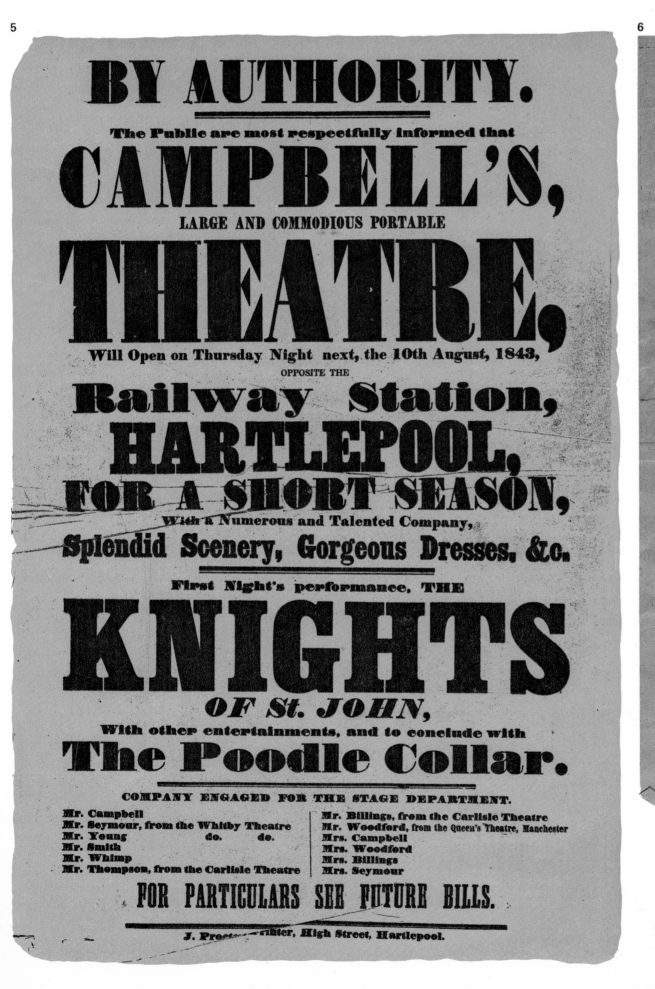

BY AUTHORITY.

The Public are most respectfully informed that

CAMPBELL'S,

LARGE AND COMMODIOUS PORTABLE

THEATRE,

Will Open on Thursday Night next, the 10th August, 1843,

OPPOSITE THE

Railway Station,

HARTLEPOOL,

FOR A SHORT SEASON,

With a Numerous and Talented Company,

Splendid Scenery, Gorgeous Dresses, &c.

First Night's performance, THE

KNIGHTS

OF St. JOHN,

With other entertainments, and to conclude with

The Poodle Collar.

COMPANY ENGAGED FOR THE STAGE DEPARTMENT.

Mr. Campbell
Mr. Seymour, from the Whitby Theatre
Mr. Young do. do.
Mr. Smith
Mr. Whimp
Mr. Thompson, from the Carlisle Theatre
Mr. Billings, from the Carlisle Theatre
Mr. Woodford, from the Queen's Theatre, Manchester
Mrs. Campbell
Mrs. Woodford
Mrs. Billings
Mrs. Seymour

FOR PARTICULARS SEE FUTURE BILLS.

J. Procter, Printer, High Street, Hartlepool.

6

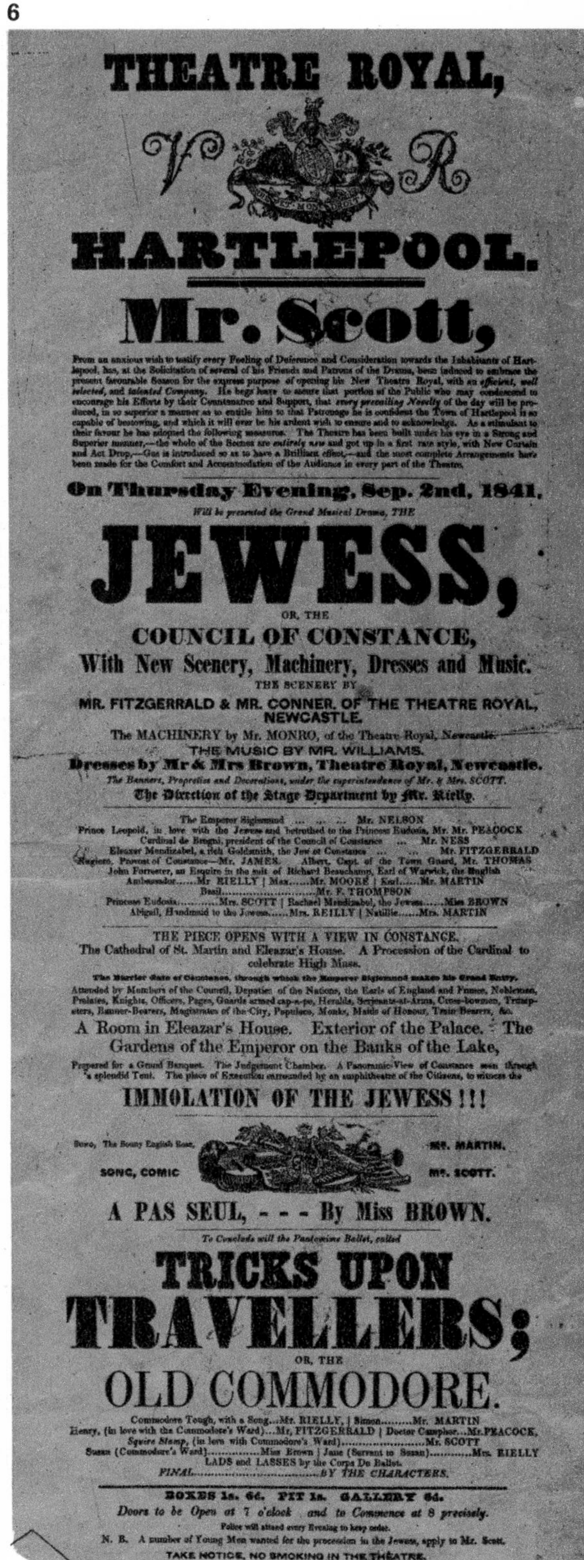

THEATRE ROYAL,

V R

HARTLEPOOL.

Mr. Scott,

From an anxious wish to testify *every* Feeling of Deference and Consideration towards the Inhabitants of Hartlepool, has, at the Solicitation of *several* of his Friends and Patrons of the Drama, been induced to embrace the present favourable Season for the express purpose of opening his New Theatre Royal, with an *efficient, well selected,* and *talented Company.* He begs leave to assure that portion of the Public who may condescend to encourage his Efforts by their Countenance and Support, that *every prevailing Novelty* of the day will be produced, in so superior a manner as to entitle him to that Patronage he is confident the Town of Hartlepool is so capable of bestowing, and which it will ever be his ardent wish to ensure and to acknowledge. As a stimulant to their favour he has adopted the following measures. The Theatre has been built under his eye in a Strong and Superior manner,—the whole of the Scenes are *entirely new* and got up in a first rate style, with New Curtain and Act Drop,—Gas is introduced so as to have a Brilliant effect,—and the most complete Arrangements have been made for the Comfort and Accommodation of the Audience in every part of the Theatre.

On Thursday Evening, Sep. 2nd, 1841,

Will be presented the Grand Musical Drama, THE

JEWESS,

OR, THE

COUNCIL OF CONSTANCE,

With New Scenery, Machinery, Dresses and Music.

THE SCENERY BY

MR. FITZGERRALD & MR. CONNER, OF THE THEATRE ROYAL, NEWCASTLE.

The MACHINERY by Mr. MONRO, of the Theatre Royal, Newcastle.

THE MUSIC BY MR. WILLIAMS.

Dresses by Mr & Mrs Brown, Theatre Royal, Newcastle.

The Banners, Properties and Decorations, under the superintendence of Mr. & Mrs. SCOTT.

The Direction of the Stage Department by Mr. Rielly.

The Emperor Sigismund ... ... Mr. NELSON
Prince Leopold, in love with the Jewess and betrothed to the Princess Eudosia, Mr. Mr. PEACOCK
Cardinal de Brogni, president of the Council of Constance ... Mr. NESS
Eleazer Mendizabel, a rich Goldsmith, the Jew of Constance ... ... Mr. FITZGERRALD
Rugiero, Provost of Constance—Mr. JAMES. Albert, Capt. of the Town Guard, Mr. THOMAS
John Forrester, an Esquire in the suit of Richard Beauchamp, Earl of Warwick, the English Ambassador......Mr RIELLY | Max......Mr. MOORE | Karl......Mr. MARTIN
Basil..........................Mr. F. THOMPSON
Princess Eudosia...........Mrs. SCOTT | Rachael Mendizabel, the Jewess......Miss BROWN
Abigail, Handmaid to the Jewess......Mrs. REILLY | Natillie......Mrs. MARTIN

THE PIECE OPENS WITH A VIEW IN CONSTANCE.
The Cathedral of St. Martin and Eleazar's House. A Procession of the Cardinal to celebrate High Mass.

The Barrier Gate of Constance, through which the Emperor Sigismund makes his Grand Entry.

Attended by Members of the Council, Deputies of the Nations, the Earls of England and France, Noblemen, Prelates, Knights, Officers, Pages, Guards armed cap-a-pe, Heralds, Serjeants-at-Arms, Cross-bowmen, Trumpeters, Banner-Bearers, Magistrates of the City, Populace, Monks, Maids of Honour, Train Bearers, &c.

A Room in Eleazar's House. Exterior of the Palace. The Gardens of the Emperor on the Banks of the Lake,

Prepared for a Grand Banquet. The Judgement Chamber. A Panoramic View of Constance seen through a splendid Tent. The place of Execution surrounded by an amphitheatre of the Citizens, to witness the

IMMOLATION OF THE JEWESS!!!

Song, The Bonny English Rose, Mr. MARTIN.
SONG, COMIC Mr. SCOTT.

A PAS SEUL, - - - By Miss BROWN.

To Conclude with the Pantomime Ballet, called

TRICKS UPON TRAVELLERS;

OR, THE

OLD COMMODORE.

Commodore Tough, with a Song...Mr. RIELLY, | Simon.........Mr. MARTIN
Henry, (in love with the Commodore's Ward)...Mr. FITZGERRALD | Doctor Camphor...Mr. PEACOCK,
Squire Stamp, (in love with Commodore's Ward)........................Mr. SCOTT
Susan (Commodore's Ward)..............Miss Brown | Jane (Servant to Susan)...........Mrs. RIELLY
LADS and LASSES by the Corps De Ballet.
FINAL................................BY THE CHARACTERS.

BOXES 1s. 6d. PIT 1s. GALLERY 6d.

Doors to be Open at 7 o'clock and to Commence at 8 precisely.

Police will attend every Evening to keep order.

N. B. A number of Young Men wanted for the procession in the Jewess, apply to Mr. Scott.

TAKE NOTICE, NO SMOKING IN THE THEATRE.

J. PROCTER'S OFFICE, WEST END OF HIGH STREET, HARTLEPOOL.

7
Mr. Blanchard certainly moved around. With Mrs. Blanchard and Master Blanchard he appears at the George with Mr. Ponisi from March 8th to May 1st 1838, then with Mr. Adams from October 1st to November 9th in the same year. In the years following they are to be found in Mr. Campbell's Company.

8
A fortnight after Mr. Blanchard and Mr. Ponisi had left Hartlepool Mr. Procter received the following:
Dear Sir,
It is with extreme regret that I am obliged to inform you Middlesbrough has turned out very indifferent for us. Since our arrival business has been so bad that it has deceived my most distant calculation. I am extremely sorry that it is not in my power at present to send you a remittance but as soon as chance offers, you may depend upon hearing from me.

Your well wisher.
S. Ponisi
May 12th, 1838.

8A
A poster proclaiming a show on the fringe of the professional theatre. Notice that it is advertised at the Mechanics Hall, an equivalent to the modern Working Man's Club. The figure suggests Nigger Minstrels yet the bill promises the appearance of the Champion Step Dancer of the World: and dancing was important. Clog Dancing and Step dancing had its aficionados in those days.

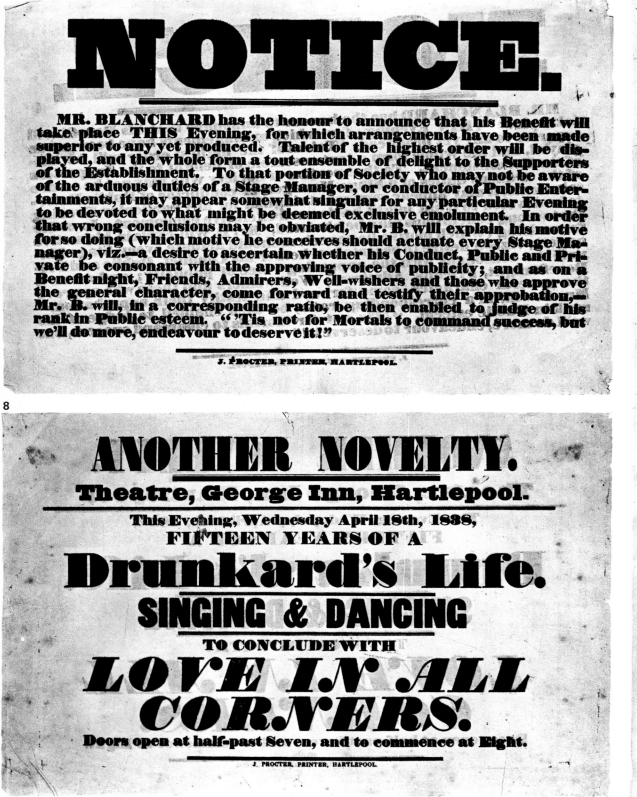

7

NOTICE.

MR. BLANCHARD has the honour to announce that his Benefit will take place THIS Evening, for which arrangements have been made superior to any yet produced. Talent of the highest order will be displayed, and the whole form a tout ensemble of delight to the Supporters of the Establishment. To that portion of Society who may not be aware of the arduous duties of a Stage Manager, or conductor of Public Entertainments, it may appear somewhat singular for any particular Evening to be devoted to what might be deemed exclusive emolument. In order that wrong conclusions may be obviated, Mr. B. will explain his motive for so doing (which motive he conceives should actuate every Stage Manager), viz.—a desire to ascertain whether his Conduct, Public and Private be consonant with the approving voice of publicity; and as on a Benefit night, Friends, Admirers, Well-wishers and those who approve the general character, come forward and testify their approbation,—Mr. B. will, in a corresponding ratio, be then enabled to judge of his rank in Public esteem. "'Tis not for Mortals to command success, but we'll do more, endeavour to deserve it!"

J. PROCTER, PRINTER, HARTLEPOOL.

8

ANOTHER NOVELTY.
Theatre, George Inn, Hartlepool.
This Evening, Wednesday April 18th, 1838,
FIFTEEN YEARS OF A
Drunkard's Life.
SINGING & DANCING
TO CONCLUDE WITH
LOVE IN ALL CORNERS.
Doors open at half-past Seven, and to commence at Eight.

J. PROCTER, PRINTER, HARTLEPOOL.

8A

Mechanics' Hall, Hartlepool.
TOM HANDFORD'S
COMIC CONCERT
To-Night! the Last Night!
LITTLE TONY!
The Champion Step Dancer of the World.
PRICES:—1s., 6d., and 3d.
Hartlepool: J. PROCTER, Printer.

9
The Ticket-of-Leave Man was first produced in 1865 and was one of the outstandingly successful social life dramas of the time. The Rifle Dance would have been highly topical in view of the formation of national rifle clubs (Chapter 4) which later became Volunteer Corps. A benefit poster of unusual design.

9

THEATRE ROYAL, NORTHGATE, HARTLEPOOL.

TUESDAY, DEC. 10th,
BENEFIT OF
MISS MADGE ANTOINETTE
WHEN WILL BE PERFORMED TH CELEBRATED DRAMA OF THE
TICKET-OF-LEAVE MAN

☞ Come and See Mr. W. H Pitt in his Great Part of Bob Brierley ! ☞ Come and See Mr. G. F. Charles as Hawksha
☞ Come and See Mr. Edmund Grace as Melter Moss ! ☞ Come and See Miss Georgina Robertson as May Edwar
☞ Come and See Little Madge as Sam Willoughby ! ☞ Come and See Mrs. M. Blandford as Mrs. Willoug
☞ COME AND SEE EVERYBODY DO THEIR BEST TO MAKE THIS NIGHT THE

NIGHT OF ALL NIGHTS!

After which, Miss Madge Antoinette will Dance, for the first time in Hartlepool, her Cele d
RIFLE DANCE !

TO CONCLUDE WITH THE
RENDEZVOUS!
In which MISS ANTOINETTE will appea
SUPPORTED by the COMPANY

HARTLEPOOL: J. PROCTER, PRINTER
BY STEAM POWER.

10
Few posters of this period attempt to portray the artists. This is an exception and a most strikingly successful one. It is of the same family as the usual 'Jump Jim Crow' illustration but whereas that is a stick figure of a negro dancer this has obviously been drawn from the life.

11
A typical sentimental play which explored the seamy side of life. There wouldn't be a dry eye in the house! In fact, the citizens would probably boast of going to 'have a good cry'. Notice the proud announcement 'Real water and real boats'.

10

Theatre Royal, West Hartlepool.
JIM BROWN & HIS TALENTED SON,
SONGS!
DANCES!
ON MONDAY, APRIL 10, 1865,
DURING THE WEEK.
J. PROCTER, PRINTED BY STEAM POWER, SOUTHGATE.

11

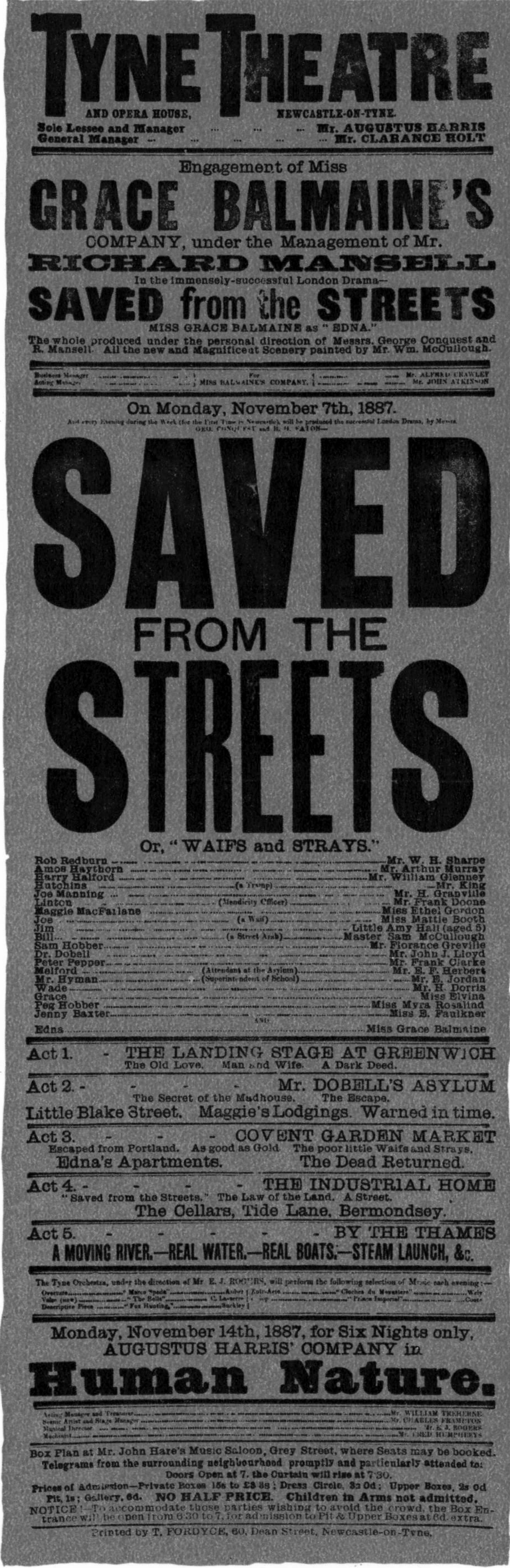

12
It must be remembered that the early years of Victoria's reign saw a massive increase in the number of Irish immigrants. Although Irishmen had been coming over since the previous century during the summer months to help with the various harvests, it was not until the Potato Famines of the 1840s that there was a mass exodus of families from Ireland to America and England. Irish entertainers were sure of a warm welcome from their compatriots in any provincial town.

13
A typical music hall handbill for the passer by. It contains very little information and appears to suffer from the somewhat limited imagination and vocabulary of the copy writer. Note that the traditional harlequinade is still with us.

12

MICHAEL. HAYNES

IRISH PRIZE DANCER.

13

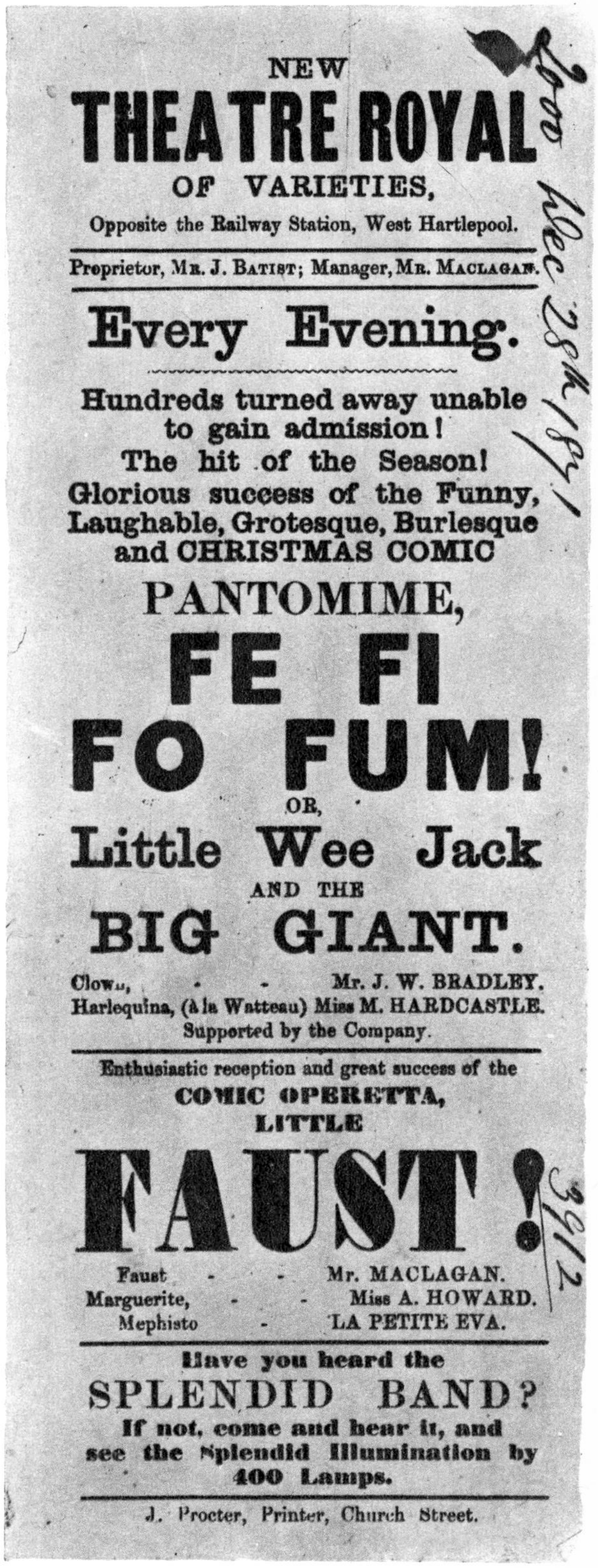

NEW

THEATRE ROYAL

OF VARIETIES,

Opposite the Railway Station, West Hartlepool.

Proprietor, Mr. J. Batist; Manager, Mr. Maclagan.

Every Evening.

Hundreds turned away unable to gain admission!

The hit of the Season!

Glorious success of the Funny, Laughable, Grotesque, Burlesque and CHRISTMAS COMIC

PANTOMIME,

FE FI FO FUM!

OR,

Little Wee Jack

AND THE

BIG GIANT.

Clown, - - Mr. J. W. BRADLEY.

Harlequina, (à la Watteau) Miss M. HARDCASTLE.

Supported by the Company.

Enthusiastic reception and great success of the

COMIC OPERETTA,

LITTLE

FAUST!

Faust - - Mr. MACLAGAN.

Marguerite, - - Miss A. HOWARD.

Mephisto - LA PETITE EVA.

Have you heard the

SPLENDID BAND?

If not, come and hear it, and see the Splendid Illumination by 400 Lamps.

J. Procter, Printer, Church Street.

14
The Victorians enjoyed nothing more than a good moral drama on social evils. It justified their attendance at the theatre which their evangelical consciences might otherwise have jibbed at and it gave them the opportunity to be self righteous. Drunkenness was an evil which had its roots in the vile living conditions in which some of the working classes existed, but the drunk aroused more indignation than the slums.

15
There has rarely been a time in England since the reign of James I when some member of the Lupino family has not been entertaining an audience as acrobat, dancer, or actor, or as all three. This bill places them in the newly-built theatre which also presented the Compton Comedy Company and so made it possible for Sir Compton Mackenzie to be born a native of West Hartlepool.

16
Another exponent of the negro breakdown dance 'Jim Crow'. The 'gimmick' of the 500 surtouts to be given away is connected with the singing for the first time of an original song 'My New Surtout'.

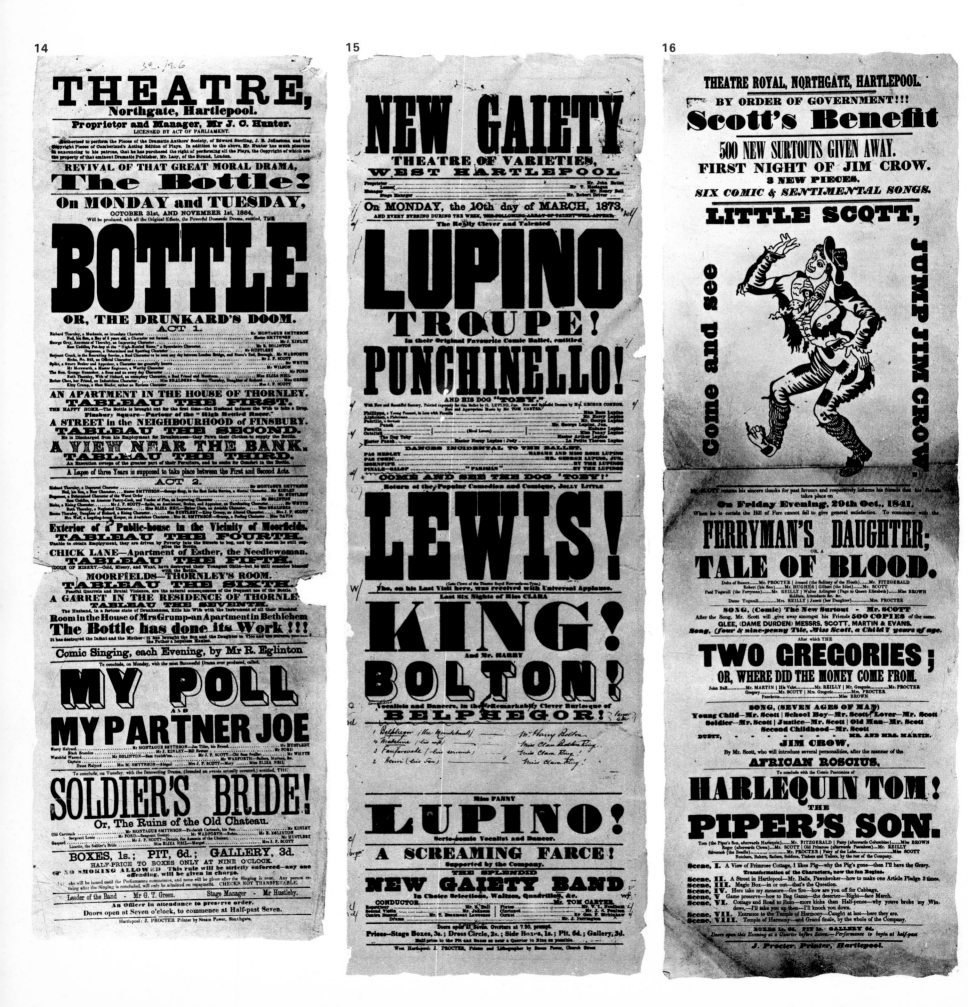

14

THEATRE,
Northgate, Hartlepool.
Proprietor and Manager, Mr J. C. Hunter.
LICENSED BY ACT OF PARLIAMENT.

Authorised to perform the Pieces of the Dramatic Authors' Society, of Edward Sterling, J. B. Johnstone, and the Copyright Pieces of Cumberland's Acting Edition of Plays. In addition to the above, Mr. Hunter has much pleasure in announcing to his patrons, that he has purchased the right of performing all the Plays, the Copyright of which are the property of that eminent Dramatic Publisher, Mr. Lacy, of the Strand, London.

REVIVAL OF THAT GREAT MORAL DRAMA,
The Bottle!
On MONDAY and TUESDAY,
OCTOBER 31st, AND NOVEMBER 1st, 1864,
Will be produced, with all the Original Effects, the Powerful Domestic Drama, entitled, THE
BOTTLE
OR, THE DRUNKARD'S DOOM.

ACT 1.

Richard Thornley, a Mechanic, an irresolute Character ... Mr MONTAGUE SMYTHSON
Ned, his Son, a Boy of 5 years old, a Character not formed ... Master SMYTHSON
George Gray, Associate of Thornley, an Improving Character ... Mr J. KINLEY
Sam Coddles, Pot-boy at the "High-Mettled Racer," a Speculative Character ... Mr R. EGLINTON
Dogsnose, a Determined and Sporting Character ... Mr HUSTLEBY
Serjeant Crank, in the Recruiting Service ... Mr WADFORTH
Binks, No. 243, an Official Character ... Mr J. F. SCOTT
Spike, a Sworn Broker and Appraiser, a Character too generally known ... Mr WHYTE
Mr Moreworth, a Master Engineer, a Worthy Character ... Mr WILSON
The Hon. George Hounslow, a Beau and an every day Character ... Mr FORD
Ruth Thornley, Wife of Richard, an exemplary Character, a Real Friend and Mentress ... Miss ELIZA NEIL
Esther Clare, her Friend, an Industrious Character ... Miss SHALDERS—Emma Thornley, Daughter of Richard ... Miss GREEN
Kitty Crump, a Shoe Binder, rather an Envious Character ... Mrs J. F. SCOTT

AN APARTMENT IN THE HOUSE OF THORNLEY.
TABLEAU THE FIRST.
THE HAPPY HOME.—The Bottle is brought out for the first time—the Husband induces the Wife to take a Drop.
Finsbury Square—Parlour of the "High Mettled Racer."
A STREET in the NEIGHBOURHOOD of FINSBURY.
TABLEAU THE SECOND.
He is Discharged from his Employment for Drunkenness—they Pawn their Clothes to supply the Bottle.
A VIEW NEAR THE BANK.
TABLEAU THE THIRD.
An Execution sweeps of the greater part of their Furniture, and he seeks for Comfort in the Bottle.

A Lapse of three Years is supposed to take place between the First and Second Acts.

ACT 2.

Exterior of a Public-house in the Vicinity of Moorfields.
TABLEAU THE FOURTH.
Unable to obtain Employment, they are driven by Poverty into the Streets to beg, and by this means he still supplies the Bottle.
CHICK LANE—Apartment of Esther, the Needlewoman.
TABLEAU THE FIFTH.
ABODE OF MISERY.—Cold, Misery, and Want, have destroyed their Youngest Child—but he still consoles himself with the Bottle.
MOORFIELDS—THORNLEY'S ROOM.
TABLEAU THE SIXTH.
Fearful Quarrels and Brutal Violence, are the natural consequences of the frequent use of the Bottle.
A GARRET IN THE RESIDENCE OF THORNLEY.
TABLEAU THE SEVENTH.
The Husband, in a furious state of Drunkenness, Kills his Wife with the Instrument of all their Mischief.
Room in the House of Mrs Grump—an Apartment in Bethlehem
The Bottle has done its Work!!!
It has destroyed the Infant and the Mother—it has brought the Son and the Daughter to Vice and the streets, and has left the Father a hopeless Maniac.

Comic Singing, each Evening, by Mr R. Eglinton

To conclude, on Monday, with the most Successful Drama ever produced, called,
MY POLL
AND
MY PARTNER JOE

Harry Halyard ... Mr MONTAGUE SMYTHSON—Joe Tiller, his Friend ... Mr HUSTLEBY
Black Brandon ... Mr J. KINLEY—Bill Bowser ... Mr FORD
Watchful Waxend ... Mr EGLINTON—Sam Snatch'em ... Mr J. F. SCOTT—Old Sam Sculler ... Mr WHYTE
Captain ... Mr WADFORTH—Sailors, Marines, &c.
Dame Halyard ... Mrs M. SMYTHSON—Abigail ... Mrs J. F. SCOTT—Mary ... Miss ELIZA NEIL

To conclude, on Tuesday, with the Interesting Drama, (founded on events actually occured,) entitled, THE
SOLDIER'S BRIDE!
Or, The Ruins of the Old Chateau.

Old Cartouch ... Mr MONTAGUE SMYTHSON—Frederick Cartouch, his Son ... Mr KINLEY
Sergeant Louis ... Mr FORD—Sergeant George ... Mr WADFORTH—Robin ... Mr R. EGLINTON
Gaspard ... Mr J. F. SCOTT—Dennis, the Assassin of the Chateau ... Mr HUSTLEBY
Lisette, the Soldier's Bride ... Miss ELIZA NEIL—Margot ... Mrs J. F. SCOTT

BOXES, 1s.; PIT, 6d.; GALLERY, 3d.
HALF-PRICE TO BOXES ONLY AT NINE O'CLOCK.
NO SMOKING ALLOWED This rule will be strictly enforced—any one offending, will be given in charge.
...cks will be issued until the Performance commences, and none will be given after the Singing is over. Any person retiring after the Singing is concluded, will only be admitted on repayment. CHECKS NOT TRANSFERABLE.
Leader of the Band - Mr G. T. Green. Stage Manager - Mr Hustleby.
An Officer in attendance to preserve order.
Doors open at Seven o'clock, to commence at Half-past Seven.
Hartlepool: J. PROCTER Printer by Steam Power, Southgate.

15

NEW GAIETY
THEATRE OF VARIETIES,
WEST HARTLEPOOL

Proprietor ... Mr. John Batist
Lessee ... Mr T. Hastagan
Manager ... Mr. Henry Bell
Stage Manager ... Mr. Robert Driver

On MONDAY, the 10th day of MARCH, 1873,
AND EVERY EVENING DURING THE WEEK, THE FOLLOWING ARRAY OF TALENT WILL APPEAR.
The Really Clever and Talented
LUPINO
TROUPE!
In their Original Favourite Comic Ballet, entitled
PUNCHINELLO!
AND HIS DOG "TOBY."
With New and Beautiful Scenery, Painted expressly for this Ballet by G. LUPINO, Jun. New and Splendid Dresses by Mr. GEORGE CONNOR. New and Appropriate Music by Mr. TOM CARTER.

Phillippo, a Young Peasant, in love with Feralla ... Miss Rose Lupino
Alphonso, a Fisherman ... Mr. Harry Lupino
Pedrillo, a Servant ... Mr. George Lupino
Punch ... Mr. George Lupino, Jun.
Feralla ... (Rival Lovers) ... Madame Lupino
Catalina ... Miss Fanny Lupino
The Dog Toby ... Master Arthur Lupino
Master Punch ... Master Harry Lupino | Judy ... La Petite Theresa Lupino

DANCES INCIDENTAL TO THE BALLET.
PAS MEDLEY ... MADAME AND MISS ROSE LUPINO
PAS COMIC ... MR. GEORGE LUPINO, JUN.
HORNPIPE ... BY THE LUPINOS
FINALE—GALOP ... "PARISIAN" ... BY THE LUPINOS

COME AND SEE THE DOG 'TOBY!'

Return of the Popular Comedian and Comique, JOLLY LITTLE
LEWIS!
(Late Clown of the Theatre Royal Newcastle-on-Tyne,)
Who, on his Last Visit here, was received with Universal Applause.

Last Six Nights of Miss CLARA
KING!
And Mr. HARRY
BOLTON!
Vocalists and Dancers, in the Remarkably Clever Burlesque of
BELPHEGOR!

Miss FANNY
LUPINO!
Serio-comic Vocalist and Dancer.

A SCREAMING FARCE!
Supported by the Company.

THE SPLENDID
NEW GAIETY BAND
In Choice Selections, Waltzes, Quadrilles, &c.
CONDUCTOR ... Mr. TOM CARTER.
Repetiteur ... Mr. T. Ball | Flutes ... Mr. V. T. Needham
Second Violin ... Mr. Johnson | Clarionet ... Mr. J. R. Poulton
Contra Basso ... Mr. T. Beaumont Lawrence | Cornet ... Mr Geo. F. Birkinshaw
Drums ... Mr. J. Farrington

Doors open at Seven. Overture at 7.20, prompt.
Prices—Stage Boxes, 3s.; Dress Circle, 2s.; Side Boxes, 1s.; Pit, 6d.; Gallery, 3d.
Half-price to the Pit and Boxes as near a Quarter to Nine as possible.
West Hartlepool: J. PROCTER, Printer and Lithographer by Steam Power, Church Street

16

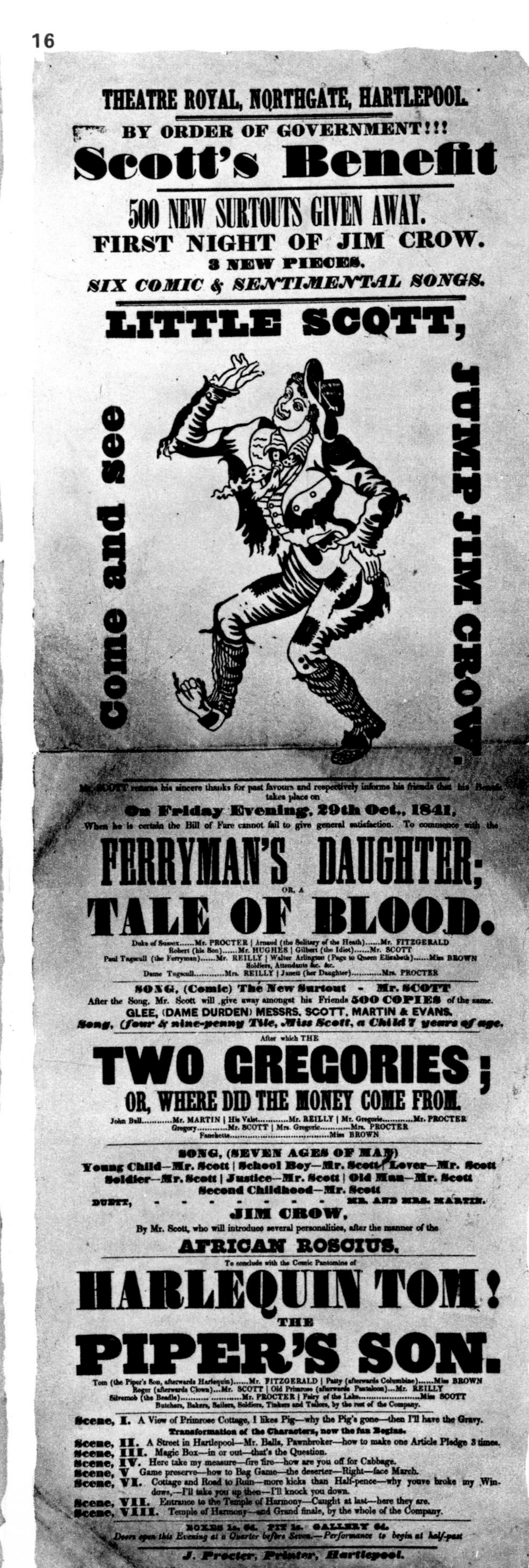

THEATRE ROYAL, NORTHGATE, HARTLEPOOL.
BY ORDER OF GOVERNMENT!!!
Scott's Benefit
500 NEW SURTOUTS GIVEN AWAY.
FIRST NIGHT OF JIM CROW.
3 NEW PIECES.
SIX COMIC & SENTIMENTAL SONGS.
LITTLE SCOTT,
Come and see
JUMP JIM CROW.

Mr. SCOTT returns his sincere thanks for past favours and respectively informs his friends that his Benefit takes place on
On Friday Evening, 29th Oct., 1841,
When he is certain the Bill of Fare cannot fail to give general satisfaction. To commence with the
FERRYMAN'S DAUGHTER;
OR, A
TALE OF BLOOD.

Duke of Sussex......Mr. PROCTER | Arnaud (the Solitary of the Heath)......Mr. FITZGERALD
Robert (his Son)......Mr. HUGHES | Gilbert (the Idiot)......Mr. SCOTT
Paul Tagscull (the Ferryman)......Mr. REILLY | Walter Arlington (Page to Queen Elizabeth)......Miss BROWN
Soldiers, Attendants &c. &c.
Dame Tagscull..........Mrs. REILLY | Janett (her Daughter)............Mrs. PROCTER

SONG, (Comic) The New Surtout - Mr. SCOTT
After the Song, Mr. Scott will give away amongst his Friends 500 COPIES of the same.
GLEE, (DAME DURDEN) MESSRS. SCOTT, MARTIN & EVANS.
Song, (four & nine-penny Tile, Miss Scott, a Child 7 years of age.
After which THE
TWO GREGORIES;
OR, WHERE DID THE MONEY COME FROM.

John Bull............Mr. MARTIN | His Valet............Mr. REILLY | Mr. Gregorie............Mr. PROCTER
Gregory............Mr. SCOTT | Mrs. Gregorie............Mrs. PROCTER
Fanchette..Miss BROWN

SONG, (SEVEN AGES OF MAN)
Young Child—Mr. Scott | School Boy—Mr. Scott | Lover—Mr. Scott
Soldier—Mr. Scott | Justice—Mr. Scott | Old Man—Mr. Scott
Second Childhood—Mr. Scott
DUETT, - - - - - - - - MR. AND MRS. MARTIN.
JIM CROW,
By Mr. Scott, who will introduce several personalities, after the manner of the
AFRICAN ROSCIUS.

To conclude with the Comic Pantomine of
HARLEQUIN TOM!
THE
PIPER'S SON.

Tom (the Piper's Son, afterwards Harlequin)......Mr. FITZGERALD | Patty (afterwards Columbine)......Miss BROWN
Roger (afterwards Clown)...Mr. SCOTT | Old Primrose (afterwards Pantaloon)...Mr. REILLY
Silvernob (the Beadle)........................Mr. PROCTER | Fairy of the Lake........................Miss SCOTT
Butchers, Bakers, Sailors, Soldiers, Tinkers and Tailors, by the rest of the Company.

Scene, I. A View of Primrose Cottage, I likes Pig—why the Pig's gone—then I'll have the Gravy.
Transformation of the Characters, now the fun Begins.
Scene, II. A Street in Hartlepool—Mr. Balls, Pawnbroker—how to make one Article Pledge 3 times.
Scene, III. Magic Box—in or out—that's the Question.
Scene, IV. Here take my measure—fire fire—how are you off for Cabbage.
Scene, V Game preserve—how to Bag Game—the deserter—Right—face March.
Scene, VI. Cottage and Road to Ruin—more kicks than Half-pence—why youve broke my Windows,—I'll take you up then—I'll knock you down.
Scene, VII. Entrance to the Temple of Harmony—Caught at last—here they are.
Scene, VIII. Temple of Harmony—and Grand finale, by the whole of the Company.

BOXES 1s. 6d. PIT 1s. GALLERY 6d.
Doors open this Evening at a Quarter before Seven.—Performance to begin at half-past
J. Procter, Printer, Hartlepool.

17
An example of the decorative and dainty handbill to be compared with the crude utility of No. 26. In addition to the usual programme of domestic drama, dances (including the polka) and the thrilling nautical drama 'Black-eyed Susan', it will be noted that Captain Edward Robinson is to sing 'Spottee'. The North-east coastal region of England has always been proud of its songs and 'Spottee's Hole' is still pointed out in Roker Park at Sunderland.

18
Five complete changes of programme in a week, concluding with a Saturday night of almost unbearable suspense! Even if the heroine in the sawmill survived the circular saw there was no escape for the customers in the ghastly melodrama of Sweeney Todd the Demon Barber.

17

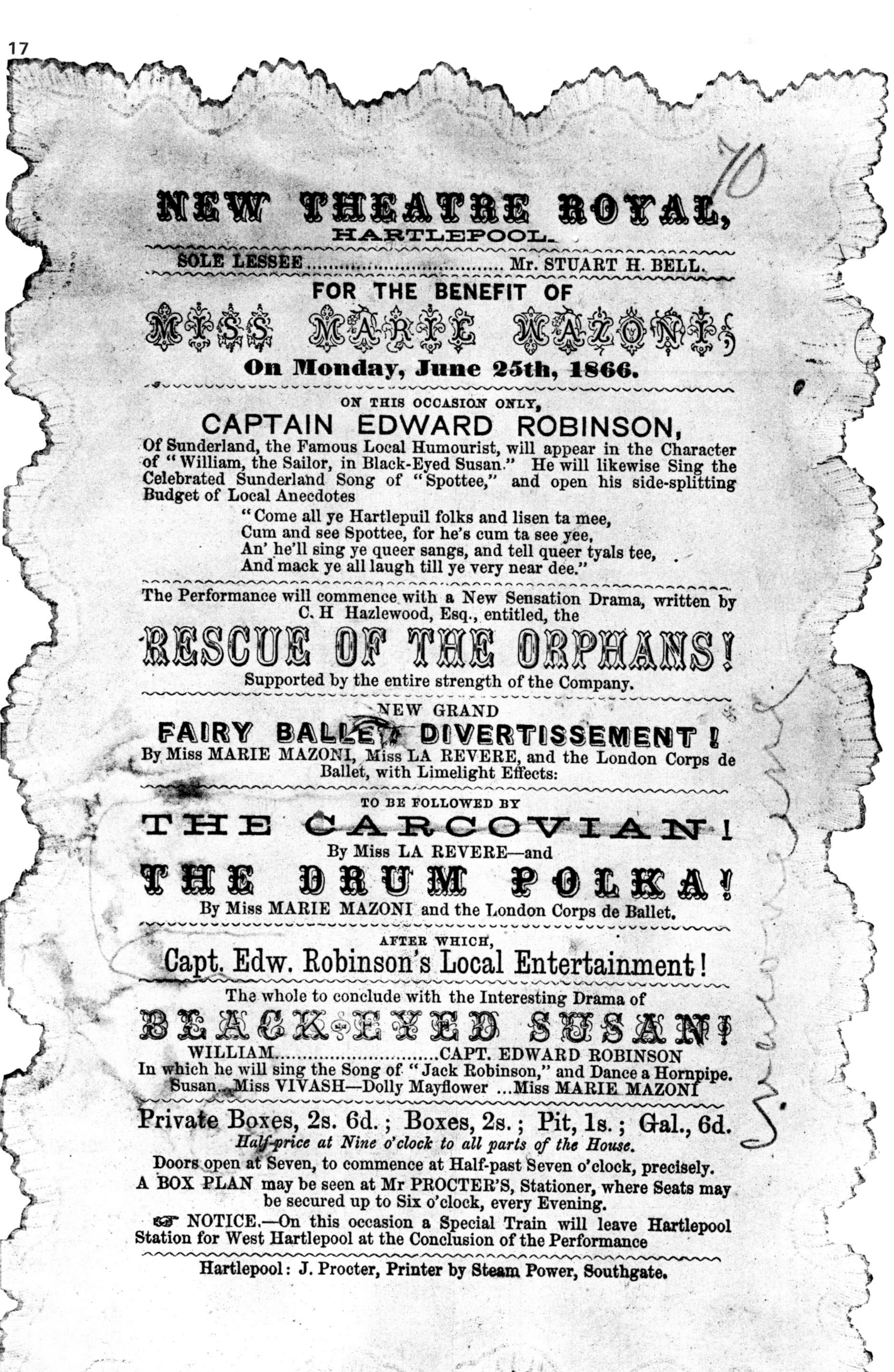
NEW THEATRE ROYAL,
HARTLEPOOL.
SOLE LESSEE.................................. Mr. STUART H. BELL.
FOR THE BENEFIT OF
MISS MARIE MAZONI,
On Monday, June 25th, 1866.
ON THIS OCCASION ONLY,
CAPTAIN EDWARD ROBINSON,
Of Sunderland, the Famous Local Humourist, will appear in the Character of "William, the Sailor, in Black-Eyed Susan." He will likewise Sing the Celebrated Sunderland Song of "Spottee," and open his side-splitting Budget of Local Anecdotes

"Come all ye Hartlepuil folks and lisen ta mee,
Cum and see Spottee, for he's cum ta see yee,
An' he'll sing ye queer sangs, and tell queer tyals tee,
And mack ye all laugh till ye very near dee."

The Performance will commence with a New Sensation Drama, written by C. H Hazlewood, Esq., entitled, the
RESCUE OF THE ORPHANS!
Supported by the entire strength of the Company.
NEW GRAND
FAIRY BALLET DIVERTISSEMENT!
By Miss MARIE MAZONI, Miss LA REVERE, and the London Corps de Ballet, with Limelight Effects:
TO BE FOLLOWED BY
THE CARCOVIAN!
By Miss LA REVERE—and
THE DRUM POLKA!
By Miss MARIE MAZONI and the London Corps de Ballet.
AFTER WHICH,
Capt. Edw. Robinson's Local Entertainment!
The whole to conclude with the Interesting Drama of
BLACK-EYED SUSAN!
WILLIAM.............................CAPT. EDWARD ROBINSON
In which he will sing the Song of "Jack Robinson," and Dance a Hornpipe.
Susan...Miss VIVASH—Dolly Mayflower ...Miss MARIE MAZONI
Private Boxes, 2s. 6d.; Boxes, 2s.; Pit, 1s.; Gal., 6d.
Half-price at Nine o'clock to all parts of the House.
Doors open at Seven, to commence at Half-past Seven o'clock, precisely.
A BOX PLAN may be seen at Mr PROCTER'S, Stationer, where Seats may be secured up to Six o'clock, every Evening.
☞ NOTICE.—On this occasion a Special Train will leave Hartlepool Station for West Hartlepool at the Conclusion of the Performance
Hartlepool: J. Procter, Printer by Steam Power, Southgate.

18

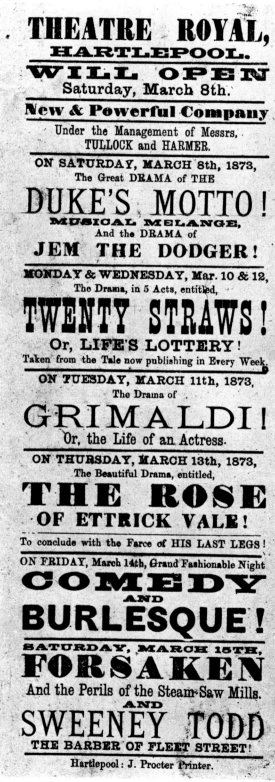

THEATRE ROYAL,
HARTLEPOOL.
WILL OPEN
Saturday, March 8th.
New & Powerful Company
Under the Management of Messrs.
TULLOCK and HARMER.
ON SATURDAY, MARCH 8th, 1873,
The Great DRAMA of THE
DUKE'S MOTTO!
MUSICAL MELANGE,
And the DRAMA of
JEM THE DODGER!
MONDAY & WEDNESDAY, Mar. 10 & 12,
The Drama, in 5 Acts, entitled,
TWENTY STRAWS!
Or, LIFE'S LOTTERY!
Taken from the Tale now publishing in Every Week.
ON TUESDAY, MARCH 11th, 1873,
The Drama of
GRIMALDI!
Or, the Life of an Actress.
ON THURSDAY, MARCH 13th, 1873,
The Beautiful Drama, entitled,
THE ROSE
OF ETTRICK VALE!
To conclude with the Farce of HIS LAST LEGS!
ON FRIDAY, March 14th, Grand Fashionable Night
COMEDY
AND
BURLESQUE!
SATURDAY, MARCH 15TH,
FORSAKEN
And the Perils of the Steam-Saw Mills.
AND
SWEENEY TODD
THE BARBER OF FLEET STREET!
Hartlepool: J. Procter Printer.

19
Like the never-ending closing down sales to be found along Oxford Street in London, this bill must not be taken seriously. It is an indication that business is declining and the stock company may move elsewhere. But if the audiences pick up, those last three nights will be extended.

20
Choppington is a colliery in Northumberland near Ashington which is sometimes unkindly described as the largest pit village in England.
Scotland Gate was a small hamlet and therefore it seems fair to claim that this bill is for a portable theatre. The programme would suggest that the audience liked its drama hot and strong.

19

LORAINE'S BENEFIT!!!

Theatre Royal,
WEST HARTLEPOOL.

Mr W. J. GLYDON begs to announce the appearance, and most positively the

LAST THREE NIGHTS OF
MR. H.
LORAINE
PRONOUNCED BY THE PUBLIC AND THE PRESS TO BE THE GREATEST
LEGITIMATE ACTOR OF THE AGE;
Supported by a Combination Company of Specially Selected Star
DRAMATIC ARTISTES!!
Doors open at 7, commencing at 7.30, except on Saturday, when the doors will open at 6.30, commencing at 7.

NOTICE:-
The Manager begs to announce that, in deference to a very generally expressed wish, THE PRICES OF ADMISSION for the Three following Nights will be, *Centre Boxes, 2s.! Side Boxes, 1s.!! The whole of the Pit, 6d.!!! The whole of the Gallery, 3d.!!!! Half-price to Boxes only.*

On THURSDAY EVENING, JULY 27th, 1871,
Will be Performed the Fine Play, entitled, THE
STRANGER
Count Walbourgh, the Stranger, Mr H. LORAINE
Francis ... Mr GLYNDON
Count Winterson ... Mr DOULAS
Baron Steinfort ... Mr SIDNEY VAUGHAN
Mr Solomon ... Mr FOWLER
Peter, Solomon's Son ... Mr W. ELLIOTT
Tobias ... Mr MIDDLETON
Mrs Haller ... Miss ADA NEILSON
Countess Winterson ... Miss EDITH KINGSLEY
Charlotte ... Miss MILLER

To conclude with the Great and Extraordinarily-interesting Historical Drama, specially translated and adapted from the Celebrated Play of the same name, by ALEXANDER DUMAS, entitled,
CATHERINE HOWARD!
OR,
THE TOMB! THE THRONE!! THE SCAFFOLD!!!
Henry VIII, King of England ... Mr. J W. GLYNDON
... Mr SIDNEY VAUGHAN
Archbishop Cranmer ... Mr FOWLER
Duke of Sussex ... Mr MIDDLETON
Duke of Norfolk ... Mr DOUGLAS
Grand Chamberlain ... Mr GODDY
Lieutenant of the Tower ... Mr JOHNSON | Fleming, an Alchemist ... Mr SMITHSON
Page to Athelwold ... Miss BRAND | Simon Kreutzer, a Weaver ... Mr G. FISHER
Martin Krinckley, a Cordwainer ... Mr J. W. ELLIOTT
Captain of the Guard ... Mr ROBINSON | Executioner ... Mr LUNT
Princess Margaret, Sister to the King ... Miss ALTON
Catherine Howard, the King's Fifth Wife ... Miss ADA NEILSON
Dame Kennedy, her Nurse ... Mrs. G. H. MILLER | Winifred Krinckley, Wife to Martin ... Miss BENSON

ON FRIDAY EVENING, JULY 28th,
For the BENEFIT of
MR.
H. LORAINE
ON WHICH OCCASION HE WILL APPEAR IN TWO OF HIS CELEBRATED CHARACTERS.

The Performance will commence with the celebrated and beautiful Play, entitled,
INGOMAR
THE SON OF THE WILDERNESS.
"Two souls with but a single thought, Two hearts that beat as one."
INGOMAR, the Son of the Wilderness - Mr H. LORAINE
Trinobantes ... Mr FORRESTER
Alastor ... Mr SIDNEY VAUGHAN
Novio ... Mr SMITH
Samo ... Mr JACKSON
Theodes ... Mr CAVILLE
Myron... ... Mr ROGERS
Polydore ... Mr J. W. ELLIOTT
Timarch of Massilia ... Mr J. W. GLYNDON
Philaster ... Mr MIDDLETON
Parthenia ... Miss ADA NEILSON
Theano ... Mrs G. H. MILLER
Theo ... Miss BENSON
Alemanni, Citizens, Soldiers, Pages &c.

The Performances will conclude with Lord Lytton's beautiful Play, in five acts, entitled, THE
LADY OF LYONS
OR, LOVE AND PRIDE!
Beauseant, a wealthy gentleman of Lyons ... Mr SIDNEY VAUGHAN
Glavis, his friend ... Mr W. J. GLYNDON
Colonel, afterwards General Damas, of the French Army ... Mr W. ELLIOTT
Claude Melnotte - - - - Mr H. LORAINE
M. Deschapelles, father of Pauline ... Mr ROGERS
Gaspar ... Mr MIDDLETON | Landlord of the Golden Lion ... Mr M. FORRESTER
1st Officer ... Mr. CAVILLE | 2nd Officer ... Mr Wilkinson | Notary ... Mr BROMLEY
Pauline, the Lady of Lyons ... Miss EDITH KINGSLEY
Madame Deschapelles ... Mrs G. H. MILLER
Widow Melnotte ... Miss WENTWORTH

On Saturday Evening, July 29th, the Last Night of Mr H. Loraine,
GRAND MONSTER ENTERTAINMENT!
DOORS OPEN ON THIS OCCASION AT 6-30, TO COMMENCE AT 7 PRECISELY.
SHAKESPEAR'S Historical Tragedy in 5 Acts, entitled,
The Life and Death of RICHARD III.
RICHARD, DUKE OF GLO'STER, AFTERWARDS KING RICHARD III .... MR H. LORAINE
To conclude with, by SPECAL DESIRE, with the Drama, entitled,
The Duke's Motto: "I AM HERE."
CAPTAIN HENRI DE LAGARDERE .... Mr H. LORAINE

Acting Manager - - Mr. A. FISHER—Stage Manager - - Mr. SIDNEY VAUGHAN—Prompter - - Mr. FORRESTER

West Hartlepool: J. PROCTER, Printer and Lithographer by Steam Power, Church Street.

FRIDAY, JULY 28TH.

20

THEATRE,
SCOTLAND GATE, CHOPPINGTON.

On Saturday Evening,
APRIL 19TH, 1873,
The Sensation Drama of
FORSAKEN
OR, THE
PERILS OF THE STEAM SAW MILL!
AND A
DRAMA!

MONDAY, APRIL 21st,
SHAKESPERE'S Tragedy of
HAMLET!
Prince of Denmark!

Tuesday Evening, April 22nd,
SHAKESPERE'S Play of THE
MERCHANT OF VENICE! OR, THE CRUEL JEW
AND A
FARCE!

On Wednesday Evening, April 23rd,
The Beautiful Play of THE
STRANGER
Or, Misanthropy and Repentance.

On Thursday Evening, April 24th,
THE
MARQUIS & THE COBBLER
AND A FARCE!

On Friday Evening, April 25th,
GRAND FASHIONABLE NIGHT!
COLMAN'S Beautiful Comedy, entitled,
JOHN BULL
Or, an Englishman's Fireside.

MUSICAL MELANGE!!
EACH EVENING.

Reserved Seats, One Shilling; Body of the Hall, 6d.

Hartlepool: J. PROCTER, Printer by Steam Power.

21
This bill was not printed in Hartlepool and was most probably handed over by some theatrical manager as a sample of what they wished the local printer to do. Actors had their own way of making up a bill. They cut out the various acts and play titles from former bills and stuck them together, frequently with stamp edging, and then handed over the result, which often looked more like the tail of a kite than a theatre bill, for the printer to follow as best he might.

22
Dogs have always delighted us with their tricks. In early days there were even dog dramas such as 'The Dog of Montargis' in which the whole play revolved around certain simple tricks carried out by Dragon the dog. In 1814 the non-appearance of the dog in Dublin caused riots. It would seem that Monsieur Artois' dogs were not of the same calibre. He needed something else to bring in the customers. Hence the offer to give away a live pig to the best amateur comic singer providing he sings with the pig under his arm. This is an echo of the crude rustic humour of the fairs.

21

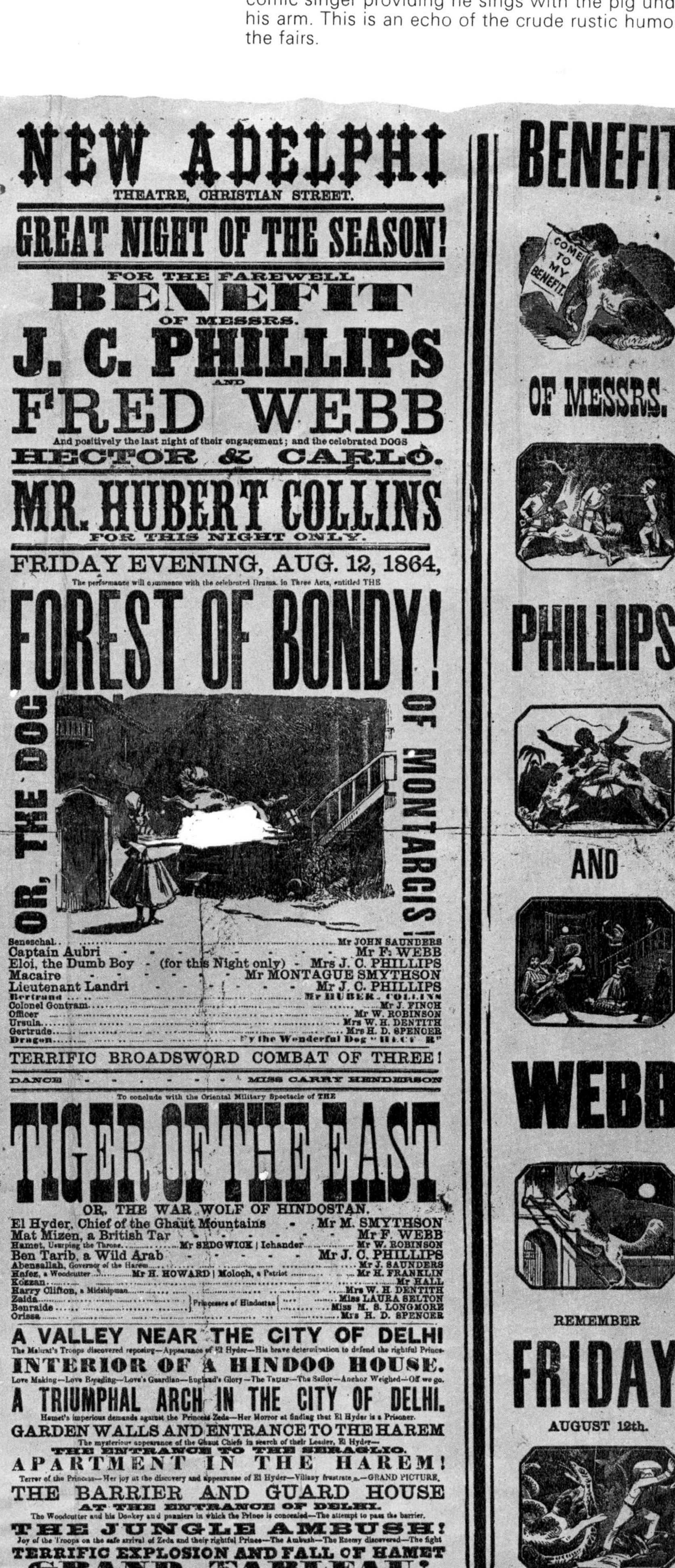

22

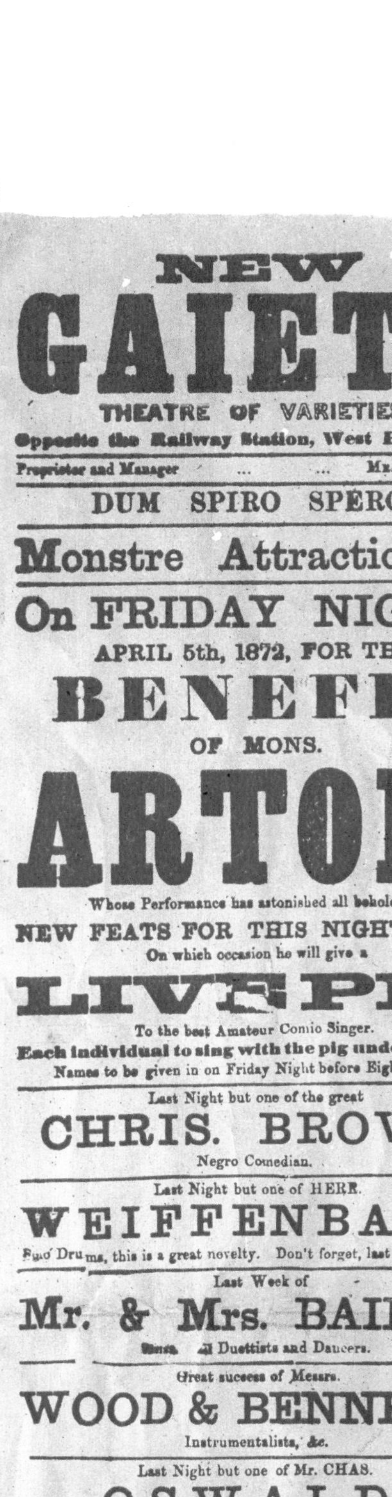

23
This is the sort of entertainment which one would expect to find in a colliery village of the period. Clog dancers were always popular and the great London drama would have its devotees.
It is strange to think that this village later provided a subject for the drama as it was here that Elizabeth Barrett Browning was born in 1806.

24
In addition to the 'Liliputian Band' we have the beautiful drama in which the theatre manager J. H. Hudspeth plays a part followed by comic songs from Farmer Tom Fancourt. Then comes Pat Kinley with his ghosts and Irish policeman, which give place to 'Little Jim, The Collier's Dying Child'.
These, together with a 'Scotch Fling', an 'Irish Jig', and a ballet present as all round an entertainment as could be devised to suit all tastes.

23

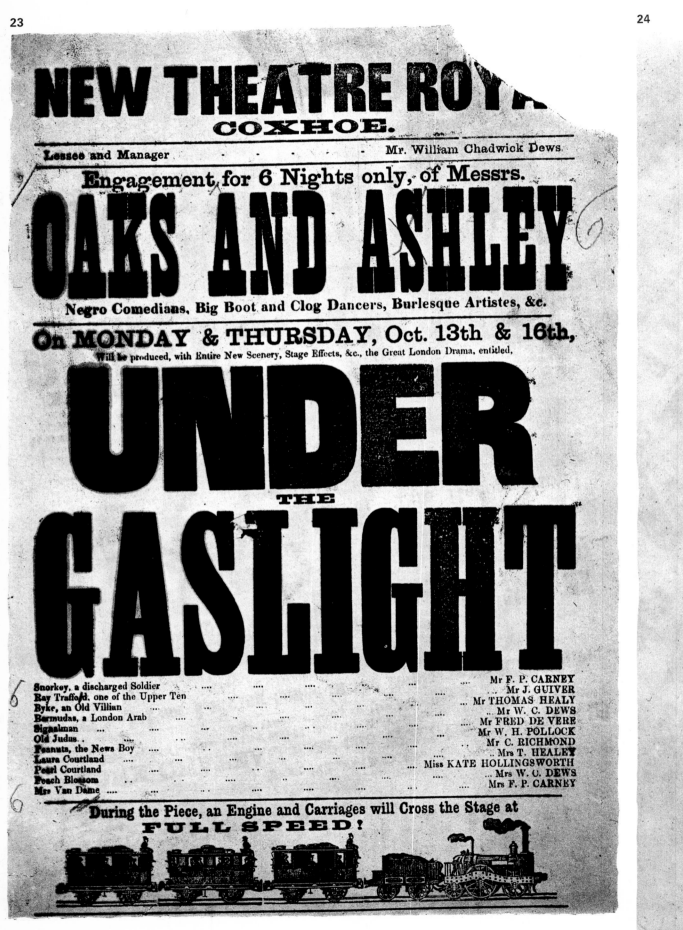

NEW THEATRE ROY[AL]
COXHOE.

Lessee and Manager - - - - - - Mr. William Chadwick Dews.

Engagement for 6 Nights only, of Messrs.
OAKS AND ASHLEY
Negro Comedians, Big Boot and Clog Dancers, Burlesque Artistes, &c.

On MONDAY & THURSDAY, Oct. 13th & 16th,
Will be produced, with Entire New Scenery, Stage Effects, &c., the Great London Drama, entitled,

UNDER
THE
GASLIGHT

Snorkey, a discharged Soldier .... Mr F. P. CARNEY
Ray Trafford, one of the Upper Ten .... Mr J. GUIVER
Byke, an Old Villian .... Mr THOMAS HEALY
Bermudas, a London Arab .... Mr W. C. DEWS
Signalman .... Mr FRED DE VERE
Old Judus .... Mr W. H. POLLOCK
Peanuts, the News Boy .... Mr C. RICHMOND
Laura Courtland .... Mrs T. HEALEY
Pearl Courtland .... Miss KATE HOLLINGSWORTH
Peach Blossom .... Mrs W. C. DEWS
Mrs Van Dame .... Mrs F. P. CARNEY

During the Piece, an Engine and Carriages will Cross the Stage at
FULL SPEED!

24

THEATRE ROYAL,
HARTLEPOOL.
Lessee and Manager - - - Mr J. H. Hudspeth

Immense & Extraordinary
ATTRACTION.

Fancourt's Liliputian Band!

Thursday, Nov. 10th,
BEING FOR THE
BENEFIT OF
FARMER TOM
FANCOURT
The Original Farmer's Son, Roving Joe, Paper Collar Joe, & 10,000 Miles away,
UNDER THE PATRONAGE OF THE
ANCIENT ORDER OF
DRUIDS!
HARTLEPOOL DISTRICT.

First and only Night of the beautiful Drama of
WILL AND THE WAY
Or, The Mysteries of Carew Abbey.

Old Martin, an old Servant ... ... Mr H. Hampton
Joe Beans ... ... Mr John H. Hudspeth
Merrin Hafez ... ...Mr Edwin Harris
Zarah, a Nurse ... ... Miss E. Hampton
Supported by the Company.

AFTER WHICH
Farmer Tom Fancourt
Will open his Comic Budget of Copyright Songs!

On this Night
PAT KINLEY
Will sing his Great Song of the "Ghost of Butcher's Wood," and introduce his "Irish Policeman," being sadly in want of a charge, must have *some one to run in.*

After which MISS EMMA HAMPTON, will deliver the beautiful Poem of LITTLE JIM, The Collier's Dying Child.

Favourite Songs, (on this occasion only,)
MISS ELLEN BELLAIR,
From the Theatre Royal, West Hartlepool.

SCOTCH FLING and IRISH JIG
Miss ANNIE MACDONALD!
From the Theatre Royal, Edinburgh.

To conclude with the Side-splitting Ballet of The
TWO ARTISANS,
Or, the Cobbler and Tailor.

Stitch, a Tailor ... ... Mr Christy Miller
Snip, a Snob ... ... Mr Daniels
Rose ... ... Miss McKenzie
William, a Sailor ... . Miss Stalman

☞ Remember THURSDAY, Nov. 10, for TOM FANCOURT'S on the move to his own True Love, 10,000 miles away.

Prices as Usual.

J. Procter, Printer by Steam Power, Hartlepool.

25
Today we have 'kitchen-sink' drama. The equivalent a hundred years ago was the play based on a social problem. Dickens had made such plots popular by means of Nicholas Nickleby and Oliver Twist and similar novels and the stage was not long in taking the hint and producing powerful social dramas such as 'The Bottle', 'Saved from the Streets' and the subject of this playbill.

26
The minstrel craze was at its height between 1850 and 1870. Towards the end of the period most audiences, even in provincial towns, had become connoisseurs of these performances. Well-drilled and smart companies could get by with hackneyed material but the slipshod artiste often attempted to whip up the waning demand by adding new extravaganzas outside the stereotyped traditional performance. This bill promises an entire change with everything fresh, but we are entitled to be sceptical about it.

25

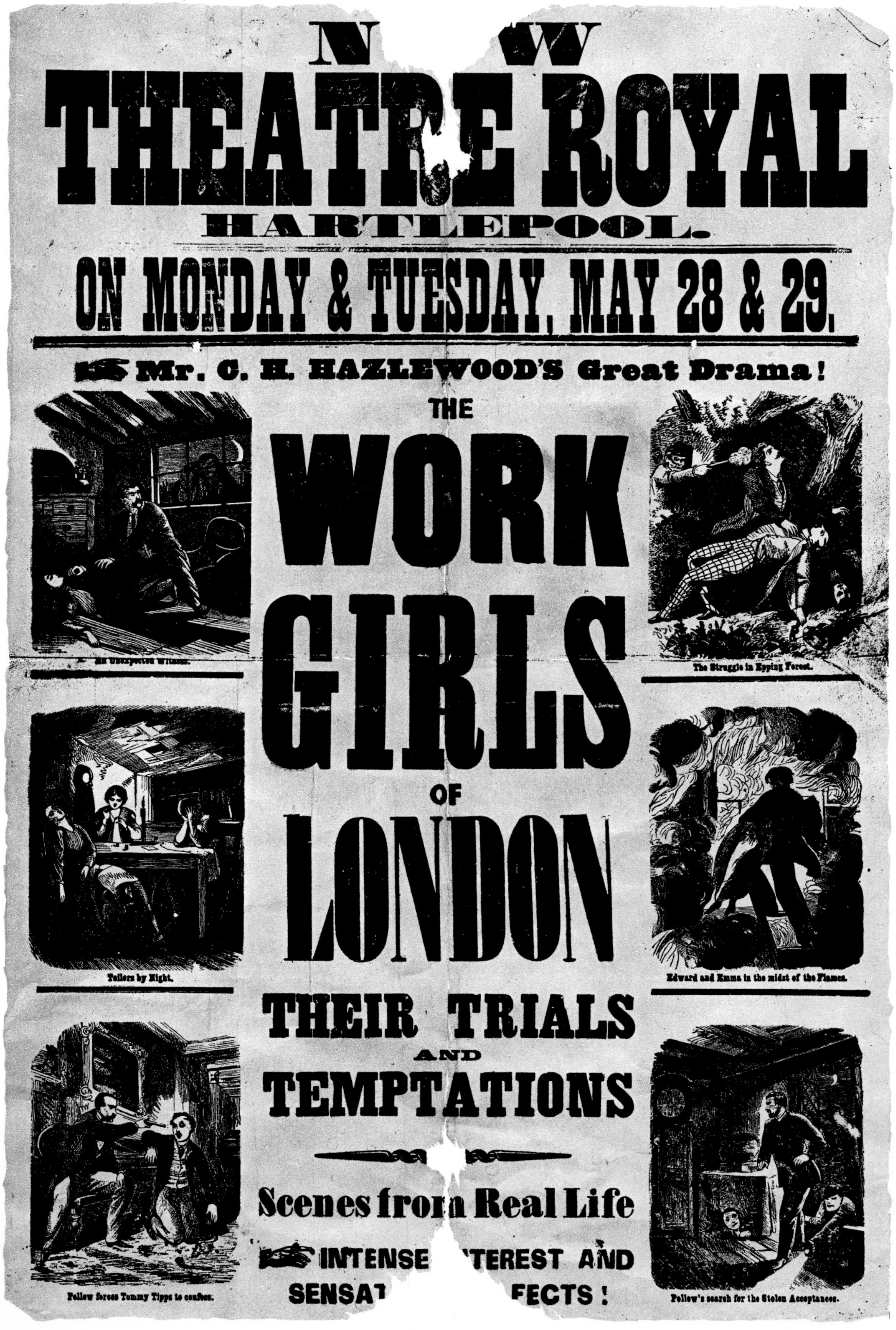

N W
THEATRE ROYAL
HARTLEPOOL.
ON MONDAY & TUESDAY, MAY 28 & 29.
Mr. C. H. HAZLEWOOD'S Great Drama!
THE
WORK
GIRLS
OF
LONDON
THEIR TRIALS
AND
TEMPTATIONS
Scenes fro a Real Life
INTENSE TEREST AND
SENSA FECTS!

The Struggle in Epping Forest.
Toilers by Night.
Edward and Emma in the midst of the Flames.
Pellow forces Tommy Tipps to confess.
Pellow's search for the Stolen Acceptances.

26

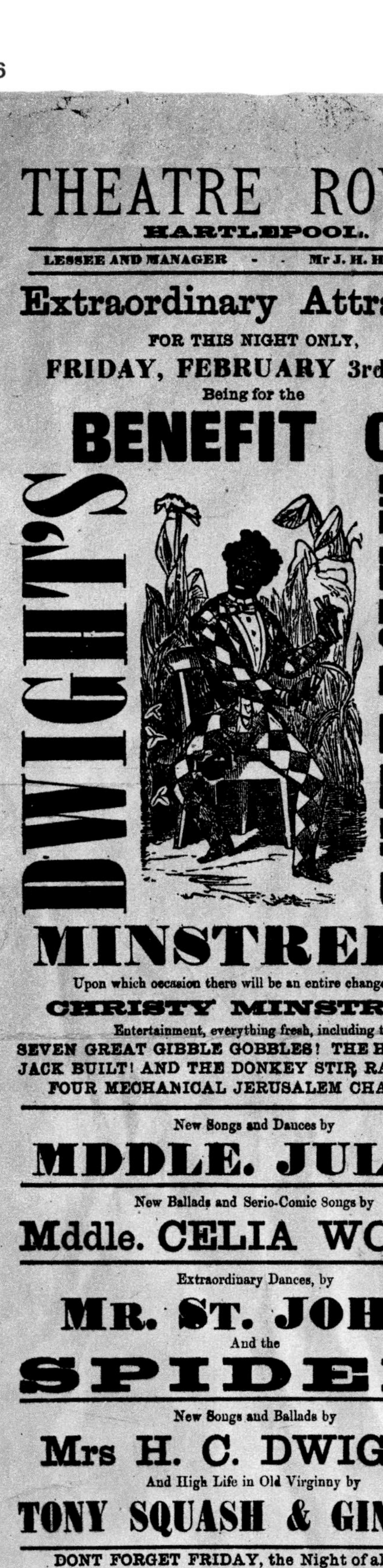

27
A true son of the music hall, for he was a mechanic from the Midlands who had graduated by way of public house sing-songs to the stage. He represented all that the street corner layabouts admired, since he came from their level of society but was now enabled by his earnings to dress immaculately and sport a monocle, whiskers, and fur collar. His favourite song was 'Champagne Charlie' and Champagne his favourite drink. He extolled the delights of dissipation and died miserably.

28
It is fairly obvious that the only stars to be found in this production are in the title! This is the bill of a typical third-rate Stock Company plodding its way steadily through its repertoire and hoping that business will get better, although those in the Company who are not incurable optimists have a shrewd suspicion it will not. They are not even playing in a proper theatre, for the Druids' Hall was hired out by its owners for fancy dress balls and exhibitions. Today it sees dramas of a different kind for it is now the County Court!

27

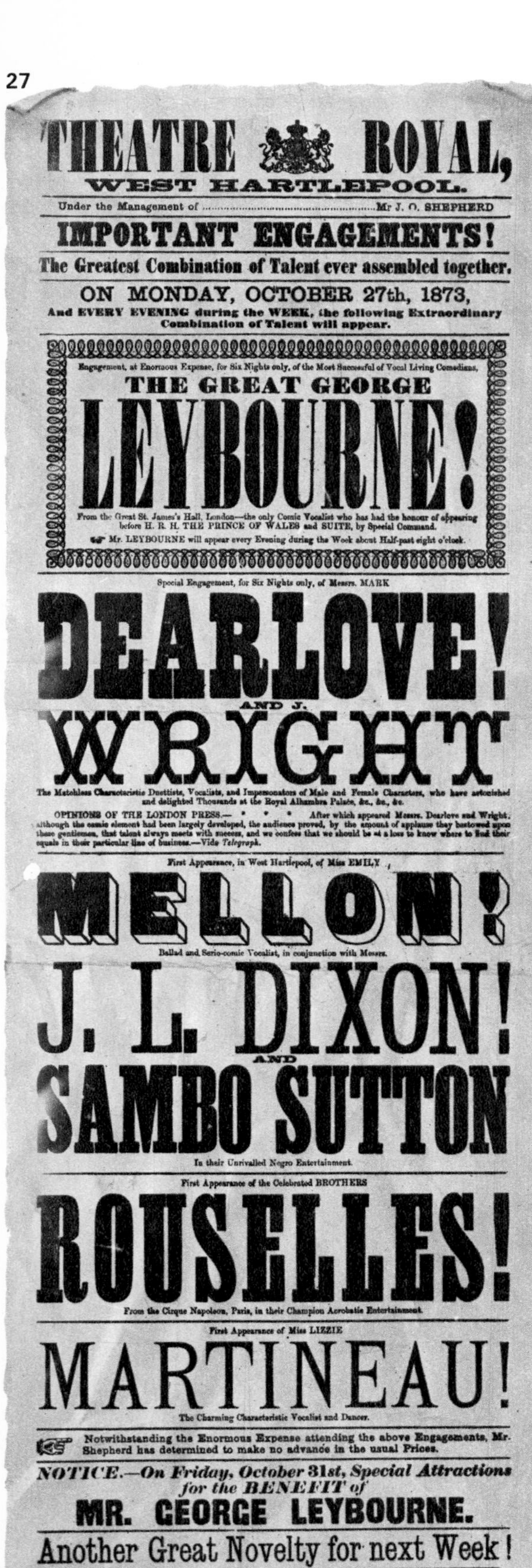

THEATRE ROYAL,
WEST HARTLEPOOL.
Under the Management of .... Mr J. O. SHEPHERD
IMPORTANT ENGAGEMENTS!
The Greatest Combination of Talent ever assembled together.
ON MONDAY, OCTOBER 27th, 1873,
And EVERY EVENING during the WEEK, the following Extraordinary Combination of Talent will appear.

Engagement, at Enormous Expense, for Six Nights only, of the Most Successful of Vocal Living Comedians,
THE GREAT GEORGE
LEYBOURNE!
From the Great St. James's Hall, London—the only Comic Vocalist who has had the honour of appearing before H. R. H. THE PRINCE OF WALES and SUITE, by Special Command.
Mr. LEYBOURNE will appear every Evening during the Week about Half-past eight o'clock.

Special Engagement, for Six Nights only, of Messrs. MARK
DEARLOVE!
AND J.
WRIGHT
The Matchless Characteristic Duettists, Vocalists, and Impersonators of Male and Female Characters, who have astonished and delighted Thousands at the Royal Alhambra Palace, &c., &c., &c.
OPINIONS OF THE LONDON PRESS.— * * * After which appeared Messrs. Dearlove and Wright, although the comic element had been largely developed, the audience proved, by the amount of applause they bestowed upon these gentlemen, that talent always meets with success, and we confess that we should be at a loss to know where to find their equals in their particular line of business.—Vide *Telegraph*.

First Appearance, in West Hartlepool, of Miss EMILY
MELLON!
Ballad and Serio-comic Vocalist, in conjunction with Messrs.
J. L. DIXON!
AND
SAMBO SUTTON
In their Unrivalled Negro Entertainment.

First Appearance of the Celebrated BROTHERS
ROUSELLES!
From the Cirque Napoleon, Paris, in their Champion Acrobatic Entertainment.

First Appearance of Miss LIZZIE
MARTINEAU!
The Charming Characteristic Vocalist and Dancer.

Notwithstanding the Enormous Expense attending the above Engagements, Mr. Shepherd has determined to make no advance in the usual Prices.

NOTICE.—On Friday, October 31st, Special Attractions for the BENEFIT of
MR. GEORGE LEYBOURNE.

Another Great Novelty for next Week!

Admission:—Centre Boxes (numbere and reservedd), 2s.; Private Boxes, 1s. 6d.; Side Boxes, 1s.; Pit, 6d.; Gallery, 3d.
BOX PLAN at Mr C. HOGGETT'S Music Warehouse, West Hartlepool, where Places may be secured. Special Arrangements for Families or Parties requiring Private Boxes. Applications to be made at the Theatre, or 21, Tower St. Doors open at 7 o'clock; Overture at 7.30., precisely. Half-price, to Boxes only, as near 9 o'clock as the termination of an ... will admit. Carriages may be ordered for 10.30.
... will be arranged to conclude in time for visitors from Hartlepool to return by last train.
... STRICTLY PROHIBITED.
... regulation carried into effect, and to maintain the Strictest Order.
... and Lithographer by Steam Power, Church Street.

28

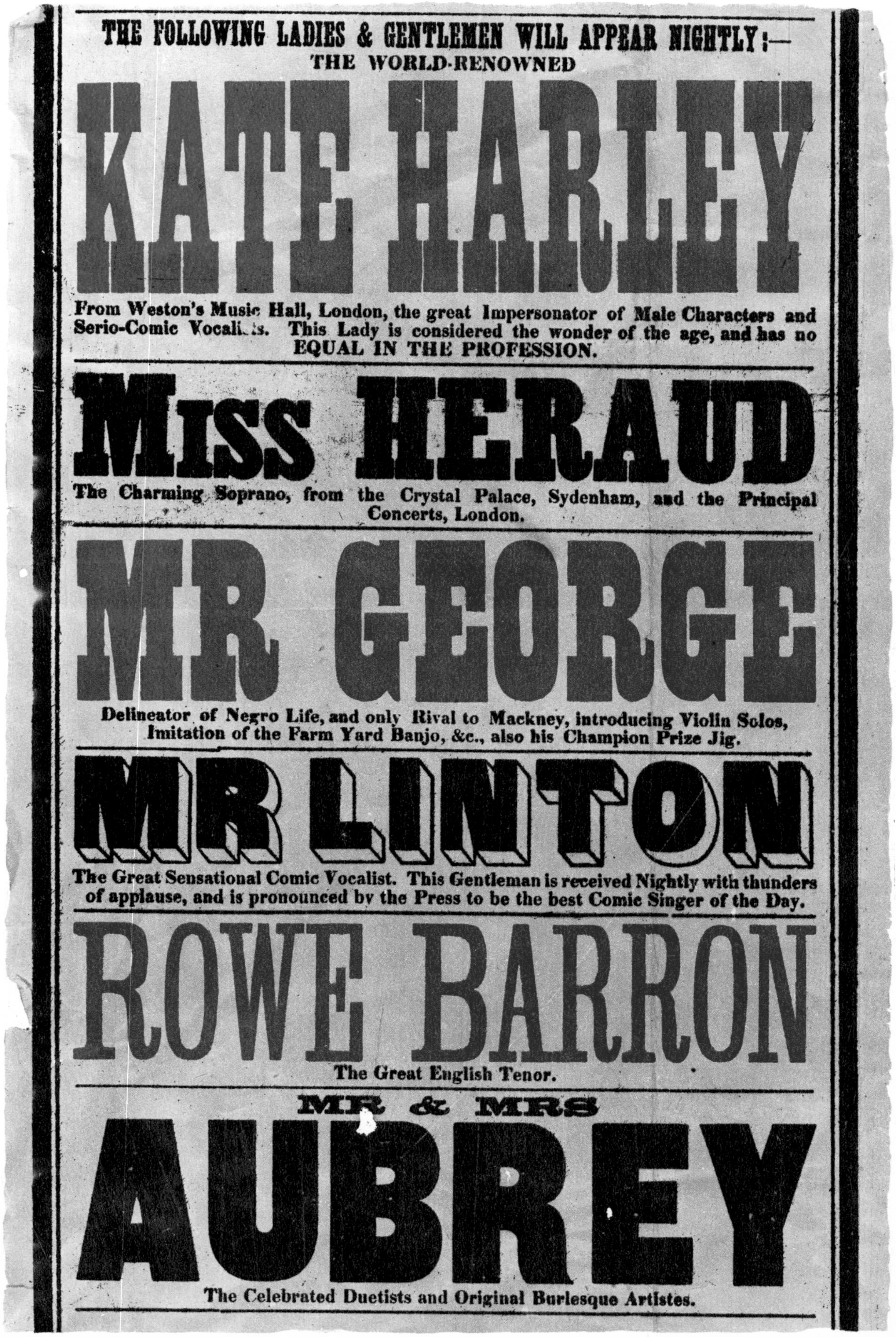

THE FOLLOWING LADIES & GENTLEMEN WILL APPEAR NIGHTLY:—
THE WORLD-RENOWNED
KATE HARLEY
From Weston's Music Hall, London, the great Impersonator of Male Characters and Serio-Comic Vocalists. This Lady is considered the wonder of the age, and has no EQUAL IN THE PROFESSION.

MISS HERAUD
The Charming Soprano, from the Crystal Palace, Sydenham, and the Principal Concerts, London.

MR GEORGE
Delineator of Negro Life, and only Rival to Mackney, introducing Violin Solos, Imitation of the Farm Yard Banjo, &c., also his Champion Prize Jig.

MR LINTON
The Great Sensational Comic Vocalist. This Gentleman is received Nightly with thunders of applause, and is pronounced by the Press to be the best Comic Singer of the Day.

ROWE BARRON
The Great English Tenor.

MR & MRS
AUBREY
The Celebrated Duetists and Original Burlesque Artistes.

29
This bill raises some problems. Here we have the Little Scott we saw in poster 16 as Jim Crow at the Royal Victoria Theatre. Is that the reason for the title of the boat? Or has he become such an enterprising publican that he attempts to steal a march on events, for the Victoria Dock was due to open in three weeks time? He is now the landlord of the Black Lion whereas in no. 36 he has the Steamboat Tavern. It is amusing to note that he could provide hot purl in a quarter of a minute but it took him an hour to get fresh water for the cask—all from the same brewery!

30
Here we have members of Purvis's Company providing an evening of entertainment at the George. The month is May and no doubt they are on tour and for some reason have a free evening. They will have become well-known in the town during the winter and a return visit for renewing old friendships and cracking old jokes will be well-patronised and neither the landlord nor the players will be out of pocket.

31
A Kamptulican was a floor covering made of india-rubber, gutta-percha, and canvas, somewhat akin to linoleum. The gaslights fitted for the purpose of lighting cigars etc, were often very ornate. A favourite was a brass figure of Billy Purvis, six inches high, which stood on a pedestal at the end of the bar. He was dressed in his knickerbocker clown costume, with a loose 'fly' or sleeveless jacket over his shoulders. Out of his white skull-cap, with its red comb running from the nape of his neck to the crown of his head, the gas-jet issued.

29

RARE NEWS!

MORE ACCOMMODATION--

AND NO FEAR OF

Bursting the

BOILERS.

ROYAL VICTORIA

Patent Purl Steam

BOAT.

MR. SCOTT,

OF THE BLACK LION INN,

Returns his kind thanks to his Friends and the Public for past favours, and in order to afford every accommodation, begs to inform them that he intends

LAUNCHING THE ABOVE BOAT

On Monday next, for the use and convenience of Mariners frequenting the Docks, and he assures them that no exertion shall be wanting to merit a continuance of their favours and support.

Mr. S. will Ply round the Docks in his Boat (wind and weather permitting) every Morning, when orders will be thankfully received.

HOT PURL READY IN A QUARTER OF A MINUTE.

Orders received for the Union Brewery.

N. B. SHIPS CASKS FILLED IN ONE HOUR'S NOTICE.

Hartlepool, 20th. Nov. 1840.

J. PROCTER, PRINTER, HARTLEPOOL.

30

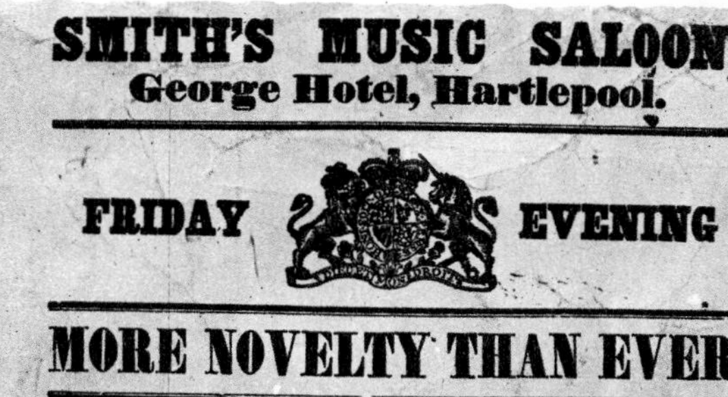

SMITH'S MUSIC SALOON,

George Hotel, Hartlepool.

FRIDAY EVENING

MORE NOVELTY THAN EVER

The Public are respectfully informed that at the request of many parties Mr. SMITH has been induced to engage, FOR ONE NIGHT ONLY,

MR. W.

THOMPSON,

Of Mr. Purvis's Theatre, who will appear

On Friday Evening

MAY 18TH, 1849,

And perform one of his favourite parts in a

NEW PETITE

COMEDY

Who will be supported by Messrs. BILLINGS, COVERDALE, &c. He will likewise sing several NEW SONGS, including

"The Wonderful Telescope," "Trip to California," &c., &c.

With his whole budget of

Punning Songs and Witty Jokes,
That will keep alive Hartlepool Folks.

31

NOTICE.

Gentlemen are particularly requested not to place Cigars on the Table.

Not to Spit on the Floor or Kamptulican, but use the Spittoon.

Not to take Lights from the Chandeliers, but from the Gas-lights fixed for that purpose near the Fires.

Not to engage the Tables verbally, but put the Name down on the Slate to avoid mistakes.

Not to stand round the Tables to the annoyance of the Players, as well as obstructing the views of those who like to see the Game.

Not to toss any Coins on the Table, as the Cloth being very tight is liable to get Cut.

In passing the Ball along the Table, please do not toss the same but roll it gently.

Gentlemen will greatly oblige, and at the same time add to their own comfort and convenience, by complying with the above Rules.

32
Although public houses were first known by the signs which were hung outside for the customer to see, it became the fashion at the latter end of the eighteenth century and well into the nineteenth for superior houses to be known by the names of their landlords. Later this practice was discontinued. This bill shows the process in reverse. Earlier posters of the same saloon which will be seen on subsequent pages give the name of the landlord but here it is dropped, although Mr. Billings is still the manager.

33
Mr. Tom Handford and Mr. J. H. Hudspeth were both well-known and highly respected players who had appeared with various companies. It is likely that they had taken the local Mechanics' Hall as a speculation, hoping to attract sufficient old friends to make their appearance profitable.

34
The coat of arms looks dignified and respectable and makes a magnificent heading for a bill. The printer does not appear to have used it on any posters except those of the Royal Music Saloon and therefore it is quite likely that it belonged to Mr. Billings or Mr. Smith. It was quite usual for a player to send a block along for the printer to use but in most cases it was one with some special reference to the performance. Whatever the reason, this coat of arms certainly gives impact to the poster.

32

ROYAL MUSIC SALOON,
GEORGE HOTEL, NORTHGATE,
HARTLEPOOL.
UNDER THE SOLE MANAGEMENT OF MR. J. BILLINGS.

GREAT ATTRACTION!
ENGAGEMENT OF
MISS ALISON,
From the Theatre Royal Newcastle; and
MRS HOWELL
From the Theatres Royal York, Leeds, and Hull;
WHO WILL MAKE THEIR FIRST APPEARANCE
On MONDAY Evening, June 24th, 1850.

Mr. B. again takes the opportunity of returning his sincere thanks for past favours, and begs most respectfully to call the attention of the Public to the variety of Talent he has selected for their entertainment, and which will be found to excel all other Establishments. And, as Philosophers assert that well-conducted Places of Amusement are calculated to produce the best results, it may also be asserted, from the well-known excellency of the Concerts that have hitherto been produced at the above Establishment, the lovers of rational recreation may anticipate treats of no ordinary merit. He assures those Friends who may patronise him in future, that nothing shall be wanting on his part to render each Evening's Amusement worthy of the Patronage it is always his study to merit.

Amongst the Company, the following highly talented Artists will appear nightly:—
Mrs. SINCLAIR
The much-admired and pleasing Sentimental Singer,
Whose sweetness and feeling in her Songs have been the theme of admiration by all who have heard her, and who have pronounced her to be emphatically a first-rate Singer.
MISS ALISON,
The very popular Comic and Sentimental Singer,
From the THEATRE ROYAL NEWCASTLE, where, as at other Provincial Theatres, she was nightly received with loud bursts of approbation.
MR. J. BILLINGS,
The most humourous Comic Singer of the Day,
Whose Whimsicalities and numerous Hits have been the constant theme of admiration with every laughter-loving Son of Momus, will on each evening amuse the Audience with his Funny Jokes, Quaint Sayings, Laughable Songs, &c.
Mrs. Howell
The Favourite Danseuse,
From the TREATRES ROYAL YORK, LEEDS, HULL, &c., where she has, by her graceful and spirited Performances, created an immense impression, to which the repeated shouts of approval which hailed her upon each appearance loudly testified.
MR. SINCLAIR,
The celebrated and highly popular Violinist,
Mr WILSON
The talented Pianist and Scottish Ballad Singer.

Refreshments of every description and of a Superior Quality.
ADMISSION FREE!
Entertainments to commence each Evening at SEVEN o'clock.
PROPRIETOR, Mr. SMITH——MANAGER, Mr. BILLINGS.
From the Office of J. PROC[illegible], Printer, High Street, Hartlepool.

33

[illegible]ECHANICS' HALL,
HARTLEPOOL.
GREAT ATTRACTION FOR TWO NIGHTS ONLY.
MR. TOM. HANDFORD!
IN CONJUNCTION WITH MR.
J. H. HUDSPETH
WILL GIVE TWO COMIC
CONCERTS!
ON FRIDAY & SATURDAY, July 21 & 22, 1871.
The following Talented Artistes will appear:—
MDLLE. MAUDE ROSIERE
MISS MARIE BRAMAH! MR MACINTIRE!
MR. J. H. HUDSPETH! MR. G. F. COOKE.
AND
TOM. HANDFORD
THE ORIGINAL
BLAC[illegible] DIAMOND!
AND EX-CHAMPION DANCER; ALSO, THE GREAT MULTUM IN PARVO,
TOM HANDFORD, JUN.,
ALIAS,
LITTLE TONY!
Seven Years of age, the Champion Step Dancer of the World.
Doors open at Half-past Seven, the Performance to commence at Eight o'clock.
PRICES:—Reserved Seats, 2s.; Front Seats, 1s.; Second do., 6d.; Gallery, 3d

34

SMITH'S ROYAL MUSIC

SALOON.
UNDER THE SOLE MANAGEMENT OF MR. J. BILLINGS.
EXTRAORDINARY ENGAGEMENT OF
SIGNOR SAMPSON BOLENO!!!
THE CELEBRATED PANTOMIMIST, &c.,
WHO WILL MAKE HIS FIRST APPEARANCE ON MONDAY NEXT,
SEPTEMBER, 30TH, 1850.
J. B. takes this Opportunity of returning Thanks to the numerous Friends and Patrons who visit the MUSIC SALOON, and begs most respectfully to inform them that it is his Determination to use every laudable Method Ingenuity can devise, and Experience accomplish, to render the above Establishment the most complete Place of INSTRUCTIVE AND RATIONAL AMUSEMENT in the North. It is a Matter of infinite Gratification that the Public fully appreciate his continued Efforts for their Amusement; and he refers with Feelings of Pride to the uninterrupted Marks of Approbation and Support from the "*Elite* of Society," which continue to increase nightly, testifying that his Attempt to introduce a superior Class of
MUSICAL ENTERTAINMENTS
In this Town, has merited public Approval.
The Manner in which this Establishment is conducted, prevents the most fastidious from being offended; in fact, admiring Audiences, and the eulogistic Encomiums of the Press, have pronounced this magnificent Saloon the *ne plus ultra* of Elegance and Execution; and it is allowed by all who witness a Night's Performance, that it cannot be surpassed by any in the Metropolis.
THE FOLLOWING TALENTED PERFORMERS, VOCALISTS, AND MUSICIANS WILL APPEAR NIGHTLY:—
SIGNOR
SAMPSON BOLENO,
TAE SPANISH HERCULES, ONLY WEIGHING 8 STONE,
Who will go through the Whole of his wonderful Performances, including the extraordinary STONE FEAT, in which a large Stone is broken on his Chest by the Blow of a sledge Hammer; also, the Herculean Task of bearing on his Chest FIFTEEN 56lbs. WEIGHTS at one Time! He will also give his unrivalled Imitation of the
ROMAN AND GRECIAN STATUES,
This talented Artiste whilst executing his pleasing, though very arduous Performance, gives a striking proof of the Herculean power the human frame is vested with; and the Manager begs to call the attention of the Public to the peculiar nature of the Performance, being an attempt to combine a great display of skill and muscular strength, with illustrations of the most classic models of antiquity. Signor Boleno will present to the audience the reward in renewed industry and perseverance; and it is confidently asserted that the wonderful power he will exhibit cannot be surpassed by any Professors of the present day. The firmness and Herculean power of muscle required for the original and other balances, while executing the beautiful and classic groups of animated sculpture, would appear, at first sight, as physical impossibilities. Also, in the course of each Evening,—
Signora Boleno,
Will give several beautiful Representations of the
POSES PLASTIQUES & TABLEAUX VIVANTS,
(From Pictures in the Royal Academy, London.)
MISS KATE MARTIN,
The Fasinating Characteristic Singer
Well Deserves the Rapturous Applause with which she is Nightly Honoured.
Miss Bloomfield,
The much admired and pleasing little Ballad Singer, from the Royal Casino, Manchester:
MRS. HOWELL,
The Favourite Danseuse,
From the Theatres Royal York, Leeds, Hull, &c., where she has, by her graceful and spirited Performances, created an immense impression, to which the repeated shouts of approval which hailed her upon each appearance loudly testify.
YANKEE BROOKS!!
As the Delineator of the Songs and Melodies of the Ethiopian Race, and inimitable Juba Dancer, leaves all his Predecessors in his peculiar Line at an immeasurable Distance.
MR. BILLINGS,
The most Humourous Comic Singer of the Day,
Who only Lost his Election for Bradford by making his Constituents Laugh so that they could not give him a Vote.
Mr. David Ord!!
The English Paganini,
Whose Performances on the Violin are hailed Nightly with Deafning Shouts of Applause.

Mrs. HOWELL will preside at the Piano Forte.—Violin Primo Mr. D. ORD.—Violin Seconda Mr. GOMERSELL.—Cornet a Piston Mr. WRIGHT.—Double Bass Mr. BATHURST.

The Host of the above delightful and splendid Saloon, feeling certain in the above Resources, trusts that the talented Performers who appear nightly, will, by their united Abilities, yield to the Lovers of Mirth, an Abundance of Wit and Humour; to the Lovers of Music, an increasing Source of Delight; to the Lovers of Dulcet Notes, a Feast Worthy of their Acceptance; to the Lovers of Terpsichore, such Poetry of Motion as to prove truly fascinating; and, lastly, to the Lovers of Good Cheer, such Excellence in that Department as even an Epicure might envy. Thus, by gratifying the Mirthful, pleasing the Musical, and catering for the Pleasures of all, he flatters himself that his Establishment will continue to be the most fashionable Place of AMUSEMENT, ENJOYMENT, and COMFORT, in the NORTH of ENGLAND.
Mr. BILLINGS, in answer to several questions sent to him last week, begs leave to state, that in the course of a Fortnight, the SALOON, will be NEW SEATED, RE-PAINTED, VENTILATED, &c., &c., after the style of the ROYAL CASINO, Manchester, also to impress on their minds, that great preparations are making for the Winter Season.

Proprietor. . Mr. SMITH.—Manager. . Mr. BILLINGS.—Mechanist. . SIGNOR BOLENO.—Artist. . Mr. T. YOUNG, late of PURVIS'S ESTABLISHMENT.—Carpenter. . . . . Mr. MARSHALL.
From the Office of J. PROCTER, High Street, Hartlepool.

35
Here we see the music hall in the making. Mr. Billings was one of Purvis's players in 1849 and Mr. Smith was the enterprising landlord of the George. A later bill shows him promoting a boxing match on the premises with an individual rejoicing in the very un-Victorian nickname of Apple Daddy. But here he has put Mr. Billings in sole charge of his Royal Music Saloon and that gentleman displays his knowledge of the seamy side of show-business by guaranteeing 'No Puff!', 'No Gammon!', 'No Lies!' about the programme.

36
The career of this little man has now been covered in three posters. We saw him first in 16 as Jim Crow, then as landlord of the Black Lion in 29 with an ambitious project to cruise round the docks offering shipbound seamen 'patent purl', which was a concoction of hot spiced gin and beer. Now we return to a poster revealing his introduction to the publican's business, taking over the Steamboat Tavern.

35

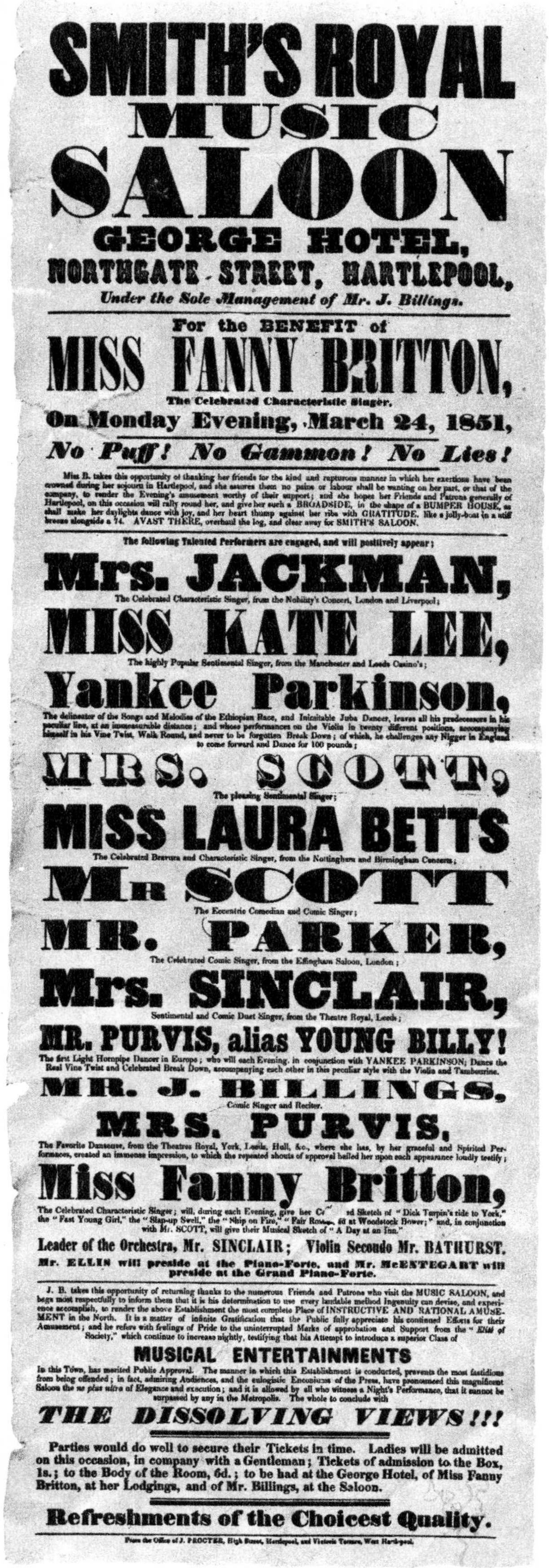

SMITH'S ROYAL
MUSIC
SALOON
GEORGE HOTEL,
NORTHGATE-STREET, HARTLEPOOL,
Under the Sole Management of Mr. J. Billings.

For the BENEFIT of
MISS FANNY BRITTON,
The Celebrated Characteristic Singer,
On Monday Evening, March 24, 1851,
No Puff! No Gammon! No Lies!

Miss B. takes this opportunity of thanking her friends for the kind and rapturous manner in which her exertions have been crowned during her sojourn in Hartlepool, and she assures them no pains or labour shall be wanting on her part, or that of the company, to render the Evening's amusement worthy of their support; and she hopes her Friends and Patrons generally of Hartlepool, on this occasion will rally round her, and give her such a BROADSIDE, in the shape of a BUMPER HOUSE, as shall make her daylights dance with joy, and her heart thump against her ribs with GRATITUDE, like a jolly-boat in a stiff breeze alongside a 74. AVAST THERE, overhaul the log, and clear away for SMITH'S SALOON.

The following Talented Performers are engaged, and will positively appear;

Mrs. JACKMAN,
The Celebrated Characteristic Singer, from the Nobility's Concert, London and Liverpool;
MISS KATE LEE,
The highly Popular Sentimental Singer, from the Manchester and Leeds Casino's;
Yankee Parkinson,
The delineator of the Songs and Melodies of the Ethiopian Race, and Inimitable Juba Dancer, leaves all his predecessors in his peculiar line, at an immeasurable distance; and whose performances on the Violin in twenty different positions, accompanying himself in his Vine Twist, Walk Round, and never to be forgotten Break Down; of which, he challenges any Nigger in England to come forward and Dance for 100 pounds;
MRS. SCOTT,
The pleasing Sentimental Singer;
MISS LAURA BETTS
The Celebrated Bravura and Characteristic Singer, from the Nottingham and Birmingham Concerts;
MR SCOTT
The Eccentric Comedian and Comic Singer;
MR. PARKER,
The Celebrated Comic Singer, from the Effingham Saloon, London;
Mrs. SINCLAIR,
Sentimental and Comic Duet Singer, from the Theatre Royal, Leeds;
MR. PURVIS, alias YOUNG BILLY!
The first Light Hornpipe Dancer in Europe; who will each Evening, in conjunction with YANKEE PARKINSON; Dance the Real Vine Twist and Celebrated Break Down, accompanying each other in this peculiar style with the Violin and Tambourine.
MR. J. BILLINGS,
Comic Singer and Reciter.
MRS. PURVIS,
The Favorite Danseuse, from the Theatres Royal, York, Leeds, Hull, &c., where she has, by her graceful and Spirited Performances, created an immense impression, to which the repeated shouts of approval hailed her upon each appearance loudly testify;
Miss Fanny Britton,
The Celebrated Characteristic Singer; will, during each Evening, give her C[illegible]ed Sketch of "Dick Turpin's ride to York," the "Fast Young Girl," the "Slap-up Swell," the "Ship on Fire," "Fair Ros[illegible] at Woodstock Bower;" and, in conjunction with Mr. SCOTT, will give their Musical Sketch of "A Day at an Inn."

Leader of the Orchestra, Mr. SINCLAIR; Violin Secondo Mr. BATHURST.
Mr. ELLIS will preside at the Piano-Forte, and Mr. McENTEGART will preside at the Grand Piano-Forte.

J. B. takes this opportunity of returning thanks to the numerous Friends and Patrons who visit the MUSIC SALOON, and begs most respectfully to inform them that it is his determination to use every laudable method Ingenuity can devise, and experience accomplish, to render the above Establishment the most complete Place of INSTRUCTIVE AND RATIONAL AMUSEMENT in the North. It is a matter of infinite Gratification that the Public fully appreciate his continued Efforts for their Amusement; and he refers with feelings of Pride to the uninterrupted Marks of approbation and Support from the "*Elite of Society*," which continue to increase nightly, testifying that his Attempt to introduce a superior Class of
MUSICAL ENTERTAINMENTS
In this Town, has merited Public Approval. The manner in which this Establishment is conducted, prevents the most fastidious from being offended; in fact, admiring Audiences, and the eulogistic Encomiums of the Press, have pronounced this magnificent Saloon the *ne plus ultra* of Elegance and execution; and it is allowed by all who witness a Night's Performance, that it cannot be surpassed by any in the Metropolis. The whole to conclude with
THE DISSOLVING VIEWS!!!

Parties would do well to secure their Tickets in time. Ladies will be admitted on this occasion, in company with a Gentleman; Tickets of admission to the Box, 1s.; to the Body of the Room, 6d.; to be had at the George Hotel, of Miss Fanny Britton, at her Lodgings, and of Mr. Billings, at the Saloon.

Refreshments of the Choicest Quality.

From the Office of J. PROCTER, High Street, Hartlepool, and Victoria Terrace, West Hartlepool.

36

HOW'S YOUR BOILERS?

John Scott

Little Scott

~~The funny little Man~~, takes this liberty to inform the Public, ~~that at the request of several respectable Friends~~, he has taken the

STEAM BOAT
TAVERN

Where he trusts that a glass of good Beverage, a cheerful Landlord, ~~a smiling Landlady~~ and good Accommodation, will gain him a Share of Public Patronage and Support. which it shall ever be his study to merit
~~Little Scott~~ will commence Business on Monday, the 3rd December, 1838.
Don't forget the VEGETABLE PILLS.

J. Procter, Printer, Hartlepool.

37

Altogether, we have in this book quite a few examples of the showman instinct of the landlord of the George IV in Hartlepool who had the sense to entrust the running of his Royal Music Saloon to a professional, Mr. Billings of Billy Purvis's Company. This programme does not tell us much. It makes great play with a selection of blocks but beyond the fact that Mr. Pymer was a clown and that the show involved what appears to have been a ventriloquist and his dummy, there is little to learn.

38

It was a wise patron who read his theatre bill carefully and made sure that what appeared in large type was, in fact what would appear on the boards. The Brothers Davenport could be expected to top any music hall bill programme with their magic and revelations of the spiritualist phenomena which were so popular. It is therefore not surprising to see them in the most prominent position on the bill. It is still less surprising on re-reading it to find that they are not going to appear at all.

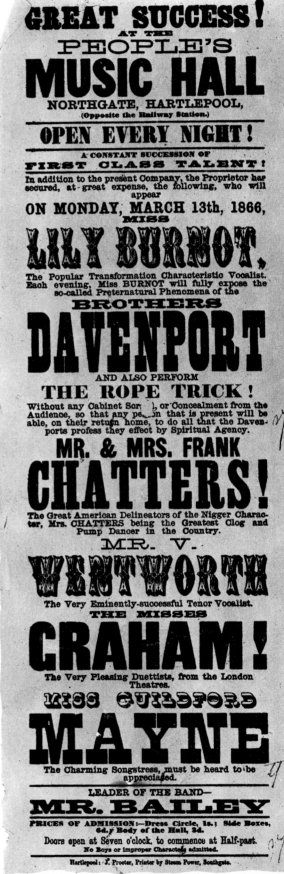

37

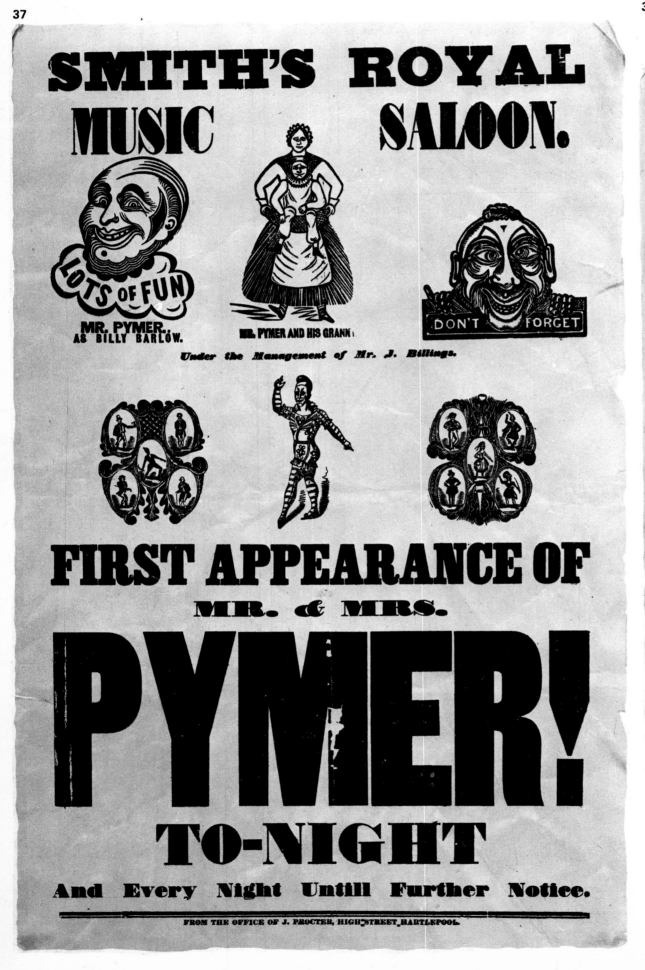

SMITH'S ROYAL

MUSIC SALOON.

MR. PYMER, AS BILLY BARLOW.

MR. PYMER AND HIS GRANN

Under the Management of Mr. J. Billings.

FIRST APPEARANCE OF

MR. & MRS.

PYMER!

TO-NIGHT

And Every Night Untill Further Notice.

FROM THE OFFICE OF J. PROCTER, HIGH STREET, HARTLEPOOL.

38

GREAT SUCCESS!

AT THE

PEOPLE'S

MUSIC HALL

NORTHGATE, HARTLEPOOL,

(Opposite the Railway Station.)

OPEN EVERY NIGHT!

A CONSTANT SUCCESSION OF

FIRST CLASS TALENT!

In addition to the present Company, the Proprietor has secured, at great expense, the following, who will appear

ON MONDAY, MARCH 13th, 1866,

MISS

LILY BURNOT,

The Popular Transformation Characteristic Vocalist. Each evening, Miss BURNOT will fully expose the so-called Preternatural Phenomena of the

BROTHERS

DAVENPORT

AND ALSO PERFORM

THE ROPE TRICK!

Without any Cabinet Scr[illegible], or Concealment from the Audience, so that any pe[illegible]on that is present will be able, on their retu[illegible]n home, to do all that the Davenports profess they effect by Spiritual Agency.

MR. & MRS. FRANK

CHATTERS!

The Great American Delineators of the Nigger Character, Mrs. CHATTERS being the Greatest Clog and Pump Dancer in the Country.

MR. V.

WENTWORTH

The Very Eminently-successful Tenor Vocalist.

THE MISSES

CRAHAM!

The Very Pleasing Duettists, from the London Theatres.

MISS GUILDFORD

MAYNE

The Charming Songstress, must be heard to be appreciated.

LEADER OF THE BAND—

MR. BAILEY

PRICES OF ADMISSION:—Dress Circle, 1s.; Side Boxes, 6d.; Body of the Hall, 3d.

Doors open at Seven o'clock, to commence at Half-past.

No Boys or improper Characters admitted.

Hartlepool: J. Procter, Printer by Steam Power, Southgate.

39
Smith's Royal Saloon did not enjoy a monopoly of public house entertainment. Here we have the Royal Casino at the Dock Hotel. Its bill is well planned and tasteful with a smaller and rather raffish coat of arms in the centre but embellished with a border complete with decorated corners which include additional coats of arms. If heraldry helps to attract the crowds the Royal Casino is going to give the Royal Saloon a run for its money!

40
Here we have another mystery. Professor Leotard is supposed to have drawn crowds to the Alhambra Palace in London when it opened in 1860. He performed without a net over the tables at which the audience ate and drank. He is reported to have died of smallpox in his native France at the age of 28. If that is true it is amazing that he should appear on this bill in 1871. Or is it another artist plagiarizing a famous name?

41
An early example of a typical Music Hall bill. Mademoiselle Austin's troupe was the nineteenth century equivalent of our chorus girls. Probably Madame Cerito put on an act perilously near to the modern nude and strip shows.

39

40

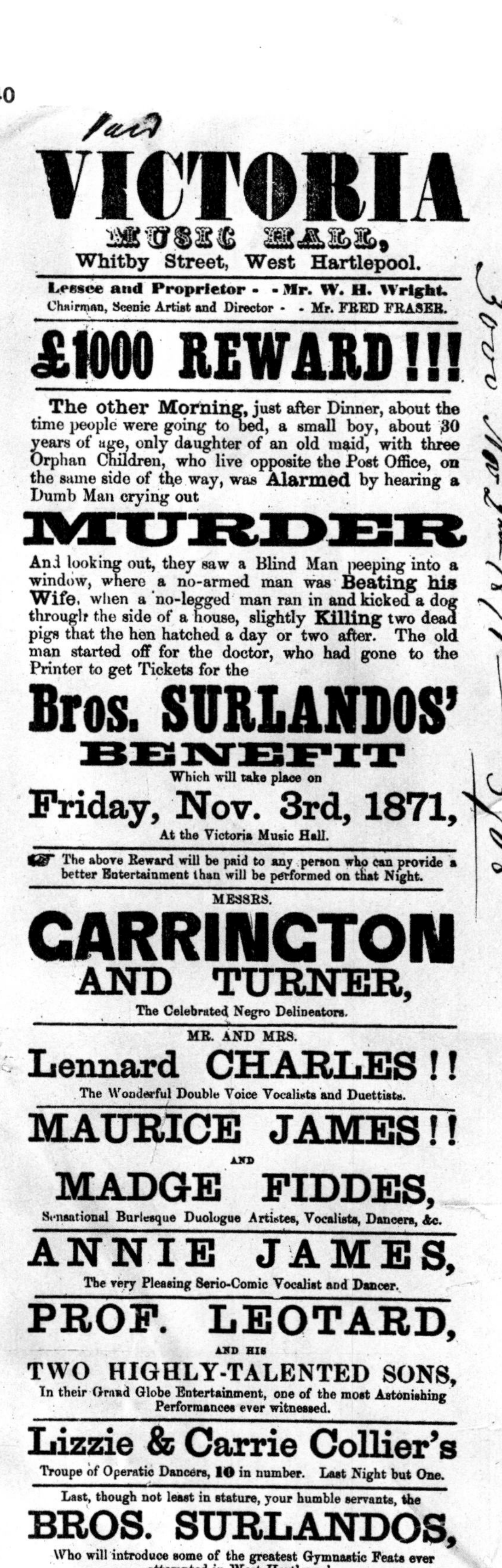

41

42
Why 'The Strike! The Strike!' should head this bill is a mystery which may be solved by reference to current events. The whole performance is a benefit and the bill of fare is not very attractive: the show appears to be far too static with too many vocalists and insufficient movement.

43
A benefit of a different kind. No one can say that there is not plenty of movement in this programme.

44
A comparison with the two former benefit bills does not tell us much. The artist was supposed to see to his own publicity on an occasion like this and it most frequently took a more personal turn. He wrote letters to all the friends he had made and the tradesmen he had patronised and especially to the local 'big-wigs' whose presence at a performance might induce sycophantic members of local society to hasten to jump on the band-wagon. Another and more certain way was to have his own tickets printed and sell them himself.

42

PEOPLE'S
MUSIC HALL,
NORTHGATE, HARTLEPOOL
(Opposite the Railway Station).

THE STRIKE! THE STRIKE!!

On Thursday next
MESSRS.
BRYDGE
AND
HALLIBURTON
Singers, Reciters, Instrumentalists, Duologue Artistes, &c., will take their FAREWELL
BENEFIT
In the above Hall, Assisted by the following Artistes, for this Night only.

MISS BROWN,
The Pleasing Soprano Vocalist.

YOUNG
MASTER BATES
Who won the Prize at the Concert, will perform a Solo on the Cornet.

MR.
RICHARDSON,
The Great Tenor Singer.

Mr. O'Neil
The Hibernian Vocalist.

LORD
ADOLPHUS CRUSHINGTON
The Howling Swell.

MISS LIZZIE HIRST
The Charming Operatic Dancer, will introduce her Castinet and Skipping-Rope Dance.

MISS MAYNE
The Ballad and Serio-Comic Vocalist.

THE YOUNG PHENOMENON,
The Great Clog Dancer.

MESSRS.
SEBASTIAN & FERDINAND,
The Great Trapeze Performers, in their NEW ENTERTAINMENT.

MR.
HALLIBURTON,
Patter Vocalist.

MR. T. BRYDGE
In his Refined Negro Entertainment, introducing the Harmonium, Organaphonican, Guiter, &c., likewise the GREAT STUMP SPEECH.

In consequence of the Length of the Performance the Curtain will rise at Seven o'clock.

PRICES OF ADMISSION:—Dress Circle, 1s.; Side Boxes, 6d.; Body of the Hall, 3d.
No Boys or improper Characters admitted.
CHECKS NOT TRANSFERABLE.

Hartlepool: J. Procter, Printer by Steam Power, Southgate.

43

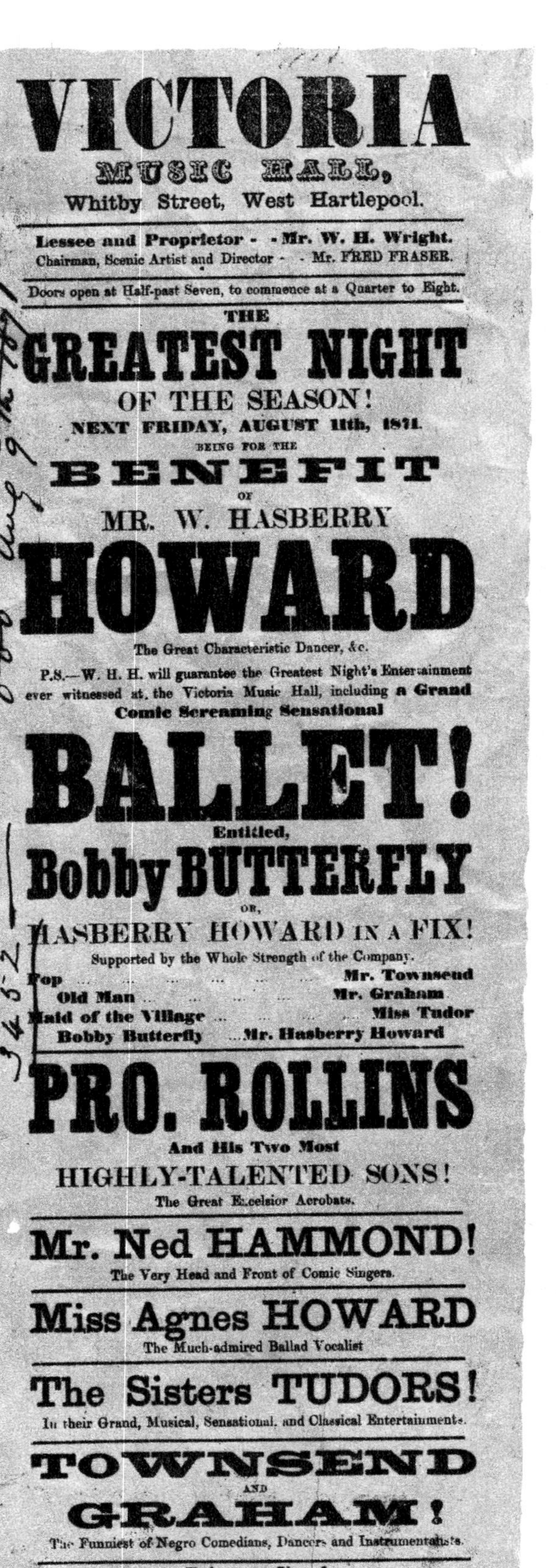

VICTORIA
MUSIC HALL,
Whitby Street, West Hartlepool.

Lessee and Proprietor - - Mr. W. H. Wright.
Chairman, Scenic Artist and Director - - Mr. FRED FRASER.

Doors open at Half-past Seven, to commence at a Quarter to Eight.

THE
GREATEST NIGHT
OF THE SEASON!
NEXT FRIDAY, AUGUST 11th, 1871.
BEING FOR THE
BENEFIT
OF
MR. W. HASBERRY
HOWARD
The Great Characteristic Dancer, &c.

P.S.—W. H. H. will guarantee the Greatest Night's Entertainment ever witnessed at the Victoria Music Hall, including a Grand Comic Screaming Sensational

BALLET!
Entitled,
Bobby BUTTERFLY
OR,
HASBERRY HOWARD IN A FIX!
Supported by the Whole Strength of the Company.

Fop ...	Mr. Townsend
Old Man ...	Mr. Graham
Maid of the Village ...	Miss Tudor
Bobby Butterfly ...	Mr. Hasberry Howard

PRO. ROLLINS
And His Two Most
HIGHLY-TALENTED SONS!
The Great Excelsior Acrobats.

Mr. Ned HAMMOND!
The Very Head and Front of Comic Singers.

Miss Agnes HOWARD
The Much-admired Ballad Vocalist

The Sisters TUDORS!
In their Grand, Musical, Sensational, and Classical Entertainments.

TOWNSEND
AND
GRAHAM!
The Funniest of Negro Comedians, Dancers and Instrumentalists.

Prices as Usual.

Doors open at Half-past Seven. Come Early.

West Hartlepool: J. Procter, Printer by Steam Power.

44

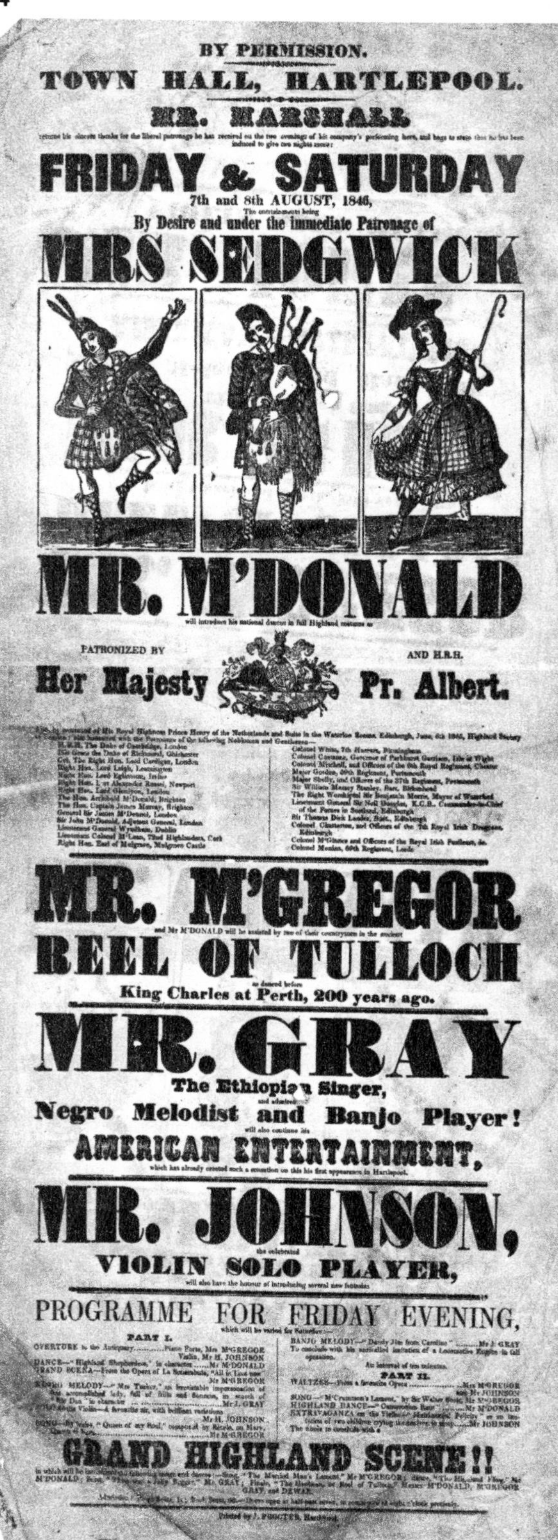

BY PERMISSION.
TOWN HALL, HARTLEPOOL.
MR. MARSHALL
returns his sincere thanks for the liberal patronage he has received on the two evenings of his company's performing here, and begs to state that he has been induced to give two nights more:
FRIDAY & SATURDAY
7th and 8th AUGUST, 1846,
The entertainments being
By Desire and under the immediate Patronage of
MRS SEDGWICK

MR. M'DONALD
will introduce his national dances in full Highland costume as

PATRONIZED BY
Her Majesty
AND H.R.H.
Pr. Albert.

MR. M'GREGOR
and Mr M'DONALD will be assisted by two of their countrymen in the ancient
REEL OF TULLOCH
as danced before
King Charles at Perth, 200 years ago.

MR. GRAY
The Ethiopian Singer,
and admired
Negro Melodist and Banjo Player!
will also continue his
AMERICAN ENTERTAINMENT,
which has already created such a sensation on this his first appearance in Hartlepool.

MR. JOHNSON,
the celebrated
VIOLIN SOLO PLAYER,
will also have the honour of introducing several new fantasias

PROGRAMME FOR FRIDAY EVENING,
which will be varied for Saturday:—

PART I.
OVERTURE to the Antiquary ... Piano Forte, Mrs M'GREGOR; Violin, Mr H. JOHNSON
DANCE—"Highland Shepherdess," in character ... Mr M'DONALD
GRAND SCENA—From the Opera of La Sonnambula, "All is Lost now" ... Mr M'GREGOR

BANJO MELODY—"Dandy Jim from Caroline" ... Mr J. GRAY
An interval of ten minutes.

PART II.
WALTZES—From a favourite Opera ... Mrs M'GREGOR and Mr JOHNSON
HIGHLAND DANCE ... Mr M'DONALD

GRAND HIGHLAND SCENE!!

Printed by J. PROCTER, Hartlepool.

'Penny Gaffs'

GRAND EXPOSURE
OF
MAGIC, &c.

Here we enter the shadowy No Man's Land of the Juggler, the Magician, the Ventriloqist and the dubious Exhibition. Shadowy because we know little about them beyond the reminiscences of various wandering actors and the fond memories found in autobiographies of the last century. Most certainly a No Man's Land because for most of these travellers, unlike companies of actors, a stage was not a necessity. They could perform equally well in an inn parlour or a gentleman's mansion.

Whereas present day magicians and jugglers have the advantage of a good stage with properly designed apparatus and specially trained assistants to help them perform their tricks successfully, these Victorian enterprises had to make do with what opportunity placed before them. Like the jongleurs of mediaeval times, of whom they were the descendants, they depended on their own good-fellowship, and the desire of most people to assist in a good joke at the expense of their friends to enable them to get that surreptitious collaboration without which their 'astounding feats' would have been impossible.

Billy Purvis claimed that he learned the Science of Legerdemain, as he called it, whilst running a dancing school in the Long Room of the Golden Lion at Hexham. It was the most suitable room in the town for exhibitions and theatricals and, since he rented it, these travellers had to apply to him for permission to use it. He was often good natured enough to let them have it without payment, and in their gratitude the magicians sometimes disclosed to him the secret of their tricks – perhaps his generosity was a sprat to catch a mackerel!

His first tutor was Monsieur Peru, a Frenchman, who performed the time-honoured tricks with cups and balls which every magician since Pharaonic days has made part of his stock-in-trade. Billy Purvis learned from Monsieur Peru tricks with cards and coins, rings, and watches. He also learned a great deal from Sanshias, a German conjuror, who is reputed to have walked on the ceiling like a fly.

In the peaceful, uneventful lives of the villager the illusionists came as refreshing interludes and their exploits would be talked over and wondered at for months afterwards. One of them met a gentleman farmer who was amused by his sly humour and offered to lend him his granary for a show. In addition, he went round the countryside advising his friends of the treat he had arranged for them. Naturally he was willing to assist in any hocus-pocus, and so he was given the task of slipping a card in the parson's pocket as a necessary part of the trick that was to follow. Having chosen a card from the magician's pack then replacing it, the parson later discovered a card of the same value in his pocket, much to everyone's amazement and satisfaction.

Conjurors have often delighted in outlandish apparel and a description of Mr. Ingleby who flourished early in the nineteenth century shows that he was no exception. 'He was a fine looking man, and arrayed in his black breeches, scarlet coat, silk stockings and silver buckles, with large gold seals hanging from a gold chain, cocked hat and sword, he had a conspicuous and imposing appearance'.

In great contrast to the likes of Mr. Ingleby was the humble, but cheerful Mr. Billy Purvis who did not disdain cutting a hole in a rival's green curtain to see how he made his puppets work. These were sometimes known as French Figures or Fantoccini, and when Billy was satisfied that he knew how to manipulate them, he began to carve his own puppets with the assistance of a wood carver who helped with the heads. Being a man of the coaly Tyne his first choice was inevitable – 'Ben Block, the Sailor', then came 'The Grand Mogul Turk', 'The Indian Juggler', 'Morgiana, the Musical Rope Dancer', 'Pantaloon and Pantalina', 'Scaramouch', 'The Boy and the Butterfly', and 'Death, or The Skeleton'.

These artists would perform anywhere and there is one amusing tale told concerning a show given in a smithy, where the hearth became the theatre. The figures were manipulated from inside the chimney in which the operator was concealed by green baize. All went well until the final act which was being concluded by Scaramouch. A large bird tumbled down the chimney and covered everything with soot, burst its way through the cloth curtain, flapped its great wings and clawed at everything within reach. The operator, blinded with soot, staggered out, and all the women shrieked and fled, being sure that the devil himself had come for them!

As the century wore on, the casual, unsophisticated arrangements of the old troupes gave way to the precise and business-like methods of the new generation. Even a man of the reputation and substance of Barnardo Eagle, was slack in his arrangements, as this letter of 1847 shows

Sun Inn,
Darlington
Jan. 7th

Sir,
As I wish to visit Hartlepool in a short time I should like to know if I can get the George the Fourth's Large Room for two nights about Monday and Tuesday, January 18th and 19th, or if you think the Town Hall could be got. But I should like to go to the most likely place to draw custom. An answer by return will greatly oblige.
Yours most obed.
Barnardo Eagle
P.S. Direct your letter to me at the Cock Inn, Darlington, which inn I am staying at. I send you an old bill as I cannot lay hold of one of this town.

Compare this with that of Powis Royle of ten years later.

Bishop Auckland
Thursday

Dear Sir,
Be kind enough to arrange for Wednesday and Thursday if the Town Hall is not engaged for Thursday, if it is, ***for Wednesday only.*** I herewith enclose a copy of a bill. The posters and blocks you will get on Saturday morning from Stockton, so get the bills ready for the block so that they can be posted and distributed on Saturday afternoon. The time will be short enough to give publicity to the affair. Enclose bills in envelopes to all the principal families and let the bill-sticker deliver them on Monday at the latest. The posters must be posted with a day bill on each side of them, and as many may be posted singly as convenient. Should you require tickets before I arrive you can write them, signing your own name to them. Let me know by return of post respecting Wednesday evening – your attention will oblige,
Yours obtly
Powis Royle

And so the intimate and friendly atmosphere of the old troupers disappeared.

45
Monsieur Gerhard appears to protest too much. Note the insistence on the improvement of the moral and intellectual faculties.
At Bishop Auckland on February 20th 1849 we find him taking
'This present opportunity of informing the Public that he is authorised by the Tradesmen of the Town, who have witnessed his Exhibition nearly every night, to state their Universal Satisfaction, all agreeing that it is the most Rich, Elegant, and Refined Treat ever offered to the Public.'

45

PROCLAMATION.

WHEREAS, it has been the practice of all Her Majesty's Subjects, particularly in that part of the United Kingdom called DURHAM, in and around the good Town of HARTLEPOOL, and the places adjacent, to visit such places of amusement as were calculated to improve the moral and intellectual faculties.

AND WHEREAS, information has been lodged by several well-disposed persons, expressing the highest gratification and delight on beholding GERHARD'S GRAND UNEQUALLED TABLEAUX VIVANTS, or LIVING REPRESENTATIONS OF CELEBRATED PAINTINGS AND SCULPTURES, the Manager has been induced to LOWER THE PRICES OF ADMISSION to FRONT SEATS, 6d.; BACK SEATS, 3d.; in order to give all classes an opportunity of witnessing this Instructive Exhibition. THEREFORE BE IT KNOWN TO ALL WHOM IT MAY CONCERN, that the Manager challenges the whole World, and hereby offers

To any person who shall produce an Exhibition displayed with as much Brilliancy, Amusement, and Instruction.

GOD SAVE THE QUEEN.

OBSERVE!—FRIDAY and SATURDAY, March 23rd and 24th, being the LAST TWO NIGHTS the Company can appear in HARTLEPOOL.—To commence at half-past 8 o'clock.

Hartlepool, March 22nd, 1849.

PRINTED AT THE OFFICE OF J. PROCTER, HIGH STREET, HARTLEPOOL.

46
All of Barnardo's bills have that old world charm which only a wood-cut can give to a poster. The figures are stiff and the design would be considered old fashioned in the more progressive cities, but Barnardo at this period was making his living by visiting the small country towns and this sort of poster, with its details of marvellous feats, would be very well received.

46A and 46B
Details from poster 46 showing the fanciful lettering and a wood-cut.

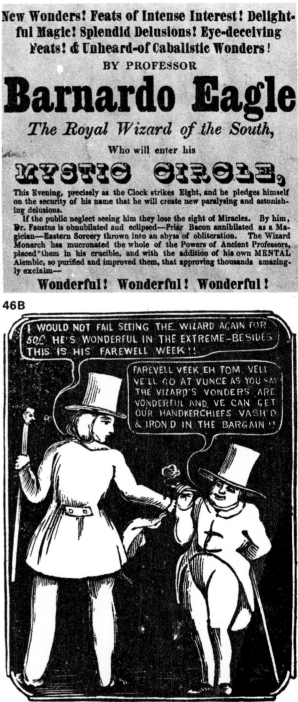

46

TOWN [torn] LL, [torn]RTLEPOOL.

TRIUMPHANT [torn]CCESS OF T[torn] MYSTERIOUS LADY.

TUESDAY, Jan. 26th, 1847.

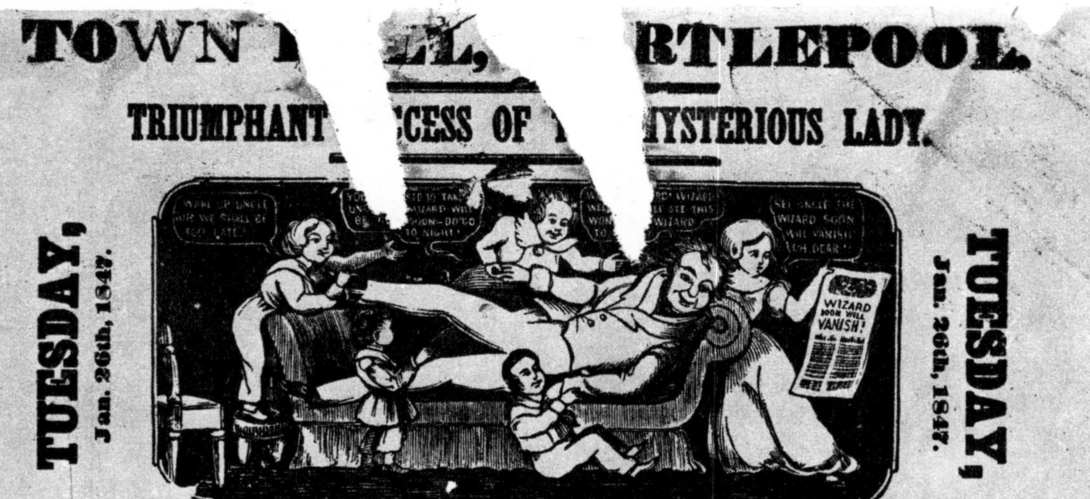

TUESDAY, Jan. 26th, 1847.

GRAND FASHIONABLE NIGHT.

This Present TUESDAY, January 26th, 1847, the Performances will be under the Immediate Patronage of the Worshipful the

Mayor of Hartlepool.

New Wonders! Feats of Intense Interest! Delightful Magic! Splendid Delusions! Eye-deceiving Feats! & Unheard-of Cabalistic Wonders!

BY PROFESSOR

Barnardo Eagle

The Royal Wizard of the South,

Who will enter his

MYSTIC CIRCLE,

This Evening, precisely as the Clock strikes Eight, and he pledges himself on the security of his name that he will create new paralysing and astonishing delusions.

If the public neglect seeing him they lose the sight of Miracles. By him, Dr. Faustus is obnubilated and eclipsed—Friar Bacon annihilated as a Magician—Eastern Sorcery thrown into an abyss of obliteration. The Wizard Monarch has mucronated the whole of the Powers of Ancient Professors, placed them in his crucible, and with the addition of his own MENTAL Alembic, so purified and improved them, that approving thousands amazingly exclaim—

Wonderful! Wonderful! Wonderful!

To-night the Wizard will Out-Herod Herod!

Between the Parts of the Wizard's Amusements will be introduced that extraordinary Novelty, the

MYSTERIOUS LADY,

Do you wish to be in the Fashion? If so, Go To-Night.

THE WONDER OF THE AGE,

Miss Georgiana Eagle,

Who has caused such a great sensation in every town in which she has had the honour of appearing, with her exp[torn] Mesmerism—Clairvoyant knowledge of the Four Quarters of the Gl[torn], Asia, Africa, and America—Reading, blindfolded, all language[torn] different Liquids described—Transfer of the Thoughts of any Individual in the world, all performed momentarily by the Mysterious Lady.

THE LADY PERFORMS ALL HER FEATS BANDAGED AND BLINDFOLDED.

Coins of all Nations Described,

Their Value, Dates, Impression, &c.

READING BLINDFOLDED.

Articles of all Descriptions, Foreign or English, described, with or without contact.

COMMUNITY OF TASTE

FULLY ILLUSTRATED.

MENTAL TRANSFER OF THOUGHT

From any Person to the Lady—the whole world, or any Country in the Four Quarters of the Globe, may be taken as a subject.

DESCRIPTION OF COLOURS, METALS, ETC.

Concluding by giving the exact time by half a dozen Watches, though all different.

Doors open at half-past 7, and commence at 8 o'clock.

FRONT SEATS, 1s. 6d. SECOND SEATS, 1s. BACK SEATS, 6d.

Printed by J. PROCTER, Hartlepool.

46A

New Wonders! Feats of Intense Interest! Delightful Magic! Splendid Delusions! Eye-deceiving Feats! & Unheard-of Cabalistic Wonders!

BY PROFESSOR

Barnardo Eagle

The Royal Wizard of the South,

Who will enter his

MYSTIC CIRCLE,

This Evening, precisely as the Clock strikes Eight, and he pledges himself on the security of his name that he will create new paralysing and astonishing delusions.

If the public neglect seeing him they lose the sight of Miracles. By him, Dr. Faustus is obnubilated and eclipsed—Friar Bacon annihilated as a Magician—Eastern Sorcery thrown into an abyss of obliteration. The Wizard Monarch has mucronated the whole of the Powers of Ancient Professors, placed them in his crucible, and with the addition of his own MENTAL Alembic, so purified and improved them, that approving thousands amazingly exclaim—

Wonderful! Wonderful! Wonderful!

46B

47

Many of these shows display two facets of showmanship combining a lecture with an entertainment. The Victorians were filled with a burning desire to learn and a strong conviction that everything could be known and explained in terms of science. Many a paterfamilias would have been extremely angry if his children had wished to attend a magical entertainment or listen to a ventriloquist and yet would have been extremely gratified if they showed any desire to attend a lecture on electricity, philosophy, hydraulics, chemistry, or mechanics.

47A

The heading from another of Taylor's bills shows how the 'showman' moved around from hall to hall prescribing his entertainment.

48

We see yet again the Victorian entertainer's preoccupation with presenting himself as 'royal' or 'by the patronage of . . .'

49 and 49A

The versatility of some of these itinerant players was astonishing. Barnardo Eagle gave his audiences value for their money. The trick with the twenty or thirty handkerchiefs appears to have been lost but some of the others are still with us, including the 'Great Gun Delusion'. It may be that some student of magic knows what the Grand Belzonian Delusion was, but it has us baffled. The extemporary tale of 'One! Two! Three!' proves that Barnardo was also a mimic and probably a ventriloquist, too.

47

FUN! FUN!! FUN!!!

TAYLOR'S

NOVELTIES!!

AT THE ATHENÆUM,

WEST HARTLEPOOL,

ON SATURDAY, NOV. 15th, 1862.

NEW WONDERS!

M. LEO TAYLOR,

THE GREAT ORIENTAL

WIZARD

AND VENTRILOQUIST!!!

Has the honour of announcing to the Public that he will give his Splendid

DRAWING ROOM

ENTERTAINMENT,

At the above-named place, and by using every exertion in his power to please, trusts that the liberal and pleasure-loving Inhabitants of this Town will give him their generous support

LAUGHABLE SCENES IN VENTRILOQUISM,

FEATS

OF MAGIC!

The Grand Temple of Mystery and Science

Will open with the Superb Entertainment of the Great Oriental Wizard. And he trusts that the name he has acquired will be a guarantee that whatever he promises he will perform. As a Magician he is unequalled, being capable of performing the whole of his incomprehensible Feats of ANCIENT NECROMANCY and MODERN MAGIC in a New and Beautiful Style.

M. LEO TAYLOR will Perform his astonishing Experiments in

Electricity, Philosophy, Hydraulics, Chemistry, Mechanism, and Science,

On the same extensive scale of Grandeur and Effects that have distinguished his Exhibitions throughout Europe and America.

THE VENTRILOQUISM

Will be of the most laughable character, surpassing in extent and variety the sanguine expectations of all—NOVEL SCENES! NUMEROUS DIALOGUES! LAUGHABLE INCIDENTS! IMITATIONS! &c., illustrating the power of the human Voice, both Amusing and Instructive.

It is universally acknowledged that M. LEO TAYLOR'S Entertainments are the most Elegant, Scientific, and Strictly Moral, being replete with the most beautiful and interesting experiments of the deepest scientific research.

The Programme constitutes a brilliant and refined series of illustrative Magic Deceptions, Necromantic Illusions, of the first order, which, together with his costly and magnificent PARAPHERNALIA, afford a treat never surpassed in this or any other country.

Front Seats, 2s.; Second Seats, 1s.; Back Seats, 6d.

Doors open at Half-past Seven, to commence at Eight precisely.

J. PROCTER, Printer, Hartlepool and West Hartlepool.

47A

FUN! FUN!! FUN!!!

TAYLOR'S

NOVELTIES!!

At the Temperance Hall,

HARTLEPOOL,

On Monday and Tuesday, Nov. 17th and 18th, 1862.

48

Great Novelty,

TOWN HALL, HARTLEPOOL.

BARNARDO EAGLE,

THE

ROYAL ILLUSIONIST,

Will have the honour of giving his Entertainment in this Town,

On THURSDAY, FRIDAY, & SATURDAY,

the 26th, 27th, and 28th inst.

COMMENCING AT 8 O'CLOCK.

49

FAREWELL

Fail not this Night to behold the Wizard's Daughter, the Mysterious Lady.

All who see him are delighted with his astounding Feats of Magic.

The Temple of the Wizard is nightly crowned with Beauty to see his Wonders.

The opinion is we shall never see again his extraordinary Dexterity.

Lose not this Chance the last of seeing the Palace of Pleasure and Delusion.

Do not have to say, when you hear of his mighty Feats, I wish I had gone to see his Last Night.

None in Europe can equal the Southern Wizard and his Mysterious Child.

Remember the last! the last!! and only opportunity of seeing the Palace of Pleasure and Delight.

49A

Between the parts of Magic, Mystery, and Music, Mr. B. EAGLE, (by particular desire) will introduce his extempore tale of

ONE! TWO! THREE!

DON'T YOU UNDERSTAND.

In which he will imitate the following different voices.

Mr. Jollyface, Landlord of the Gloucester Hotel .... The WIZARD!
Jonathan Snufflenose, Waiter .... The WIZARD!!
Mr. Crotchet, a musician and music seller .... The WIZARD!!!
Sally Giggle, Chambermaid at the Hotel .... The WIZARD!!!!
Humphrey Gubbins, Oastler .... The WIZARD!!!!!

The whole to conclude with the most wonderful DELUSION ever attempted by man, entitled

THE GREAT GUN DELUSION,

The 1615th time of Mr. BARNARDO EAGLE performing this extraordinary delusion.

Shoot the Wizard!—Ha! ha!! ha!!!—The barrel is not founded—the bullet is not moulded, to bring him to destruction—No! he defies the deadly ball, and holds as nought the "WINGED MESSENGER OF FATE." Bring your own Bullets, No. 25.

Doors open at half-past 7, and commence at 8 o'clock.

FRONT SEATS, 1s. 6d. SECOND SEATS, 1s. BACK SEATS, 6d.

Printed by J. PROCTER, Hartlepool.

50
This bill contains all the information necessary for the reader. Needless to say, this is not Barnum's General Tom Thumb but his country cousin. On such a plain announcement it is rather disconcerting to encounter this delicate distinction in the prices of admission. Who separated the sheep from the goats?

51
A rather archaic but pleasant poster, even if someone has blundered over the spelling of leger de main. The tricks are all old favourites such as the frequenters of country inns would be familiar with and pleased to see again. As usual the magician included some ventriloquism in his act.

50

NOW EXHIBITING,

AT THE HOPE INN,

WEST HARTLEPOOL,

FOR A

Short Time Only,

THE GREATEST

PHENOMENON!!!

Ever seen in this part of the Country, the

ENGLISH TOM THUMB,

OR LEICESTERSHIRE

DWARF!

MR. JOHN WARDLE.

He is a native of Cloughton, in Leicestershire, is now in his 42nd year, and in good health; measures

38 Inches in Height, and Weighs 28 Pounds.

He is small in stature, in no part deformed, but proportionate throughout the frame, and is considered, by all who have seen him, one of the greatest wonders of the world. He has a pleasant appearance, and is able to converse with any lady or gentleman who may honour him with a visit. He appeared before his Majesty George IV., at Brighton, twenty years ago, and was called by him "Tom Thumb the First." Since then he has travelled through all the principal towns in England, Ireland, Scotland, and Wales, and has also been four years in America.

To enable all parties to witness this matchless and wonderful curiosity, the Price of Admission will be—

Ladies and Gentlemen, 6d; Tradesmen, 3d; Working People and Children, 1d.

51

The GREA[illegible] WIZAR[illegible] the South

Will perform every Evening during the Week
IN THE

LARGE ROOM, BLACK LION, TOWN WALL, HARTLEPOOL.

PART 1.

MAGICAL ILLUSIONS;

Or the ART of LEDGERDEMAIN

With Cards, Rings, Money, Watches, Medals, Dice, Handkerchiefs, Birds Magic Pedestal, &c. &c.

Mons. A. will command a Key, borrowed from any person in the Company, from the Black Lion to the inside of a Loaf, Bought from any Baker's Shop in Hartlepool. Various other Deceptions.

THE CELEBRATED

GUN TRICK.

Mons. A. will allow any Gentlemen in the Town to bring his own fowling piece, load it, and fire at him, and he will Catch the marked Ball between his Teeth.

Singing and Recitations.

PART 11.

ASTONISHING FEATS OF VENTRILOQUISM.

Mons. A. will command his Voice to all parts of the Room—likewise an exact Imitation of the Saw, Plane,—

BIRDS, AND THE BRUTE CREATION:

Concluding with the laughable Dialogue of the

OLD LADY & HER SON TOMMY.

The Performance to commence at half past 7.
FRONT SEATS. 6d.—BACK SEATS, 3d.

Good Fires,—Music, & Refreshments.

HARTLEPOOL: PRINTED BY J. PROCTER.

52
Note that the bill is headed 'Grand Exposure' and sets the cue for the performance. Mr. Shaw does not pretend to be a magician. He is giving an educational lecture on the origin, development, and explanation of magic, with illustrations and demonstrations. In other words he is giving a performance of magic disguised as an educational lecture. Assisted by Miss Shaw who plays the piano and a New Musical Instrument, together they sing duets. Altogether the performance is an attractive one, but it must be stressed that it is educational.

53
The Witham Testimonial still stands in the main street of Barnard Castle, a rather austere building which would seem to be the last place on earth in which to find 'Soirees Fantastique'. But Victorian England contains many surprises. Opposite the Testimonial is the King's Head Inn where Dickens stayed when he was investigating the horrors of the Yorkshire schools before writing Nicholas Nickelby. Nearby was the shop where he set his watch by Master Humphrey's Clock and three miles along that same road was Mr. Shaw's Academy, better known as Dotheboys Hall.

54
A letter from Professor Jacobs to the printer states 'I have forwarded a Parcel containing Posters and Lithographs which I will thank you to get out immediately. Tell the Bill Poster to promise a ticket to each Person who exposes a Lithograph, which will be given on the day of performance, when they will be collected in again—print as many of the enclosed bills as will do the Town well—enclose same in envelopes to all the principal families in the place and send by post to those who live in the vicinity. Please to answer the receipt of the Parcel'.

52

GRAND EXPOSURE

BY PERMISSION OF THE MAYOR.

TOWN HALL, HARTLEPOOL.

ON MONDAY, TUESDAY, WEDNESDAY, & THURSDAY,

October 25th, 26th, 27th, & 28th, to commence at EIGHT o'Clock.

ARRANGEMENTS HAVE BEEN MADE FOR

MR. SHAW,

Formerly known as the

ROYAL MAGICIAN,

TO EXHIBIT HIS WONDERFUL

Magical Delusions, Cabalistic Surprises, and Philosophical Recreations,

IN

NATURAL, ARTIFICIAL, AND MECHANICAL

MAGIC

To be followed by an EXPLANATION of the manner in which the Tricks are performed, unfolding the Mystic Art, and exposing the credulity of those who superstitiously rely upon Fortune-tellers, Witchcraft, and Miracles, as performed by modern Wizards.

SYLLABUS,—INTRODUCTION.

Early Stages and Origin of Magic.

Moses' Rod changed into a Serpent—Saul and the Witch of Endor—Ancient Oracles—Natural, Artificial, and Mechanical Magic—Legerdemain Jugglery, and how used at the present time—by whom practised—Ignorance of the Professors—Scientific Investigation of the Feats of the Modern Magician—the Mystic Art confined to a few—Credulity of the Public—Nostrum, Doctor, and Patient—Exposure of Fortune Telling—Injurious effects produced by a belief in Witchcraft—Overthrow of Superstition and Magic, and an Exposure of its Trickery.

Mr. Shaw's object being to counteract the pernicious consequences of a belief in Supernatural Agency, in the performance of Magical Delusion, he will gladly explain any trick he may happen to overlook, upon being requested by any of the audience; and respectfully requests the attendance of Sabbath and Public Schools.

SYNOPSIS, diversified each Evening:—

The Dissolving Ball,

MAGIC METHOD OF PRINTING, without the use of Ink or Press—Sympathetic Balls and Mystic Egg—the Enchanted Handkerchief—the Lost Wedding Ring Discovered.

MAGIC CALDRON,

Or Cold Water Trick,

One of the most astonishing Feats ever produced! A Caldron of large dimensions is shown to be empty, and will be filled with water, in the presence of the spectators; immediately after will be brought forth a number of Animals alive.

FLORA'S GIFTS,

CELEBRATED LOAF TRICK,

In which articles borrowed from the Spectators may be found in any Loaf procured from any Baker's Shop in the town.—Watch Delusion, or Magic Power—Deceiving Dice—Bottle of Asmodeus, or Wine and Handkerchief—Dissolving Dice, and Cutting out the Crowns of Hats—Menagerie in a Hat—Lemon of Restoration—Incendiary or Wax Candle—Flying Coins—the Witch Pigeon—Invisible Postman—Cut Handkerchief—Dancing and Speaking Money—Miraculous Water—with numerous other Wonderful and Incomprehensible Feats.

☞ Miss SHAW will preside at the PIANO-FORTE, and during each Evening Mr. & Miss Shaw will introduce the New Musical Instrument, called the

MOUSICON XZULON!!

Compose of rough pieces of Deal Boards laid upon Hay Bands, the tone of which is powerful, the compass 5½ octaves, with semitones, played upon by two performers, and which has caused the greatest astonishment to all who have heard its powers.

SONG—"Kate Kearney,"............Miss SHAW——DUET—"Meet me my Moonlight,"............Mr. and Miss SHAW.
DUET, on Piano-forte—"Reminiscences of England and Scotland,"............Mr and Miss SHAW.
SONG, Comic ....Mr. SHAW——DUET—"Through the Wood,"............................Mr. and Miss SHAW.

Reserved Seats, 1s.—Back Seats, 6d.—Children, Half-price. Tickets to be had of Mr. PROCTER, Printer.

☞ SCHOOLS LIBERALLY TREATED.

[Printed by J. PROCTER, Hartlepool.

53

FOR TWO NIGHTS ONLY.

WITHAM TESTIMONIAL

BARNARD-CASTLE.

SOIREES FANTASTIQUE

ON

Monday and Tuesday, November 28th and 29th, 1853.

PROFESSOR

POWIS ROYLE

THE RENOWNED WIZARD OF ALL EUROPE!

Who has been giving his Fashionable Soirees for 16 weeks at Manchester to crowded audiences, and whose unsurpassed Performances have gained for him golden opinions, the Public and the Press in each City and Town he has visited having pronounced him to be the ONLY LEGITIMATE ILLUSIONIST OF THE PRESENT DAY! has the honour to announce his Unparalleled Entertainment of New and

Startling Illusions—Astonishing Experiments—Inconceivable Transformations—Astounding Wonders—and Great Cabalistic Novelties!!

The APPARATUS is on a Scale of Magnificence not to be surpassed, the whole forming a perfect

Oriental Palace of Enchantment!

The EXPERIMENTS are new and unique, embracing the various sciences of Chemistry, Hydraulics, Pneumatics, Acoustics, Electricity, Galvanism, Mechanism, &c.

The Programme will be varied each evening, and selected from the following incomprehensible feats of Ambidextrous Prestidigitation.

THE MAGIC LOAF, OR SNAKE-LIKE HANDKERCHIEF!!

THE MINNIE RIFLE

OR ENCHANTED BULLET.

THE MAGIC CAULDRON, OR COOKING EXTRAORDINARY!

THE CRYSTAL CASH BOX,

THE UNLUCKY UMBRELLA, OR ENCHANTED SNUFF BOX.

THE INVISIBLE POSTMAN.

Illusion with Cards, Persons' Thoughts discovered, or Futurity developed.

ZAMIEL'S PROJECT, OR TEMPUS FUGIT.

ROBERT THE SORCERER!!!

THE MAGIC KALEIDOSCOPE. THE ELECTRIC CHAIR, OR SEAT OF TIME.

MYSTIC CHAPEAU, OR PIGEONS & CANNON BALLS!

THE INVISIBLE BIRD OF THE PRAIRIE.

THE MYSTERIOUS TAPER, OR SIGNATURE OF MEPHISTOPHILES!!

THE FIRE-PROOF HANDKERCHIEF.

THE EXHIBITION BOTTLE OF 1851.

FLIGHT AT THE RATE OF 50 MILES A SECOND.

FREAKS OF THE MERRY JACK OF HEARTS.

THE MAGIC PUNCH BOWL!!

THE INVISIBLE SUPPLY, OR THE BASKET OF ABUNDANCE.

The ENCHANTED CRAVAT, producing Feathers, &c.

THE MAGNETIC BELL. THE ÆRIAL CLOCK!

GARLAND OF FLOWERS!

THE COLUMN AND GLOVE, &c., &c.

THE ENTERTAINMENTS WILL BE VARIED

WITH VOCAL AND INSTRUMENTAL MUSIC.

MISS R. SCOTT will preside at the PIANO-FORTE.

54

TEMPERANCE HALL,

HARTLEPOOL.

FOR ONE NIGHT ONLY,

Thursday, February 14th, 1861.

FAREWELL VISIT

OF

PROFESSOR

JACOBS

THE WORLD-RENOWNED

WIZARD OF WIZARDS,

VENTRILOQUIST,

GREAT MODERN MAGICIAN

Improvisatore, Professor of Experimental and Scientific Philosophy,

Whose Fame is established throughout Europe, Australia, California, New Zealand, United States of America, Canada, New Brunswick, Novia Scotia, &c., who has weathered both Cape Horn, and the Cape of Good Hope, Crossed the Line several times, and who, on Board the

GREAT EASTERN

Steam Ship on her Return Voyage,

FOR THE BENEFIT OF THE DREADNOUGHT HOSPITAL,

And the Amusement of the Passengers, presented one of his Unrivalled Entertainments in the middle of the NORTH ATLANTIC OCEAN, LATITUDE 50 deg. 30 min. NORTH, LONGITUDE 38 deg. 30 min. WEST, an unprecedented and wonderful undertaking in those Regions, has the honor to announce his RETURN TO ENGLAND for the purpose of making a FINAL VISIT to all the Cities in which his early attempts were made, and by way of a Farewell to his old and kind Patrons, previously to retiring from his profession.

PROFESSOR JACOBS FOR YEARS HAS BEEN, AND STILL IS, THE NE PLUS ULTRA OF MAGICIANS. Many Imitators have tried to copy his Experiments, but the original still holds the Palm of his profession, performs such Feats, and in so improved a style, that detection is impossible. Old and Young, Simple and Wise, are alike held by him in the dark. Posterity will speak of him as the Great Wonder of the Nineteenth Century. The Stage on which his marvels are performed will resemble

A TEMPLE OF

ENCHANTMENT

THE APPARATUS IS OF

MASSIVE SILVER,

The DECORATIONS in the STYLE of LOUIS QUATORZE

And the Tout Ensemble alone a Treat!

A pleasing and varied feature in the Entertainment is the Performance of the

GOBLIN SPRIGHTLY

Who for Twenty years has accompanied the WIZARD JACOBS, as his attendant SPRITE. The Press has given him the title of the

MODERN LISTON

And not without cause, his peculiar part being a conception of his own, matured by travelling through the World, and aided by extraordinary powers of Wit and Imitation; his drolleries are beyond conception, roars of laughter the Audience are compelled to endure, and the fixed attention of all eyes upon SPRIGHTLY, is in itself a proof of his extraordinary powers.

Many have said that Dickens must have selected him for the Fat Boy in "Pickwick."

Thus the truly Wonderful Inventions, Manipulations, Improvisatorial, and Ventriloquial Powers of WIZARD JACOBS, together with the irresistible attractions of GOBLIN SPRIGHTLY, render this Entertainment unapproachable,—and when it is withdrawn from public patronage, as it positively will be after this Tour, the Poet's words will be realised—

"You shall not look upon the like again."

Doors open at Half-past Seven; the Wizard and his Goblin appear at Eight.

Reserved Seats, 2s.; Second Seats, 1s.; Back Seats, 6d.

Children under 12 Years of Age, Half-price to the First and Second-class Seats only.

Tickets (and for Reserved Seats Numbered) may be had of the Printer.

On MONDAY & TUESDAY Evenings, Jan. 25th & 26th, 1847.

FIRST APPEARANCE OF THE NAPOLEON OF WIZARDS,

AND THE

MYSTERIOUS LADY!

Who will give her complete Expose of Mesmerism, Clairvoyance, Animal Magnetism, &c., for particulars of which read the following Paragraphs.

THE ROYAL WIZARD,

Mr. BARNARDO EAGLE,

Who has been Patronised by THREE CROWNED HEADS,

GEORGE IV., WILLIAM IV., AND QUEEN VICTORIA,

Begs to inform the Public that his Apartments are most costly and complete, and the whole of his Arrangements on a scale of unparalleled Splendour and Magnificence.

Opinions of the Press.

From the *York Courant*, Dec. 11th, 1846.

THEATRE ROYAL.—The Theatre Royal, York, has been open during the assize week with rather a novel exhibition, conjuring and clairvoyance, by a Mr Barnardo Eagle, accompanied by his daughter, a little girl of eleven years of age, who is styled by her father "The Mysterious Lady;" and, judging from her exhibitions, the title is not unworthily or inaptly applied. The young lady appears on the stage, and any person in the theatre is allowed to blindfold her, and then commences a series of the most inexplicable mysteries which we ever witnessed. Mr Eagle, in the course of his own incantatory tricks, "makes our eyes the fools o' the other senses;" but his daughter makes the audience the fools of their own *ears*. She sits on the stage, as we have said, blindfolded; her father goes to any part of the theatre and desires one of the audience to whisper to him the name of any particular country or city, or of any remarkable man, and the "Mysterious Lady," still remaining on the stage, on being asked what the gentleman has whispered, instantly speaks out, and with a correctness that, in another and in a darker age, would have induced people to believe she had dealings with a certain personage. A gentleman present handed to Mr Eagle some antique coins of a scarce kind, and on his asking his daughter to "describe the coin this gentleman has handed to me, and name its date," the reply came instantly, and in almost every instance most correctly. Coins bearing the "image and superscription" of the Cæsars, nobles, and other curious specimens of old English coinage, although held at the opposite end of the theatre, were told with a truth most startling to the hearer. Signet rings, with heraldic bearings, could not eseape her mystic gaze: and throughout the exhibition the young enchantress absolutely perplexed her audience with her startling and most unaccountable revelations. Mr Eagle does not attempt to conceal that the whole is the result ot a pre-arrangement, and this he asserts the more freely in order to put the public on their guard against the elucidators of mesmerism and clairvoyance. Whatever may be the means of communication employed between Mr Eagle and his daughter, they are silent and motionless means, and we will not hazard a conjecture upon them. We see, by an advertisement in another column, the performances will be repeated during the next week, and parties who have not yet seen the lady will have an opportunity of doing so.

From the *Yorkshireman*, Dec. 13th, 1846.

THE MYSTERIOUS LADY, OR CLAIRVOYANCE UNVEILED.—We have had much pleasure in witnessing the "conjuring," as it used to be called, of the Wizard of the South, a gentleman of the name of Barnardo Eagle. He rivals all the apparently impossible feats of his class. But what we would especially recommend to the notice of those who have not yet visited him, is the unmasking of what is called "Clairvoyance" by the little daughter of the conjuror. From what we witnessed on Monday evening, we fully believe what her father stated—namely, that wherever they had had an opportunity of being in the same town with Adolph, Alexis, and other mesmeric miracle workers, the mysterious lady has always astonished the public far more by her performances than the adepts at clairvoyance: while Mr Eagle acknowledges his and his daughter's exhibition to be a deception, the mesmeric people put forth their conjuring as true, honest facts. Miss Georgiana Eagle is blindfolded *secundem ardem*, and her father moves about among the audience gathering all sorts of things, which the lady names without hesitation, giving the inscriptions of datas on coins, and doing other similar miracles, which to a professor of clairvoyance would be invaluable. The crowning feat, however, is the telling the thoughts of the company; and, by way of illustration, we will just say that a gentleman in the theatre, whom we know (with others who took the *trouble* to think also) to be incapable of any confederacy with the Eagles, *thought* he should like to drink a glass of *Lachryma Christi* at Naples at that moment. The lady paused a moment and then gave the correct answer. Let it be observed that this is *avowed* to be a trick; but it is a most ingenious one, requiring a presence of mind, clearness of intellect, and rapid judgment, which few of the mesmerisers possess. We have no hesitation whatever in saying that any person, after witnessing the young lady's performance, will be satisfied that, at all events, it is possible to simulate the most difficult feats of clairvoyance; whether any person shall be credulous enough to believe in such unnecessary powers after *her* exhibition, is of very little consequence to any body. All the other entertainments are very pleasing. We understand that these entertainments will be repeated next week; therefore advise the curious in such matters to go and judge for themselves.

From the *Anti-Mesmerist*, Edited by James Quilton Rumball, Esq, Surgeon.

January 25th, 1845.—MR. BARNARDO EAGLE, a celebrated Conjurer, is at this time amusing the good folks at Bath, by an exhibition of Clairvoyance in addition to his own conjurations, which may really give the Mesmerisers a wrinkle if they will but visit him; it is too faithful a copy of their own proceedings to be mistaken, the only difference between them being that his performance as far excels theirs as does his honesty, in acknowledging the whole to be a complete trick; not only making our eyes the fools of other senses, but making us the fools of our own ears. A little girl is blindfolded on the stage, her father goes among the audience, and asks any one for anything; if it be a coin, he asks of what metal it is composed, what is the date, value, reign, country, &c., to all of which she answers correctly, and various articles from different pockets, scissors, keys, sweetmeats, tools, reptiles, &c., &c., enough in number and variety to stock a curiosity shop, are given to him, and a simple unaccented question, elicits from her an unhesitating and accurate description of their nature. Steel, copper, gold, satins, silks, velvets, are all apparently seen, and when we were present she actually stated that one half crown had been found in the Ruins of the late disastrous fire, which was the fact. Go, see the Wizard, ye wretched bunglers,* then hide your diminished heads for ever.

* Mr. Rumball alludes to Messrs. Brooks, Owen, Vernon, Spencer Hall, and a host of travelling Mesmerisers.

55
Barnardo Eagle again! It is interesting to compare the arrogance of this his first appearance with announcements on later posters (49 and 49A).

56
Mr. J. H. Devon is an entertainer of a different breed. It is obvious from his bill that this is a show for the family; his lecture on the Physiology of the Human Voice is just a pretext for a performance of human and farmyard imitations. No doubt this sort of thing was enjoyed in the public houses too, but the sad truth remains that when Mr. Devon wrote to the printer from Darlington and Northallerton he was patronising Temperance Hotels.

57
The Brothers Hutchinson have something to boast about and make sure that everyone knows they are patronised by the best people. They make a presentable performance of their own contribution by adding a negro singer, a fiddler, a contortionist, and something mysterious which rejoices in the title of Tranca Espaniola. A section of the poster is shown overleaf.

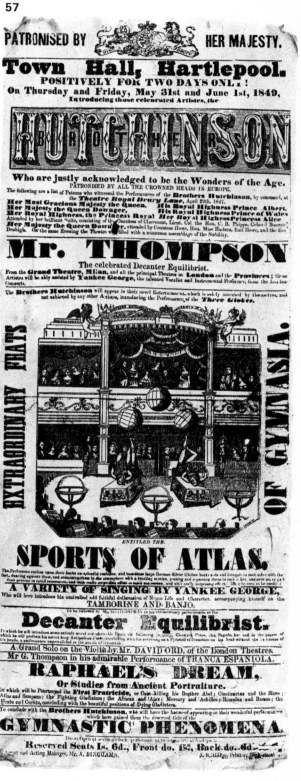

56

ATHENÆUM,
WEST HARTLEPOOL.

MONDAY, NOV. 5, 1855

GRAND
VENTRILOQUIAL EVENING.

FOR ONE NIGHT ONLY.

GO & HEAR THE MODERN VALENTINE VOX.

ADMISSION :—Reserved Seats, 1s. 6d.; Second do., 1s.; Back do., 6d.
Children and Schools, Half-price to the Second Seats. Commencing at Eight, and concluding at Ten.

MR. J. H. DEVON,

The Renowned Ventriloqist and Polyphonist,

Respectfully intimates to the Nobility, Gentry, and Inhabitants of this Town and Vicinity, that he intends giving his truly ORIGINAL ENTERTAINMENTS on the above Evening, which he is confident will be found a Treat of no ordinary description, commencing with

INTRODUCTORY REMARKS
ON THE PHYSIOLOGY OF THE HUMAN VOICE!

Definition of the Voice and Speech—Circumstances necessary to the formation of the Voice—Its Organs and Illustrations, explaining that Wonderful Phenomenon of Nature, so called

Ventriloquism

The Entertainment, entitled

AN EVENING WITH THE OLD SQUIRE & HIS PARTY,

Will be found to suit all ages, on the nature, origin, extent, and power of which the Human Voice is capable; combining the intermediate voices from a Lisping Child to Venerable Age; from a Mewing Kitten to a Snarling Mastiff; from a Single Fly to a Hive of Bees; producing the effect of several imaginary characters in such quick succession, and emanating from different places and opposite directions, that it is almost impossible to avoid thinking the dialogues are performed by real individuals.

57

PATRONISED BY HER MAJESTY.

Town Hall, Hartlepool.
POSITIVELY FOR TWO DAYS ONLY!
On Thursday and Friday, May 31st and June 1st, 1849,
Introducing those celebrated Artistes, the

BROTHERS HUTCHINSON

Who are justly acknowledged to be the Wonders of the Age.
PATRONISED BY ALL THE CROWNED HEADS IN EUROPE.

The following are a list of Patrons who witnessed the Performances of the Brothers Hutchinson, by command, at the Theatre Royal Drury Lane, April 29th, 1847.
Her Most Gracious Majesty the Queen. His Royal Highness Prince Albert.
Her Majesty the Queen Dowager. His Royal Highness Prince of Wales
Her Royal Highness, the Princess Royal Her Royal Highness Princess Alice
Attended by her brilliant Suite, consisting of the Countess of Claremont, Lieut. Col. the Hon. C. B. Phipps, Colonel Bouvrie, Her Majesty the Queen Dowager, attended by Countess Howe, Hon. Miss Hudson, Earl Howe, and the Earl Denbigh. On the same Evening the Theatre was filled with a numerous assemblage of the Nobility.

Mr. THOMPSON

The celebrated Decanter Equilibrist.
From the Grand Theatre, Milan, and all the principal Theatres in London and the Provinces; these Artistes will be ably assisted by Yankee George, the talented Vocalist and Instrumental Performer, from the London Concerts.

The Brothers Hutchinson will appear in their novel Entertainment, which is solely invented by themselves, and not achieved by any other Artistes, introducing the Performance of the Three Globes,

EXTRAORDINARY FEATS OF GYMNASIA.

ENTITLED THE

SPORTS OF ATLAS.

The Performers recline upon their backs on splendid cushions, and toss three large German Silver Globes backwards and forwards to each other with the feet, dancing against them, and sustaining them in the atmosphere with a twirling motion, passing and repassing them to each other, and over every part of their persons in rapid succession, and with really surprising effect.

A VARIETY OF SINGING BY YANKEE GEORGE,
Who will here introduce his unrivalled and faithful delineation of Negro Life and Character, accompanying himself on the
TAMBORINE AND BANJO.

To be followed by Mr. G. THOMPSON in his extraordinary performances as the

Decanter Equilibrist.

In which he will introduce some entirely novel and admirable Feats, viz. balancing, juggling, Classical Poses, the Pagoda, &c. and in the course of which he will perform his astonishing Antipodean Feats, concluding with his revolving on a Pyramid of Decanters on his head without the assistance of his hands, a performance unparalleled in the annals of Gymnastic.

A Grand Solo on the Violin by Mr. DAVID ORD, of the London Theatres.
Mr G. Thompson in his admirable Performance of TRANCA ESPANIOLA.

RAPHAEL'S DREAM,
Or Studies from Ancient Portraiture.

In which will be Pourtrayed the First Fratricide, or Cain killing his Brother Abel; Cincinnatus and the Slave; Atlas and Sampson; the Fighting Gladiators; the African and Ajax; Mercury and Achilles; Romulus and Remus; the Eratu and Curatu, concluding with the beautiful positions of Dying Gladiators.

To conclude with the Brothers Hutchinson, who will have the honor of appearing in their wonderful performances which have gained them the deserved title of the

GYMNASTIC PHENOMENA.

Doors Open at seven o'clock, performance to commence at half-past.
Reserved Seats 1s. 6d., Front do. 1s., Back do. 6d.
Agent and Acting Manager, Mr. A. BINGHAM. J. R. Hodge, Printer, High-street.

57A
Perhaps the Brothers Hutchinson, and Mr. Thompson with his decanters, will forgive us if we suggest that the programme is not well-balanced. This expression is rather unfortunate, bearing in mind the nature of the entertainment, and we apologise in advance for any damage done to their feelings

57A

Introducing those celebrated Artistes, the

Who are justly acknowledged to be the Wonders of the Age.
PATRONISED BY ALL THE CROWNED HEADS IN EUROPE.

The following are a list of Patrons who witnessed the Performances of the **Brothers Hutchinson**, by command, at the ***Theatre Royal Drury Lane***, April 29th, 1847.

Her Most Gracious Majesty the Queen, His Royal Highness Prince Albert,
Her Majesty the Queen Dowager, His Royal Highness Prince of Wales
Her Royal Highness, the Princess Royal *Her Royal Highess* Princess Alice
Attended by her brilliant Suite, consisting of the Countess of Claremont, Lient. Col. the Hon. C. B. Phipps, Colonel Bouvrie, ***Her Majesty the Queen Dowager,*** attended by Countess Howe, Hon. Miss Hudson, Earl Howe, and the Earl Denbigh. On the same Evening the Theatre was filled with a numerous assemblage of the Nobility.

Mr. THOMPSON

The celebrated Decanter Equilibrist,

From the **Grand Theatre, Milan,** and all the principal Theatres in **London** and the **Provinces**; these Artistes will be ably assisted by **Yankee George,** the talented Vocalist and Instrumental Performer, from the London Concerts.

The **Brothers Hutchinson** will appear in their novel Entertainment, which is solely invented by themselves, and not achieved by any other Artistes, introducing the Performance of the ***Three Globes,***

58 and 59

Although the register of the colour blocks is not accurate and the slight misalignment gives a rather bizarre effect, it probably adds to the impact of the picture on the passer-by. All is out of joint, in a world where a woman's head can be cut off in public, and if the printing is out of register also, it is merely part of a pattern. Let us hope that no one was naive enough to imagine that this is what they would actually see! Such a situation did arise when the same sort of poster was exhibited in Mexico. The audience rioted because there was no blood! In 58 Rubini takes full advantage of the opportunity to use red ink. This poster foreshadows the technical virtuosities of the 1880s but Rubini cannot refrain from using the verbal extravagances of the 1840s. A 'Cagliostromantheum of Prestidigitation' indeed! 59 shows the most effective use of yellow and blue characteristic of Victorian typographers. The bolder, but less elegant type faces of this poster are typical of those which tended to be used in preference to the Bodoni-like founts of the early part of the nineteenth century.

58

NEW THEATRE ROYA
WEST HARTLEPOOL.
FOR 4 NIGHTS ONLY!
COMMENCING ON SATURDAY,
MAY 1st, 1869.
Performance to commence at 8 o'clock each Evening.
THE REAL, RENOWNED, ORIGINAL, AND ONLY

THE GREAT & FAMOUS CONJUROR,
Having just terminated a Brilliant Season of nearly 200 Representations at the ST. JAMES'S, ST. GEORGE'S, & EGYPTIAN HALLS, LONDON,
To Crowded and Fashionable Audiences, will appear in his Delightful Entertainment the
MARVELS OF MAGIC,
AND HIS GREAT NEW FEAT OF

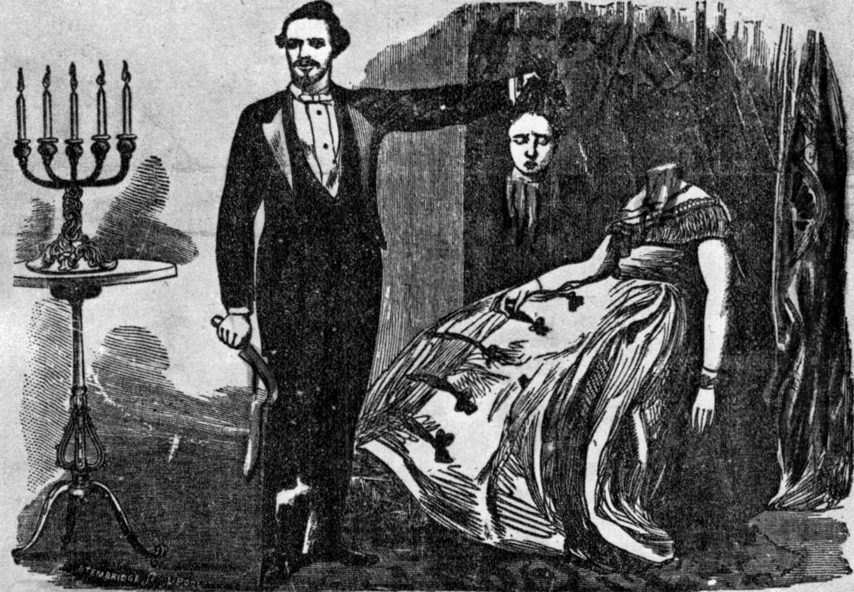

BEHEADING A LADY
THE GREATEST SENSATIONAL ACHIEVEMENT OF THE AGE, NOVEL AND ORIGINAL BEYOND ALL PRECEDENT:
ALSO INCLUDING
RUBINI'S GLOBES OF GOLD FISH!
RUBINI'S SHOWER OF MONEY!!
RUBINI'S INDIAN BASKET FEAT!!!
RUBINI'S GIRL OF THE PERIOD!!!!
TWO HOURS IN THE FAIRY PALACE OF DAZZLING BEAUTY,
RUBINI'S RESPLENDENT WIZARDIAN CAGLIOSTROMANTHEUM OF PRESTIDIGITATION !!
The Hall will be transformed into a TEMPLE OF MAGIC, fitted up in th
same manner as at the ST. JAMES' & EGYPTIAN HALLS, LONDON.
Pianist ... ... Mr. THEODO
Agent in Advance ... ... Mr. C.
Manager ... ... Mr.
ADMISSION:— Reserved Seats - 2s., Second Seats - 1s., Thi
DOORS OPEN MORNINGS AT HALF-PAST TWO EVENINGS AT HALF-PAST

59

CENTRAL HALL,
DARLINGTON.
THURSDAY, FRIDAY, AND SATURDAY,
May, 6th, 7th, and 8th, at Eight o'clock.
MORNING PERFORMANCE!
ON SATURDAY, AT THREE O'CLOCK.
V. R.
The World-Renowned
RUBINI!
The Great and Famous Conjurer,
From the Egyptian Hall, London, in his Highly-successful and Popular Entertainment, the
MARVELS
OF
MAGIC!
INCLUDING
RUBINI'S GLOBES OF GOLD FISH!
RUBINI'S SHOWER OF MONEY!!
RUBINI'S INDIAN BALL!!!
And many ASTOUNDING WONDERS, concluding with RUBINI'S GREAT NEW FEAT (which has created such a Sensation in London), entitled,
BEHEADING
A LADY!
The Greatest Sensational Achievement of the Age! Novel Original beyond all precedent!
Doors open—Mornings, at Half-past Two; Evenings, at Half-past Seven.
RESERVED SEATS, 2s.; SECOND SEATS, 1s.; THIRD SEATS, 6d.

60

This bill is a good example of how the great technical advances, both in the art of printing and stage production, had outstripped that of writing 'copy' designed to bring in the customers. Monsieur Gerhard's bill of 1843 (page 41) is for a show of exactly the same character, and in comparison with Professor Wheeler shows clearly the changes in style that occur over a twenty year period. Yet it is difficult to believe that Monsieur Gerhard would have allowed the printer to make such a typographic mess of the four words around the fountain. Perhaps it was necessary to reassure the reader that the nymphs were truly living ones for the specimens illustrated are obviously the work of an artist who could not make up his mind which sex they should be. The brief mention of the Suez Canal reminds us that there is another world beyond that of show business and that the enterprising showman is ready to go anywhere if business warrants it. The 'Crowned Heads of Europe' is a cliché which has become almost historical.

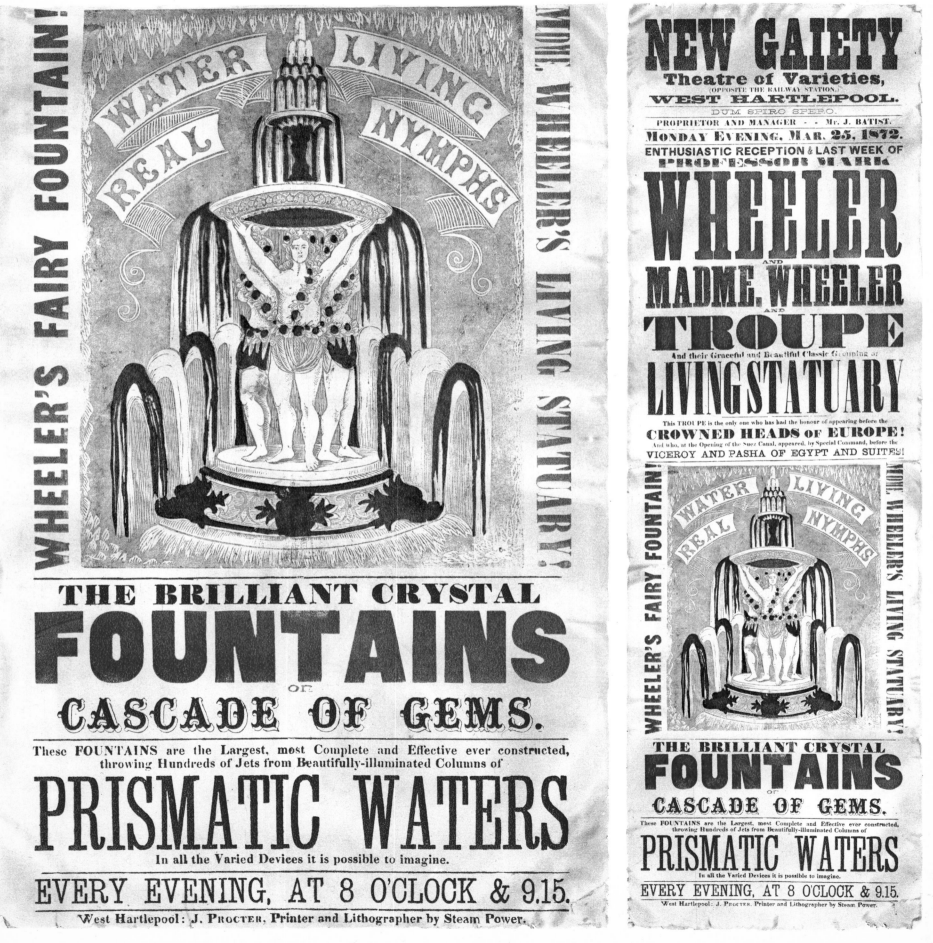

60

THE BRILLIANT CRYSTAL

FOUNTAINS

or

CASCADE OF GEMS.

These FOUNTAINS are the Largest, most Complete and Effective ever constructed, throwing Hundreds of Jets from Beautifully-illuminated Columns of

PRISMATIC WATERS

In all the Varied Devices it is possible to imagine.

EVERY EVENING, AT 8 O'CLOCK & 9.15.

West Hartlepool: J. PROCTER, Printer and Lithographer by Steam Power.

NEW GAIETY

Theatre of Varieties,

(OPPOSITE THE RAILWAY STATION.)

WEST HARTLEPOOL.

DUM SPIRO SPERO.

PROPRIETOR AND MANAGER - - Mr. J. BATIST.

MONDAY EVENING, MAR. 25, 1872.

ENTHUSIASTIC RECEPTION & LAST WEEK OF

PROFESSOR MARK

WHEELER

AND

MADME. WHEELER

AND

TROUPE

And their Graceful and Beautiful Classic Grouping of

LIVINGSTATUARY

This TROUPE is the only one who has had the honour of appearing before the

CROWNED HEADS OF EUROPE!

And who, at the Opening of the Suez Canal, appeared, by Special Command, before the

VICEROY AND PASHA OF EGYPT AND SUITES!

THE BRILLIANT CRYSTAL

FOUNTAINS

or

CASCADE OF GEMS.

These FOUNTAINS are the Largest, most Complete and Effective ever constructed, throwing Hundreds of Jets from Beautifully-illuminated Columns of

PRISMATIC WATERS

In all the Varied Devices it is possible to imagine.

EVERY EVENING, AT 8 O'CLOCK & 9.15.

West Hartlepool: J. PROCTER, Printer and Lithographer by Steam Power.

3

Circuses and Waxworks

There were many early examples of animals being used in arenas for entertainment purposes. The Romans had their circuses and wild animals were hunted in their arenas. Byzantium rejoiced in chariot racing and the Minoans are famed for their bull leapers, but none of these amusements can claim to be the precursor of the modern circus.

The riding masters of the eighteenth century began the true art of the circus by giving displays of trick riding at village fairs and London pleasure gardens in their efforts to earn additional income. These occasional shows soon became permanent attractions presented in fields adjoining prosperous public houses.

Sergeant-Major Astley was of a more independent breed and he branched out in the Westminster Bridge Road with his own riding school which very shortly became the Amphitheatre of the Arts. Later one of his riders opened the Royal Circus in opposition and although it did not survive for very long its name was a little more meaningful than 'amphitheatre' and has remained the generic term for all such shows since.

At first the audience in these establishments was housed in boxes arranged in the plan of a horseshoe within which was the circle that we now call the Ring. A stage was built at the open end.

At this time the stages of both theatre and circus showed musical spectacles. In fact the stage of the circus was still more important than the Ring.

After Philip Astley died in 1814 his son Philip introduced a new style display of horsemanship which became known as 'Equestrian Drama', but he died in 1821, and it was his successor, Andrew Ducrow, who brought this to perfection. He had a remarkable flair for publicity and an equally remarkable egotism. In the awe-inspiring majesty and dignity of the Ring Master we can still see the faint shadow of Ducrow. He made the riding school exercises into an exciting spectacle with his Poses Plastiques and the Courier of St. Petersburg. Van Amburgh the lion tamer appeared for him as 'The Brute Tamer of Pompeii with his Kings of the Jungle'. That great Victorian favourite 'Mazeppa and the Wild Horse', was first in the limelight at Astley's in 1831.

Fire destroyed Astley's in 1841 and Ducrow died, but a new Astley's arose which was managed by William Cooke, grandson of Thomas Cooke who had started to tour in the North of England during the latter part of the eighteenth century. The second generation was headed by Thomas Taplin Cooke, who toured abroad. He had nineteen children and returned home leaving his eldest son Thomas Edwin to found a dynasty in America. With Cookes innumerable there is no wonder that this was the circus family par excellence, for by intermarriage they were related to nearly every circus management in the world.

James Sanger, a sailor who fought at Trafalgar, travelled round the fairs with a peep-show. His sons were more ambitious and owned a Welsh pony which was well trained in the art of picking out the biggest rogue in the company, and a horse which would trot in a circle. This nucleus of a show was filled out by adding clowning, rope-walking, and juggling to the programme. Soon, however, the Sangers were able to buy more horses and George Sanger was able to play Mazeppa.

Another circus which found its origins in Astley's was Hengler's. The first Hengler was a rope-dancer who had been employed there. The Ginnetts were descendants of another Waterloo warrior who had appeared at Astley's.

These were the great names in the circus world. There were many others who went on tour in the spring and summer. Myer's, Pinder's, Batty's, Swallow's, Powell and Clarke's, and Fossett's, besides the host of small family concerns which made a living jogging from village to village. One or two still survive to give the authentic flavour of the old, intimate family circus.

But the modern Big Top which tours today seems to lack the variety of acts which the old shows offered. This opinion may be mistaken, for the circus folk were always adepts at advertising. All that appears on a showbill may not necessarily have been there to see, although the variety of animals on show was important for the cinema and television had not yet made the forms of most animals and birds familiar in every home. The educational element appears to have departed from the modern circus and the programme is essentially one of spectacle.

Perhaps this waning interest in the caged living animal on tour accounts for the disappearance of the travelling menagerie. Nowadays the public can easily visit any number of zoological gardens and see the animals in much better surroundings than the old wild beast shows could offer.

Of course, there was a time when Wombwell's three collections of wild animals and birds were all continuously on tour round the countryside, and even small towns were likely to be honoured by an annual visit. George Wombwell, who founded his business by buying two boa-constrictors for £75 and exhibiting them in premises off Piccadilly, London over a century and a half ago, made enough money in that way to buy a small collection of beasts. He was a methodical man who manged to visit all the great fairs of the British Isles. He also attended all the great race-meetings.

When he died in 1850 he left his entire collection to his niece, Mrs. Edmonds, who had for years managed his Number 2 collection. When she retired her son James Edmond managed the Number 1 collection and Mrs. Bostock, his mother's sister, took charge of Number 2. whilst her son, Edward Bostock, ran Number 3. This was the creation of Bostock and Wombwell's which many Victorians delighted in.

Another popular menagerie in the North of England was that of Mander's.

In the world of the menagerie the technique of presentation was in great contrast to that of the circus. Just as the zoo visitor wanders round as he pleases, so did the provincial who came to Bostock and Wombwell's show.

The cages were arranged in the shape of a rectangle and the entire area was covered with a large canvas roof after the fashion of the Big Top. The organ, the box-office and the administrative wagons formed one narrow side in which were the entrances for the public.

There was no attempt to induce the customer to spend more money by including side-shows. The only 'performance' that the visitor was likely to see, was that of the animals being fed, the times of which were displayed. The atmosphere was one of decorum and dedication. The showman had brought the animals to be seen and the customer could feast his eyes without interruption.

61

The following Artistes are engaged, and will positively appear, each of whom is at the head of his or her Profession:—

ALF. EUGENE COOKE

Mr EDWARD SIDNEY. Mr HARRY BOSWELL. Mr E. SULLY.

Signor EDWARDO. Mons. LORENZO. Mr FRED COOKE. Mr ROBINSON.

Master GEORGE BATTY. Mr WALTER H. CLARKE.

The Proprietor calls particular attention to the Noble Stud of

70 HORSES & 20 PONIES

Which for Beauty, Condition, and Training, are unequalled in England!

SIX GOOD CLOWNS

Headed by the Modern Grimaldi, FRED COOKE, and the Great Funny LITTLE JULIAN with his TROUPE of

EDUCATED DOGS, GOATS, AND MONKEYS.

Miss CLARA JOHNSON. Miss CARTER. Madlle. ANNETTO. Madam GAERTNER.

MADLLE. LEATITIA

MONS EUGENIO GAERTNER

MADLLE. GAERTNER

With her Highly-Trained Trick and Menage Horses, "SUPERB," "MAYFLOWER," and "BRONZE," the Highest Leaping Horses in Europe! Will appear at each Performance.

Everybody who has a taste for the Beautiful must see the GRAND PUBLIC ENTREE and

PROCESSION

Which will start from the Marquee (Weather permitting) A, ONE o'clock precisely, headed by the Splendid BAND, seated in the Magnificent

EGYPTIAN BAND CAR!!

Followed by the Ladies and Gentlemen of the Establishment on their beautiful Steeds, attired in the richest Costumes of Satin, Silk, and Velvet, ornamented with Gold and Silver.

MAGNIFICENT CARRIAGES! Beautiful Horses, adorned with Silver and Gold-Mounted Harness, Several Grand Allegorical Tableaux, Comic Carriages, drawn by Comic Ponies and Driven by COMIC CLOWNS.

THE WHOLE WILL POSITIVELY APPEAR ON THE DAY ANNOUNCED IN

TWO GRAND REPRESENTATIONS

MID DAY PERFORMANCE 2 30; EVENING 7 30.

Reserved Seats, (Splendidly Fitted up and Carpeted.) 3s. First Class, 2s. Second Class, 1s. Third Class, 6d.

Children under Ten Years of Age, Half-price to Reserved Seats, 1s 6d; First Class, 1s; Second Class, 6d. No Half-price to Third Class.

Agent in Advance, - Mr JOHN McDOWELL. Secretary, - Mr C. H. REED, Stud Groom, - Mr BUTCHER. Band Master, - Mr G. SPENCER

Manager, Mr A. E. COOKE. SOLE PROPRIETOR, Mr THOMAS BATTY (Nephew of the Late WM. BATTY, Esq. of Astley's Royal Amphiteatre, London.

T. C. BARLOW, Designer, Engraver, and Colour Printer, 341 St. Vincent Street, Glasgow.

61 (page 53)
In the 1850s William Cooke, grandson of the original Thomas Cooke, managed the new Astley's but in 1860 his desire to travel again was very strong and he went on tour. The show wintered in Portsmouth where there was a disastrous fire in the circus building. Alfred Eugene Cooke climbed on to the roof and managed to get inside through a skylight to open the doors but the horses were so terrified of the flames that they refused to move and fourteen of them were burned to death. Alfred Eugene Cook is reputed to be the original 'daring young man on the flying trapeze.'

62, 62A, 62B and 62C
This remarkable travelling show has everything likely to attract a crowd. It proclaims itself as an exhibition of Wax Figures and includes Mechanical Works or Art. A close examination of the bill reveals that it also possesses a Panorama.
The Wax Figures are arranged to suit all tastes. There are the Royal Family, various Heads of State, Religious and Military leaders and other people in the news for various reasons. The Tichborne claimant and his adviser Dr. Kenealy share their notoriety with the Siamese Twins. No doubt the Turkish Slave Market introduced an erotic element.
The detailed description of the movements of the lion in Androcles and the Lion enables us to imagine the sort of action which could be expected in the other scenes of Joseph and Abraham, although the episode of the Grecian daughter is rather puzzling. If it is the classical story of the imprisoned father it is difficult to imagine how it could be shown without giving offence.
The panoramic oil paintings of American scenes and cities would appeal particularly to those whose nearest and dearest had emigrated there, and to those who were contemplating making the plunge.

62A

The Interior of the Exhibition comprises, in addition to the above features, a most Magnificent Series of

PANORAMIC OIL PAINTINGS

Of American Cities and Scenery!

These Beautiful Works of Art are of large size, and are painted by H MORLEY, Esq., of Nottingham, from Sketches taken in the various localities during Mr. ROWLAND'S recent Tour through the United States.

N.B.—Mr. ROWLAND, in submitting this novel, interesting, instructive, and amusing assemblage of Works of Art, respectfully announces that no expense has been spared to render the Promenade as attractive as it is possible for the most strenuous efforts to accomplish.

☞ The attention of Parents and Guardians is especially called to this Exhibition, as a means of impressing upon the minds of the young a vivid and lasting impression of the principal events in Sacred and Secular History, indispensable to a genuine education.

A SPLENDID BRASS BAND

Under the Leadership of Mr. T. LONSDALE, travels with the Exhibition, and the repertoire of Music will be found worthy of public notice & approval. This Beautiful Exhibition has afforded universal satisfaction to the thousands who have witnessed it, and it has been visited by the Nobility, Clergy, and Gentry, both in Great Britain and on the Continent.

62

ROWLAND'S
COLOSSAL EXHIBITION OF AUTOMATIC
WAX
FIGURES
AND
Mechanical Works of Art,
By far the LARGEST AND BEST TRAVELLING, consisting of 500 LIFE-SIZED MODELS, in Eight Large Caravans, Drawn by Twenty Magnificent Draught Horses,
WILL VISIT
EAST HARTLEPOOL,
ONE DAY ONLY,
WEDNESDAY, SEPTEMBER 29th, 1875.
QUEEN VICTORIA
Seated in the Coronation Chair, habited in Magnificent Robes of State; HIS ROYAL HIGHNESS, the late lamented PRINCE ALBERT,
The MARQUIS & MARCHIONESS of LORNE
THE PRINCE & PRINCESS OF WALES, THE CROWN PRINCE PRINCESS OF PRUSSIA,
The DUKE & DUCHESS of EDINBURGH, THE PRINCE LEOPOLD,
And the other Members of the Royal Family.
NAPOLEON
LATE EMPEROR OF THE FRENCH;
THE EMPRESS EUGENIE; AND THE PRINCE IMPERIAL.
THE SHAH OF PERSIA.
NAPOLEON BUONAPARTE.
NICHOLAS, LATE EMPEROR OF RUSSIA.
PRESIDENT LINCOLN.
HIS GRACE THE LATE DUKE OF WELLINGTON.
HIS ROYAL HIGHNESS THE LATE DUKE OF CUMBERLAND.
Uncle to Her Majesty.
THE LATE LORD PALMERSTON,
Prime Minister of England.
A Pair of Beautiful Models illustrating the
JOYS & SORROWS OF INFANCY.
REV. JOHN WESLEY,
The Eminent Divine.
General Havelock.
A GROUP OF SURPASSING MAGNITUDE AND RICH BEAUTY, REPRESENTING
A TURKISH SLAVE MARKET!

62B

First time of the Representation of a Magnificently Modelled Group, entitled,

KING BELSHAZZAR'S IMPIOUS FEAST!

"Belshazzar, the King, made a great feast to a thousand of his Lords, and drank wine before the thousand. Belshazzar, whilst he tasted the wine, commanded them to bring the Golden and Silver Vessels which his father Nebuchadnezzar had taken out of the temple which was in Jerusalem; that the King and his Princes, his Wives and his Concubines, might drink therein."—DANIEL V. 1, 26.

62C

Ladies and Gentlemen, 1s. Working People, 6d. Children, Half-price.

When the Exhibition only remains One Day at each place, it will open from Four until Five, to oblige Families that cannot make it convenient to come in the Evening; when more than One Day, from Two till Five, and from Six until Ten in the Evening.

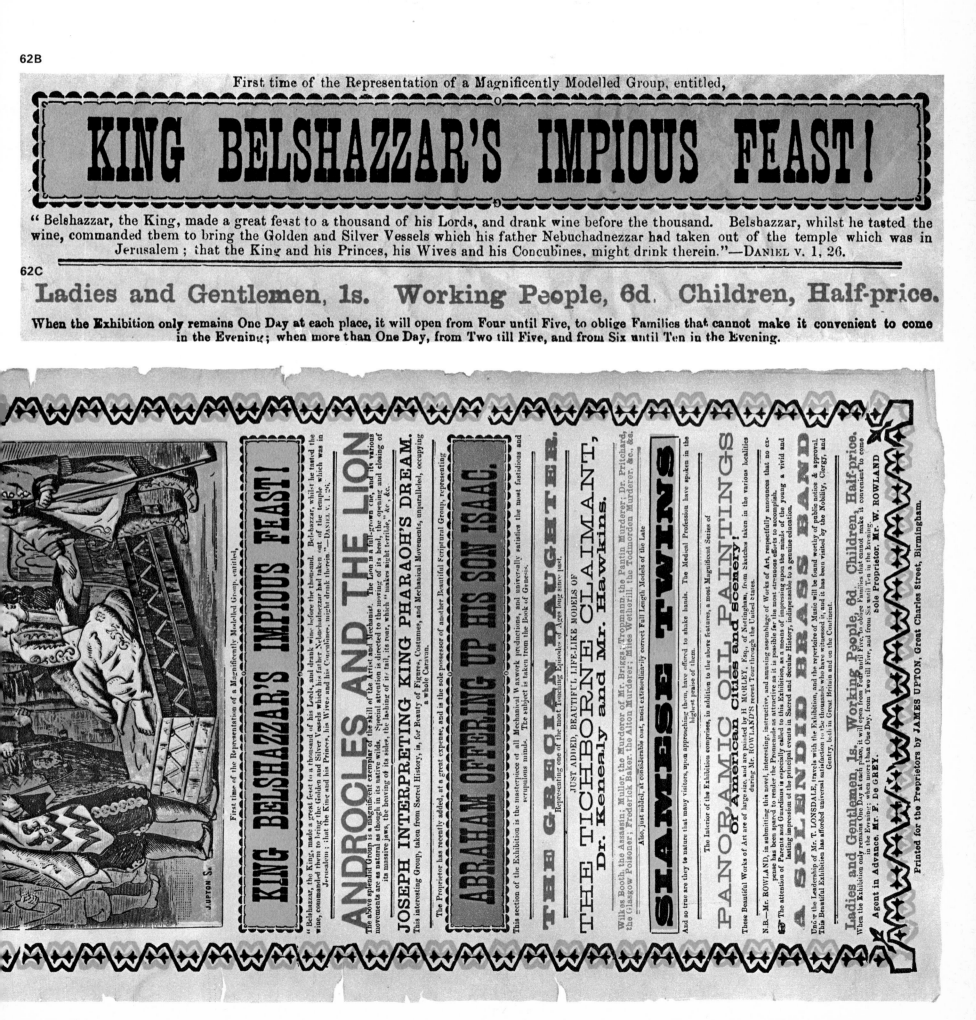

J. UPTON Sc.

First time of the Representation of a Magnificently Modelled Group, entitled,

KING BELSHAZZAR'S IMPIOUS FEAST!

"Belshazzar, the King, made a great feast to a thousand of his Lords, and drank wine before the thousand. Belshazzar, whilst he tasted the wine, commanded them to bring the Golden and Silver Vessels which his father Nebuchadnezzar had taken out of the temple which was in Jerusalem; that the King and his Princes, his Wives and his Concubines, might drink therein."—DANIEL V. 1, 26.

ANDROCLES AND THE LION

The above splendid Group is a magnificent exemplar of the skill of the Artist and Mechanist. The Lion is a full-grown one, and its various movements are as natural as though in its native wilds. Special attention is directed to the moving of its head, the opening and closing of its massive jaws, the heaving of its sides, the lashing of its tail, its roar, which "makes night terrible," &c. &c.

JOSEPH INTERPRETING KING PHARAOH'S DREAM.

This interesting Group, taken from Sacred History, is, for Beauty of Figures, Costumes, and Mechanical Movements, unparalleled, occupying a whole Caravan.

The Proprietor has recently added, at a great expense, and is the sole possessor of another Beautiful Scriptural Group, representing

ABRAHAM OFFERING UP HIS SON ISAAC.

This section of the Exhibition is the masterpiece of all Mechanical Waxwork productions, and universally satisfies the most fastidious and scrupulous minds. The subject is taken from the Book of Genesis.

THE GRECIAN DAUGHTER.

Representing one of the most Touching Episodes of Ages long since past.

JUST ADDED, BEAUTIFUL LIFE-LIKE MODELS OF

THE TICHBORNE CLAIMANT,

Dr. Kenealy and Mr. Hawkins.

Wilkes Booth, the Assassin; Mullor, the Murderer of Mr. Briggs; Tropmann, the Pantin Murderer; Dr. Pritchard, the Glasgow Poisoner; Frederick Baker, the Alton Murderer; Miles Wetherill, the Todmorden Murderer, &c. &c.

Also, just added, at considerable cost, most extraordinarily correct Full Length Models of the Late

SIAMESE TWINS

And so true are they to nature that many visitors, upon approaching them, have offered to shake hands. The Medical Profession have spoken in the highest praise of them.

The Interior of the Exhibition comprises, in addition to the above features, a most Magnificent Series of

PANORAMIC OIL PAINTINGS

of American Cities and Scenery!

These Beautiful Works of Art are of large size, and are painted by H. MORLEY, Esq., of Nottingham, from Sketches taken in the various localities during Mr. ROWLAND'S recent Tour through the United States.

N.B.—Mr. ROWLAND, in submitting this novel, interesting, instructive, and amusing assemblage of Works of Art, respectfully announces that no expense has been spared to render the Promenade as attractive as it is possible for the most strenuous efforts to accomplish.

☞ The attention of Parents and Guardians is especially called to this Exhibition, as a means of impressing upon the minds of the young a vivid and lasting impression of the principal events in Sacred and Secular History, indispensable to a genuine education.

A SPLENDID BRASS BAND

Under the Leadership of Mr. T. LONSDALE, travels with the Exhibition, and the repertoire of Music will be found worthy of public notice & approval. This Beautiful Exhibition has afforded universal satisfaction to the thousands who have witnessed it, and it has been visited by the Nobility, Clergy, and Gentry, both in Great Britain and on the Continent.

Ladies and Gentlemen, 1s. Working People, 6d. Children, Half-price.

When the Exhibition only remains One Day at each place, it will open from Four until Five, to oblige Families that cannot make it convenient to come in the Evening; when more than One Day, from Two till Five, and from Six until Ten in the Evening.

Agent in Advance, Mr. F. De GREY. Sole Proprietor, Mr. W. ROWLAND

Printed for the Proprietors by JAMES UPTON, Great Charles Street, Birmingham.

63, 63A, 63B and 63C

The history of this circus has been told elsewhere and all that remains for us to do is admire the poster and ponder upon its announcements. The old quarrel between the legitimate theatre and its provincial proletarian rivals seems to have transferred itself in some peculiar way to the circus. Here we have Thomas Batty claiming that he has the only legitimate equestrian troupe, as arrant a piece of nonsense as it is possible to come across. The bill shows a tendency to 'knock' other shows when it boasts that no expense has been spared to secure the best performers and promises 'No useless trash'.

Like the previous gaudily printed bill this is a product of some better equipped printer's office than Procter's and just sent to him to print in the name of the town and the date.

Notice the announcement of the Grand Public Entree and Procession which was the highlight of the visit of the circus to any town and which became a thing of the past as the traffic increased in the early days of this century.

63A

The whole will positively appear on the day announced in

TWO GRAND REPRESENTATIONS

The first to take place at TWO o'clock in the Afternoon, which is particularly recommended to heads of Families, Schools, &c., it being in every respect equal to the night performance, and will avoid the crowding which must necessarily attend this the grandest Exhibition that ever travelled. The Evening Representation will commence precisely at Half-past Seven. The Pay Office at the exterior will open one hour previous to the Performances, where Tickets can be obtained. **No Money taken at the Doors.** Notwithstanding the enormous and unheard-of expense, and to give all parties an opportunity of seeing the brilliant amalgamation of Novelties, the following will be the low tariff of Admission:—

Reserved Seats (Splendidly fitted up and carpeted), 3s. First Class, 2s. Second Class, 1s. Third Class, 6d

Children under Ten Years of Age, Half-price to Reserved Seats, 1s 6d; First Class, 1s; Second Class, 6d. No Half-price to Third Class.

63

63B

200 MEN & HORSES

NOTICE TO THE PUBLIC.

Mr THOMAS BATTY (nephew of the late Wm. Batty, Esq., of Astley's Royal Amphitheatre, London,) commenced a Provincial Tour, from London, in 1874, after an absence of 15 years from England, and has received the most flattering reception in every Town he has visited, every individual who has been fortunate enough to witness his Grand Entertainment having unhesitatingly declared it to be the ONLY LEGITIMATE EQUESTRIAN TROUPE TRAVELLING and to be decidedly

The BEST CIRCUS thev EVER BEHELD

The Proprietor never studies expense in order to gain the high esteem of his Patrons, and therefore engages Artistes ONLY of the highest reputation. It is a FACT that Mr BATTY pays more Money Weekly to REAL PERFORMERS than any other TWO Travelling Circuses put together in England. The Performance is therefore not made up of useless trash, which is neither amusing nor instiuctive

63C

64, 64A, 64B

Sanger could be described as the English Barnum and his 1860 visit to Hartlepool illustrates the clannishness of the circus artistes and strolling players, their sentimentality, and their devious ways of obtaining publicity.

Billy Purvis, the beloved strolling player, had died at Hartlepool in 1853. During his career as an entertainer he had played in Cooke's circus in Dundee and at Hartlepool. There was no stone marking his grave, so the circus had a special matinee performance to raise the necessary money. No better way could have been found of winning the hearts of the countryside's population. They thronged to see the show and honour Billy's memory, and in due course the stone was erected and is there to this very day, a subtle advertisement for Sangers' Circus. 'Take him for all in all, we ne'er shall look upon his like again.'

Here lies
WILLIAM PURVIS
better known as Billy Purvis,
Clown and Jester of the North,
who departed this life the 16th Dec. 1853
Aged 70 years
'Where be your gibes now? Your gambols?
Not one now—quite chap-fallen'

This stone was erected by J. G. Sanger, circus proprietor, May, 1860, to mark the last resting place of him who was always a friend of the fatherless, the widow, and the distressed. Requiescat in pace.

64A

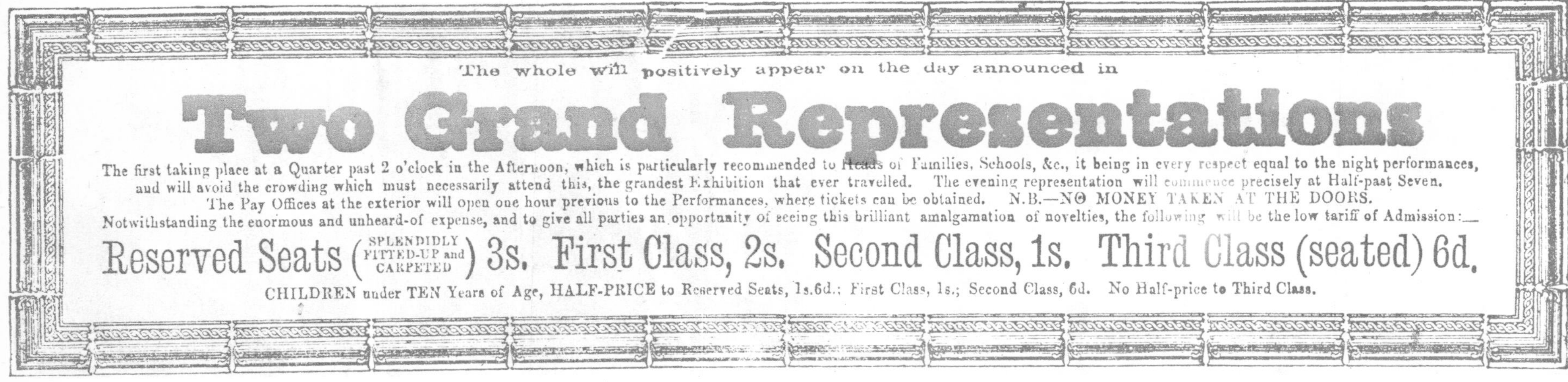

The whole will positively appear on the day announced in

Two Grand Representations

The first taking place at a Quarter past 2 o'clock in the Afternoon, which is particularly recommended to Heads of Families, Schools, &c., it being in every respect equal to the night performances, and will avoid the crowding which must necessarily attend this, the grandest Exhibition that ever travelled. The evening representation will commence precisely at Half-past Seven.

The Pay Offices at the exterior will open one hour previous to the Performances, where tickets can be obtained. N.B.—NO MONEY TAKEN AT THE DOORS.

Notwithstanding the enormous and unheard-of expense, and to give all parties an opportunity of seeing this brilliant amalgamation of novelties, the following will be the low tariff of Admission:—

Reserved Seats (SPLENDIDLY FITTED-UP and CARPETED) 3s. First Class, 2s. Second Class, 1s. Third Class (seated) 6d.

CHILDREN under TEN Years of Age, HALF-PRICE to Reserved Seats, 1s.6d.; First Class, 1s.; Second Class, 6d. No Half-price to Third Class.

64

SANGERS'
GREAT INTERNATIONAL
CIRCUS & HIPPODROME
Under the distinguished Patronage of the Queen, the Late Prince Consort, &c.
WILL VISIT THIS TOWN ON
MONDAY, May 29, 1865.

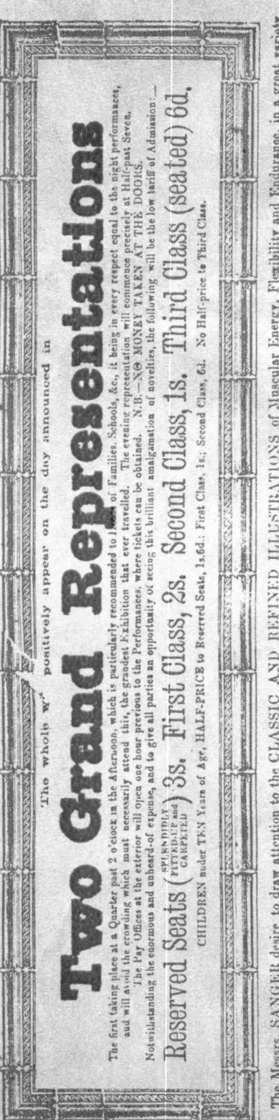

£900 per week and the £200 per week

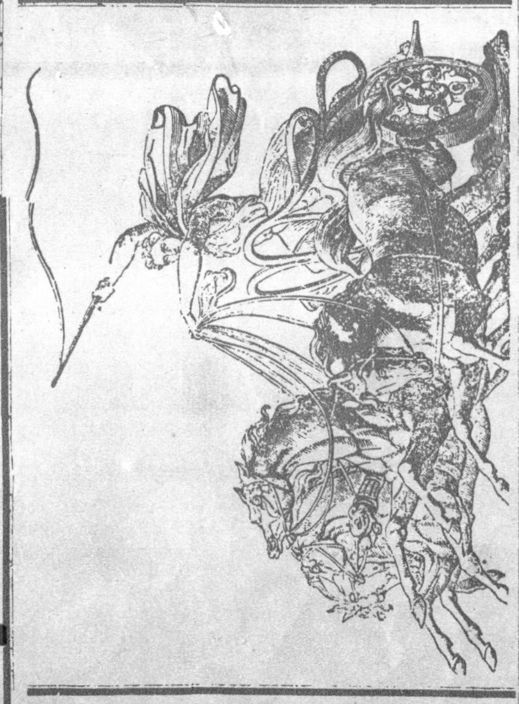

EXTENDING NEARLY
ONE MILE
IN LENGTH,
Which will start from the Circus at One o'clock.
PROCESSION

CONTINENTAL FEMALE RIDERS

LADY FRANCES ANNETTE | MDLLE. GUERSTINE,

64B

The Messrs. SANGER desire to draw attention to the CLASSIC AND REFINED ILLUSTRATIONS of Muscular Energy, Flexibility and Endurance, in a great variety of Athletic exercises by a selection of the First Artistes Living, introducing a great diversity of healthful, invigorating and diverting exhibitions of Courage and Address. This exhibition is so entirely unexceptionable in its character and influence, as to receive universal command and approval in all parts of the country, and acknowledged everywhere the most popular, instructive and economical of all public Amusements, being free from all features which are considered so objectionable in many exhibitions, by the refined and educated classes of the community.

The Messrs. SANGER also, in making this, their fifteenth annual tour, are desirous that the public should remember the inexhaustible routine of novelties they have produced on each and every occasion of their visit. Howes & Cushing, Mdme. McCarte, R. Bell, H. Brown, Pablo Fanque, Hernandez, Stone and Newsome, Cooke, and many others, who contended for the laurels, have sunk into insignificance, while this establishment, greater than on any former occasion, has the pleasure of offering to the inhabitants of this town a performance far eclipsing anything on record in point of grandeur, variety, brilliancy, and startling novelties, being a grand programme of the most daring acts of the day. Some idea may be formed of the greatness of this NE PLUS ULTRA exhibition when the weekly expenditure amounts to the enormous sum of

£900 per week and the wear and tear to **£200 per week**

The great Bare-back Rider, who will execute terrific flights over banners, through Balloons, &c., &c., acknowledged to be the Princess of Equestriennes, the epitome of grace, daring, and feminine perfection.

MDLLE. PERNETTAI, THE BEAUTIFUL SYLPH.

MDLLE. ARLONA, THE GEM.

MDLLE ADELINA, THE JEWEL.

MDLLE. CAROLINE

The most daring Equestrienne of this or any other age, therefore named the Diana of the Cirque, who will appear in her terrific Bare-Back Act.

CONTINENTAL MALE RIDERS.

Signor de Sotto, The great Somersault Rider, from the Cirque Imperial, St. Petersburgh.
Sig. Nicolo, The Great Rider and Vaulter.
Mons. Zweicker, From the Cirque Royal, Turin.
Mons. Mellilli, The Great Antipodean Performer.

Signor Potenio, The Talented and Popular Scene Rider, who will appear in his Great Exciting Act, on Two Horses.
Mons de Boss, The Great Tight-rope Artiste.
Monsieur Auguzi, The Flying Man.
Young Bertini, The Great Contortionist.

The Brothers Auguzi, The Ladder Sprites.
Chang Wyu, From Hong Kong, the Famous Balancer and Tumbler.
THE RENOWNED Ridalgo Family, In their Drawing-Room Entertainment.

ENGLISH FEMALE RIDERS.

Miss Matilda Emily Dashwood
Mrs. Williams
Miss Helena Charlotte Murray
Miss Rachel Saunders

Mrs. Dovedale
Miss Julia Atkin
Miss Francis Charlton
Miss Amelia Linsey Aldridge

Mrs. Emedy
Mrs. William Atkin
Miss Lucy Jane Twigg

Miss HARRIET SANGER, In her admired characteristic Sketch, entitled "The Warrior of Old, or The Standard Bearer."

Miss GEORGINA SANGER, In her dashing and truly astounding Backward and Forward Feats of Wonder.

ENGLISH MALE RIDERS.

Mr. A. Powell, England's greatest Horseman, who will ride and drive one, two, three, and four Horses at one time.
Mr. Alfred Clarke, The Model Rider, and great Somersault Thrower.
Mr. John Clarke, The great English Scene Act Rider.
Mr. Joseph Ashly, The renowned Bare-back Rider and Vaulter.

The Brothers Carlo, The most astounding Gymnasts of the Age.
Mr. Alfred William Spencer, The Flying Horseman.
Mr. George Henry Twigg, The World's Wonder.
Mr. Samuel James Tomkins, The Irresistible.

Mr. Edward Kerwin, The Champion Elephant Trainer.
Master John Samuel Sanger, In his great Somersault Act, on his Rampant Charger.
Master Samuel Watson
Master John Watson

FRENCH CLOWNS

Mons. Oriello, Mons. Devani, and Mons. Camilla.

ENGLISH CLOWNS

Funny Footitt, J. Clarke, Tom Dexter, and the great Burlesque Clown and

QUEEN'S JESTER

The whole of the above great Artistes will appear, together with the great

Performing Elephants, Camels, Dromedaries, &c., &c.

The Public are requested to expect much, and they will no doubt be prepared to indulge in one of the greatest entertainments in Europe.

Agent in Advance, ... Mr. J. TWIGG. Acting Manager, ... Mr. G. KNIGHT. Sole Proprietors, J. & G. SANGER

VIVAT REGINA.

Martin Billing, Son, & Co., Printers, Livery Street, Birmingham.

65

The strange and magical creatures of legends and heraldry lingered in the popular imagination for many years. Indeed, there is a link between heraldry and the menagerie, for the Tower beasts, the first wild beast show in England, began when the Emperor gave Henry III three living leopards as a delicate compliment, for the identical three were on Henry's shield.

If the common people could swallow the wyvern and the hippogriff, and the lion and the unicorn could fight for the Crown, who was ready to argue when a showman claimed to exhibit the maned colobus or the noble casheware, the rioboscay from Russia, or the bonassus? The Vlacke Vark is another of the same breed of beasts with noble and outlandish names.

John Cooper is a famous name among lion tamers and it is fitting that he should be presented adjacent to Van Amburgh. John was born in 1833 in the Midlands and became an orphan at the age of ten. He ran away from whatever apprenticeship the parish had destined him for and joined a circus. Its pride was a lion so fierce that it had to be secured by an iron collar and chain even when it was in its cage. It occasionally broke loose and terrified everybody. It did so at Leeds and John Cooper, a boy of eleven, slipped into the cage and fastened the collar round its neck without the beast making the slightest objection. From that moment he was the lion tamer of the show and rose to the height of his profession. He lived to the substantial age of 87.

65

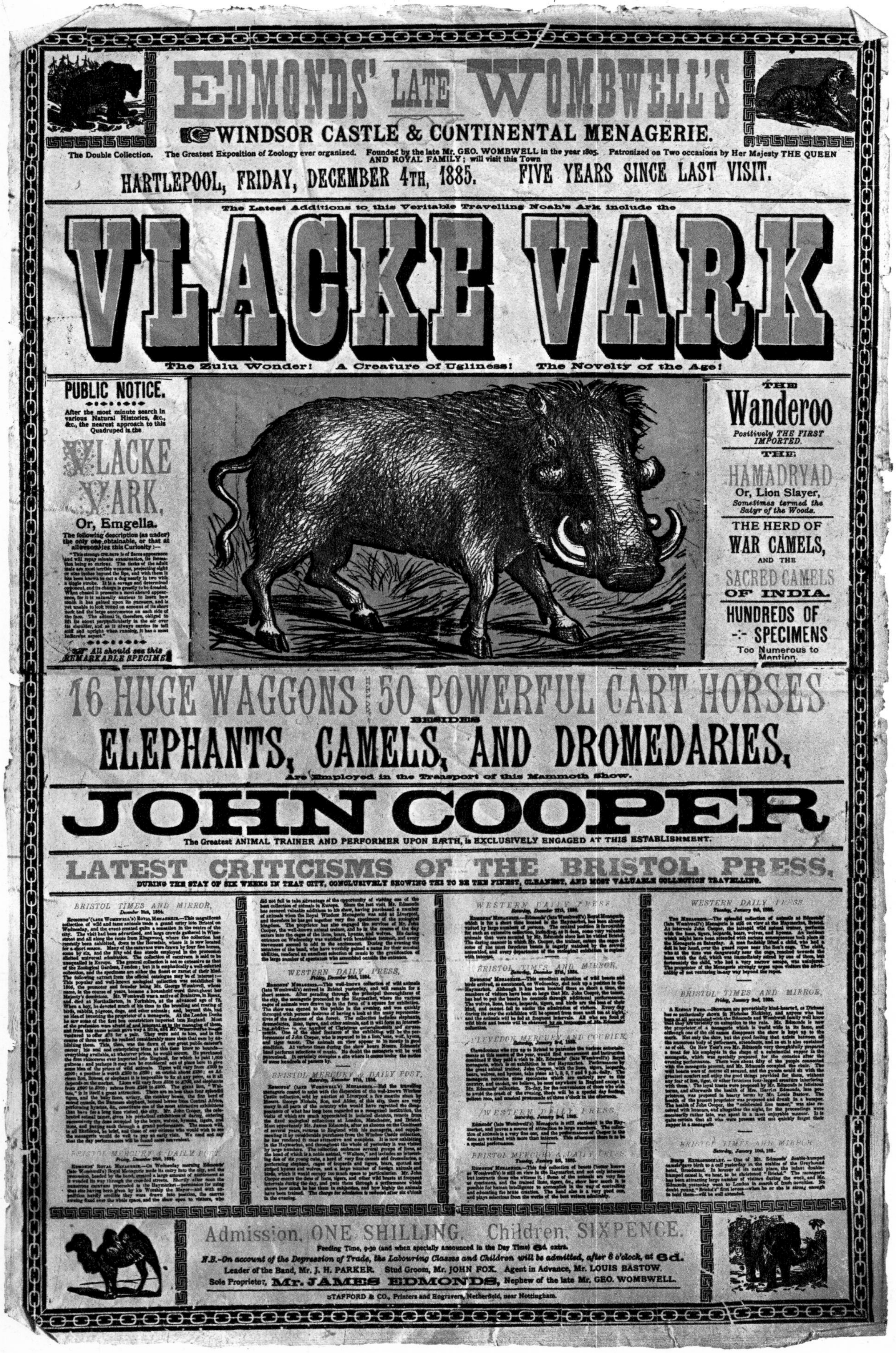

EDMONDS' LATE WOMBWELL'S

WINDSOR CASTLE & CONTINENTAL MENAGERIE.

The Double Collection. The Greatest Exposition of Zoology ever organized. Founded by the late Mr. GEO. WOMBWELL in the year 1805. Patronized on Two occasions by Her Majesty THE QUEEN AND ROYAL FAMILY; will visit this Town

HARTLEPOOL, FRIDAY, DECEMBER 4TH, 1885. FIVE YEARS SINCE LAST VISIT.

The Latest Additions to this Veritable Travelling Noah's Ark include the

VLACKE VARK

The Zulu Wonder! A Creature of Ugliness! The Novelty of the Age!

PUBLIC NOTICE. After the most minute search in various Natural Histories, &c., &c., the nearest approach to this Quadruped is the VLACKE VARK, Or, Emgella.

THE Wanderoo Positively THE FIRST IMPORTED.

THE HAMADRYAD Or, Lion Slayer, Sometimes termed the Satyr of the Woods.

THE HERD OF WAR CAMELS, AND THE SACRED CAMELS OF INDIA.

HUNDREDS OF SPECIMENS Too Numerous to Mention.

16 HUGE WAGGONS 50 POWERFUL CART HORSES

BESIDES

ELEPHANTS, CAMELS, AND DROMEDARIES,

Are Employed in the Transport of this Mammoth Show.

JOHN COOPER

The Greatest ANIMAL TRAINER AND PERFORMER UPON EARTH, is EXCLUSIVELY ENGAGED AT THIS ESTABLISHMENT.

LATEST CRITICISMS OF THE BRISTOL PRESS,

DURING THE STAY OF SIX WEEKS IN THAT CITY, CONCLUSIVELY SHOWING THIS TO BE THE FINEST, CLEANEST, AND MOST VALUABLE COLLECTION TRAVELLING.

Admission, ONE SHILLING. Children, SIXPENCE.

Feeding Time, 9-30 (and when specially announced in the Day Time) 6d. extra.

N.B.—On account of the Depression of Trade, the Labouring Classes and Children will be admitted, after 8 o'clock, at 6d.

Leader of the Band, Mr. J. H. PARKER. Stud Groom, Mr. JOHN FOX. Agent in Advance, Mr. LOUIS BASTOW.

Sole Proprietor, Mr. JAMES EDMONDS, Nephew of the late Mr. GEO. WOMBWELL.

STAFFORD & CO., Printers and Engravers, Netherfield, near Nottingham.

65A

PUBLIC NOTICE.

After the most minute search in various Natural Histories, &c., &c., the nearest approach to this Quadruped is the

VLACKE VARK,

Or, Emgella.

The following description (as under) the only one obtainable, or that at all resembles this Curiosity:—

"This strange creature is of fierce appearance and will repay minute examination, its formation being so curious. The tusks of the adult male are most terrible weapons, projecting eight or nine inches beyond the lips, and with them it has been known to cut a dog nearly in two with a single stroke. It is a savage and determined opponent, and its charge is greatly to be dreaded. When chased it presents a most absurd appearance, for it is naturally anxious to learn how much it has gained upon its pursuers, and is yet unable to look round on account of its short neck and the large excrescence on each side of the face. The animal is, therefore, obliged to lift its snout perpendicularly in the air over its shoulder, and as it always carries its tail stiff and upright when running, it has a most ludicrous aspect."

65B

BRISTOL TIMES AND MIRROR,

Saturday, December 27th, 1884.

EDMONDS' MENAGERIE.—This excellent collection of wild beasts and birds arrived, as announced, on Wednesday, and took up a position in the Haymarket. Although it has been located there so short a time, the numbers of visitors have been so large that Mr. John Cooper, the tamer, has had to put the beasts he controls through additional performances. The wolves, lions, bears, leopards, tigers, and birds are the best of their kind, and cannot fail to excite the admiration of visitors. Every day during its stay the exhibition will be opened from noon until ten at night, and the animals will be fed at frequent intervals. All who are fond of wild birds and beasts will be charmed by an inspection of Mr. Edmonds' collection.

CLEVEDON MERCURY AND COURIER,

Saturday, January 3rd, 1885.

Clevedonians who run up to Bristol to patronise the various entertainments at this season of the year, would find amusement and instruction combined if they paid a visit to Mr. Edmonds' (late Wombwell's) Royal menagerie, which is on exhibition in the Haymarket. Performances by the great animal trainer, John Cooper, with the lions, tigers, leopards, bears, wolves, and hyenas, take place at 1, 3, 5, 7 and 9 p.m. daily. The menagerie contains some specimens which are entirely new to this country, and cannot, we believe, be seen anywhere in England except in Mr. Edmonds' collection. To-day, for the convenience of those who wish to avoid the crush of the evening, there will be a special day feeding, pelican race, and musical promenade at three o'clock in the afternoon.

WESTERN DAILY PRESS,

Saturday, January 3rd, 1885.

Edmonds' (late Wombwell's) Menagerie is still stationed in the Haymarket, and proves a source of attraction to large numbers. The collection of animals is a very fine one, and the performances of Cooper in the dens are watched with more than interest. This afternoon there is to be a special performance.

66
The usual gammon for a benefit.

67
Van Amburgh visited the North of England in June and July, 1843 giving performances in every town as far north as Berwick-on-Tweed. His appearances called forth the inhabitants en masse to behold the splendid show, the hero of the day driving a superb team of ten beautiful cream-coloured and piebald horses, harnessed two abreast. He restrained and guided the motions of these fiery steeds as easily as though he had been guiding a pair of ladies' ponies, and was followed by some twenty light caravans, picked out splendidly in green and gold, and drawn likewise by handsome horses, harnessed in furniture ornamented with silver.

66

TAKE NOTICE!

COOKE'S CIRCUS, HARTLEPOOL,

On TUESDAY, FEB. 29, 1848,

IT IS EXPECTED THAT UPWARDS OF

5000

Persons will attend, it being for the Benefit of Mr. Emidy, Ring Master and Equestrian, who hopes that his Friends will

REWARD

Him with a bumper. He wishes them not to

RUN AWAY

With an idea that every one in

HARTLEPOOL

Will be there, his only desire is that the Circus may be comfortably filled, and his friends enjoy themselves.

Mr EMIDY pledges himself that a greater variety of Unprecedented Novelties than was ever witnessed on any former occasion will be brought forward. In order to render this the greatest night of the season, there will be a Grand Parade in the course of the day, when Mr Emidy (the only person who ever drove **28 Horses in hand** through the streets of London) will have the honour of driving **14 Horses in hand.**

In the Evening there will be a **RACE** between TWO LARGE **MONTGOLFIER BALLOONS,** which will be dispatched from the Circus at a Quarter before Seven o'Clock precisely.

UNDER THE PATRONAGE OF THE

INDEPENDENT ORDER OF ODD FELLOWS.

PRINTED BY J. PROCTER, HIGH STREET, HARTLEPOOL.

67

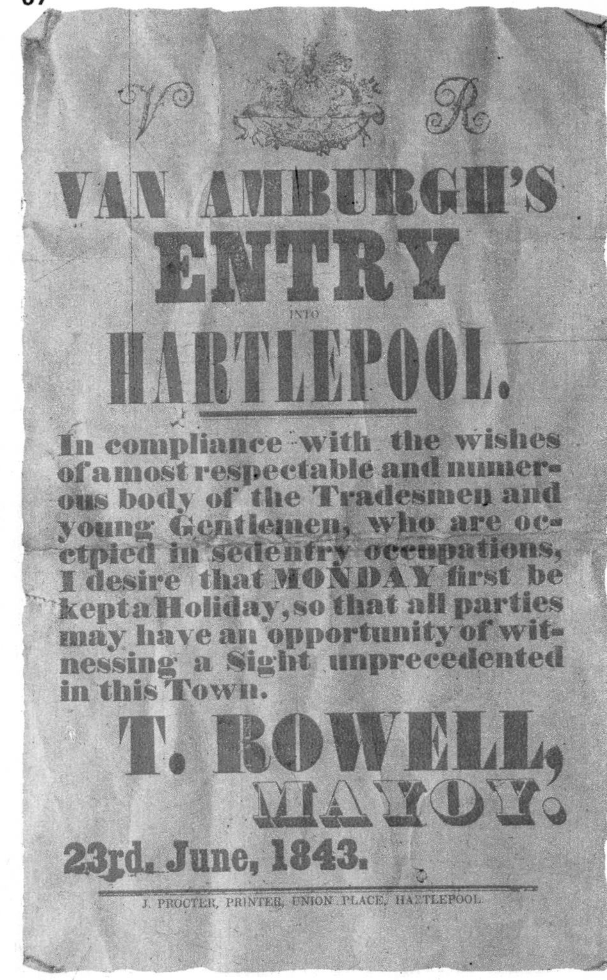
V R

VAN AMBURGH'S ENTRY INTO HARTLEPOOL.

In compliance with the wishes of a most respectable and numerous body of the Tradesmen and young Gentlemen, who are occupied in sedentry occupations, I desire that MONDAY first be kept a Holiday, so that all parties may have an opportunity of witnessing a Sight unprecedented in this Town.

T. ROWELL, MAYOY.

23rd. June, 1843.

J. PROCTER, PRINTER, UNION PLACE, HARTLEPOOL.

68
When George Sanger was in Liverpool in 1857 the circus of Howes and Cushing arrived from America with a large company. Such were the crowds that all the shops on the processional route closed. The band headed the parade in a carriage drawn by forty horses, followed by the performers in golden cars, and with a group of Indians running alongside and behind.
Sanger recognised in one of the Indian chiefs an African that he had picked up on the London docks a dozen years before and decided to recruit his 'savages' in a similar manner. He went round the slums and recruited as bizarre a band of toughs as possible. With red ochre, skin tint, long black hair, feathers, skins and beads they were transformed and taught war dances and tribal rites. Were these genuine real wild men at Stockton? It didn't really matter so long as they continued to make the customers shudder.

69
In the early days of the circus there was a craze for American Circuses. Not surprisingly such companies always put on a liberal display of eagles and Stars and Stripes. In fact Howes and Cushing were astute enough to insist that the American flag should be flown outside every house at which one of their performers lodged. The circuses themselves seemed to follow the familiar pattern since the appeal of cowboys and Indians had not been realised. Possibly they were not familiar to Victorians at this time.

68

V. R.

EXTRAORDINARY ATTRACTION!!!

THE GREAT SHOW!!!

EDMUNDS' late WOMBWELL'S

ROYAL

WINDSOR CASTLE MENAGERIE,

WILL ARRIVE FOR EXHIBITION, AT

East Hartlepool, ON SATURDAY, SEPTEMBER 15th, | West Hartlepool, MONDAY, SEPTEMBER 17th,

STOCKTON, TUESDAY 18th,

For the First Time since 1842, Accompanied by that Extraordinary Race of Men the ZULU KAFFIRS, or

WILD MEN!!

Of Africa, the only men of their Race ever brought to this Country, who will go through their Wonderful and Extraordinary Performances at each Exhibition during the stay of the Managerie; Representing in their Native Costume the MANNERS and CUSTOMS OF KAFFIR LIFE, Viz:—The War Signal, Modes of Warfare, War Dances, & Exercises, Songs of War, Peace, &c.

THE KAFFIRS.

In describing a race, as with any other object of Natural History, it must always be of importance to ascertain clearly their geographical position; for on being shown a plant, or a rare animal, our first question naturally is, from whence does it come? is it aboriginal to that spot, or does it come from some other place? and, if so, what place? Secondly we naturally enquire into the qualities, natural or acquired, of the specimen before us.

To pass the mighty cape of South Africa formed the main object of ambition to the Portuguese, in their celebrated voyage of discovery along the continent; and, after a century passed in vain, Andrew Bartolomew Dies obtained a view of that great promontory; but the stormy sky in which it was enveloped, and the fearful swell produced by the conflict of contending oceans, appalled even that stout navigator; he called it Cape Tempest, and returned home. His King (King John,) to fan the flame of discovery, called it the Cape of Good Hope. Vasco de Gama, true to his nature—a prudent, calculating Dutchman—following the steps of the indolent Portuguese, pushed his way into the Indian seas, and, with much difficulty, affected a landing. Following this, we find, that when the Dutch seized upon the Cape of Good Hope, and located themselves there as settlers and farmers, true to their natures, they set down on farms as far apart as they well could—a practice we see followed by our Anglo-Saxon brethren in America; driving before them the aborigines, seizing their flocks and herds, and, finally, their lands; reducing the poor natives to miserable bondage,—the necessary fate of all races of men deprived of and refused the privilege of defensive arms. To the powerful fire-arms and sinews of the Dutch Boor, the wretched Hottentot could only oppose the bow and poisoned arrow, and perhaps, an assegai,—the only resort of that feeble and helpless race.

Retiring, therefore, before the Saxon race (that is, the Dutch boor,) towards the east, he there encountered the Kaffirs, the warlike Kaffirs; tall, stout, robust, of a deep bronze colour, enterprising, chivalrous, and bold, freemen in fact, who have since, more than once, driven back the British troops, and with whom, till lately, we waged a war of extermination; but, be assured of this, the Kaffir will never become the slave of the white man; he will never, with life yield his lands to the British and Dutch now gaping for them. Where the lions roar and the hyenas howl, his song is still to be heard—

"No white man shall drink our milk,
No white man shall eat the bread of our children,
Ho how, ho how, ho how, ho how!"

By a series of mismanagements, almost without parallel in the history of ... we have crushed the wretched Hottentot to the dust, and converted ... minded Kaffirs into a nation of tigers. Subjugating first, destroying aft... prey alike of the European settler and the native intruder—the... domesticated ferret or wild stoat ravage, with equal fe... timid rabbit.

ADMISSION, One Shilling.—Children under Ten Years of Ag...

From the Office of J. PROCTER, Printer, Southgate, Hartlepo...

69

POSITIVELY

FOR

ONE DAY ONLY!

MR. SANDS,

Proprietor of the New York Amphitheatre, and late Lessee of the English Opera House, London.

Most respectfully informs the Visitors and Inhabitants of HARTLEPOOL, and its Vicinity, that his Company of unequalled

AMERICAN EQUESTRIANS

AND HIS HIGHLY TRAINED STUD OF

FORTY AMERICAN HORSES!

WILL PERFORM AT

HARTLEPOOL

On WEDNESDAY, July 17th, 1844,

FOR ONE DAY ONLY,

Under a spacious and novel Pavilion, erected in a Field belonging to Mr. John Grey, near the Church.

Doors open at Two o'clock, and to commence at Half-past Two in the Afternoon, and Half-past Seven in the Evening.

The Fearless and Pre-eminent Stud of Beautiful Horses and Fairy Ponies (Forty in number) were landed at Liverpool, March 8th, 1842; and the Company commenced their Performance with the most unbounded and brilliant success, for Eight Weeks, at the Royal Amphitheatre, after which they made a Summer Tour through the principal Towns, where they met with the same liberal support. During the Winter Months they have performed at the English Opera House, London, and received the patronage of Royalty, and all the Distinguished Nobility of the Great Metropolis.

Mr. Sands has the pleasure of announcing, that he has, at an enormous expense, had a Splendid and novel Pavilion made after an entirely new style, with the most costly interior Decorations and appointments forming at once a magnificent spacious Roman Amphitheatre and Arena of Arts, the whole of which is erected in a few hours, and capable of holding several thousand persons. The Box Seats neatly covered and Ornamented, are so well arranged, that each person commands a free and uninterrupted view of the whole Performance, the safe and easy access to which, combined with every possible attention to avoid accidents, has given universal satisfaction. Mr. Sands particularly invites Ladies and Gentlemen to inspect the Pavilion, previous to the Performance.

The Unique and splendid Carriages, built by Mr. Troylett, of Manchester, and the Richly-ornamented and Costly Harness, made by Messrs. Filligan, Whitechapel Road, London, are justly admired for their novelty of design and construction, and for grandeur cannot be surpassed. Mr. Sands's Private Carriage, built in America, is a rare specimen of the art.

Mr. SANDS in introducing to a generous British Public, an Establishment that stands unrivalled in all the World, hopes they will not see in his programme, those extravagant announcements which have lately been adopted in similar details, but trusts the reputation and advantageously known encomiums of the Press, which this Establishment has ...ned since his arrival in England will be sufficient proofs to vouch for this, as well as for the Talent to be brought forward; he is aw... there are opinions at variance with entertainments of this description, yet he begs to assure the Public, there is nothing in his perfo... to which the most fastidious can object.

THE CAVALCADE

Will arrive in HARTLEPOOL, on Wednesday Morning, July 17th, at Eleven o'clock, from Stockton, and make a

GRAND PROCESSION

Through the principal Streets, accompanied by his justly

CELEBRATED BRASS BAND

IN A CARRIAGE DRAWN BY

TEN SPLENDID CREAM-COLOURED HORSES,

DRIVEN IN HAND BY MR. R. BROWN.

Equestrian Director—Mr. C. RIVEA. Leader of the Band,—Mr. SWAN. Secretary and Treasurer—Mr. A. SMITH, to whom all communications must be addressed.

☞ Admission to First Seats, 2s. Second Seats, 1s. 6d. Standing Places, 1s. Children under 10 years of age, Seats, 1s. Standing Places, 6d.

Mr. Sands will also be at Scarborough, July 11th and 12th; Whitby, July 13th; Guisbro', July 15th, and Stockton, on the 16th.

J. Procter, Printer, Union Place, High Street, Hartlepool.

70
A close examination of the woodcut will reveal in the centre of the lower edge 'F. Ginnett' which was a name to conjure with in the circus world. John Frederick Ginnett's father was a French prisoner after Waterloo who by sheer pertinacity acquired a circus of his own and made a name for himself as a trainer of horses. His son was the Infant Equestrian Prodigy in Monsieur Ducrow's 'Cupid and Zephyr' Act and he prospered to such an extent that he left his three sons three circuses, £80,000, 274 horses, and a large touring show.

71
A Bailey's Circus existed long before Barnum and Bailey had ever been heard of, but whether this Exhibition had anything to do with either it must be left for the reader to decide.
This bill is unusual because it is the product of Procter's office, although it is nothing to be proud of unless other corrections were made in the proof. Some of the animals would puzzle a modern zoologist. The cameleopard was an old term familiar in the eighteenth century, but what was a cameleon or a chinkertoe? The price of admission suggests that it was a Penny Gaff not a menagerie.

70

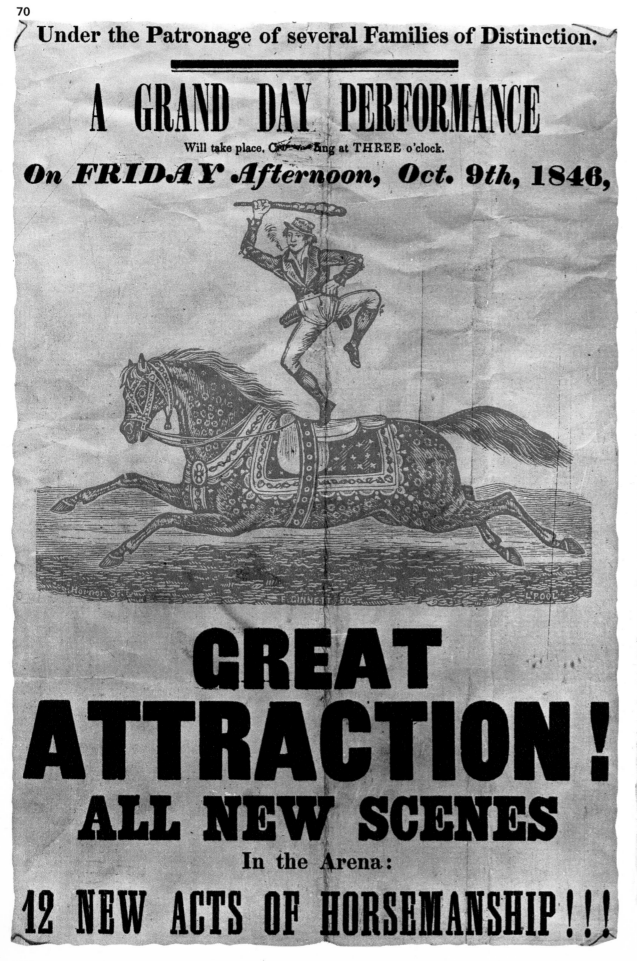

Under the Patronage of several Families of Distinction.

A GRAND DAY PERFORMANCE

Will take place, C[illegible]ing at THREE o'clock.

On FRIDAY Afternoon, Oct. 9th, 1846,

Horner Sc. F. GINNETT [illegible] L'POOL

GREAT

ATTRACTION!

ALL NEW SCENES

In the Arena:

12 NEW ACTS OF HORSEMANSHIP!!!

71

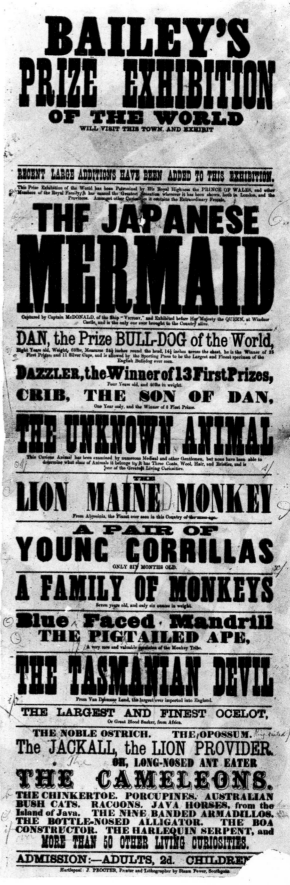

BAILEY'S

PRIZE EXHIBITION

OF THE WORLD

WILL VISIT THIS TOWN, AND EXHIBIT

RECENT LARGE ADDITIONS HAVE BEEN ADDED TO THIS EXHIBITION.

This Prize Exhibition of the World has been Patronized by His Royal Highness the PRINCE OF WALES, and other Members of the Royal Family, it has caused the Greatest Sensation wherever it has been shown, both in London, and the Provinces. Amongst other Curiosities it contains the Extraordinary Female,

THF JAPANESE

MERMAID

Captured by Captain McDONALD, of the Ship "Victory," and Exhibited before Her Majesty the QUEEN, at Windsor Castle, and is the only one ever brought to the Country alive.

DAN, the Prize BULL-DOG of the World,

Eight Years old, Weight, 68lbs, Measures 24½ inches round the head, 14½ inches across the chest, he is the Winner of 23 First Prizes, and 11 Silver Cups, and is allowed by the Sporting Press to be the Largest and Finest specimen of the English Bulldog ever seen.

DAZZLER, the Winner of 13 First Prizes,

Four Years old, and 40lbs in weight.

CRIB, THE SON OF DAN,

One Year only, and the Winner of 3 First Prizes.

THE UNKNOWN ANIMAL

This Curious Animal has been examined by numerous Medical and other Gentlemen, but none have been able to determine what class of Animals it belongs to, it has Three Coats, Wool, Hair, and Bristles, and is one of the Greatest Living Curiosities.

THE

LION MAINE MONKEY

From Abyssinia, the Finest ever seen in this Country of the same age.

A PAIR OF

YOUNC CORRILLAS

ONLY SIX MONTHS OLD.

A FAMILY OF MONKEYS

Seven years old, and only six ounces in weight.

Blue Faced Mandrill

THE PIGTAILED APE,

A very rare and valuable specimen of the Monkey Tribe.

THE TASMANIAN DEVIL

From Van Diemans Land, the largest ever imported into England.

THE LARGEST AND FINEST OCELOT,

Or Great Blood Sucker, from Africa.

THE NOBLE OSTRICH. THE OPOSSUM.

The JACKALL, the LION PROVIDER.

OR, LONG-NOSED ANT EATER

THE CAMELEONS.

THE CHINKERTOE. PORCUPINES. AUSTRALIAN BUSH CATS. RACOONS. JAVA HORSES, from the Island of Java. THE NINE BANDED ARMADILLOS. THE BOTTLE-NOSED ALLIGATOR. THE BOA CONSTRUCTOR. THE HARLEQUIN SERPENT, and

MORE THAN 50 OTHER LIVING CURIOSITIES.

ADMISSION:—ADULTS, 2d. CHILDREN

Hartlepool: J. PROCTER, Printer and Lithographer by Steam Power, Southgate.

72, 72A and 72B

Henry Hengler was a tight rope dancer with Astley in 1807 and in due course had three sons, two of whom, Edward and John, he trained in his own speciality under Ducrow when the latter ran Astley's. Charles Hengler (the third son) was a horseman and a good businessman and the sons and their father separated from Ducrow and joined the circus of Price and Powell. Powell married Henry's daughter and when the concern went bankrupt Edward and Charles bought and ran it.

They were competing with stiff opposition for Ducrow was established in the larger cities whilst they had to tour throughout the summer, and spend the winter in temporary wooden buildings in large towns. They worked hard and made themselves famous for the perfection of their acts. In 1857 they had saved sufficient money to enable them to open a permanent Cirque Varieties in Liverpool. They continued to prosper and moved to London in 1876. This bill is a relic of their early tenting days before they had achieved security.

72

HENGLER'S
CIRCUS ROYAL
Colossal Equestrian Establishment of Foreign and British Artistes,
TROUPE OF LADIES,
And a STUD of HIGHLY TRAINED HORSES and PONIES.

Mr. C. HENGLER respectfully announces that his TALENTED COMPANY will perform their OLYMPIC WONDERS in a SPACIOUS AMERICAN PAVILION, ERECTED

15th October 1850

FOR ONE DAY ONLY

The Company will arrive into this Town precisely at 12 O'CLOCK on the above named day, preceded by the Splendid Brass Band in a Carriage drawn by BEAUTIFUL VARIEGATED PALFREYS, followed by the Unique Tandem. The Ladies of the Stag Hunting Chase in Splendid Scarlet Costume, mounted on Black, Bay, and Grey, thorough-bred Coursers, the Infant Wonders on the diminutive Burmese Ponies. The extraordinary Performing Monkey, Mons. Mushapug, on his Trained Pony, Sir Tatton Sykes. The Superb Stag Carriage, drawn by Skewbald Horses.

Beautiful White ARABIAN STEED, IBRAHIM PACHA,

In sumptuous Trappings. Also, the Royal Pony, BLACKAMOOR, presented to Mr. CHARLES HENGLER by Her Most Gracious Majesty, Queen VICTORIA, in Windsor, February, 1849. The Grand Equestrian Procession brought up by the

Magnificent Pony Equipage,
The exact Model of Prince Albert's Shooting Break,
Conveying the Zoological Curiosity, BEESWING, only 24 inches high, the incomparable Equine Atom, or Fractional Horse, being the smallest Horse in the World, drawn by Four handsome Fairy Steeds, with New and Richly Silver-mounted Harness.

ONE DAY ONLY — ONE DAY ONLY

ROUTINE of HENGLER's unparalleled Entertainment of Equestrian Sports, Tourneys, Chases, and the most extensive Concentration of Talent ever produced in any Establishment of the kind in One Day!!

The First Performance will commence at TWO o'clock, including the inimitable Artiste on the Tight Rope, Herr HENGLER; likewise the Grand Stag-hunting Scene, called the Dames of the Chase, by the principal Ladies of the Menage.

The Second Performance will take place at SEVEN in the Evening, including the Brilliant Equestrian Spectacle, entitled TURPIN'S RIDE TO YORK and the DEATH OF BONNY BLACK BESS, the most extraordinary Horse in Europe. The wonderful Training of this BONNY BLACK BESS is pronounced by all who witness her to be a Wonder of the Age—the anxiety she shows when her master is in apparent danger—the beautiful leap over a five-barred gate—her feigning of lameness, then death, and allowing herself to be dragged on to a platform, and carried away upon the shoulders of Twenty Men! is a portion of the Performance of this wonderful Horse, showing the very acme of Horse Training, and the representation is so imposing and faithfully delineated, that hundreds who have witnessed it have actually gone away with the impression that BLACK BESS WAS REALLY DEAD!

All Accounts to be presented for liquidation at 8 o'clock in the Evening. Box Usher, Mr. Frowde, of whom places may be secured after the arrival of the Establishment. First Class Seats 2s. Second do. 1s. Arena, 6d. Children under 10 years of age and schools half-price to First and Second Class. Charity Schools admitted Gratis to the Day Exhibition on application being made to Mr. Hengler after his arrival.

[R. Harrison, Printer, 44, Tyne Street, North Shields.]

72A

To conclude in the Evening, with the Grand Equestrian Spectacle, with an entirely new and appropriate Costumes, Music, Decorations, Dresses, &c, entitled

TURPIN'S RIDE TO YORK,
AND DEATH OF BLACK BESS

"Let the lover his mistress's beauty rehearse,
And laud her attractions in languishing verse;
Be it mine in rude strains, but with truth to express
The love that I bear to my bonny Black Bess."

Dick Turpin .... Mr. C. HENGLER
Tom King .... Herr HENGLER

Timothy Gudgeon, Ralph, Simon, Sharpscent, Young Sharpscent, Luke Rookwood, Landlord of the Falstaff, Dolly Gudgeon, Constables, &c. by the rest of the Company.

The succession of Incidents and Events will commence with the Village of Kilburn. REWARD for TURPIN and KING—arrival of Turpin at Kilburn on his black mare Bess—

"Mark her skin, sleek as velvet, and dusky as night;
Its jet undisfigured by one spot of white;
Mark that throat branched with veins, prompt to charge or caress;
Is she not beautiful? my bonny Black Bess."

The Cockney fishmonger—Turpin robs him of his money—the polite highwayman and the robbery—Turpin and King's friendship—seizure of King—Dick shoots his friend—death of Tom King—commencement of

TURPIN'S UNPARALLELED FLIGHT TO YORK!

The Pursuit—Beadles, Tinkers, Sweeps, &c.

"She knows not distance—she cares not for distress;
Show me a courser to match with Black Bess."

Turnpike at Hornsey—leaping the gate—continued flight—Stamford—the stable—Turpin's stratagem—the beefsteak in Bess's mouth—escape of Turpin and sagacity of the mare.

"By moonlight, by darkness, by night or by day,
Her headlong career there's nothing can stay.'

The Gipsies' home—Turpin's struggle with the mare—his despair—she falls—she is dead..the Gipsies form a bier with branches, on which Black Bess is placed and carried from the Circle—allowed to be a most imposing scene, and showing the Acme of Horse Training.

"O'er highways and by-ways, in rough and smooth weather,
Some thousands of miles we've journey'd together:
Our couch the same straw—our meal the same mess,
No couple more constant than I and Black Bess."

72B

MID-DAY PROGRAMME,
Commencing at 2 o'Clock.

Master Powell the Precocious Youth, as
THE HIGHLAND LADDIE.

Mr J. Ryan will introduce his Feats of
EQUIPOISE AND JUGGLING.

THE WONDERFUL PERFORMING MONKEY.
Mons. Mushapug, on his highly Trained Pony, Sir Tatton Sykes.

The Dames of the
Stag Hunting Chase; Or, The Stag Hunt of Windsor Castle.

Mr. J. Frowde, as the
FLEXIBLE MORTAL; Or, The Man from the Red Mountains.

Mr Hengler will attend and instruct his graceful
LEOPARD STEED, SPOT BEAUTY;
Or, The Horse of the Drawing Room.

Herr Hengler universally acknowledged the first Rope Dancer in Europe, will go through his Extraordinary and difficult Evolutions on
THE BOUNDING CORD.

Mr Young and Young Polaski on Two Swift Coursers, as
THE TROJAN YOUTHS.

The Matchless Stud of Ponies, will here be put through some pleasing Feats, likewise will be introduced Beeswing, the Smallest Horse in the World, only 24 Inches high.

Mr Young and his *Infant Pupils* in their Grand
DRAWING ROOM ENTERTAINMENT

The Renowned BRITISH HORSEMAN
Mr Powell will ride and drive four RAMPANT HORSES, as
APOLLO.

A Humourous Equestrian Scene will terminate the Performance

EVENING PROGRAMME,
Commencing at 7 o'Clock.

The graceful Equestrians Miss Powell and Young Polaski will appear in a splendid Scene of Riding, on two horses, as
DONALD AND JESSY.

Mr J. Ryan's novel Entertainment with
THE LA TRANCA HISPANIOLA.

Mr Hengler Master of the Horse, will introduce his magnificent highly tutored Spotted Steed, surnamed from his beauty and wonderful exercises,
THE DIAMOND OF THE DESERT
The training of this noble animal will present a new era in the School of the Menage. The precision, grace, and pleasing exercises cannot be described, but must be admired when witnessed.

Young Polaski, considered the only Rival to Young Hernandez will perform his
MIRACULOUS LEAPS,
Backwards and Forwards, from a Galloping Horse.

Mr Young the great CALEDONIAN HORSEMAN, in a bold Scene of Riding, as Phæton
DRIVING THE HORSES OF THE SUN.

Mr Ryan the Celebrated Artiste, will execute his daring Feats on
THE ELASTIC CORD.

A Grand Military Scene of Horsemanship by *Mr Powell*, called
THE DEATH OF SHAW THE LIFE GUARDSMAN.
Or, The Glorious 18th of June at Waterloo.

THE WONDERFUL PERFORMING MONKEY,
Mons. Mushapug on his highly trained Steed of the Menage.

Mr Frowde
THE MAN OF MANY FORMS.
In his surprising exercises.

Messrs Adrian and Thatcher the TWO FIRST CLOWNS in ENGLAND, will enliven the various Scenes with their *Original Whimsicalities, Burlesque Speeches, & Comic Doings.*

73A and 73B

One of the oldest and most popular circuses in the North of England, Cooke's, well knew the value of publicity and were lavish with their bills. They made use of all the gimmicks and had a few extra ones for good measure. The leg-pull about the tradesmen kindly consenting to close their shops 'at the usual hour' in very small print was a well established joke. The first circus clown of whom we have much knowledge was Dicky Usher who performed at Astley's. Two episodes of his career illustrate something which is characteristic of clowns. Firstly they are clever men and secondly they achieve a reputation because they have a 'gimmick'. In 1842 when Astley's was burned down, William Batty bought the site and decided to rebuild it. The man he chose as architect was Dicky Usher.
Usher developed a highly successful publicity stunt in which he was towed in a washing tub from Westminster Bridge to Waterloo Bridge by four geese named Gibble, Gabble, Gobble, and Garble, to be drawn from there in his chariot by Four Thoroughbred Mousers. The crowds were so great that his chariot wasn't able to move. The gimmick was copied by his successor, the Irish Joker named Tom Barry, and also by Nelson and Twist. Here we have Nelson's performance. Although the geese were harnessed to the tub and the clown appeared to drive them with a small whip, the tub was really drawn by a small steamboat, the rope being weighted so that it was underwater. The act had a tragic conclusion at Yarmouth in 1846 when a similar performance was promised on the River Yare. Such was the crowd that congregated on the suspension bridge that it collapsed into the river and large numbers were drowned.

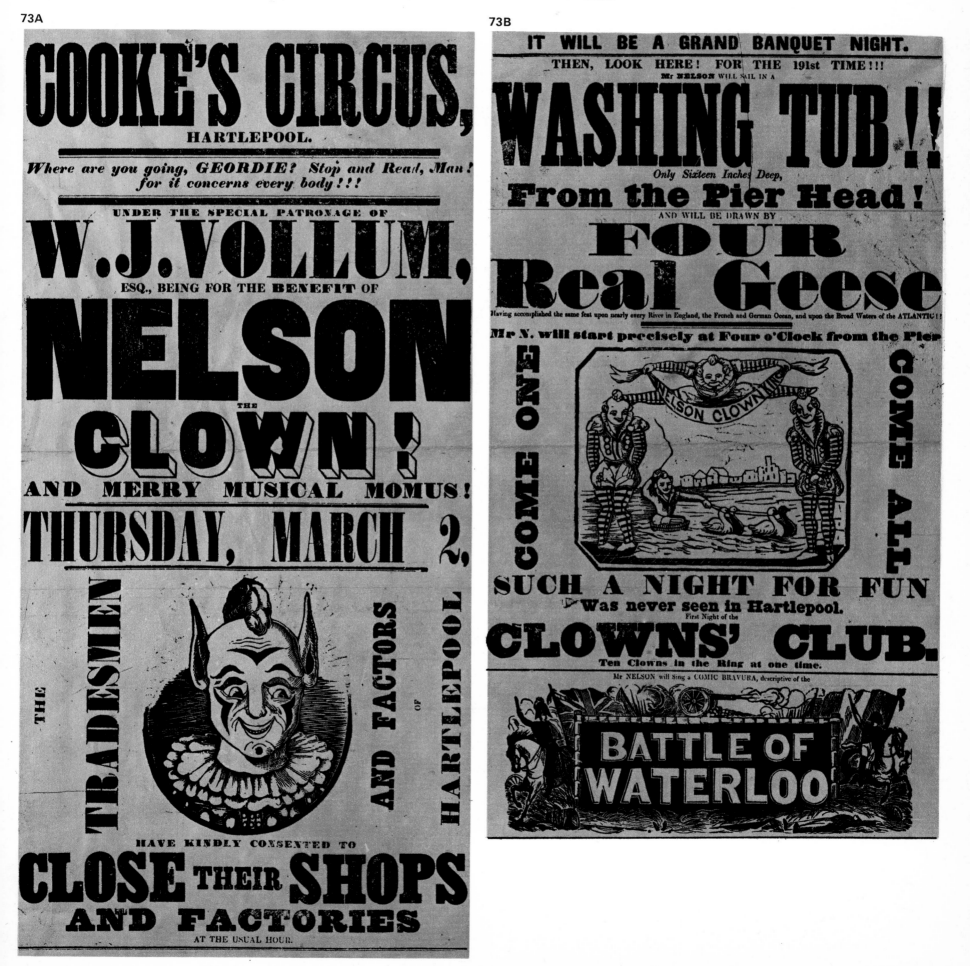

73A

COOKE'S CIRCUS,
HARTLEPOOL.
Where are you going, GEORDIE? Stop and Read, Man! for it concerns every body!!!
UNDER THE SPECIAL PATRONAGE OF
W. J. VOLLUM,
ESQ., BEING FOR THE BENEFIT OF
NELSON
THE
CLOWN!
AND MERRY MUSICAL MOMUS!
THURSDAY, MARCH 2,
THE TRADESMEN AND FACTORS OF HARTLEPOOL
HAVE KINDLY CONSENTED TO
CLOSE THEIR SHOPS
AND FACTORIES
AT THE USUAL HOUR.

73B

The Tin Circus. Such was the title by which Charles Weldon's show was remembered. It neither achieved fame nor went bankrupt; it quietly disappeared at the end of the 70s. Charles Weldon claimed to have been secretary of the Permanent Free and International Fine Art and Scientific Exhibition in London at Argyle Street off Oxford Circus in London. How he came with his company to the North of England and West Hartlepool is a mystery. They built a temporary wooden erection on a vacant piece of land and, much to the chagrin of the local theatre owners, did very good business. On one occasion in 1877 the audience literally brought the house down, for the gallery collapsed under their weight.

This establishment was so popular that it took on a semi-permanent appearance. Although it is ninety years ago since Charles Weldon's circus last appeared, there are still people in Hartlepool who talk of the Tin Circus. By the early days of this century it had degenerated into a booth which was used for all sorts of ventures from boxing tournaments to evangelistic meetings and even a skating rink, but this bill shows that in its more prosperous days it could put on a good programme.

But Weldon's Circus deserves to be remembered for another reason. It is claimed, on fairly good authority, that Dan Leno first played the part of Pongo the Monkey here thus being launched on the path to stardom. Dan did not like his step-father and in this particular sketch he had to appear as a very lively and mischievous monkey. The sketch obtained its laughs when the monkey belaboured the man with a roll of brown paper and Dan used to spend much of his spare time lovingly rolling the paper as tightly as he could so that he could get in some substantial smacks at his step-father as part of the

74

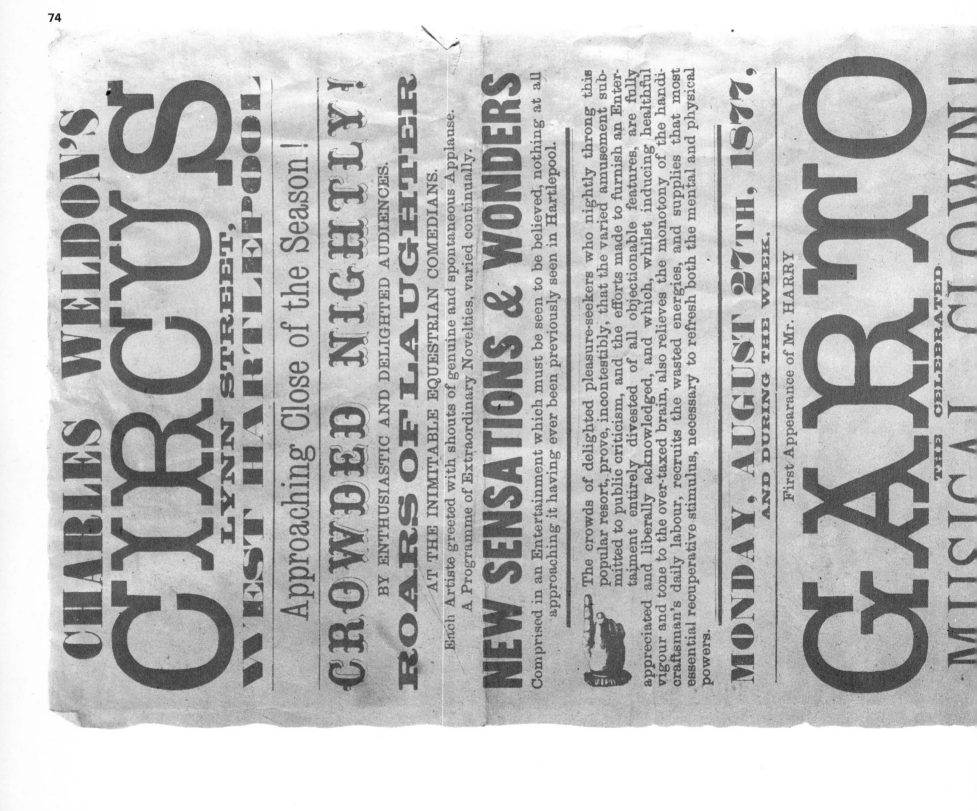

CHARLES WELDON'S
CIRCUS
LYNN STREET,
WEST HARTLEPOOL
Approaching Close of the Season!
CROWDED NIGHTLY!
BY ENTHUSIASTIC AND DELIGHTED AUDIENCES.
ROARS OF LAUGHTER
AT THE INIMITABLE EQUESTRIAN COMEDIANS.
Each Artiste greeted with shouts of genuine and spontaneous Applause.
A Programme of Extraordinary Novelties, varied continually.
NEW SENSATIONS & WONDERS
Comprised in an Entertainment which must be seen to be believed, nothing at all approaching it having ever been previously seen in Hartlepool.

The crowds of delighted pleasure-seekers who nightly throng this popular resort, prove, incontestibly, that the varied amusement submitted to public criticism, and the efforts made to furnish an Entertaiment entirely divested of all objectionable features, are fully appreciated and liberally acknowledged, and which, whilst inducing healthful vigour and tone to the over-taxed brain, also relieves the monotony of the handicraftsman's daily labour, recruits the wasted energies, and supplies that most essential recuperative stimulus, necessary to refresh both the mental and physical powers.

MONDAY, AUGUST 27TH, 1877,
AND DURING THE WEEK.
First Appearance of Mr. HARRY
THE CELEBRATED
CARTO
MUSICAL CLOWN!

stage business and avenge himself for the discipline he had received.

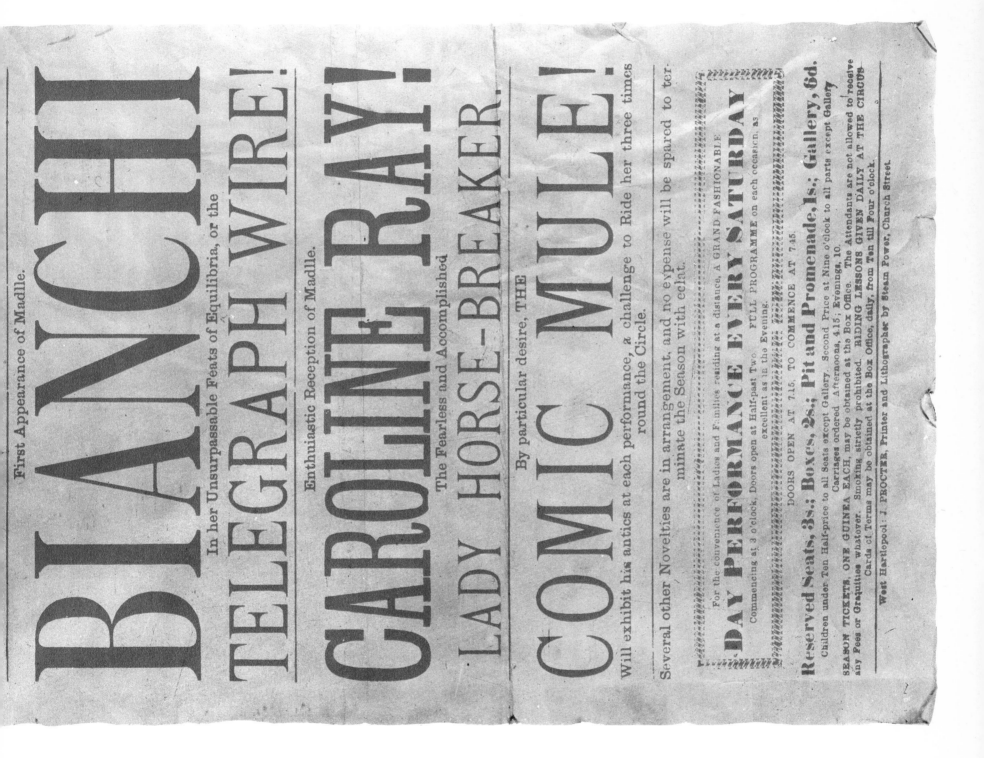

First Appearance of Madlle.

BIANCHI

In her Unsurpassable Feats of Equilibria, or the

TELEGRAPH WIRE!

Enthuiastic Reception of Madlle.

CAROLINE RAY!

The Fearless and Accomplished

LADY HORSE-BREAKER.

By particular desire, THE

COMIC MULE!

Will exhibit his antics at each performance, a challenge to Ride her three times round the Circle.

Several other Novelties are in arrangement, and no expense will be spared to terminate the Season with eclat.

For the convenience of Ladies and Families residing at a distance, A GRAND FASHIONABLE

DAY PERFORMANCE EVERY SATURDAY

Commencing at 3 o'clock, Doors open at Half-past Two. FULL PROGRAMME on each occasion, as excellent as in the Evening.

DOORS OPEN AT 7.15, TO COMMENCE AT 7.45.

Reserved Seats, 3s.; Boxes, 2s.; Pit and Promenade, 1s.; Gallery, 6d.

Children under Ten Half-price to all Seats except Gallery. Second Price at Nine o'clock to all parts except Gallery. Carriages ordered Afternoons, 4.15; Evenings, 10.

SEASON TICKETS, ONE GUINEA EACH, may be obtained at the Box Office. The Attendants are not allowed to receive any Fees or Gratuities whatever. Smoking strictly prohibited. **RIDING LESSONS GIVEN DAILY AT THE CIRCUS.** Cards of Terms may be obtained at the Box Office, daily, from Ten till Four o'clock.

West Hartlepool: J. PROCTER, Printer and Lithographer by Steam Power, Church Street.

75
Mathewson the Clown must have been a very popular figure for it was on the occasion of his benefit that the gallery collapsed under the weight of the assembled crowd. When Weldon was summoned to appear before the magistrates for having erected a building without submitting a plan to the officers of the Improvement Commissioners who ran the town, his solicitor argued that because it was a temporary building no such plans needed to be submitted. History does not record the result of the debate.

76
A typical example of the kind of letter distributed by an actor or performer on the occasion of his or her benefit. Few could afford to have an invitation of this sort printed and the curious may be amused by the masonic emblems at the head of the invitation. People of the time would have accepted this as a matter of course, for tradesmen and actors often had their masonic honours printed on their private and trade cards and did not hesitate to take advantage of any fraternal feeling which might prove helpful.

75

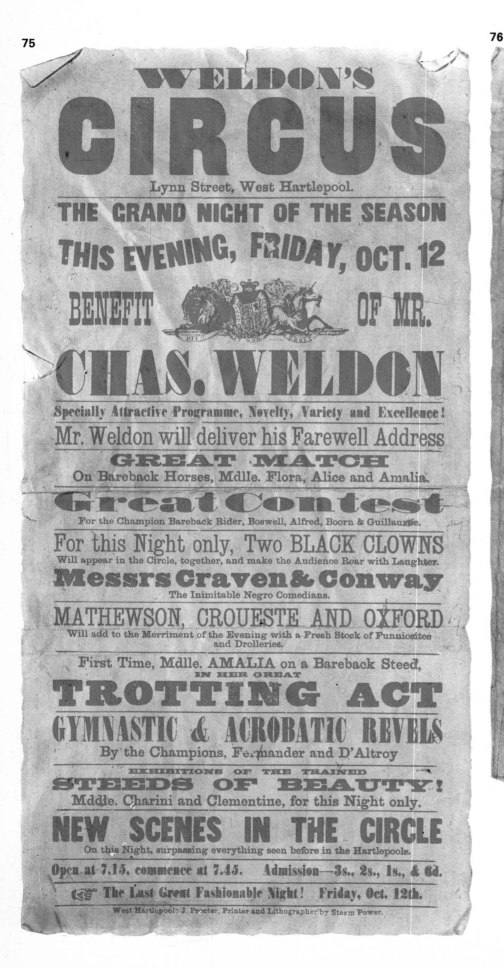

WELDON'S

CIRCUS

Lynn Street, West Hartlepool.

THE GRAND NIGHT OF THE SEASON

THIS EVENING, FRIDAY, OCT. 12

BENEFIT  OF MR.

CHAS. WELDON

Specially Attractive Programme, Novelty, Variety and Excellence!

Mr. Weldon will deliver his Farewell Address

GREAT MATCH

On Bareback Horses, Mdlle. Flora, Alice and Amalia.

Great Contest

For the Champion Bareback Rider, Boswell, Alfred, Boorn & Guillaume.

For this Night only, Two BLACK CLOWNS

Will appear in the Circle, together, and make the Audience Roar with Laughter.

Messrs Craven & Conway

The Inimitable Negro Comedians.

MATHEWSON, CROUESTE AND OXFORD

Will add to the Merriment of the Evening with a Fresh Stock of Funniosites and Drolleries.

First Time, Mdlle. AMALIA on a Bareback Steed,

IN HER GREAT

TROTTING ACT

GYMNASTIC & ACROBATIC REVELS

By the Champions, Fernander and D'Altroy

EXHIBITIONS OF THE TRAINED

STEEDS OF BEAUTY!

Mddle. Charini and Clementine, for this Night only.

NEW SCENES IN THE CIRCLE

On this Night, surpassing everything seen before in the Hartlepools.

Open at 7.15, commence at 7.45. Admission—3s., 2s., 1s., & 6d.

☞ The Last Great Fashionable Night! Friday, Oct. 12th.

West Hartlepool: J. Procter, Printer and Lithographer by Steam Power.

76

COOKE'S ROYAL CIRCUS,

HARTLEPOOL.

Sir and Brother,

I take the liberty of informing you, that my BENEFIT *is fixed for* TUESDAY, FEBRUARY 29TH, 1848, *when I trust the Pieces selected for the Evening's Entertainment, will merit the approbation of those Brethren who may please to favour me with their support.*

Your attendance on this occasion will confer an obligation on,

Sir and Brother,

Your's fraternally,

J. H. EMIDY.

77
This is a striking bill with a woodcut after the Grecian style and some very interesting descriptions of the acts, although no doubt nowadays Mr. Thomas Lee would object to being described as an Æriel Bounder. The mixed collection of various founts of type seems to have been a convention of this style of circus bill.

77

CROWDED HOUSES—UNCEASING APPLAUSE—ATTRACTION EXTRAORDINARY.

COOKE'S GREAT CIRCUS ENTERTAINMENTS!

AND UNPRECEDENTED EQUESTRIAN MIRACLES!!!

SPLENDID CHANGE OF AMUSEMENTS!

THURSDAY, FRIDAY, & SATURDAY, Feb. 10, 11, & 12.

The Attractions of the Arena will consist of the most exhilarating **DISPLAYS OF SCENIC HORSEMANSHIP**, by the celebrated Company of Equestrians, with the beautiful Stud of Horses, showing many New and **MAGNIFICENT PERFORMANCES**, rendering each Night's Exhibition one of extraordinary Attraction and Beauty.

Doors open every Evening at a Quarter before 7 o'Clock, and commence at Half-past 7 to a minute. Good Fires constantly in the Circus.

***OBSERVE! THERE WILL BE A GRAND EQUESTRIAN TREAT AND SPLENDID NOON PERFORMANCE, ON SATURDAY, FEB. 12th, DOORS OPEN AT 1, AND AMUSEMENTS TO COMMENCE AT 2 O'CLOCK.

Mr. ALFRED PALMER, the **STAR RIDER** and **FIRST HORSEMAN** in **EUROPE**, is **ENGAGED**, and will make his first appearance here on Monday, Feb. 14th.

☞ Mr. COOKE has the pleasure of announcing, that his Establishment will be honoured with the Presence and **PATRONAGE** of the **MAYOR OF HARTLEPOOL**, on TUESDAY EVENING, Feb. 15.

The Brilliant Scenes in the Circle will present an unprecedented striking Arenic Scene, pourtraying some daring Equestrian Pastimes, entitled

GAMES OF THE HIPPODROME

Or the **Horse Races of the Curriculum at Rome**, performed by **Messrs. Thomas Lee, Clarke, and Barlow**, on **Six Prancing and Highly-trained Coursers.** These able Equestrians will perform some extraordinary evolutions. They will advance in solid columns; anon they disperse, and execute various movements with the greatest precision; then essemble, pass, and repass, and whirl in erratic motion—now towards the centre of the circle, and afterwards to its extremities; the whole being graceful as it is ingenious. The New Circus Piece will conclude with the RAPID CHARGE and FLIGHT of the RACERS round the GRAND CORSO. The whole will be accompanied by appropriate Costume, characteristic of the Roman Rider.

A highly pleasing Scene of the Manege, in which **Mr Cooke** will appear as the

Warrior Saladin,

With his sagacious and beautiful Barb, **Prince Albert,** allowed by every connoisseur to be one of the most perfectly-trained Horses ever presented to public notice. A full description of all the feats of extraordinary intelligence performed by "Prince Albert," would tend to detract from the pleasure of surprise.

The Peerless Horsewoman, **Mrs Woolford,** will appear in her matchless Act of Riding, entitled the

For the first time, a highly amusing Piece called the Anniversary of

HODGE'S BRIDAL MORN;

Or, The Miller's Merrymaking,

Introducing the full Company of Equestrian Artistes.

First time here, the talented little Equestrian, **Miss Woolford,** will enact on her beautiful Steed, a Grand Pas, as

FLORA, the GODDESS of FLOWERS.

Mr Thomas Lee, the Æriel Bounder and

FLYING VAULTER!

Will throw in rapid succession his Æriel Torbillons and extraordinary Battou acquirements.

THE JUVENILE EQUESTRIAN ASPIRANT

Master Powell, will make his first appearance on a Rapid Courser.

THE AMPHI GYMNASIENS

Messrs Butler and Dean, designated the **Sons of Milo,** wi

78

PROCLAMATION.

W.  R.

WILLIAM, THE FOURTH

by the grace of God, of the *United Kingdom* of
Great Britain and Ireland, King Defender of the
Faith. To the *Lovers* of ARTS and SCIENCES,
GREETING, *We command You* and every of
you, that all other things set aside, and ceasing every *excuse*, you and
every of you to be and appear in your *proper persons* at Mr BATTY'S
CIRCUS ROYAL, *Bath Lane, Westgate, Newcastle*, on TUESDAY,
the 2nd June, 1835, by half-past six o'clock in the evening of the same
day, to *testify* the TRUTH according to your knowledge of the evening's ENTERTAINMENTS provided for you, and to WITNESS a
number of NEW SCENES that have just arrived from DUCROW'S
ROYAL AMPHITHEATRE, *London*, and likewise the whole of the
talented COMPANY of Artistes, at the same time and place aforesaid,
pursuant *to the bills of the day* in that case printed and published;
And this you nor any of you shall in nowise OMIT, under the PENALTY
of every of you, of the LOSS of one of the *best Night's Amusements*
that has ever been offered to a British Audience.

Documemts will be delivered, with full details of each particular scene, in proper
form. To commence at half-past 7 o'clock.

Witness, JAMES FURLONG, Clown,

The chief person interested, and for whose **BENEFIT** the above night is appointed, by desire and under the patronage of **EVERYBODY**, in the fifth year of Our
Reign.

By the Court of Gymnastc and Equestrian Sciences,

W. PLEASANT, Clerk Of the Places.

78
The spaciousness and dignity of the format of this poster proclaim that we are in another age. We have trespassed into the reign before that of Queen Victoria when the sailor-king, William IV, was on the throne. Ducrow at this time was in charge of Astley's and Batty was on tour. By 1843 William Batty will be in charge of a new Astley's for the old one will be in ashes and Ducrow dead.

79, 79A and 79B
A number of circuses toured England in Victorian times and then disappeared, unrecorded and forgotten except as one of an old man's boyhood memories. Freeman's Circus would appear to be such a case for no mention of it can be found. The phrase Cirque Varieties would suggest a connection with Hengler's Liverpool establishment of that name, but that may not be so, imitation being the sincerest form of flattery.

79

"Pleasures that please on reflection."

V. R.

FREEMAN'S

GRAND ATHLETIC AND GYMNASTIC

CIRQUE VARIETIES

WILL VISIT THIS TOWN ON

Mr FREEMAN in introducing this Entertainment to the Public, begs most respectfully to inform them that it is calculated to please the most fastidious. The Artistes are carefully selected for their efficiency, and no labour or expense is spared in making this Entertainment agreeable to his patrons. "NO OUTSIDE SHOW."

The Evening's Entertainment will be selected from the following:—Miss

LAURA CHARLOTTA

Mr J. DURO, Comic Vocalist

OPEN

EVERY EVENING

Mons. ELNO, Equilibrist and Great Flying Wonder

FUNNY FRED

BROTHERS

MARIO

AND

VICINI

In their Graceful and Daring Performance on the Horizontal Bar

Clown, - Mons. ZIG

Comic Interlude, the "SPANISH BULLFIGHT," by

Mr G. BULL

Brothers R. & J. HELENI

Funny Fred and Funny Duro

In their "COMIC TUB" Performance

The Living Wheelbarrow

MISS

ROSANNA FREEMAN

FREEMAN'S

Grand Troupe of Acrobats

And Athletic Wonders

Introducing Acrobats, Benders, Posturers, and FEATS of STRENGTH, &c., &c., finishing with the GRAND STEEPLECHASE, by the Three Funny Clowns

The Boneless Wonder

OF THE AGE. SEE HIM

The Evening's Performance will conclude with a Laughable Sketch, side-splitting Extravaganza, or Negro Burlesque. Introducing the entire strgength of Company

BRASS BAND............Leader, Mr C. FREEMAN

Doors Open at SEVEN, Commencing at Half-Past SEVEN.

Admission-Front Seats, 6d. Gallery, 3d

Special Performance for Children only on SATURDAYS at 3 o'clock

ADMISSION, 1d, SATURDAYS ONLY

NOTICE TO FETE AND GALA PROPRIETORS.—C. FREEMAN is prepared to supply the above First-Class Entertainment on reasonable Terms at the shortest Notice.

Agent in Advance, Mr HENRY STRAND. Business Manager, Mr C. FREEMAN. Stud Groom, Mr H. ALLEN. Lamp Man, Mr G. BIRD
Sole Proprietress - - - Mrs FREEMAN

T. C. BARLOW, Designer, Engraver, Litho. and Letterpress Printer, 103 Bath Street, Glasgow.

79A

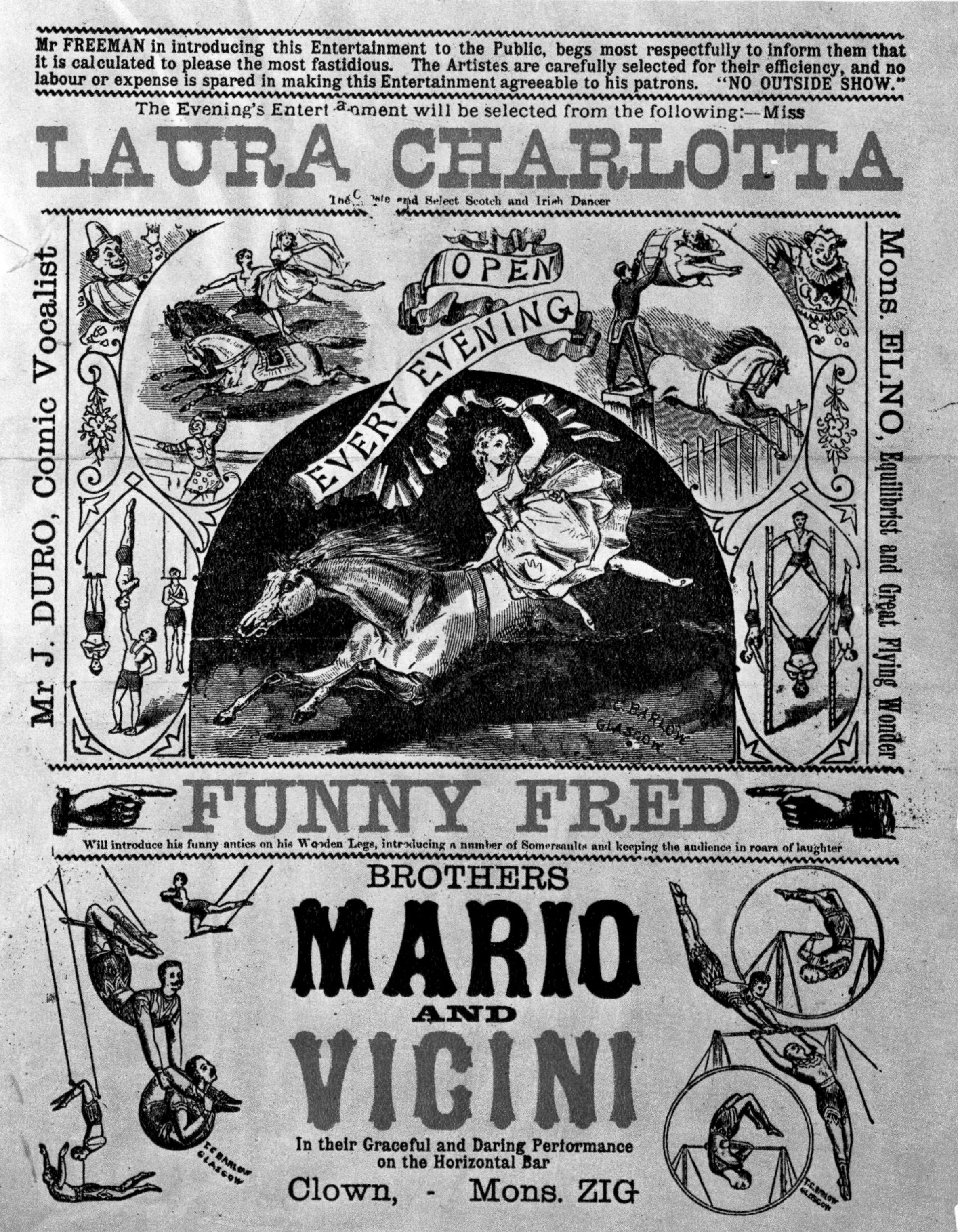
Mr FREEMAN in introducing this Entertainment to the Public, begs most respectfully to inform them that it is calculated to please the most fastidious. The Artistes are carefully selected for their efficiency, and no labour or expense is spared in making this Entertainment agreeable to his patrons. "NO OUTSIDE SHOW."

The Evening's Entertainment will be selected from the following:—Miss

LAURA CHARLOTTA

The Celebrated Select Scotch and Irish Dancer

Mr J. DURO, Comic Vocalist

OPEN

EVERY EVENING

Mons. ELNO, Equilibrist and Great Flying Wonder

T. C. BARLOW GLASGOW

FUNNY FRED

Will introduce his funny antics on his Wooden Legs, introducing a number of Somersaults and keeping the audience in roars of laughter

BROTHERS

MARIO

AND

VICINI

In their Graceful and Daring Performance on the Horizontal Bar

Clown, - Mons. ZIG

79B

Doors Open at SEVEN, Commencing at Half-Past SEVEN.

Admission-Front Seats, 6d. Gallery, 3d

Special Performance for Children only on SATURDAYS at 3 o'clock

ADMISSION, 1d, SATURDAYS ONLY

NOTICE TO FETE AND GALA PROPRIETORS.—C. FREEMAN is prepared to supply the above First-Class Entertainment on reasonable Terms at the shortest Notice.

Agent in Advance, Mr HENRY STRAND. Business Manager, Mr C. FREEMAN. Stud Groom, Mr H. ALLEN. Lamp Man, Mr G. BIRD
Sole Proprietress - - - - - - - - - Mrs FREEMAN

T. C. BARLOW, Designer, Engraver, Litho. and Letterpress Printer, 103 Bath Street, Glasgow.

80
Another unknown establishment proclaims its identity some years later. If it had wintered in the Liverpool Zoological Gardens we see it in the spring of 1865 on the start of its summer tour. Mr. Procter printed bills for its appearances at most of the towns in County Durham and as far west as Haltwhistle, so it may be surmised that they were en route for the Lowlands of Scotland. The woodcuts of the animals are particularly attractive. It is not generally known that some of Thomas Bewick's best animal blocks were made for circuses. Bewick was a noted Victorian printer.

81
Van Amburgh was an American Indian who was the first and most talented of the lion tamers. He came to England in 1838 and was fêted by the greatest in the land. Queen Victoria came to see him feed his lions and the great Duke of Wellington was not satisfied until Landseer himself promised to paint a great picture of 'Van Amburgh and his Lions'. Perhaps in the great bronze lions in London's Trafalgar Square we may see some memory which Landseer retained of the painting he did for the Duke of Wellington.

80

81

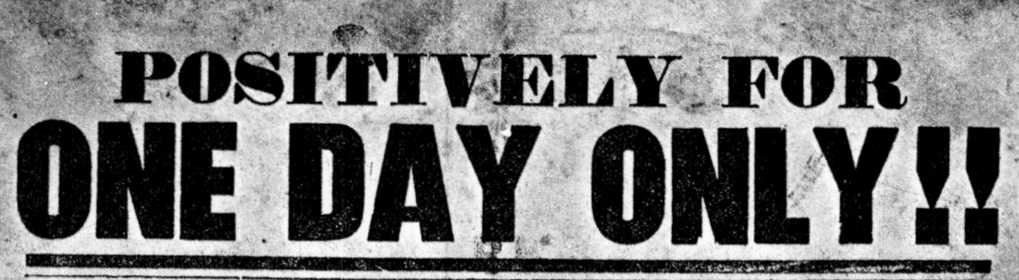

UNDER THE PATRONAGE OF

HER MAJESTY THE QUEEN!

MR. VAN AMBURGH

Begs most respectfully to inform the Nobility, Gentry, Clergy, and Inhabitants of ~~DURHAM~~ and its Vicinity that he will have the honour of exhibiting his ROYAL COLLECTION of TRAINED

LIONS,

TIGERS, LEOPARDS, &c.,

IN HIS SPLENDID MARQUEE,

TO BE ERECTED

~~IN THE COURT YARD~~,

~~OLD ELVET~~, DURHAM,

On ~~SATURDAY~~, 24th June, 1843,

From 2 to 4 in the Afternoon, and from 7 to 9 in the Evening.

The Performance to commence half an hour after opening.

Mr. VAN AMBURGH will arrive in ~~Durham~~ from ~~Bishop Auckland~~ on ~~Saturday~~, June 24th, at 11 o'clock, and make a

GRAND PROCESSION

~~Down New Elvet, across Elvet Bridge, through Fleshergate, the Market Place, up Claypath and Gilesgate, and then return, proceeding up Old Elvet~~ to the Pavilion,

DRIVING IN HAND

EIGHT

Beautiful Cream-Coloured HORSES,

Accompanied by his Band of First-rate Musicians, &c.

The astonishing performances of Mr. VAN AMBURGH need no panegyric, they have attracted the admiration of all who have witnessed them; the repeated presence of

OUR MOST GRACIOUS SOVEREIGN,

And a distinguished list of the Nobility, attest the unequalled splendour of his Daring Feats; any attempt at description would be almost superfluous: it will be sufficient to state before him the "LORDLY LION" and the "FEROCIOUS TIGER" forget their savage nature, and crouch in trembling submission.

Associated with the above is a

LIVING GIRAFFE.

The existence of this extremely rare and valuable Animal was, until the last few years, deemed almost fabulous, and the most intense sensation was created by the arrival of the one presented to HIS MAJESTY GEORGE THE FOURTH BY THE PACHA OF EGYPT, its death and previous seclusion prevented its being much seen, and in all probability the present will be the only occasion (from the immense expense and extreme difficulty in procuring them) that the Public will have an opportunity of gratifying their curiosity.

To render the Exhibition at once surpassing and unrivalled, Mr VAN AMBURGH has included his celebrated Performing

ELEPHANT,

4

The Sporting World

Nowadays every daily newspaper has its sports pages, and sport abounds on television and radio.

A hundred years ago, sport, as entertainment, played a much smaller part in the life of the townsman than it does today. Newspaper reports covered horse-racing, hunting, coursing, cricket, and rowing, but of these hunting was for the élite and rowing could only be indulged in by those living near a river or by the sea. It was not that there was any lack of interest for many of the inhabitants of the new industrial towns had once been villagers, and they had a keen appreciation and knowledge of horses.

From the middle of the eighteenth century the farming community had been particularly interested in improving its livestock, animal husbandry was a subject which caused long and passionate debate. Horse racing was an easy and obvious way of publicly demonstrating the superiority of one strain of animal in comparison with another, and there was the added excitement of backing one's opinion with a bet. In Napoleonic times most villages had their races. The farmers brought forth their favourites, chose some suitable piece of land, advertised the event, charged pedlars and hucksters for permission to set up their booths, threatened stray dogs with immediate destruction, and generally provided the villagers with a red-letter day to be remembered in company with the local fair.

A contemporary account of races in the rising industrial port of Hartlepool in September 1841 runs as follows:

'The weather on the first day, Thursday, was delightful, and long before the appointed hour crowds of smartly dressed and happy looking people thronged to the course where booths, gaily decorated with flags, shows with all manner of inconceivable curiosities, and stalls spread with the most tempting dainties, whiled away the interval previous to the racing.

The weather on the second day was wet, but not sufficiently so to deter a great number of spectators from assembling, and the racing was held to be fully equal to that of the previous day. The wind, which had been boisterous all the afternoon, rose during the night to a heavy gale, and the scene on Saturday morning was desolate in the extreme. Most of the booths had been unroofed by the violence of the hurricane, and the wreck of a vessel which had struck upon the rocks gave additional evidence of the disastrous tempest. The rain poured in torrents during the whole day, yet at the signal hour of starting a few brave sons of the turf, enveloped in costumes more useful than ornamental, came plodding to the course with an energetic determination to see the end of the sport. The greatest satisfaction was expressed by all parties who were unanimous in opinion that better sport had never been witnessed at any races in the kingdom.'

So ended a typical race meeting of this kind. It may appear amateurish but don't be misled for many a townsman in those days was a better judge of horses than regular race-goers today, and the organisers were extremely knowledgeable. A steward, Robert Stephenson of Hart, owned Voltigeur which won the 1850 Derby, the St. Leger, and the Doncaster Cup. It is doubtful if a finer horse has since been produced in the North of England.

Coursing was a sport which appealed to the working man lacking the capital to breed as expensive an animal as a horse and any rough field or piece of waste ground provided a suitable meeting place.

Regattas were enjoyed in those places which had access to a navigable piece of waterway. Yachting was the sport of the rich, but in the days of sail the niceties of seamanship were understood and appreciated by the majority of the spectators. Rowing matches were keenly contested, for in those days champion oarsmen received the adulation reserved for today's 'pop' singers. Humorous items were added to give diversity to the programme, 'novelty races' as they were called, 'greasy poles', and 'all the fun of the fair'.

Football was not yet an organised sport, but simply a barbaric relic of mediaeval times. It achieved official recognition only on time-hallowed occasions such as Shrove Tuesday. Cricket, on the other hand, was something more serious for a great deal of money could be won or lost over a match. The reversal of the roles of these two popular English mass entertainments is one of the eccentricities of history.

Although the game laws prevented most people in towns from enjoying any shooting, itinerant showmen with shooting galleries gave those who wished, the chance to show their skill. In the late 50s the bellicose utterances of the French Emperor caused patriots of all classes to combine in what were first known as national rifle clubs but later became duly constituted volunteer corps.
In those days of peace the art of soldiering was looked upon as a commendable form of sport and the various reviews held throughout England were social occasions for all classes. Special excursions were run for admiring wives and sweethearts.

In the smaller towns and villages the old fairs continued as usual under their traditional names of feasts, hoppings, or wakes. The programmes of events which have survived show that, in their rural surroundings, the old sports and pastimes remained unchanged. Fives, quoits, and bowls were played whilst the races went on. Similar activities are enjoyed at the annual village flower shows today.

Although boxing became popular in the eighteenth century in urban areas it was always regarded by the countryman as a cruel and unwholesome sport. He preferred the equally athletic and more skilful wrestling matches where men could pit themselves one against the other and display their skill without reducing each other to bloody wrecks.

Running was also a sport which provided sizeable monetary rewards for talented youngsters and athletic clubs which fostered this sort of activity by young men became very popular.

In the late 60s music hall artistes presented an act showing the velocipede and their skilful riding of it, but this did not become a popular sport until the 'safety' bicycle was introduced and pneumatic tyres made it comfortable to ride. But well before this most people were familiar with the velocipede through having seen it used for trick riding on the stage, or in races arranged by enterprising landlords, on special tracks near public houses, much as Philip Astley had started his circus.

There were occasional exhibitions of rare and archaic sports such as hawking and archery, but it was impossible for ordinary folk to indulge in the former whilst the latter became, like tennis and croquet, the pastime for the country-house lawn.

82, 83 and 84

These three posters concern the same small village of Stranton which in 1831 had a population of 381, in 1841, 1491, and in 1851, 4008.

That of 1835 is a very modest affair suited to a small village, the prizes are the very minimum likely to be offered on such an occasion, and the procedure very much as usual. There were three inns, the Blacksmith's Arms, the Seven Stars, and the Anchor, and there seems to have been an arrangement whereby the landlords each took their turn in accepting the entries. In 1835 it was the task of the landlord of the Blacksmith's Arms.

What is most unusual is the large sum of £50 staked on a cricket match between Stranton and the neighbouring small village of Greatham.

In 1835 the first dock opened in the adjoining port of Hartlepool and the Hartlepool Railway brought coal down to the ships. This created more employment and the small settlement of New Stranton, midway between the village and Hartlepool, grew larger. Perhaps this is why we find in 1838 'Old Stranton' at the top of the poster. The races were run on the sands, a most convenient spot, depending on the state of the tide, and this was why entries were made 'between the hours of 10 and 12 o'clock in the Forenoon'. No doubt Mr. Cummins would not be pleased to see his inn the Anchor, rechristened the Anker, though no doubt either title was appropriate.

The bill ends with the typical 'Plays and Assemblies as usual' though it is doubtful if there would be a play in Stranton, unless it took place in one of the long rooms of the inns. There would certainly be Assemblies at which everyone would dance to the fiddle.

The 1846 bill includes West Dock which in the following year was to become West Hartlepool.

82

THE STRANTON AND WEST DOCK

RACES

Will take place, over the new course, on the 20th and 21st days of July, 1846.

Further particulars in future bills.

£50

has already been subscribed, and a further addition to that sum is expected to be given to the above meeting.

84

OLD STRANTON

RACES.

TO BE RUN FOR

ON THE

Sands at Stranton,

On Monday, the 19th Nov. 1838,

A

PURSE

OF

Gold,

Not less than 3 Sovereigns, for Horses not thorough bred, that never won the value of £5, at any one time. Matches excepted.

Three-year-old to carry 8 stone
Four — — 9 —
Five — — 10 —

ALSO,

10 Shillings

FOR

PONIES.

On account of the Tide, parties are requested to enter their Horses, &c. at Mr. George Cummins's, Sign of the Anker, Old Stranton, between the hours of 10 and 12 o'clock in the Forenoon.

FIVE SHILLINGS ENTRANCE.

Three to start or no race, unless by the consent of the Stewards.

Plays and Assemblies as usual.

J. Procter, Printer, Hartlepool.

83

85
The days of the Regency were not forgotten and the gambling spirit was still very strongly entrenched. Here we have two men, Mr. White, a publican, and Mr. Tate, a shipowner, deciding to settle an argument by matching their two horses—('Owners on',) i.e. the owners would ride. The match could have been arranged to take place without any fuss, early one morning in the presence of an umpire, but quite obviously the argument has become well-known and there is no doubt that much more money than appears on the bill will change hands, whoever wins!

86
This is the occasion referred to in the introduction (page 74) when a ship was wrecked within sight of the race-course. Those familiar with the Turf's history will be well acquainted with the names of the stewards, for Blakelock was a famous breeder of racehorses at Hart, a village three miles away. Robert Stephenson's farm was next to his, and he took over Blakelock's stock when the latter died. John Lawrenson was a typical John Bull both in looks and temperament and controlled most things in Hartlepool yet still found time to organise races and regattas, soirées and concerts.

85

MATCH FOR £25.

A

MATCH

FOR £12 10s. A SIDE,

Between Mr. WHITE'S, (Fleece Inn,) b. f. "BLUE STOCKING," and Mr. TATE'S, bl. h. "TOM BOY," (Owners on,) to come off on Hartlepool Race Course, on Thursday, the 30th inst., at Two o'clock.

DISTANCE TWO MILES.

Hartlepool, Nov. 25, 1854.

From the Authorized List of the Stewards and the Clerk of the Course.

GEORGE BLAKELOCK, ESQ.
ROBERT STEPHENSON, ESQ. } **Stewards.**

Mr. John Lawrenson, Clerk of the Course.

Thursday, Friday & Saturday 2nd. 3rd. & 4th. days of September, 1841

TO START EACH DAY AT TWO O'CLOCK.

FIRST DAY,—THURSDAY.

The Members Stake of 2 sov. each, with 20 sov. added by the Members of the Southern Division. Three-years-old 7st. 4lb; four 8st. 2lb; five 8st. 10lb; six and aged 9st. Mares and Geldings allowed 3lb. The Second to receive back his Stake. Heats, about 1 Mile and a half.

Mr. Osborne's c. c. Emperor, 3 y. o. *blue and black cap.* ... JOHN STORY, 2 1 2 1
Mr. Hepple's bl. c. Bush Ranger, 4 y. o. by The Mole, *crimson, white, black cap.* ... 4 4 1 dr.
Mr. Hutchinson's c. f. Maria Monk, by Revolution, 4 y. o. *pink and black cap.* ... 1 2 dist.
Mr. Lambert's c. f. Annulet, by Velocipede 4 y. o. *blue body, red sleeves.* ... ... 3 3 dr.

The Innkeeper's Plate of 15 sov, with 3 sov. added for the Second. The Winner of the Members Stake to carry 5lb extra; Weights, &c. the same as the Members Stake. Heats, 1 Mile and a half. Entrance 10s. 6d.

Mr. Hutchinson's c. f. Maria Monk, 4 y. o. *pink and black cap.* ... JOHN JOY, 1 1
Mr. Lambert's b. f. Parisina by Voltaire, 4 y. o. *blue body, and red sleeves.* 2 2
Mr. Osborne's c. c. The Em[illegible]
Mr. Lambert's c. f. Annulet, 4 y. o. *blue body and red sleeves.*
Mr. J. Hepple's br. g. Black Heddon, aged. *crimson and white, black cap.*
Mr. Burnett's b. m. Hartlepool Lass, aged. *blue and crimson.*

The Hartlepool Plate of 10 sov. with 2 sov. added for the second. Weights, &c. same as Innkeeper's Plate; except that the Winner of the Innkeeper's Plate or Members Stake will not be allowed to start. Heats, 1 Mile and a half. Entrance [illegible] 6d.

Mr. Lambert's c. f. Annulet, 4 y. o. *blue body, and red sleeves.* ... THOMAS CLERL, 1 [illegible] 1
Mr. Osborne's b. f. Ten Pound Note, 3 y. o. *blue and black cap.* ... 2 0
Mr. J. Hepple's br. g. Black Heddon, aged *crimson and white, black cap.* 4 3 2
Mr. Lister's b. m. Eliza, aged *buff and blue.* ... ... 3 dr.
Mr. Osborne's c. c. The Emperor 3 y. o. *blue and black cap.*
Mr. Lambert's b. f. Parisina, 4 y. o. *blue body and red sleeves.*
Mr. Burnett's b. m. Hartlepool Lass, aged *scarlet and black stripes, black cap.*

SECOND DAY,—FRIDAY.

The Raby Stake of 1 sov. each, with 10 sov. added by His Grace the Duke of Cleveland, for Horses, &c. that never won £50. at any one time; the second to receive back his Stake. The Winner of a Stake on the previous day to carry 7lb extra—if a Winner of two Stakes 10lb. Three-years-old 7st. 2lb; four 8st. 5lb; five 8st. 12lb; six and aged 9st. 2lb. Mares and Geldings allowed 3lb. Heats, 1 Mile and a half.

Mr. Osborne's b. f. Ten Pound Note, 3 y. o. *blue and black cap* ... WM. ABDALE ... 1 1
Ms. Hutchinson's c. f, Maria Monk, 4 y. o. *pink and black cap* 2 2
Mr. J. Hepple's br. g. Black Heddon, aged. *crimson and white, black cap* 3 3
Mr. Burnett's b. m. Hartlepool Lass, aged. *scarlet and black stripes, black cap*

The Ingleborough Stakes of 10s. 6d. each, with £5. added by James Farrer, Esq. Conditions as above. The Winner of the Raby Stake, not allowed to start.

Mr. France's b. c. Hard Bargain, 3 y o. *crimson.* ... JOHN JOY 1 1
Mr. Burnett's b. m. Hartlepool Lass, aged. *scarlet and black staipes* ... ... 2 dr.
Mr. Osborne's b. f. Ten Pound Note, 3 y. o. *blue and black cap*

Ten Guineas for Horses, &c. not thorough bred, Stake and Draw. Three Heats of one Mile and a half each. The Winner of each Heat to receive £2. the second £1. and the third 10s. Three-years-old 7st. 8lb; four 8st. 10lb; five 9st. 3lb; six and aged 9st. 7lb Entrance 5s. each.

Mr. Lister's b. m. Eliza, aged. *buff and blue* ... HODGSON 1 1 1
Mr. J. Hepple's br. g. Black Heddon, aged. *crimson and white bl. cap* 2 2 2
Mr. Burnett's b. m. Hartlepool Lass, aged. *scarlet and bl. cap* 3 3 3
Mr. Harrison's bk. m. Fisher Lass, 5 y, o. *blue.*

THIRD DAY,—SATURDAY

A Free Handy-Cap of 1 sov. each, with 10 sov. added and 2 sov. for the second. Heats, once round and a distance

Mr. Hutchinson's c. f. Maria Monk, 4 y. o. 7st 11lb. *pink and black cap*
Mr. Osborne's b. f. Ten Pound Note, 3 y. o. 6st. 7lb. *blue and black cap*
Mr. France's b. c. Hard Bargain, 3 y. o. 5st. 10lb. *crimson*

A Plate of 7 sov. with 1 sov. added for the second, for the beaten Horses of the Week—Weights according to the Member's Stake, Heats once round and a distance. Enterance 5s.

Mr. Humble's br. g. Black Heddon, aged 9st. *crimson and white, black cap*
Mr. Burnett's b. m. Hartlepool Lass, aged 9st. *scarlet and black stripes, black cap*
Mr. Hepple's bl. c. Bush Ranger, 4 y. o. 8st. 2lb. *crimson white black cap*
Mr. Lister's b. m. Eliza, aged 9st. 7lb. *buff and blue*

☞ Three reputed Running Horses to start for each Stake or no Race, unless otherwise agreed upon by the Stewards. Disputes (if any) to be determined by the Stewards, or whom they may appoint, and their decision to be final.

A BELL will ring for Saddling, aud again for the Horses Coming to the Post, and those ready Five Minutes after the Second Bell, shall be started without waiting for others.

On Ringing the Bell for Saddling, the Course to be cleared. Half an hour allowed between each Heat.

The THEATRE ROYAL, North-end of Northgate, will be opened during the Races.

87
A most imposing poster for a not very significant place. Hart Bushes was certainly not a village and scarcely merited the description of a hamlet. The names of the stewards, who were local farmers, may well provide a clue. If they were able to arrange their work so that they had a free day they were quite entitled to organise a little race meeting for their own amusement and that of their friends. The ubiquitous John Lawrenson would willingly act as judge and everyone would enjoy themselves.

88 and 88A
Just south of Hartlepool, on the opposite side of the channel leading into the docks, was a large tongue of sand named Middleton after a miller whose windmill was sited there. The narrow peninsula on which Hartlepool stands caused industrialists to build an iron works at Middleton in 1838. The races held there seem to have been of a very happy-go-lucky nature because it was outside the jurisdiction of the Corporation of Hartlepool. There were more amusements than was usual at races and on most of the bills they are fully described.

87

HART BUSHES RACES.

Stewards :—

Mr. J. STEELE

Mr. G. SWINBURN

Secretary and Clerk of the Course :—

Mr. WM. SHORT

JUDGE:—JOHN LAWRENSON, ESQ.

ON MONDAY, AUGUST 15th, 1859.

THE HART BUSHES STAKE

Of 4s. each, with £4 added;

For Horses of all denominations—to be Handicapped by the Stewards. (The Second to save his Stake.)

THE HURWORTH PLATE

Of 2s. 6d. each, with £2 added;

For Horses of all denominations, that never won the value of £10, in Plate or Stake, at any one time—to be Handicapped by the Stewards. (The Second to save his Stake.)

The NURSERY STAKE

Of 1s. 6d each, with £1 added:

For Ponies under 14 hands high—to be Handicapped by the Stewards.

No Winning Horse will be allowed to start for more than one Race; and all the above Races will be run for in Heats.

All Disputes to be settled by the Stewards, and their decision to be final.

The Horses to be entered at Mr. J. ARROWSMITH'S, Colliery Inn, not later than Two o'clock. To Start at Four o'clock.

QUOIT AND BALL PLAYING, AND OTHER SPORTS.

No Person will be allowed to Erect a Tent or Stall on the Course, without paying the usual Fee to the Clerk of the Course.

HARTLEPOOL: J. PROCTER, PRINTER, SOUTHGATE.

88

MIDDLETON JULY MEETING.

TO BE RUN FOR
ON THE SANDS AT MIDDLETON NEAR HARTLEPOOL,
On MONDAY & TUESDAY,
The 5th and 6th, days of JULY, 1841,

TO START PRECISELY AT 2 O'CLOCK.

A

SILVER CUP

Of £5. in Specie, for Horses not thorough bred; 3 years-old 7st. 6lb; 4 Years-old 8st. 12lb.; 5 years-old 9st. 3lb.; 6 and aged 9st. 8lb. A winner of £10 at any one time to carry 3lb. extra—if twice, 5b—if three times 7lb.

Heats 1½ Miles. Entrance 5s. each. Three to start or no race.

THE

INNKEEPERS' STAKE Of THREE POUNDS

For Horses not thorough bred;—weights as above; heats 1½ Miles, entance 2s. 6d. each; three to start or no race; the winner of the Cup will not be allowed to Start.

A SPLENDID

DOUBLE REINED Bridle, or 10s.

At the option of the winner, for Ponies not exceeding 14 hands high; euther weights; heats 1 mile; entrance 1s. each; the second to recive 2s. 6d. Three to start or no race.

ON TUESDAY THE FOLLOWING PRIZES

WILL BE CONTENDID FOR, VIZ;—

A Circle will be formed 20 yards diameter, and a person will go into it with four Bells attached to him—then four persons blind-folded to try to catch him, and if any of them do so in 10 minutes, to receive the amount of 10s. but should he not be caught in the above named time, the person who has tne Bells attached to him to receive the 10s.

Also, a Beautiful Gown Piece

To be run for by Ladies not exceeding 50 years of age nor less than 15. Distance 100 yards; three to start or no race.

ALSO, A PRIZE of 10s. will be given for Shooting at a TARGET, with No 4 Shot, at a distance to be fixed by the Stewards. Entrance 6d. each.

ALSO, A PRIZE of 5s. will be given to the Winner of a Race in Sacks; distance 100 yards; Four to start or no race.

Also a prize of a **NEW HAT**, to be contended for by climbing up a Greased Pole. If the prize is not won in an hour, to be run for in a foot race.

Also, a race Blindfold, with Wheel-barrows for 5s.

To enter at the Lord Seaham Inn, Middleton, between the hours of Ten and Two of Monday, the 5th July, and none will be allowed to enter after that time. Disputes if any, to be determined by the Stewards, or whom they may appoint, and their decision to be final.

All Dogs found on the Course will be destroyed.

The Prizes to be paid **(only)** at the Lord Seaham and the Commercial Inns, Middleton, at the conclusion of the Races.

Stewards.--J. Burtoft & J. Outhwaite,

FRANCIS ESKEW, CLERK OF THE COURSE.

N. B. No Tents allowed to be erected but by Subscribers of 10s. each, to be paid to the Clerk of the Course.

A Band of Music will play on the Ground.

J. PROCTER'S OFFICE, HARTLEPOOL.

88A

A SPLENDID

DOUBLE REINED Bridle, or 10s.

At the option of the winner, for Ponies not exceeding 14 hands high; feather weights; heats 1 mile; entrance 1s. each; the second to receive 2s. 6d. Three to start or no race.

ON TUESDAY THE FOLLOWING PRIZES

WILL BE CONTENDID FOR, VIZ;—

A Circle will be formed 20 yards diameter, and a person will go into it with four Bells attached to him—then four persons blind-folded to try to catch him, and if any of them do so in 10 minutes, to receive the amount of 10s. but should he not be caught in the above named time, the person who has the Bells attached to him to receive the 10s.

Also, a Beautiful Gown Piece

To be run for by Ladies not exceeding 50 years of age nor less than 15. Distance 100 yards; three to start or no race.

ALSO, A PRIZE of 10s. will be given for Shooting at a TARGET, with No 4 Shot, at a distance to be fixed by the Stewards. Entrance 6d. each.

ALSO, A PRIZE of 5s. will be given to the Winner of a Race in Sacks; distance 100 yards; Four to start or no race.

Also a prize of a **NEW HAT,** to be contended for by climbing up a Greased Pole. If the prize is not won in an hour, to be run for in a foot race.

Also, a race Blindfold, with Wheel-barrows for 5s.

To enter at the Lord Seaham Inn, Middleton, between the hours of Ten and Two of Monday, the 5th July, and none will be allowed to enter after that time. Disputes if any, to be determined by the Stewards, or whom they may appoint, and their decision to be final.

All Dogs found on the Course will be destroyed.

The Prizes to be paid **(only)** at the Lord Seaham and the Commercial Inns, Middleton, at the conclusion of the Races.

Stewards.--J. Burtoft & J. Outhwaite,

FRANCIS ESKEW, CLERK OF THE COURSE.

N. B. No Tents allowed to be erected but by Subscribers of 10s. each, to be paid to the Clerk of the Course.

A Band of Music will play on the Ground.

SEDGEFIELD
Steeple Chases,

ON TUESDAY, APRIL THE 8th, 1856.

Stewards:— { H. B. BAKER, Esq.
M. ORD, Esq.

Judge:—W. H. WILLIAMSON, Esq.

Clerk of the Course:—Mr. JOHN LAWRENSON.
Clerk of the Scales:—Mr. JOHN STEELE.
Treasurer:—Mr. THOS. CHARLETON.
Hon. Secretary:—Mr. J. B. HODGSON.

A SWEEPSTAKES

Of 3 Sov. each, 1 Sov. forfeit, with 25 Sovs. added, for Horses which have been Hunted with the Durham County, Raby and Hurworth Foxhounds; Four years old, 11 stone; Five years old, 11 stone 9lbs.; Six and aged, 12 stone.—Thorough-bred Horses, 10lbs. extra.—A Winner of any Steeple Chase, 7lbs extra.—The Winner to pay 2 Sovs. towards expenses, over Three Miles of a fair Hunting Country; if not more than Three Horses enter, only 15 Sovs. will be added.

A SWEEPSTAKES

Of 1 Sov. each, with 15 Sovs. added, for Horses *bona fide*, the property of Tenant Farmers resident in the County of Durham.—Weight as above.—The Winner to pay 1 Sov. towards expenses.—If not more than Three Horses enter, only 10 Sovs. will be added.

A HURDLE RACE

For Beaten Horses, and a Race for Ponies under 14 hands high, will take place in Hardwick Park immediately, after the Steeple Chase.

Entries for the Steeple Chases to be made on or before TWELVE o'clock at noon of the Saturday previous to the Races, at Mr. THOMAS CHARLTON'S, Hardwick Inn, Sedgefield, and the other Races on Tuesday, April the 8th.

89 and 89A
This bill is unique in being the only racebill of the many that John Procter printed which relates to a meeting that has survived the years. Racehorses still go to Sedgefield. Even in those days it was a very well patronised event. The stewards are two of the local gentry. The judge is 'Billy' Williamson, brother-in-law to Lord Zetland and the man who persuaded his lordship to buy Voltigeur. Mr Lawrenson is present as Clerk of the Course.

90
The two horses to be sold were both from the stables at Hart. The stable in which the great Voltigeur was born was situated here and used to be regarded as a shrine. The cottage which now stands on the site proudly proclaims itself Voltigeur Cottage.

91
Menfolk in the North of England have always bred dogs. Even the monks of Durham Cathedral were allowed to take their greyhounds with them when they went on holiday to Finchale. Those familiar with the locality will wonder where the landlord of the Leeds Hotel could possibly organise his rabbit coursing, for the house was virtually on the sea front. It is highly probable that he used the sand-dunes to the south of his establishment.

89A

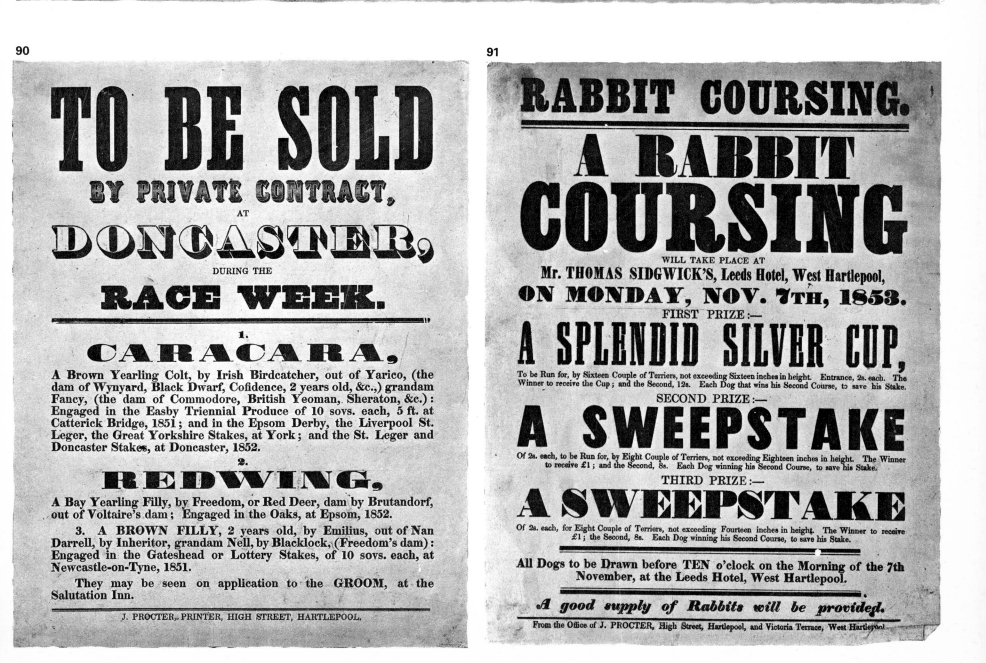

All Disputes to be settled by the Stewards, and their Decision to be Final.

Certificates will be required from the Master or Huntsman, of the above-named Hounds.

The Colours of the Riders to be declared at the time of Entry, or forfeit Ten Shillings; and a similar Fine will be imposed for Riding in a different Colour to that declared.

TO COMMENCE AT TWO O'CLOCK PRECISELY.

From the Office of J. PROCTER, Printer and Lithographer, Hartlepool and West Hartlepool

90

TO BE SOLD

BY PRIVATE CONTRACT,

AT

DONCASTER,

DURING THE

RACE WEEK.

1.

CARACARA,

A Brown Yearling Colt, by Irish Birdcatcher, out of Yarico, (the dam of Wynyard, Black Dwarf, Cofidence, 2 years old, &c.,) grandam Fancy, (the dam of Commodore, British Yeoman, Sheraton, &c.): Engaged in the Easby Triennial Produce of 10 sovs. each, 5 ft. at Catterick Bridge, 1851; and in the Epsom Derby, the Liverpool St. Leger, the Great Yorkshire Stakes, at York; and the St. Leger and Doncaster Stakes, at Doncaster, 1852.

2.

REDWING,

A Bay Yearling Filly, by Freedom, or Red Deer, dam by Brutandorf, out of Voltaire's dam; Engaged in the Oaks, at Epsom, 1852.

3. A BROWN FILLY, 2 years old, by Emilius, out of Nan Darrell, by Inheritor, grandam Nell, by Blacklock, (Freedom's dam): Engaged in the Gateshead or Lottery Stakes, of 10 sovs. each, at Newcastle-on-Tyne, 1851.

They may be seen on application to the GROOM, at the Salutation Inn.

J. PROCTER, PRINTER, HIGH STREET, HARTLEPOOL.

91

RABBIT COURSING.

A RABBIT COURSING

WILL TAKE PLACE AT

Mr. THOMAS SIDGWICK'S, Leeds Hotel, West Hartlepool,

ON MONDAY, NOV. 7TH, 1853.

FIRST PRIZE:—

A SPLENDID SILVER CUP,

To be Run for, by Sixteen Couple of Terriers, not exceeding Sixteen inches in height. Entrance, 2s. each. The Winner to receive the Cup; and the Second, 12s. Each Dog that wins his Second Course, to save his Stake.

SECOND PRIZE:—

A SWEEPSTAKE

Of 2s. each, to be Run for, by Eight Couple of Terriers, not exceeding Eighteen inches in height. The Winner to receive £1; and the Second, 8s. Each Dog winning his Second Course, to save his Stake.

THIRD PRIZE:—

A SWEEPSTAKE

Of 2s. each, for Eight Couple of Terriers, not exceeding Fourteen inches in height. The Winner to receive £1; the Second, 8s. Each Dog winning his Second Course, to save his Stake.

All Dogs to be Drawn before TEN o'clock on the Morning of the 7th November, at the Leeds Hotel, West Hartlepool.

A good supply of Rabbits will be provided.

From the Office of J. PROCTER, High Street, Hartlepool, and Victoria Terrace, West Hartlepool.

92 and 92A
In a seaport town a hundred years ago, when everyone's livelihood depended either directly or indirectly on the sea, a regatta was a notable event. If the two Members of Parliament for the Southern Division of Durham had not been patrons, they would have been very foolish men. The stewards are the Mayors, and William Vollum, the senior alderman and a most respected citizen, and John Punshon Denton, the leading shipbuilder. The statement 'Open to boats from all parts' meant what it says for entries came from all along the East coast of England.

93A and 93B
Details of superb engravings from regatta posters.

92

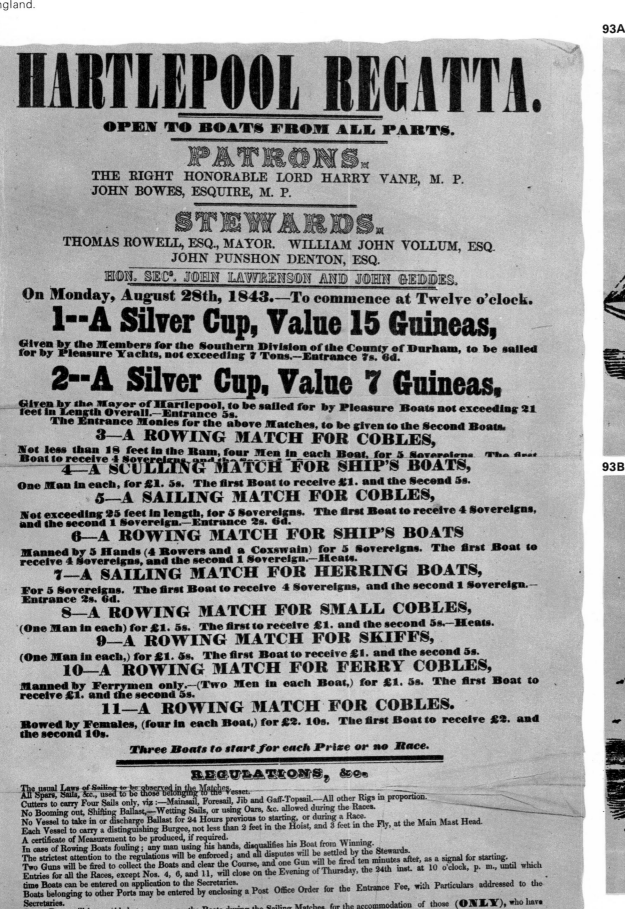

HARTLEPOOL REGATTA.

OPEN TO BOATS FROM ALL PARTS.

PATRONS.

THE RIGHT HONORABLE LORD HARRY VANE, M. P.
JOHN BOWES, ESQUIRE, M. P.

STEWARDS.

THOMAS ROWELL, ESQ., MAYOR. WILLIAM JOHN VOLLUM, ESQ.
JOHN PUNSHON DENTON, ESQ.

HON. SEC^s. JOHN LAWRENSON AND JOHN GEDDES.

On Monday, August 28th, 1843.—To commence at Twelve o'clock.

1--A Silver Cup, Value 15 Guineas,

Given by the Members for the Southern Division of the County of Durham, to be sailed for by Pleasure Yachts, not exceeding 7 Tons.—Entrance 7s. 6d.

2--A Silver Cup, Value 7 Guineas,

Given by the Mayor of Hartlepool, to be sailed for by Pleasure Boats not exceeding 21 feet in Length Overall.—Entrance 5s.

The Entrance Monies for the above Matches, to be given to the Second Boats.

3—A ROWING MATCH FOR COBLES,

Not less than 18 feet in the Ram, four Men in each Boat, for 5 Sovereigns. The first Boat to receive 4 Sovereigns, and the ...

4—A SCULLING MATCH FOR SHIP'S BOATS,

One Man in each, for £1. 5s. The first Boat to receive £1. and the Second 5s.

5—A SAILING MATCH FOR COBLES,

Not exceeding 25 feet in length, for 5 Sovereigns. The first Boat to receive 4 Sovereigns, and the second 1 Sovereign.—Entrance 2s. 6d.

6—A ROWING MATCH FOR SHIP'S BOATS

Manned by 5 Hands (4 Rowers and a Coxswain) for 5 Sovereigns. The first Boat to receive 4 Sovereigns, and the second 1 Sovereign.—Heats.

7—A SAILING MATCH FOR HERRING BOATS,

For 5 Sovereigns. The first Boat to receive 4 Sovereigns, and the second 1 Sovereign.—Entrance 2s. 6d.

8—A ROWING MATCH FOR SMALL COBLES,

(One Man in each) for £1. 5s. The first to receive £1. and the second 5s.—Heats.

9—A ROWING MATCH FOR SKIFFS,

(One Man in each,) for £1. 5s. The first Boat to receive £1. and the second 5s.

10—A ROWING MATCH FOR FERRY COBLES,

Manned by Ferrymen only.—(Two Men in each Boat,) for £1. 5s. The first Boat to receive £1. and the second 5s.

11—A ROWING MATCH FOR COBLES.

Rowed by Females, (four in each Boat,) for £2. 10s. The first Boat to receive £2. and the second 10s.

Three Boats to start for each Prize or no Race.

REGULATIONS, &c.

The usual Laws of Sailing to be observed in the Matches.
All Spars, Sails, &c., used to be those belonging to the Vessel.
Cutters to carry Four Sails only, viz:—Mainsail, Foresail, Jib and Gaff-Topsail.—All other Rigs in proportion.
No Booming out, Shifting Ballast,—Wetting Sails, or using Oars, &c. allowed during the Races.
No Vessel to take in or discharge Ballast for 24 Hours previous to starting, or during a Race.
Each Vessel to carry a distinguishing Burgee, not less than 2 feet in the Hoist, and 3 feet in the Fly, at the Main Mast Head.
A certificate of Measurement to be produced, if required.
In case of Rowing Boats fouling; any man using his hands, disqualifies his Boat from Winning.
The strictest attention to the regulations will be enforced; and all disputes will be settled by the Stewards.
Two Guns will be fired to collect the Boats and clear the Course, and one Gun will be fired ten minutes after, as a signal for starting.
Entries for all the Races, except Nos. 4, 6, and 11, will close on the Evening of Thursday, the 24th inst. at 10 o'clock, p. m., until which time Boats can be entered on application to the Secretaries.
Boats belonging to other Ports may be entered by enclosing a Post Office Order for the Entrance Fee, with Particulars addressed to the Secretaries.
Steam Boats will be provided, to accompany the Boats during the Sailing Matches, for the accommodation of those (**ONLY**), who have favoured the Committee with Subscriptions.

The Regatta Committee will be strenuous in their exertions to collect sufficient Subscriptions to enable them to give a brilliant display of Fire Works in the Evening.

Committee Room, Hartlepool, August 15th, 1843.

93A

93B

94
The Victorian attitude towards sea bathing was very different from ours. We regard it as a frolic but they approached it after medical advice and with a proper appreciation of its value if taken with care. Victorian decorum being what it was, the extraordinary business of sea bathing was surrounded with safe-guards and a due appreciation of the necessity for preserving the decencies. There were men who devoted their whole lives to establishing a reputation for running their sea bathing business in the most proper way, John Alderson was one of them.

92A

REGULATIONS, &c.

The usual Laws of Sailing to be observed in the Matches.
All Spars, Sails, &c., used to be those belonging to the Vessel.
Cutters to carry Four Sails only, viz :—Mainsail, Foresail, Jib and Gaff-Topsail.—All other Rigs in proportion.
No Booming out, Shifting Ballast,—Wetting Sails, or using Oars, &c. allowed during the Races.
No Vessel to take in or discharge Ballast for 24 Hours previous to starting, or during a Race.
Each Vessel to carry a distinguishing Burgee, not less than 2 feet in the Hoist, and 3 feet in the Fly, at the Main Mast Head.
A certificate of Measurement to be produced, if required.
In case of Rowing Boats fouling; any man using his hands, disqualifies his Boat from Winning.
The strictest attention to the regulations will be enforced; and all disputes will be settled by the Stewards.
Two Guns will be fired to collect the Boats and clear the Course, and one Gun will be fired ten minutes after, as a signal for starting.
Entries for all the Races, except Nos. 4, 6, and 11, will close on the Evening of Thursday, the 24th inst. at 10 o'clock, p. m., until which time Boats can be entered on application to the Secretaries.
Boats belonging to other Ports may be entered by enclosing a Post Office Order for the Entrance Fee, with Particulars addressed to the Secretaries.
Steam Boats will be provided, to accompany the Boats during the Sailing Matches, for the accommodation of those (**ONLY**), who have favoured the Committee with Subscriptions.

The Regatta Committee will be strenuous in their exertions to collect sufficient Subscriptions to enable them to give a brilliant display of Fire Works in the Evening.

Committee Room, Hartlepool, August 15th, 1843.

94

SEA BATHING.

JOHN ALDERSON,

Begs to inform the Inhabitants and Visitors of Hartlepool, that he has placed Two

COMMODIOUS BATHING MACHINES,

UPON THE

NORTH SANDS,

HARTLEPOOL,

And to solicit a share of their Support.

***Hartlepool 14th August,* 1844.**

J. Procter, Printer, Union Place, Hartlepool.

95
It must have been quite aggravating to travel on a long journey in the days when there were a large number of railway companies, for the passengers would often be called upon to change from one train to another, or even from one station to another. But within the boundaries of the area it served a small railway company could be extremely useful. The West Hartlepool Harbour and Railway Company owned most of the town, but served it well. If there was a late dance or some similar function, the railway put on a special train to take the dancers home. This is a very imposing special bill for the regatta.

96
What pleasure the Victorians seemed to obtain from their use of ungainly words! There are further extraordinary creations in a later chapter but fortunately they disappeared. At one time it seemed as though 'velocipede' was an established addition to our language. To this very day in Belgian coastal resorts the extraordinary four-wheel vehicles which are pedalled, but steered by a wheel, are known as 'velos'.

97
On early posters it was quite common for the client to ask the printer to leave a space where the name of the place or inn should be, so that the poster could be used in many places by simply inserting the particular names with a pen. This could claim to be a superior example for it can be used anywhere at any time without recourse to a pen. It illustrates the lowest level of advertising to which a strolling performer could descend without abandoning the poster altogether.

95

WEST HARTLEPOOL HARBOUR & RAILWAY.

WEST HARTLEPOOL ANNUAL

REGATTA.

ON

MONDAY & TUESDAY,

July 30th and 31st, 1855,

CHEAP TRAINS

	FARES, THERE AND BACK. 1st CLASS.	2nd CLASS.	3rd CLASS.
Will leave Coxhoe at 9 15, a. m.	4s.	3s.	1s. 4d.
" Ferry Hill at 9 35, a. m. and 12 30, p. m.	4s.	3s.	1s. 4d.
" Sedgefield at 9 45, a. m. and 12 40, p. m.	3s.	2s.	1s. 6d.
" Stillington at 9 55, a. m. and 12 50, p. m.	2s.	1s. 6d.	1s. 3d.
" Carlton at 10, a. m. and 12 55, p. m.	2s.	1s. 6d.	1s.
" Port Clarence at 9 40, a. m. and 12 23, p. m.	2s. 6d.	1s. 8d.	1s. 4d.
" Billingham at 10 10, a. m. and 1 5, p. m.	1s. 6d.	1s.	8d.
" Stockton at 11, a. m. and 12 55 p. m.	2s.	1s. 6d.	1s.
" Norton Junction at 11 8, a. m.	2s.	1s. 6d.	10d.
" Greatham at 11 25, a. m. and 1. 15, p. m.	1s.	7d.	

And return from West Hartlepool for Coxhoe, Ferry Hill, Sedgefield, Stillington, and Carlton at 5 20, p. m., and for Stockton, Norton Junction, Port Clarence, Billingham and Greatham at 5 20 and 7 30, p. m.

CHILDREN UNDER 12 YEARS OF AGE, HALF PRICE.

SAMUEL CHESTER,
General Manager.

West Hartlepool, 18 July, 1855.

J. Procter, Printer and Lithographer, West Hartlepool.

96

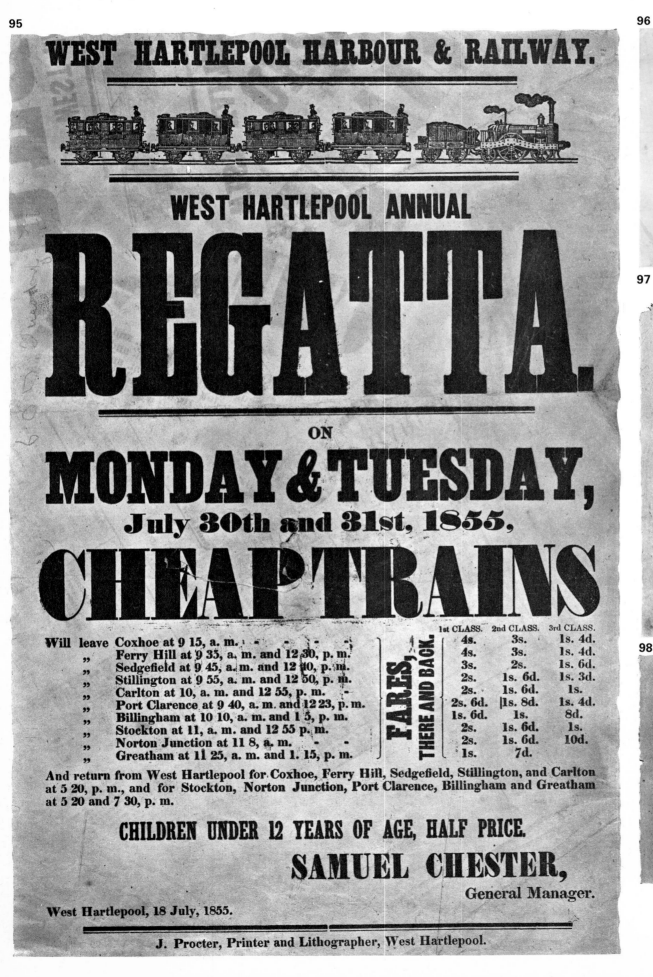

PRIZES
FOR
VELOCIPEDE
RACES,
TUESDAY, AUGUST 2ND, 1870.

97

NOVELTY!!
ON A COMMODIOUS PIECE OF GROUND.

The public are respectfully informed that there will be a performance
OF
TIGHT ROPE
DANCING,
SLACK WIRE WALKING,
&c., &c.
In the course of the performance a Grand Balloon will ascend.
TO COMMENCE AT 7 O'CLOCK.

J. Procter, Printer, Hartlepool.

98

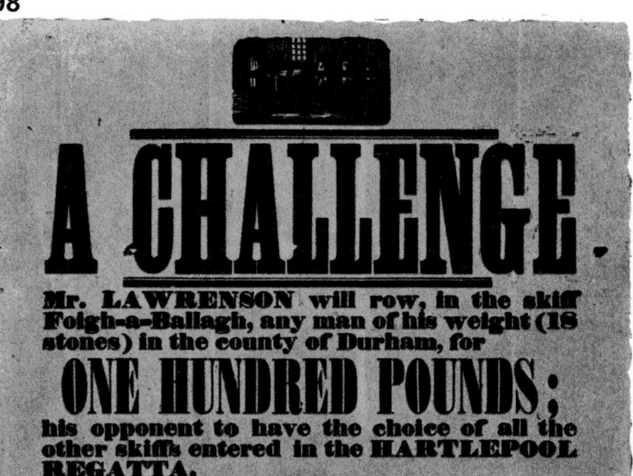

A CHALLENGE.

Mr. LAWRENSON will row, in the skiff Folgh-a-Ballagh, any man of his weight (18 stones) in the county of Durham, for
ONE HUNDRED POUNDS;
his opponent to have the choice of all the other skiffs entered in the HARTLEPOOL REGATTA.

Printed by J. PROCTER, Hartlepool.

98
A superb piece of Victorian humour. The challenge is a genuine one if the conditions are fulfilled. On this coast rowing was taken very seriously and good oarsmen became famous men. Note the block borrowed from the brewery adorning the top centre.

99
No doubt Mr. Lawson would feel aggrieved if we did not display an interest in his shooting gallery, but we are equally entitled to admire the manner in which his announcement is presented to the public. The neat design and fine discrimination in choosing a suitable type fount make this poster a pleasure to behold.

99

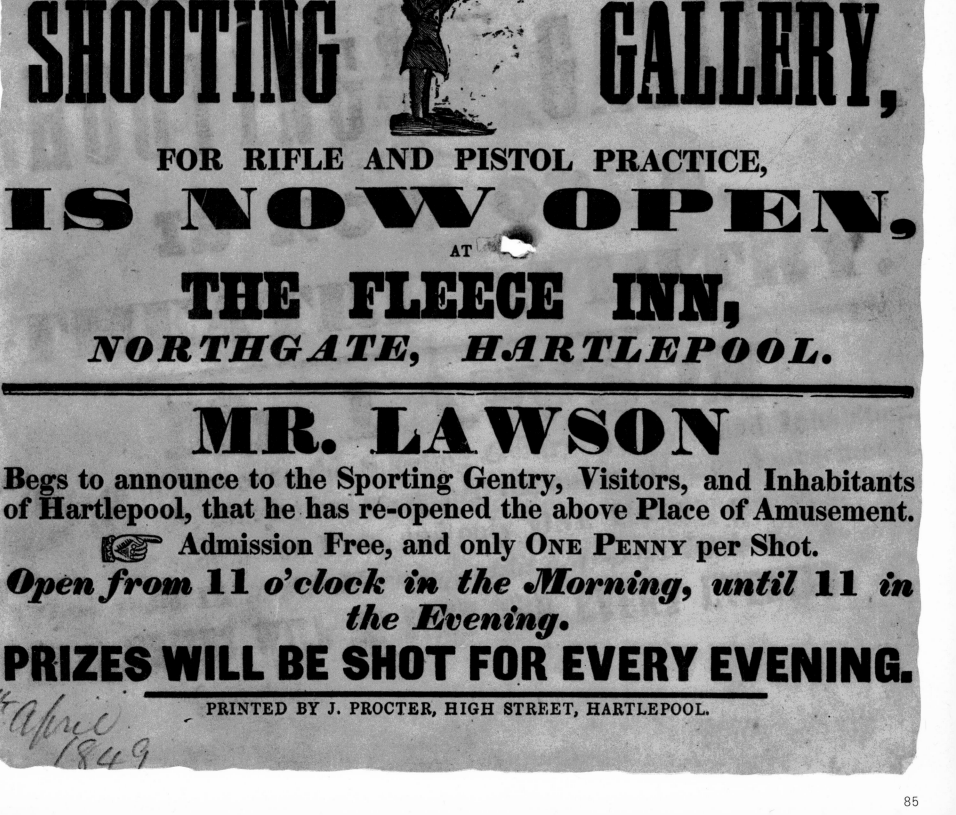

LAWSON'S

SHOOTING GALLERY,

FOR RIFLE AND PISTOL PRACTICE,

IS NOW OPEN,

AT

THE FLEECE INN,

NORTHGATE, HARTLEPOOL.

MR. LAWSON

Begs to announce to the Sporting Gentry, Visitors, and Inhabitants of Hartlepool, that he has re-opened the above Place of Amusement.

☞ Admission Free, and only ONE PENNY per Shot.

Open from 11 o'clock in the Morning, until 11 in the Evening.

PRIZES WILL BE SHOT FOR EVERY EVENING.

PRINTED BY J. PROCTER, HIGH STREET, HARTLEPOOL.

16 April 1849

100
The National Rifle Clubs originated in 1860 and from them the Volunteer movement evolved. At first the participants were very much 'week-end' soldiers and the 'General Rules and Conditions' of their Carbine Competition' betray traces of their civilian attitude. Not that the Fourth Durhams did not make good soldiers; they were a crack unit, Sergeant Scales, as he then was, and his unit, won the Volunteer Challenge Cup in 1862. The author is the proud possessor of his medal.

101
Occasionally one still sees at fairs the old fashioned shooting gallery with its endless belt of rabbit silhouettes and its array of miniature fountains each balancing a celluloid ball which dances continuously up and down until the more skilful marksman manages to shoot it down. At one time the galleries had a background of row upon row of clay pipes but these, too, have vanished.

102
Stockton v Hartlepool. William Hone wrote in 1831 'Cricket is of late years become exceedingly fashionable, being much countenanced by the nobility and gentlemen of fortune who frequently join in the division. This game, which is played with the bat and the ball, consists of single and double wicket. Of late years the wicket consists of three stumps and two bails. Single wicket requires five players on each side, and double wicket eleven; but the number in both instances may be varied at the pleasure of the two parties'.

100

Fourth Durham Volunteer Artillery

CARBINE COMPETITION.

PROGRAMME OF PRIZE MEETING,

Wednesday, May 10th, 1865.

		£	s.	d.
1. Tradesmen's Prize—Silver Cup ......value		3	0	0
2. Licensed Victuallers' Prize—Gold Albert	„	2	10	0
3. Ladies' Prize—Timepiece	„	1	15	0
4. Mr. Hill's Prize—Opera Glass	„	1	10	0
5. Sergt. Major Scales' Prize—A Portrait of the Winner..........................	„	1	10	0

General Rules and Conditions.

1. That the Competition take place on the 10th day of May, 1865, at the Range, West Hartlepool. Firing to commence at 1, p.m.

2. None but *bona fide* effective Members of the 4th D.A.V. will be allowed to compete, with the exception of Recruits, who will be allowed to shoot only by sanction of the Officer in command.

3. Prizes to be shot for with the Regulation Artillery Carbine. Each Member competing to be in uniform, excepting Recruits who are not provided with the same.

4. Each Competitor to fire five rounds at 150, 200, and 300 yards respectively. Hythe position to be observed.

5. Bull's Eyes to count 4, Centres 3, Outer 2.

6. The five Competitors making the highest scores will win the Prizes. Ties will be decided by a single shot at the longest distance.

7. The Squad will fall-in two deep, at One o'clock, and load from the word of command only, and not to cap before marching out to fire. No talking in the Ranks allowed.

N.B. The above Rule will be strictly enforced, any Member infringing the same will be find 2s. 6d., or ~~expelled~~ from Firm.

8. Each Competitor to provide himself with Ammunition before coming on the ground.

9. Competitors not present at the word *load*, will forfeit their entrance fees, and will not be allowed to fall-in on any pretence whatever.

10. Each Competitor to give in his name and pay an entrance of 1s. 6d. to Sergeant Mountford, on or before Tuesday, the 9th inst.

11. All disputes to be decided by the officer in charge of the ground, whose decision shall be final.

12. Any Competitor accidentally discharging his Carbine will forfeit his shot.

Officers' and other Prizes postponed for future Competition.

BY ORDER OF THE COMMITTEE.

HARTLEPOOL: J. PROCTER, PRINTER BY STEAM POWER.

101

PRIZE SHOOTING!

OPEN TO ALL ENGLAND.

MR. LAWSON,

Proprietor of the RIFLE SHOOTING GALLERY, (which is now open) FLEECE INN, NORTHGATE, HARTLEPOOL, respectfully informs his Friends and the Public, that he intends offering Two Prizes, as follows:—The first

A SPLENDID RIFLE

AND THE SECOND A

BRACE OF PISTOLS

TO BE SHOT FOR, AT HARTLEPOOL,

ON MONDAY, THE 21st OF JANUARY, 1850,

18 SUBSCRIBERS AT 5s. EACH.

Each Competitor to fire 3 Shots at the Target. 100 Yards Range. The nearest Shot to claim the first Prize, and the second the second Prize.

The Winner of the First Prize to pay the Third his Stake.

The Shooting to commence at TEN o'clock in the Morning.

The strictest attention will be paid to the Competitors as to fair off-hand Shooting.

Mr. L. will provide Rifles, or any Gentleman may use his own.

Each Competitor to Pay 3d. for his Three Shots.

Parties wishing to become Subscribers, may receive every Information at the Shooting Gallery, where a List is kept for the purpose.

Printed at the Office of J. PROCTER, High Street, Hartlepool.

102

CRICKET

Stockton

v.

HARTLEPOOL

A MATCH

BETWEEN THE ABOVE CLUBS, WILL BE PLAYED,

ON FRIDAY, 21ST CURRENT,

ON THE HARTLEPOOL GROUND.

Wickets Pitched at TEN, a.m., precisely.

A COLLATION will be served upon the Ground at TWO, p.m. Tickets 2s. each, which may be had of Mr. JOHN GREY, Wheat Sheaf Inn; or of the Committee.

Admittance to the Ground, 3d. each.; Ladies will be admitted Free.

All Persons found Climbing over the Wall, or Trespassing on the Field, will be Prosecuted.

R. BELL,

Hartlepool, May 13th, 1852. HON. SEC.

From the Office of J. PROCTER, High Street, Hartlepool, and Victoria Terrace, West Hartlepool.

103

One of the most amusing things about this charming piece of printing is that this particular club seems to have been so liberal in its attitudes that it took care to spare its member's feelings about discipline. There were rules and fines galore but the fact that these are the rules and regulations of the club is not stressed by the design of the bill and one is left with the impression that they would not be enforced rigidly. Rule 8 may well confirm this general impression.

104 and 104A

The Rugby Union was founded in 1871 and consisted of teams drawn chiefly from the Public Schools, Universities and the Army. Yet by 1875 there was a team in the Hartlepool area which soon had rivals. They merged in 1882 to form the famous Hartlepool Rovers. The Friarage ground within sight and sound of the sea was a great battlefield on which some of the renowned clubs of Rugby Union were honoured to play. The Rovers were the County Champions in 1885 and their match cards, in quality and production, were worthy of them and the printer. 104 shows the cover and 104A part of the inside.

103

HARTLEPOOL
Friendly Cricket Club.

At a MEETING held by the MEMBERS at the *Wheat Sheaf Inn, Hartlepool,* the 12th day of May, 1835, the following RULES and REGULATIONS were unanimously approved of and adopted.

1. That a Committee of five be chosen by the majority of the Members with a Treasurer and Secretary to be chosen annually.

2. That the Committee be appointed with power to call Special Meetings, and conduct and manage the affairs of the Club in such manner as they may think most to the advantage thereof.

3. That Committee Men not attending the Meeting as named in Rule 10th, shall forfeit 6d, if without a substitute.

4. Days of practice the Second Tuesday in every Month at 3 o'Clock in the afternoon and Members not attending without a reasonable excuse to be find 3d.

5. That all expences incurred by the Committee while acting for the Club, be reimbursed out of the funds thereof. And if they are inadequate to meet the same, a contribution to be levied on each member to meet the demands required,

6. That each playing Member shall pay at the time of his admission to the Secretary the sum of 1s., to be added to the funds of the Club, and an additonal sum of 6d per month, during the year.

7. That the number of Members be unlimited; any person wishing to become a Member, be proposed at any meeting, shall become a Member by ballot.

8. That if any Member come to the play ground tipsy, or get tipsy in the time of playing, shall be fin'd 6d., to be paid on application of the Secretary or to be excluded on non-payment, according to Rule 18th.

9. That if any Member shall retire before the close of the game in which he is engaged, without leave from one of the Committee, if present, or if absent, without the consent of those who are playing, he shall forfeit 6d; and in case any player shall refuse to obey the Bowler's orders, he shall forfeit 3d.

10. That a meeting of the Club be held precisely at Eight o'Clock, on the first Tuesday in every month during the year, at such Inn as shall be previously agreed on, when all business relating to the affairs of the Club shall be transacted.

11. That if any Member come to the ground after the hour appointed for the regular meeting of the Club to play, and the game be then commenced he shall not require to be taken as a partner in such game until done, or another player can be found to be taken in against him.

12. That all fines incurred or forfeited, shall be paid on demand of the Secretary.

13. That no match shall be made with any other Club without the attendance of 15 Members at a special or monthly meeting; and if the majority be in favour of the match, the players shall be chosen by the Committee, who shall have power to take or refuse any sum of money from the funds for the purpose of such match.

14. That if any Member withdraw or be excluded from the Club, he shall forfeit all claim to any funds or property the Club at that time may possess.

15. That at the end of the year the Secretary's accounts shall be inspected by the Committee, and the surplus (if any), in his hands, shall be disposed of as a majority of the Club shall direct.

16. That if any question or dispute shall arise relating to the affairs of the Club, which cannot be decided by those Rules, the same shall be referred to the Committee, whose decision shall be final.

17. That each Member of this Society clear the Books once in two months, or subject himself to a fine of 3d, and if not cleared in three months to be excluded.

18. That if any Member shall refuse to conform to the Rules and Regulations of the Club, a majority of the Members attending a Special Meeting shall have full power to exclude him.

HARTLEPOOL: PRINTED AT THE OFFICE OF J. PROCTER, BOOKSELLER.

104

Durham
VERSUS
Yorkshire
FRIARAGE FIELD
HARTLEPOOL,
NOVEMBER 6TH, 1886.
KICK OFF AT 2.45.
F. W. MASON, TYP.

104A

Yorkshire

Back.

C. E. FOX (Salterhebble)

Three-Quarter Backs.

Right.	*Centre*	*Left.*
R. LOCKWOOD (Dewsbury)	R. ROBERTSHAW (Bradford)	T. HASLAM (Batley)

Half Backs.

F. BONSOR (Bradford) — J. NAYLOR (Batley)

Forwards.

G. HARRISON Captain (Hull)	E. WILKINSON (Bradford)	H. WARD (Wakefield Trinity)
E. JACKSON (Batley)	P. DICKINSON (Castleford)	C. MATHERS (Bramley)
L. HICKSON (Bradford)	J. W. SYKES (Batley)	T. WATSON (Halifax)

SCORE—Under the New Rules.

A GOAL COUNTS 3 POINTS, A TRY 1 POINT.

	Goals.	Tries.	Minors.	Total Points
1st Half				
2nd Half				

Umpire—Mr. J. A. MILLER, *Hon. Sec. Yorkshire County Football Club.*

105

BURTON HOTEL RUNNING GROUNDS,

WEST HARTLEPOOL.

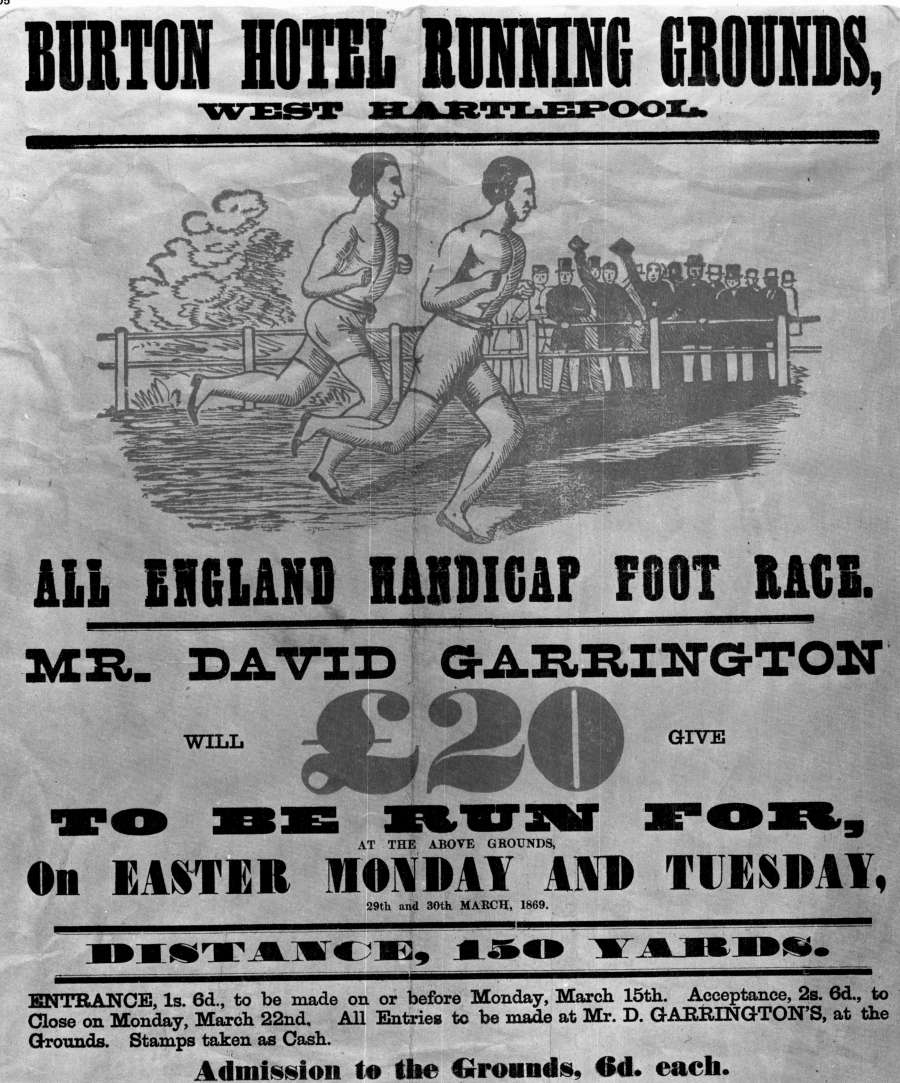

ALL ENGLAND HANDICAP FOOT RACE.

MR. DAVID GARRINGTON

WILL

GIVE

TO BE RUN FOR,

AT THE ABOVE GROUNDS,

On EASTER MONDAY AND TUESDAY,

29th and 30th MARCH, 1869.

DISTANCE, 150 YARDS.

ENTRANCE, 1s. 6d., to be made on or before Monday, March 15th. Acceptance, 2s. 6d., to Close on Monday, March 22nd. All Entries to be made at Mr. D. GARRINGTON'S, at the Grounds. Stamps taken as Cash.

Admission to the Grounds, 6d. each.

105
Burton Hotel Running Grounds. A quite superb poster.

106
In a mining village such as Wheatley Hill, where open fields had existed before the pit was sunk, there was no tradition of a fair. But even miners deserved a holiday and it was usually called a gala. To this day the Durham Big Meeting of the miners is known as the Durham Gala though nowadays they listen to political speeches. At Wheatley Hill, however, they were happy to enjoy the usual sports and competitions.

107
The village fair has a different name depending on the region in which it is held. It can be a feast or a wake or a gala or a hopping. Quite why the word 'hopping' was used at Bradbury is rather obscure. The village is certainly too far north for the successful cultivation of hops.
Quoits has always been a rustic sport to be played on a summer evening outside the village inn whose landlord could be relied upon to keep the clay round the hob properly moist. In the last century quoits infiltrated into the towns but now it appears to have become solely a country pastime.

108
It was customary on the old race bills to place at the foot of the poster in rather small letters 'Plays and Assemblies as usual'. The promoters of the races could be certain that there would be a dance in the inn at night, and that accounted for the 'Assembly'. If any strolling players arrived then there would certainly be 'Plays'. If they didn't come, then their absence provided the excuse for the lack of a play. This poster is the industrial town's equivalent to the village poster. The proletariat must have its fun, and here it is provided for them by a thoughtful Committee.

106

WHEATLEY HILL.

GRAND GALA

AND

WRESTLING

ON SATURDAY, AUGUST 8th, 1874,

The Wheatley People, beg respectfully to announce to the Inhabitants of Wheatley Hill and Neighbourhood that they intend to hold their First Annual Gala, in a Splendid Field, near to the Old Farm, Wheatley Hill, kindly granted for the occasion, by PHILIP COOPER, Esq.

WHEN THE FOLLOWING PRIZES WILL BE GIVEN:

£1 10s. for Wrestling

IN THE CUMBERLAND STYLE.

£1 10S. FOR WRESTLING

IN THE CORNISH STYLE.

OPEN TO ALL COMERS—Any Dispute arising about the Falls, to be left to the decision of the Umpire and Referee, such decision to be final—Entrance, 6d.

£1 10s. Will be GIVEN for a CRICKET MATCH

ENTRANCE. 2s. 6d. EACH CLUB.

PROGRAMME OF SPORTS:—

	First.	Second.	Entrance.
Quoit Match, not under 7 yards	15s.	5s.	6d.
Flat Race, 130 Yards	10s.	5s.	6d.
Running High Leap for Boys	5s.	2s. 6d.	6d.
Pole Leap for Youths under 20 years of age	7s. 6d.	5s.	6d.
Sack Race for Boys	5s.	2s. 9d.	6d.

A Grand Barrow Race for Old Women, 50 yards, First Prize, One Pound of Best Tea; Second, Half Pound of Tobacco—ENTRANCE, 6d.
A Cock Race for Boys under 14 years of age, each Lad to have his hands behind his back and catch the Cock with his Teeth, the Winner to have the Cock and Five Shillings. ENTRANCE, 6d.
A Grand Pig Race for a Pig, Value Two Pounds—ENTRANCE, 9d.
There will be a Dust Bag Race.

OLD AUNT SALLY AND OTHER AMUSEMENTS.

A BRASS BAND

Will be in attendance and Play some Select Music during the Day.

P.S.—The Costumes of all Competitors to meet the approval of the Stewards or be disqualified.

NO UNRULY CONDUCT ALLOWED.

Gates open at One o'clock, Sports to commence at Two.

Admittance to the Field, Adults, 6d.; Children under 12 years, 3d.

107

BRADBURY HOPPING

WILL BE HELD ON

SATURDAY, JULY 25th, 1874,

WHEN THE FOLLOWING

SPORTS

Will take place at the

PLOUGH INN,

VIZ.

Quoit Match for - - - - 15s.
First, to receive 12s. Second, 3s.

Foot Race for Men- - - 7s. 6d.
First, to receive 5s. Second, 2s. 6d.

Quoit Match for - - - - 10s.
First, to receive 7s. 6d. Second, 2s. 6d.

Entrance Fee, 6d. each.

Other Sports will take place

TOO NUMEROUS TO MENTION.

Bradbury, July 15th, 1874.

Hartlepool: J. PROCTER, Printer and Lithographer by Steam Power, Southgate.

108

FUN FOR THE MILL...

THE FOLLOWING PRIZES ARE TO BE COMPETED FOR,

On the Evening of the Regatta,

JUNE 26th, 1854,

IN FRONT OF VICTORIA TERRACE.

A

DONKEY RACE

For 15s.—First, to receive 10s.; Second, 5s.—Open to all the World.

A FOOT RACE BY WOMEN,

From 17 and upwards, for a Shawl and Bonnet. A

LEG OF MUTTON

Upon a Greasy Pole, to be Climbed for.

A FOOT RACE

By Girls, for a Pair of Shoes.

A WHEEL BARROW RACE BY MEN, BLINDF..LD,

For 5s.—Each Man to bring his own Barrow.

A Foot Race by Men,

For a Hat.

A FOOT RACE BY BOYS

Under 15, for a Pair Boy's Shoes, and a Cap.—First, to receive the Shoes; Second, the Cap.

Eating Rolls and Treacle, for 2s. 6d.

A PIG, VALUE £2,

To be Run for and Caught by the Tail.

A JINGLING MATCH FOR 5s.

SEARCHING FOR SILVER. DIPPING FOR ORANGES.

A FOOT RACE BY WOMEN

For a Gown Piece, Value 5s.

TO COMMENCE AT SEVEN O'CLOCK PRECISELY.

From the Office of J. PROCTER, Printer, 1 Victoria Terrace West Hartlepool.

109
This is the only boxing poster which has been found among John Procter's entire collection of bills. It would appear that either 'the noble art of self-defence' was not popular locally, or its exponents didn't need to print posters to attract crowds. The second suggestion is more likely because this solitary bill is the work of Mr. Smith of the George Inn who quite obviously likes to use his coat of arms. Moreover, the town-folk often saw John Gully, once Champion of All England and who owned collieries nearby, and poor Jem Mace, also a Champion, who earned a meagre salary putting on exhibitions of boxing in a local third-rate music-hall.

109

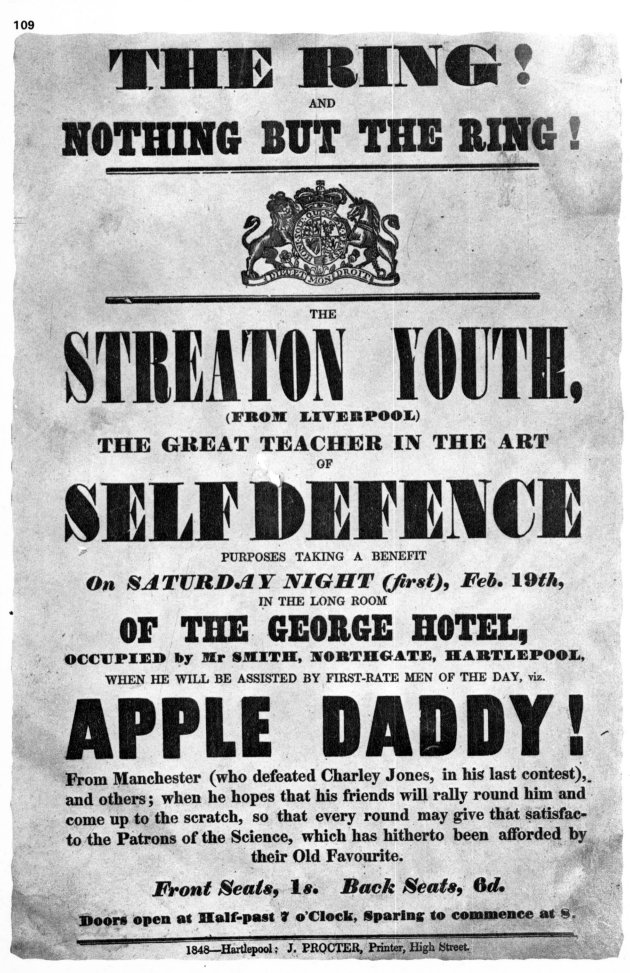

THE RING!

AND

NOTHING BUT THE RING!

THE

STREATON YOUTH,

(FROM LIVERPOOL)

THE GREAT TEACHER IN THE ART

OF

SELF DEFENCE

PURPOSES TAKING A BENEFIT

On SATURDAY NIGHT (first), Feb. 19th,

IN THE LONG ROOM

OF THE GEORGE HOTEL,

OCCUPIED by Mr SMITH, NORTHGATE, HARTLEPOOL,

WHEN HE WILL BE ASSISTED BY FIRST-RATE MEN OF THE DAY, viz.

APPLE DADDY!

From Manchester (who defeated Charley Jones, in his last contest), and others; when he hopes that his friends will rally round him and come up to the scratch, so that every round may give that satisfac-to the Patrons of the Science, which has hitherto been afforded by their Old Favourite.

Front Seats, 1s. Back Seats, 6d.

Doors open at Half-past 7 o'Clock, Sparing to commence at 8.

1848—Hartlepool: J. PROCTER, Printer, High Street.

110
It is very doubtful if Mr. Barr would make much money for there would be very few gentlemen within ten miles of the Warren who would be 'fond of this Ancient, Royal, and truly Aristocratic Sport.' The nautical element among the population would probably be too familiar with the not dissimilar activities of the seagulls at the fish quay. Nevertheless, this a neatly-designed poster displaying a variety of typefaces.

111
Fireworks constituted a very specialised form of entertainment which was extremely popular on suitable occasions. Tight-rope walkers, balloonists, and fireworks were all seen rarely but were therefore appreciated all the more.

110

UNUSUAL SPECTACLE

GRAND EXHIBITION OF

HAWKING.

MR. BARR,

The celebrated SCOTCH FALCONER,

WILL

FLY HIS PEREGRINE FALCONS,

On the WARREN, near Hartlepool,

On Saturday, 13th March, inst.

THE

First Falcon will leave the Hand,

PRECISELY AT TWO O'CLOCK, P. M.

Mr. BARR has with him SIX FALCONS, and plenty of Quarry.

☞ It is hoped that Gentlemen who are fond of this Ancient, Royal, and truly Aristocratic Sport, will honour the occasion with their presence.

ADMISSION INTO THE FIELD ONE SHILLING.

From the Office of J. PROCTER, High Street, Hartlepool, and Victoria Terrace, West Hartlepool.

BY PERMISSION OF THE WORSHIPFUL THE MAYOR.

For One Night only.

A SPLENDID DISPLAY OF

French, Italian, & Chinese

FIREWORKS

WILL TAKE PLACE

ON WEDNESDAY EVENING, JULY 30TH, 1851,

BY SUBSCRIPTION COLLECTED DURING THE DISPLAY,

IN THE MARKET PLACE,

HARTLEPOOL, BY

MR. L. V. GYNGELL

(From the Royal Gardens, Vauxhall, and the Royal Old Wells, Cheltenham,)

Who had the honor of exhibiting before the Queen at Perth, on the occasion of Her Majesty's visit to that City.

As an exhibition of this description must necessarily be attended with a very considerable expense, (saying nothing of the study and labour required to bring it to perfection) it is hoped that all who witness it will contribute to its support. Persons will be employed with Boxes to receive Subscriptions during the Display, from those persons standing in the street; and Mr. G. will feel obliged to those Ladies and Gentlemen seeing the Fireworks from the adjacent windows, by leaving their Contributions with the occupiers of the house from which they witness the Display.

Firing to commence at Half-past Nine o'clock.

Gentlemen supplied with Fireworks to any extent, for Birthday, Marriage, or other Fetes, by applying to Mr. GYNGELL, at Mrs. CUMMINS'S, Smithfield, Stockton.

From the Office of J. PROCTER, High Street, Hartlepool, and Victoria Terrace, West Hartlepool.

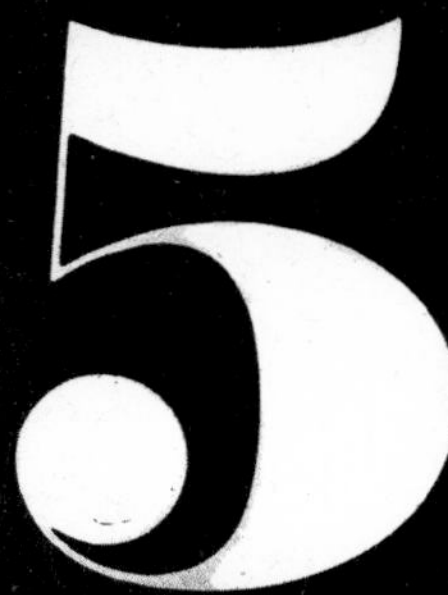

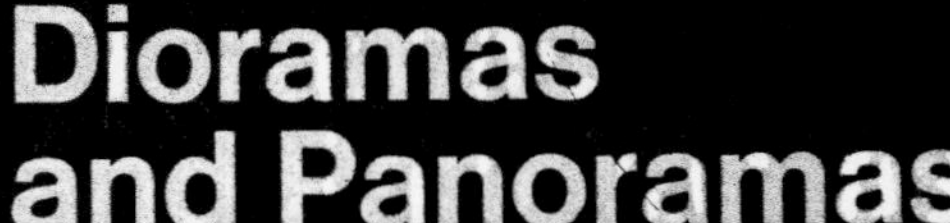

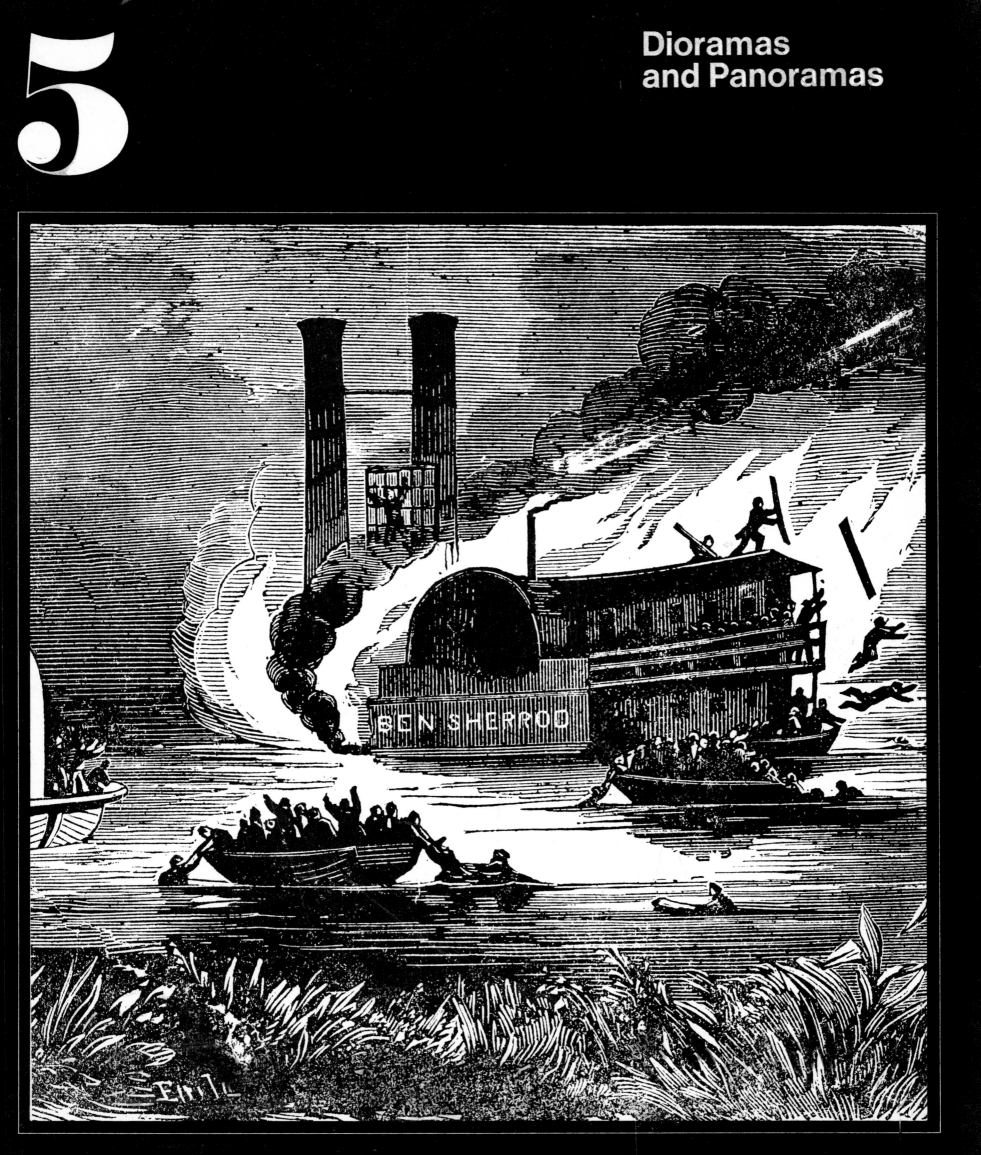

5 Dioramas and Panoramas

Dioramas and panoramas were the Victorian equivalent of television documentaries and newsreels. The history of this popular form of instructive entertainment can be traced back to the time of Queen Anne. A glance at some of the posters in this section will show how close a resemblance they bear to the show exhibited during her reign at the Great House in the Strand, alongside the Globe Tavern. Entrance, one shilling for the best places, sixpence for others.

'To be seen, the greatest Piece of Curiosity that ever arrived in England, being made by a famous engineer from the camp before Lisle, who with great labour and industry, has collected into a moving picture the following figures; first, it doth represent the confederate camp and the army lying intrenched before the town; secondly, the convoys and mules with Prince Eugene's baggage; thirdly, the English forces commanded by the Duke of Marlborough; likewise, several vessels laden with provisions for the army which are so artificially done as to seem to drive the water before them. The city and the citadel are very fine, with all its outworks, ravelins, horn-works, counterscarps, half-moons, and palisados; the French horse marching out at one gate, and the confederate army marching in at the other. The Prince's travelling coach with two generals in it, one saluting the company as it passes by; then a trumpeter sounds a call as he rides, at the noise whereof a sleeping sentinel starts and lifts up his head, but, not being espied, lies down to sleep again; besides abundance more admirable curiosities too tedious to be inserted here. In short, the whole piece is so contrived by art that it seems to be life and nature'.

By the 1830s dioramas and panoramas were really beginning to warrant a place of their own. They satisfied the great public demand for a moral, instructive exhibition which gave visual information about the world around and the events which took place in it. The automata and models of various sorts delighted the Victorians who were fascinated by mechanical marvels and delighted by the ingenuity of the craftsmen.

In the early part of the Queen's reign newspapers were still expensive and much beyond the taste and the pocket of the working classes. The sensational and the sordid still inspired broadsides and ballads which were sold in the markets to the mechanics and labourers. Dioramas and panoramas, however, supplied an agreeable compromise between these two extremes for they were the visual equivalent of the 'Family newspaper' so familiar to the generation previous to our own. Their proprietors wished to attract everyone so that their shows had to set a desirable moral tone to secure the approbation of ministers, schoolmasters and the like on whose goodwill they depended for a large proportion of their customers.

Spectacular displays such as a 'trip round Paris', the 'Overland Route to India', and the 'Battle of Trafalgar' were popular. A 'Tour of the Holy Land' was sure to attract the pious, and any programme dealing with Canada or America brought in those ambitious souls who thought of emigrating and those who were curious to see where their dear ones had settled down and the kind of new life that they might be leading. Voyages of exploration to the Polar Regions were eminently suitable, topical subjects. Battle scenes such as 'Waterloo' and 'Trafalgar' long continued to appear until in due course the canny showman was able to refurnish and refit them to provide the audience with up-to-date scenes from the 'Crimean War' and the 'Indian Mutiny'.

The more perceptive showmen were quick to exploit any local event or disaster which was suited to visual interpretation. 'The Wreck of the Forfarshire' and the 'Story of Grace Darling', and the dreadful 'Hartley Pit Disaster' were a godsend to the diorama showmen in the North of England.

A variety of methods were employed in running such a show. Whatever the name given to it – panorama, diorama, eidophusikon, eiduranion – it is safe to assume, in small towns certainly, that the show was never a true diorama, for that was an elaborate arrangement involving two circular rooms. The inner held the seated audience and revolved, allowing views to be seen through the single window into either of the two rooms arranged in the two halves of the outer circle. So complicated an arrangement was unlikely to be set up in a small town.

One kind of panorama consisted of a continuous painting on canvas round the walls of a room, with a three-dimensional foreground on which were displayed the mechanical figures which the visitors delighted in seeing. The 'Scissor grinder', the 'Boy trundling a Hoop', the Countryman' and the 'Stubborn Donkey going to Market', the 'Gamekeeper shooting the Hare' which was 'killed' at every performance, these presentations were always sufficiently popular to attract a substantial audience. This type of panorama is still to be seen at Innsbruck portraying the Tyrolean War of Independence.

Sometimes the painted backcloth was exhibited on a stage across which the scene was wound from one vertical roller to another. It is highly probable that, in all these variations of the entertainment, at stated times there was a 'performance' when the 'Professor' mounted a podium and supplied a commentary on what was passing before the eyes of the audience or alternatively took his visitors on a conducted tour of the exhibition. A band provided a background of suitable music.

But the man to tell us about dioramas is surely James Groves – the Professor Groves in this selection of bills – who wrote this in February 1843

'Sir,
Being desirous of visiting Hartlepool with my Dioramic Exhibition, now in Sunderland for the last three months (and the previous three months in Newcastle) I take the liberty of soliciting a little information as to the largest and most respectable Room or Hall to be obtained in Hartlepool for my purpose

The Exhibition is of the most Moral and Elegant description – of great mechanical ingenuity – and requires a very large Room for exhibiting the same – one about 50 foot long – 26 or 30 foot wide – about 16 high or more – also require a supply of gas for lighting the Exhibition – having my own fittings for the purpose and only require a supply from the nearest large pipe – the length of time we should require the use of the Room would be either one or two months.'

We have Procter's answer. Groves could have a room 45 ft by 21 ft and 14 ft high at a rent of six guineas. Groves must have been well satisfied for he returned again and again during the next twenty years and left Procter plenty of his bills.

112
Grace Darling and John Wesley seem rather a curious combination to place in the same programme but the showman knew his business and he was sure of an audience with 'Grace Darling and the Wreck of the Forfarshire'. Although shipwrecks were almost an everyday occurrence they always aroused interest, and on the north-east coast in particular the story of Grace Darling was well known. Is it possible that even in that pious age the career of John Wesley was not sufficiently exciting to attract the crowds without Grace Darling as a support?

113
The War in India was extraordinarily well received for its sensational details. It probably alternated with the Holy Land diorama because it is quite likely that the same oriental foreground was used for both, an arrangement which was most convenient for the showman. The local interest was very great for General Havelock, who relieved Lucknow, was of Sunderland extraction.

114
The Holy Land was an ever popular subject, as might be expected, and there was undoubtedly unending variation in the scripture stories illustrated. However, the showman was able to add something topical to the subject as a result of the Prince of Wales being escorted through Palestine, for it was always subsequently advertised as the 'Prince of Wales' Tour of the Holy Land'.

112

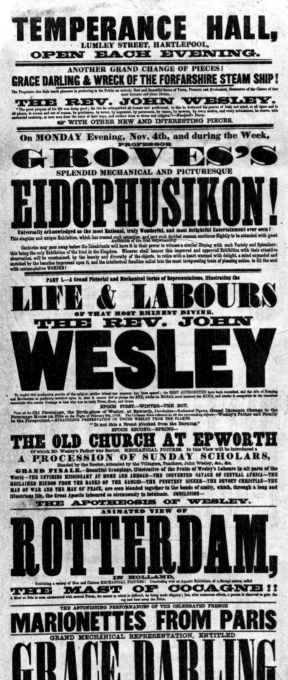

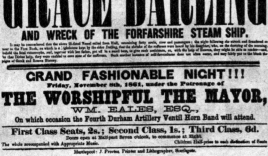

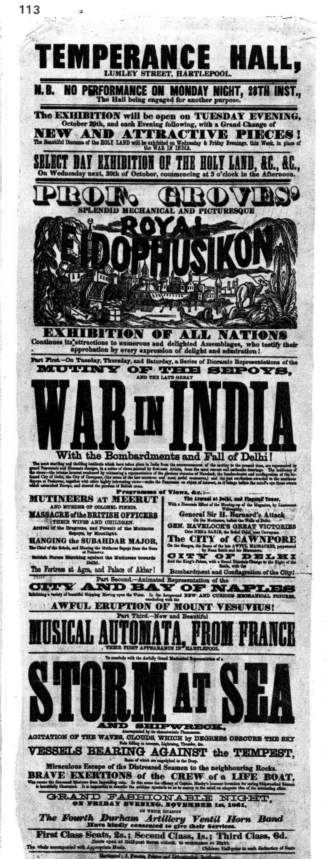

TEMPERANCE HALL,
LUMLEY STREET, HARTLEPOOL,
OPEN EACH EVENING.
ANOTHER GRAND CHANGE OF PIECES!
GRACE DARLING & WRECK OF THE FORFARSHIRE STEAM SHIP!
THE REV. JOHN WESLEY.
WITH OTHER NEW AND INTERESTING PIECES.
On MONDAY Evening, Nov. 4th, and during the Week,
PROFESSOR
GROVES'S
SPLENDID MECHANICAL AND PICTURESQUE
EIDOPHUSIKON!
PART I.—A Grand Pictorial and Mechanical Series of Representations, illustrating the
LIFE & LABOURS
OF THAT MOST EMINENT DIVINE,
THE REV. JOHN
WESLEY
EPOCH FIRST.—WINTER—THE BOY.
"Is not this a Brand plucked from the Burning."
EPOCH SECOND.—SPRING—
THE OLD CHURCH AT EPWORTH
A PROCESSION OF SUNDAY SCHOLARS,
THE APOTHEOSIS OF WESLEY.
ANIMATED VIEW OF
ROTTERDAM,
IN HOLLAND,
THE MAST OF COCAGNE!!
THE ASTONISHING PERFORMANCES OF THE CELEBRATED FRENCH
MARIONETTES FROM PARIS
GRAND MECHANICAL REPRESENTATION, ENTITLED
GRACE DARLING
AND WRECK OF THE FORFARSHIRE STEAM SHIP.
GRAND FASHIONABLE NIGHT!!!
Friday, November 8th, 1861, under the Patronage of
THE WORSHIPFUL THE MAYOR,
WM. HALES, ESQ.,
On which occasion the Fourth Durham Artillery Ventil Horn Band will attend.
First Class Seats, 2s.; Second Class, 1s.; Third Class, 6d.
Doors open at Half-past Seven o'clock, to commence at Eight.
The whole accompanied with Appropriate Music. Children Half-price to each distinction of Seats
Hartlepool: J. Procter, Printer and Lithographer, Southgate.

113

TEMPERANCE HALL,
LUMLEY STREET, HARTLEPOOL.
N.B. NO PERFORMANCE ON MONDAY NIGHT, 28TH INST.,
The Hall being engaged for another purpose.
The EXHIBITION will be open on TUESDAY EVENING, October 29th, and each Evening following, with a Grand Change of
NEW AND ATTRACTIVE PIECES!
The Beautiful Diorama of the HOLY LAND will be exhibited on Wednesday & Friday Evenings, this Week, in place of the WAR IN INDIA.
SELECT DAY EXHIBITION OF THE HOLY LAND, &C., &C.,
On Wednesday next, 30th of October, commencing at 3 o'clock in the Afternoon.
PROF. GROVES'
SPLENDID MECHANICAL AND PICTURESQUE

EXHIBITION OF ALL NATIONS
Continues its attractions to numerous and delighted Assemblages, who testify their approbation by every expression of delight and admiration!
Part First.—On Tuesday, Thursday, and Saturday, a Series of Dioramic Representations of the
MUTINY OF THE SEPOYS,
AND THE LATE GREAT
WAR IN INDIA
With the Bombardments and Fall of Delhi!
Programme of Views, &c.:—
MUTINEERS AT MEERUT
MASSACRE of the BRITISH OFFICERS
HANGING the SUBAHDAR MAJOR,
The Fortress at Agra, and Palace of Akbar!
General Sir H. Barnard's Attack
GEN. HAVELOCK'S GREAT VICTORIES
The CITY of CAWNPORE
CITY OF DELHI
Bombardment and Conflagration of the City!
Part Second.—Animated Representation of the
CITY AND BAY OF NAPLES
AWFUL ERUPTION OF MOUNT VESUVIUS!
Part Third.—New and Beautiful
MUSICAL AUTOMATA, FROM FRANCE
THEIR FIRST APPEARANCE IN HARTLEPOOL.
STORM AT SEA
AND SHIPWRECK,
AGITATION OF THE WAVES, CLOUDS, WHICH by DEGREES OBSCURE THE SKY
VESSELS BEARING AGAINST the TEMPEST,
Miraculous Escape of the Distressed Seamen to the neighbouring Rocks.
BRAVE EXERTIONS of the CREW of a LIFE BOAT,
GRAND FASHIONABLE NIGHT,
ON FRIDAY EVENING, NOVEMBER 1st, 1861,
ON WHICH OCCASION
The Fourth Durham Artillery Ventil Horn Band
Have kindly consented to give their Services.
First Class Seats, 2s.; Second Class, 1s.; Third Class, 6d.
Doors open at Half-past Seven o'clock, to commence at Eight.
The whole accompanied with Appropriate Music. Children Half-price to each distinction of Seats
Hartlepool: J. Procter, Printer and Lithographer, Southgate.

114

FOR A SHORT TIME ONLY!
AT THE
ATHENÆUM,
WEST HARTLEPOOL,
Commencing on Thursday, Friday, and Saturday Evenings next, December 5th, 6th, and 7th, 1861,
PROF. GROVES'S
SPLENDID MECHANICAL AND PICTURESQUE
EIDOPHUSIKON!
AND
THEATRE OF ARTS
CONSISTING OF
HISTORICAL ANIMATED ILLUSTRATIONS
OF THE MOST INTERESTING PARTS OF THE WORLD.
Enlivened with Thousands of Chaste Mechanical Figures
HOLY LAND!!
With Descriptive Illustrations from Scripture, by the proprietor.
NEW & WONDERFUL MOVING FIGURES!!

BETHLEHEM.	FORDS of the JORDAN.
JERUSALEM.	THE RIVER KISHON.
BROOK KEDRON.	MOUNT TABOR.
ANCIENT OLIVE TREES.	Tiberias and Sea of Galilee.
	JERICHO.

ZURICH!
FOUR SEASONS!
SPRING, SUMMER, AUTUMN, AND WINTER,
FRENCH AUTOMATA,
FROM PARIS.
CAPT. ROSS' VOYAGE
TO THE NORTH POLE,
IN SEARCH OF
SIR JOHN FRANKLIN!
FLOATING MOUNTAINS; ICEBERGS
THE PALACE OF WINTER
First Class Seats, 2s.; Second Class, 1s.; Third Class, 6d.
The whole accompanied with Appropriate Music. Children Half-price to each distinction of Seats
Hartlepool: J. Procter, Printer and Lithographer, Southgate.

115
This poster needs no introduction.

116
Threepence and a Pass! The card may have been labelled 'Half Price Ticket' but it was probably given to a shop-keeper in return for displaying one of Professor Groves' posters in his window. Such a card warranting cheap admission has always been known as a Pass.

117
Another method of obtaining custom was to send schoolmasters a letter of this sort 'Mr. Friend presents his compliments, and begs to enclose a free admission to his Beautiful Entertainment and should it be desirable that the whole of the School attend, arrangements may be entered into, to admit them at a great reduction of price.'

118
The majority of dioramas and panoramas had a band, orchestra or vocalist. Mr. Henri Nunn is advertised as 'The celebrated Pianist and Baritone Vocalist from the Pavilion, Canterbury, and Oxford Music Halls, London'. It is pardonable if we take this statement with a pinch of salt, for these were the leading music halls of the time, and if Mr. Henri Nunn had any connection with them then the citizens would surely wonder why he should so lower himself.

115

WAR
IN
INDIA
WITH THE BOMBARDMENT AND
FALL OF DELHI
Embracing all the principal and most Startling Incidents, from the commencement to the present time. Painted by first-class Artists, from the most correct and authentic Drawings. The
MUTINEERS AT MEERUT
AND MURDER OF COLONEL FINNIS.
MASSACRE OF THE BRITISH OFFICERS
THEIR WIVES AND CHILDREN.
Arrival of the Dragoons, and Pursuit of the Mutinous Sepoys, by Moonlight.
HANGING the SUBAHDAR MAJOR
The Chief of the Rebels, and Blowing the Mutinous Sepoys from the Guns at Peshawur.
British Forces Marching against the Mutineers towards Delhi.
The Fortress at Agra, and Palace of Akbar!
The Arsenal at Delhi, and Flagstaff Tower,
With a Dioramic Effect of the Blowing-up of the Magazine, by Lieutenant Willoughby.
General Sir H. Barnard's Attack
On the Mutineers, before the Walls of Delhi.
GEN. HAVELOCK'S GREAT VICTORIES
Over NENA SAHIB, the Rebel Chief, near Cawnpore.
The CITY of CAWNPORE
On the Ganges, the Scene of the late AWFUL MASSACRES, perpetrated by Nena Sahib and his Miscreants.
CITY OF DELHI
And the King's Palace, with a Grand Dioramic Change to the Night of the Battle, with the
Bombardment and Conflagration of the City
To be followed with other Interesting Performances, including the
STORM AT SEA!
AND SHIPWRECK.
First Class Seats, 2s.; Second Class, 1s.; Third Class, 6d.
Doors open at half-past Seven o'clock, to commence at Eight.
The whole accompanied with appropriate Music. Children Half-price to each distinction of Seats.

116

New Diorama of Syria and the Holy Land. City and Lake of Zurich, &c.

HALF PRICE TICKET
TO PROFESSOR GROVES'
ROYAL EIDOPHUSIKON EXHIBITION!!
Of the most interesting Parts of the World, with its WONDERFUL MECHANICAL FIGURES.
Now Open for a few Evenings at the Theatre, West Hartlepool.
This Ticket will admit the Bearer at Half the usual Price to either distinction of Seats, any Evening this Week.
Bring this Ticket and pay at the Door.

Prices without this Ticket.		Prices with this Ticket.	
First Class	2s.	First Class	1s.
Second Class	1s.	Second Class	6d.
Third Class	6d.	Third Class	3d.

Doors open at Half-past Seven, to commence at Eight.

Captain Ross's Voyage in search of Sir John Franklin, &c.

117

ATHENÆUM, WEST HARTLEPOOL,
FOR SIX DAYS ONLY,
COMMENCING ON FRIDAY, JUNE 16th, 1865.
A GRAND TREAT
For Day and Sunday School Scholars, their Parents and Friends, to DRAKE'S Magnificent Moving Pictorial and Mechanical Exhibition of the
OVERLAND ROUTE TO INDIA,
AND WANDERINGS IN THE FAR EAST,
Illustrating the manners and Customs of the Hindoos, accompanied with
SONGS AND MUSIC,
This Ticket will admit the Bearer at HALF-PRICE to any part of the Room; it will also admit Children under 12 years of age for One Penny to Afternoon Exhibitions only.
TWO EXHIBITIONS EACH DAY,
At Three and Eight o'clock. Doors open an Half-hour previous.
NOTICE.—Prices without this Ticket 2s., 1s., and 6d.

118

CONCLUDING VIEW.
One of the Wonders of the World, The Rocky Temple of Ellroa, by Day, changing by an extraordinary Dioramic Effect, to the Temple by Night, with the Shrine of the Goddess Khalee, Brilliantly Illuminated, and Representing the Adoration of the Brahmins of Khalee, the Goddess, wife of Siva the Destroyer. Words cannot do justice to the beauty of this most exquisite and Matchless Production.
MR. HENRI NUNN,
The celebrated Pianist and Baritone Vocalist, from the Pavilion, Canterbury, and Oxford Music Halls, London, will appear at each Representation, and sing a choice selection of songs.

119

The miners who went to the Londonderry Institute at Seaham Harbour were just as likely to be considering emigration across the Atlantic as they were to be increasing their geographical knowledge The local newspapers were full of long letters from obscure places in Canada and the U.S.A. written by past citizens with the express purpose of giving those left behind information about the differences of climate and the chances of employment.

120

The description of the departure of the Children of Israel bears a striking resemblance in form and manner to that of the exhibition at the Globe Tavern in Queen Anne's reign mentioned in the introduction to this section. Note the dogmatic way in which it is stated that 'Religious scruples against visiting Exhibitions are laid aside in cases of Panoramas,' and they have 'no affinity to Theatrical Performances.' These statements get to the heart of the matter and explain the popularity of such shows.

119

120

PANORAMA-LE-GRAND, FROM THE PALAIS ROYAL, RUE ST. HONORE, PARIS,

NOW OPEN,

IN THE LARGE ~~EXHIBITION~~ ROOM,

~~SADDLER-STREET, DURHAM~~ George Inn, Northgate, Hartlepool

The Director in calling Public attention to this STUPENDOUS and ELABORATE WORK OF ART, begs leave to state that during its Exhibition at the Academy of Arts, Newcastle, for the last Two Months, it has met with the most decided approbation; and at the request of several Families of ~~Distinction, it will remain~~ OPEN

FOR SIX DAYS LONGER,

Monday 12th Sept 1842 INCLUDING SATURDAY, SEPTEMBER 3, 1842.

MONSIEUR P. DAGUIRE & Co.'s

CELEBRATED HISTORICAL, PERISTREPHIC, REVOLVING, DIORAMIC

PANORAMA

PAINTED BY EMINENT FOREIGN AND BRITISH ARTISTS,

ON AN IMMENSE SHEET OF CANVASS, UPWARDS OF

16,000 SQUARE FEET.

☞ The Conductor, in calling the attention of the Public, begs leave to state that as representations of occurrences like the present can only be interesting as they are faithful, no expense or trouble has been spared to attain this object. He confidently anticipates the patronage of an enlightened public, being a faithful portrait of the most important events in ancient and modern History.

Religious scruples against visiting Exhibitions are laid aside in cases of Panoramas. The subjects being founded on facts, they are consequently patronised by Clergymen, Seminaries, and all religious classes of the community; having no affinity to Theatrical Performances.

The Subjects are as follow:—The Departure of the

CHILDREN OF ISRAEL

Out of Egypt, under the guidance of Moses and Aaron,

(From the Picture by the celebrated David Roberts, Esq.)

The Picture represents the dawn breaking; the first lighting up of the summits of the gigantic Pyramids which are seen in the distance, and then falling in slant lines across the stately Obelisk and Pinnacles, which adorn the prodigious display of Palaces and Temples which are towering above each other, and Collonades, tier on tier, forming one of the grandest sights that can possibly be imagined. The subject of this picture is one of the most memorable events recorded in the history of the Israelites. In the space of 430 years, the single family of Jacob increased to about Six Hundred Thousand Men, besides a corresponding number of Women aud Children. They are seen in a continuous mass, marching out in order, with their Banners and Ensigns, their Camels, Elephants, and Flocks; their two leaders, Moses and Aaron, are seen conspicuous, King Pharoah and the Royal party are witnessing their departure which no man dared longer to oppose.

THE HOLY CITY OF

JERUSALEM

FROM THE MOUNT OF OLIVES,

Painted from Drawings made on the Spot, by David Roberts, Esq.

It embraces the whole Town, and nearly all its most striking details. The Mosque of Omer, formerly the Golden Temple, erected by King Solomon for the Ark of the Covenant. The Mosque El Aksa, formerly the Church of the Purification. Mount Zion, on which stood the City of David. The Citadel or Stronghold of Zion. The Greek Church, on the site of which our Lord instituted the Last Supper. The Site of Herod's Palace. The Tomb of David. The Golden Gate of the Temple. The Gate of St. Stephen. The Tomb of Absalom. The Valley of Jehosaphat, at the bottom of which runs the brook Kedron, Groups of Figures are seen, Turks, Armenians, Jews, Pilgrims, and Arabs,—giving a correct idea of the Inhabitants, while the Churches and Mosques, with their dome, roofs, and splendid minarets, give an exact representation of this ancient City, the seat of our earliest civilization.

NAPOLEON'S

FUNERAL PROCESSION,

On the 15th of December, 1840, *two Miles long; from the Arc' de Triomphe to the Palace of the Tuilleries.*

The Drawing for this View was made from a platform erected on the Avenue-de-Neuilly (the most interesting position that could be chosen), embracing the TRIUMPHAL ARCH, the Barrier-de-l'Etoile, the Road to Neuilly, St. Germain, &c. The Triumphal Car was the most beautiful thing of the kind that could possibly be conceived, being entirely of burnished gold, and drawn by sixteen black horses richly caparisoned. No description can give an adequate idea of the enthusiasm which this ceremony excited: every where on the passage of the Hearse, the loudest acclamations resounded, and cries of "Vive L' Empereur!" rent the air, but more particularly when they reached the "Arc' de Triomphe." In the procession are to be noticed Prince de Joinville, General Bertrand, and many of Napoleon's old Officers. Soldiers who fought at Jena, Wagram, Friedland, and Austerlitz: —men, who seem as if risen from the dead, to figure for a moment in the Pageant. The crowd that thronged thither is beyond description, those who have endeavoured to describe it, say that it was an overwhelming torrent; wherever the eye could rest was covered with human beings.

120A
Details from 120.

121
The description of this exhibition gives us a clear picture of the sort of thing that could be found inside by the visitor. The views of cities, rivers, etc. are 'Got up in such a way as to appear at Miles distant'. There is great emphasis on the mechanical figures and the models of ships which appear in these landscapes and the moving panorama is simply described. The bill is a delight from an earlier age when such shows did not need to be described in the pretentious language of 'Eidophusikons' and 'Eiduranions'.

120A

PAINTED BY EMINENT FOREIGN AND BRITISH ARTISTS,
ON AN IMMENSE SHEET OF CANVASS, UPWARDS OF
16,000 SQUARE FEET.

☞ The Conductor, in calling the attention of the Public, begs leave to state that as representations of occurrences like the present can only be interesting as they are faithful, no expense or trouble has been spared to attain this object. He confidently anticipates the patronage of an enlightened public, being a faithful portrait of the most important events in ancient and modern History.

Religious scruples against visiting Exhibitions are laid aside in cases of Panoramas. The subjects being founded on facts, they are consequently patronised by Clergymen, Seminaries, and all religious classes of the community; having no affinity to Theatrical Performances.

The Subjects are as follow:—The Departure of the
CHILDREN OF ISRAEL
Out of Egypt, under the guidance of Moses and Aaron,
(From the Picture by the celebrated David Roberts, Esq.)

The Picture represents the dawn breaking; the first lighting up of the summits of the gigantic Pyramids which are seen in the distance, and then falling in slant lines across the stately Obelisk and Pinnacles, which adorn the prodigious display of Palaces and Temples which are towering above each other, and Collonades, tier on tier, forming one of the grandest sights that can possibly be imagined. The subject of this picture is one of the most memorable events recorded in the history of the Israelites. In the space of 430 years, the single family of Jacob increased to about Six Hundred Thousand Men, besides a corresponding number of Women and Children. They are seen in a continuous mass, marching out in order, with their Banners and Ensigns, their Camels, Elephants, and Flocks; their two leaders, Moses and Aaron, are seen conspicuous, King Pharoah and the Royal party are witnessing their departure which no man dared longer to oppose.

THE HOLY CITY OF
JERUSALEM
FROM THE MOUNT OF OLIVES,
Painted from Drawings made on the Spot, by David Roberts, Esq.

It embraces the whole Town, and nearly all its most striking details. The Mosque of Omer, formerly the Golden Temple, erected by King Solomon for the Ark of the Covenant. The Mosque El Aksa, formerly the Church of the Purification. Mount Zion, on which stood the City of David. The Citadel or Stronghold of Zion. The Greek Church, on the site of which our Lord instituted the Last Supper. The Site of Herod's Palace. The Tomb of David. The Golden Gate of the Temple. The Gate of St. Stephen. The Tomb of Absalom. The Valley of Jehosaphat, at the bottom of which runs the brook Kedron. Groups of Figures are seen, Turks, Armenians, Jews, Pilgrims, and Arabs,—giving a correct idea of the Inhabitants, while the Churches and Mosques, with their dome, roofs, and splendid minarets, give an exact representation of this ancient City, the seat of our earliest civilization.

NAPOLEON'S
FUNERAL PROCESSION,
On the 15th of December, 1840, two Miles long; from the Arc' de Triomphe to the Palace of the Tuilleries.

The Drawing for this View was made from a platform erected on the Avenue-de-Neuilly (the most interesting position that could be chosen), embracing the TRIUMPHAL ARCH, the Barrier-de-l'Etoile, the Road to Neuilly, St. Germain, &c. The Triumphal Car was the most beautiful thing of the kind that could possibly be conceived, being entirely of burnished gold, and drawn by sixteen black horses richly caparisoned. No description can give an adequate idea of the enthusiasm which this ceremony excited: every where on the passage of the Hearse, the loudest acclamations resounded, and cries of "Vive L' Empereur!" rent the air, but more particularly when they reached the "Arc' de Triomphe." In the procession are to be noticed Prince de Joinville, General Bertrand, and many of Napoleon's old Officers. Soldiers who fought at Jena, Wagram, Friedland, and Austerlitz:—men, who seem as if risen from the dead, to figure for a moment in the Pageant. The crowd that thronged thither is beyond description, those who have endeavoured to describe it, say that it was an overwhelming torrent; wherever the eye could rest was covered with human beings.

121

WILL OPEN IN A FEW DAYS,

HILL'S.

Grand Mechanical

AND OPTICAL EXHIBITION,

CONSISTING OF

Views of Cities, Rivers, &c.

Got up in such a way as to appear at Miles distant, and animated with numbers of

MECHANICAL FIGURES,

Shewing the movements of Life with great precision.—Ships of various Nations are seen on the Rivers, passing and repassing.

A GRAND MOVING PANORAMA OF

PALESTINE,

OR THE HOLY LAND,

Being 14 Views of that Country, dear to every Christian.

A COPIOUS DESCRIPTION GIVEN WITH EACH SCENE.

A BEAUTIFUL DISPLAY OF OPTICAL AND CHEMICAL

PYROTECNICS,

&c. &c.

The whole has been exhibited with unbounded applause, to crowded audiences, for the last Nine Weeks, at Shields, and highly gratified the curiosity of the discerning Public.

In this Exhibition, there is nothing to give offence to the most scrupulous religionist, but rather, while it amuses, it is calculated to instruct all classes, particularly the Panorama of that country, where the Bible was written, and where man's salvation was purchased.

Bills, descriptive of the Exhibition, will appear previous to opening.

PRINTED BY J. PROCTER, HARTLEPOOL.

122
Another panorama, but one which is only appearing for three days. The explanation for this rapid move would seem to be that Mr. Gompertz's exhibition had previously been at the Athenaeum, West Hartlepool. As that was not very far away it would have been very easy for Mr. Gompertz to arrange one show for Hartlepool whilst he was conducting another in West Hartlepool.

123
The great Mr. Friend may have given unparalleled entertainment but he did it with great haste. Most panoramas stayed for at least a month in one place, but not Mr. Friend. He wrote from Sunderland on November 7th, 1856 enquiring about the size of the best hall in Hartlepool and gave his itinerary as Durham, Darlington, Stockton, and then Hartlepool during the first week in December.

124
Sir, I shall feel truly obliged by your informing me whether any astronomical lectures have been recently given in your town, also the charge for the hire of the most eligible room, and your own terms for printing the usual number of bills for the town. If you are disposed to speculate I beg to submit the following proposition—viz That you print and circulate the bills—pay for the hire of the room—in fact be at all the expense, and that we divide the cash received for the admission of the public to the lecture equally. If the matter was well-worked I think it would prove mutually advantageous
Your obt. Servt. H. Simpson

122

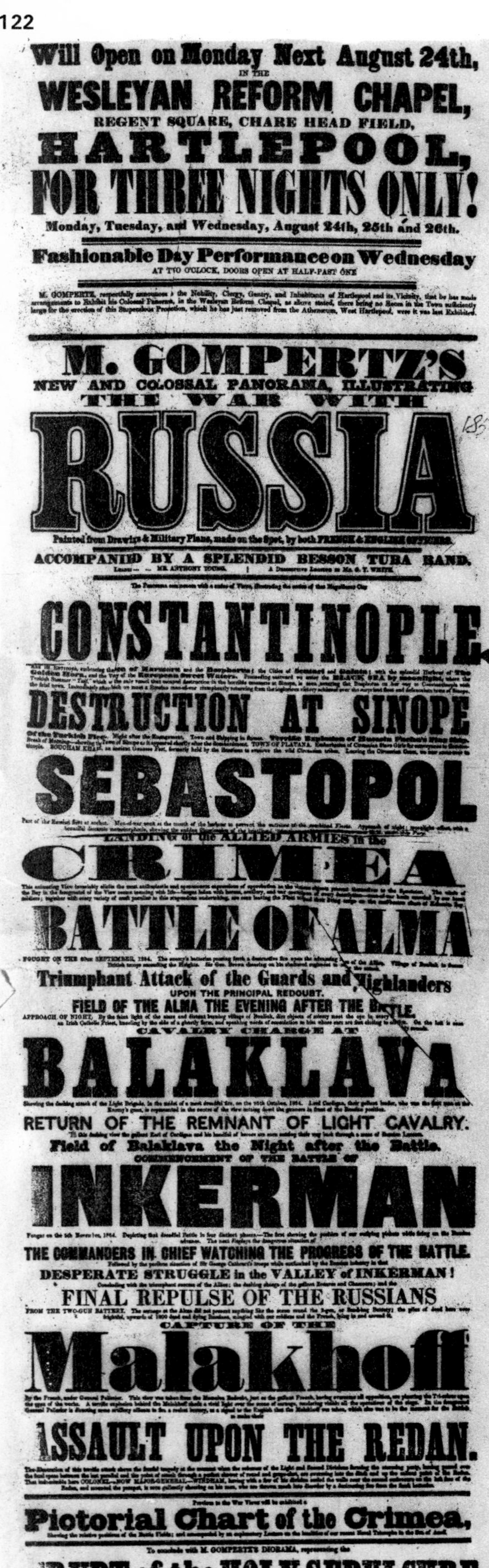

123

124

123A, 123B and 123C
These extracts from Mr. Friend's poster require no explanation. The language is deliciously Victorian.

125 (overleaf)
A Magic Lantern Show? We shall never know what the audience saw in that school room, whether they were illuminated transparencies or real lantern slides, but one thing is certain they would be watched with rapt attention.

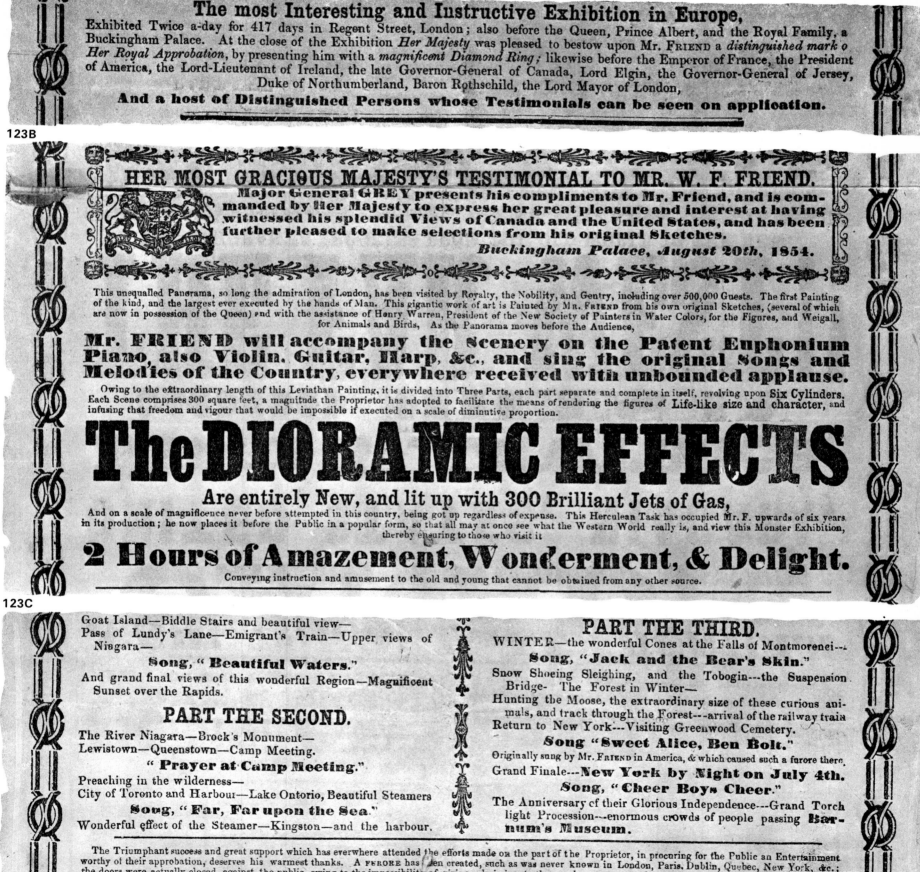

123A

The most Interesting and Instructive Exhibition in Europe,

Exhibited Twice a-day for 417 days in Regent Street, London; also before the Queen, Prince Albert, and the Royal Family, a Buckingham Palace. At the close of the Exhibition *Her Majesty* was pleased to bestow upon Mr. Friend a *distinguished mark o Her Royal Approbation*, by presenting him with a *magnificent Diamond Ring;* likewise before the Emperor of France, the President of America, the Lord-Lieutenant of Ireland, the late Governor-General of Canada, Lord Elgin, the Governor-General of Jersey, Duke of Northumberland, Baron Rothschild, the Lord Mayor of London,

And a host of Distinguished Persons whose Testimonials can be seen on application.

123B

HER MOST GRACIOUS MAJESTY'S TESTIMONIAL TO MR. W. F. FRIEND.

Major General GREY presents his compliments to Mr. Friend, and is commanded by Her Majesty to express her great pleasure and interest at having witnessed his splendid Views of Canada and the United States, and has been further pleased to make selections from his original Sketches.

Buckingham Palace, August 20th, 1854.

This unequalled Panorama, so long the admiration of London, has been visited by Royalty, the Nobility, and Gentry, including over 500,000 Guests. The first Painting of the kind, and the largest ever executed by the hands of Man. This gigantic work of art is Painted by Mr. Friend from his own original Sketches, (several of which are now in possession of the Queen) and with the assistance of Henry Warren, President of the New Society of Painters in Water Colors, for the Figures, and Weigall, for Animals and Birds, As the Panorama moves before the Audience,

Mr. FRIEND will accompany the Scenery on the Patent Euphonium Piano, also Violin, Guitar, Harp, &c., and sing the original Songs and Melodies of the Country, everywhere received with unbounded applause.

Owing to the extraordinary length of this Leviathan Painting, it is divided into Three Parts, each part separate and complete in itself, revolving upon Six Cylinders. Each Scene comprises 300 square feet, a magnitude the Proprietor has adopted to facilitate the means of rendering the figures of Life-like size and character, and infusing that freedom and vigour that would be impossible if executed on a scale of diminutive proportion.

The DIORAMIC EFFECTS

Are entirely New, and lit up with 300 Brilliant Jets of Gas,

And on a scale of magnificence never before attempted in this country, being got up regardless of expense. This Herculean Task has occupied Mr. F. upwards of six years in its production; he now places it before the Public in a popular form, so that all may at once see what the Western World really is, and view this Monster Exhibition, thereby ensuring to those who visit it

2 Hours of Amazement, Wonderment, & Delight.

Conveying instruction and amusement to the old and young that cannot be obtained from any other source.

123C

Goat Island—Biddle Stairs and beautiful view—
Pass of Lundy's Lane—Emigrant's Train—Upper views of Niagara—

Song, "Beautiful Waters."

And grand final views of this wonderful Region—Magnificent Sunset over the Rapids.

PART THE SECOND.

The River Niagara—Brock's Monument—
Lewistown—Queenstown—Camp Meeting.

"Prayer at Camp Meeting."

Preaching in the wilderness—
City of Toronto and Harbour—Lake Ontorio, Beautiful Steamers

Song, "Far, Far upon the Sea."

Wonderful effect of the Steamer—Kingston—and the harbour.

PART THE THIRD.

WINTER—the wonderful Cones at the Falls of Montmorenci---

Song, "Jack and the Bear's Skin."

Snow Shoeing Sleighing, and the Tobogin---the Suspension Bridge- The Forest in Winter—
Hunting the Moose, the extraordinary size of these curious animals, and track through the Forest---arrival of the railway train
Return to New York---Visiting Greenwood Cemetery.

Song "Sweet Alice, Ben Bolt."

Originally sung by Mr. Friend in America, & which caused such a furore there.

Grand Finale---**New York by Night on July 4th.**

Song, "Cheer Boys Cheer."

The Anniversary of their Glorious Independence---Grand Torch light Procession---enormous crowds of people passing **Barnum's Museum.**

The Triumphant success and great support which has everwhere attended the efforts made on the part of the Proprietor, in procuring for the Public an Entertainment worthy of their approbation, deserves his warmest thanks. A FURORE has been created, such as was never known in London, Paris, Dublin, Quebec, New York, &c.; the doors were actually closed against the public, owing to the impossibility of giving admission to the numbers congregated around them. A similar triumph may be anticipated, during the remainder of his short stay in this Country, from the well-known fact that it is the GREAT ORIGINAL, and only real Canvas Moving Panorama of Canada travelling.

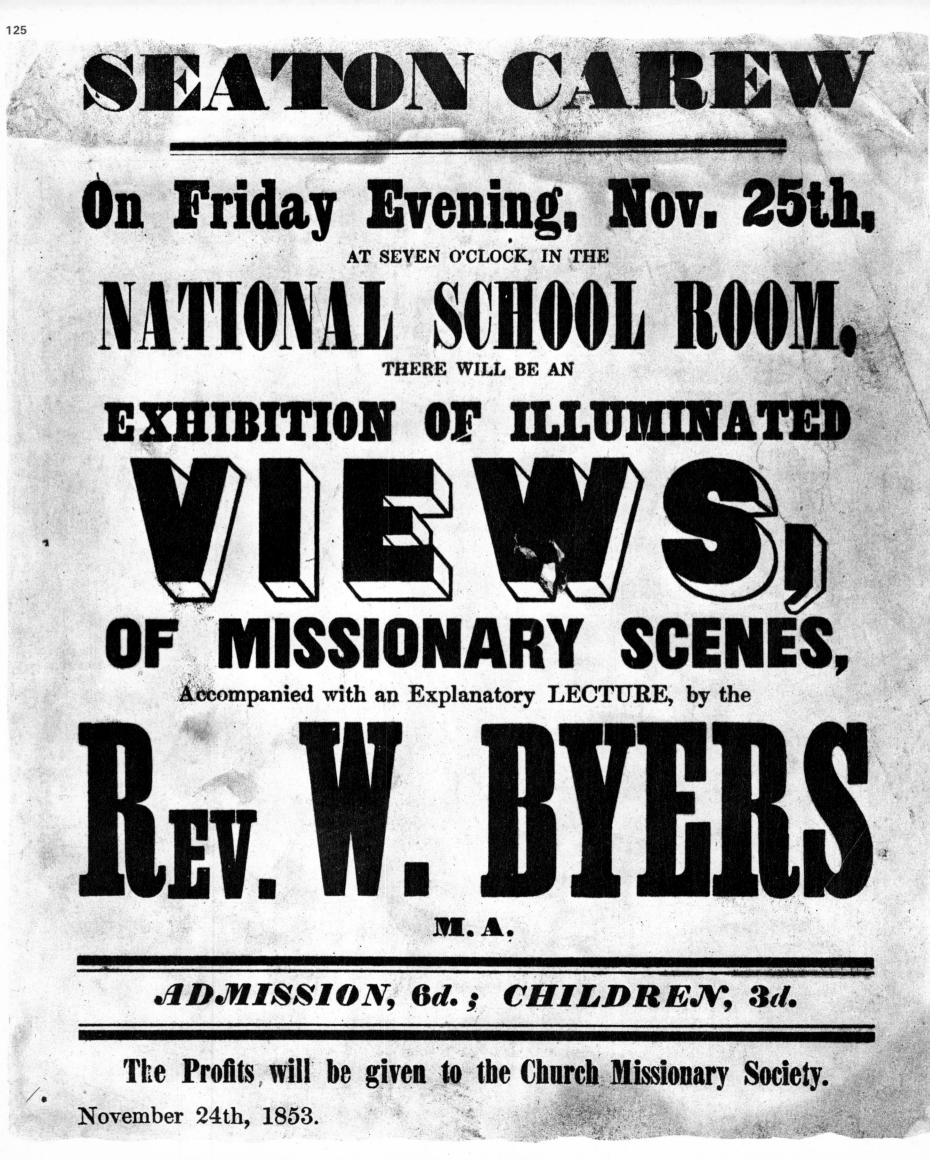

SEATON CAREW

On Friday Evening, Nov. 25th,

AT SEVEN O'CLOCK, IN THE

NATIONAL SCHOOL ROOM,

THERE WILL BE AN

EXHIBITION OF ILLUMINATED

VIEWS,

OF MISSIONARY SCENES,

Accompanied with an Explanatory LECTURE, by the

REV. W. BYERS

M. A.

ADMISSION, 6d.; CHILDREN, 3d.

The Profits will be given to the Church Missionary Society.

November 24th, 1853.

6

Music

One of the philanthropic causes pre-eminent in the minds of all responsible citizens at the beginning of Queen Victoria's reign was that of national education. Although much has been made of the insistence on instruction in the Three R's and the utilitarian nature of the curriculum, a closer examination of the subject proves that music, especially of the vocal sort, occupied an important place in the time-table of most National Schools.

The teaching of vocal music in junior schools was urged on moral and disciplinary grounds, in addition to that of improving the general taste in music and providing a happy atmosphere for the children. It was said that music 'Has a tendency to wean the mind from vicious and sensual indulgences; and if properly directed, it has a tendency to incline the heart to kindly feeling, and just and generous emotions.'

It was as a result of these beliefs in music's 'improving' qualities that there arose a general movement to make the musical instruction and education of the young, more efficient. John Hullah (1812-1884) was a pioneer with musical classes in Battersea, London, and throughout his life he endeavoured to perfect a clear and adequate system for the teaching of music to large groups, and to ensure that his methods were properly understood by the students in teacher-training colleges before they practised them in schools. Another pioneer of the mass teaching of music was Joseph Mainzer who preferred to educate the public by providing lectures and voluntary classes. Then came the Rev. John Curwen who was the great advocate of the Tonic Sol-fa System.

But the love of music had revealed itself in the working classes ever since the crowded living conditions in the towns of the Industrial Revolution, and the lack of space in which to carry on their rural recreations, had caused them to find their own amusements, as inexpensively as possible. The making of music, both vocal and instrumental, came high on their programme of enjoyable activities. The recorder of earlier days was superseded by the German flute which had a more penetrating tone quality and a wider range of notes. This instrument provided pleasure for the individual in the home, but the instruments of a band enabled a group to make music together.

Bands were popular long before Victoria came to the throne. The military bands of the eighteenth century had started the fashion, and, by the end of the reign of George III, most small towns and many villages had their own bands, as had many factories and other industrial undertakings.

On May 23rd, 1822 when the first rail of the Stockton and Darlington Railway was laid, the Yarm band headed the procession, and the band from Greatham climbed into the trucks of the first train from Stockton when it steamed into Hartlepool in 1840 and played all the way.

The lead miners of the Yorkshire dales had bands in many of the remote villages by 1825. These were subsidised by their employers, the London Lead Company. The band of a Welsh ironworks was hired for five days in 1831 to assist at a Breconshire election, whilst a Durham ironworks band frequently accompanied excursions by paddle-boat to Scarborough and Whitby.

Those town dwellers who had migrated from rural areas brought with them the ballads handed on in their villages by oral tradition, but there was also another source of supply. Throughout the eighteenth century, and well into the nineteenth, a thriving business was done by printers and hawkers of chapbooks, broadsides, and pamphlets. Although many of them were coarse and sensational their very success was the reason for the survival of some of the best British traditional folk tunes and ballads.

A more scholarly interest had been shown by Bishop Percy whose 'Reliques of Ancient English Poetry' appeared in 1765, but he did not publish any of the tunes. On the other hand 'The Scots Musical Museum' which appeared in the 1790s had a tune for each song but the words were often rewritten, some of them by Robert Burns. It was left to local enthusiasts to preserve many of the tunes we love today. The names of the Rev. Baring Gould, Cecil Sharp, Percy Grainger, and Vaughan Williams are all connected with the most active period of folksong collecting, the years between the founding of the English Folk Song Society in 1898 and the outbreak of war in 1914, but as early as 1784 Joseph Ritson published 'The Bishoprick Garland', a collection of songs and verses associated with County Durham. William Shield, a Tynesider, and a composer who became musical director of Covent Garden Theatre, in London, used some Border tunes in a publication of 1817.

Around this time there appeared a publication 'Melodies of the Tyne and Wear' which contained twenty-four tunes and the words to thirteen of them. This was the work of Robert Topliff, a native of Sunderland, a blind man who was organist of Trinity Church, Southwark, in London, and who came back to his beloved North year after year to give lectures and recitals and sing the pit songs he loved so well. One of his programmes is reproduced on a later page. To him we owe the publication of 'Bobby Shaftoe', 'The Keel Row', 'Blow the wind southerly', 'Christmas Day in the morning' and many other traditional songs.

Contemporary with this pleasure in native music was the belief that not only was the best music foreign but that the most skilled performers of it came from abroad. For generations the public taste in music had been guided by the wealth of German, Austrian, French and Italian compositions. German musicians were regarded as the finest because their training was so thorough, and many important orchestras, theatres, and churches in Britain had German conductors and organists.

This tendency to favour foreign music and musicians was amplified by the liberal opinions of the educated members of the community who saw in many of the performers refugees from the repressive regimes of the Continent and the revolutions of 1848. In addition the lower classes were often attracted to performances by foreigners if they wore their national costume and presented a few characteristic dances.

But the musical coin had another side, for there were many people with Puritanical minds who linked opera with the theatre and since so many operatic themes dealt with violent and erotic passions, they condemned it and regarded with suspicion the foreign musicians and singers connected with it. Felix Mendelssohn alone was whole-heartedly admired because his private life was exemplary, the subjects of his compositions were wholesome, he was the father of five children, and much admired by the Queen.

126

The Victorians it was who discovered children and the pleasure they could give adults. In return the grateful adults began to cater for children's tastes in literature and in doing so added 'Alice in Wonderland,' 'Treasure Island' and many other treasures to our book shelves. The world of music has always had its infant prodigies, but here we get them en masse with the typical, sentimental title of 'Little Men'. Take note of the remarkable, and misplaced, ingenuity of the designer who managed to contort the shape of musical instruments into an alphabet. (see page 103)

126

PROGRAMME.

PART 1.

- OVERTURE ....Der Freichutz..............................Weber.
- SOLO VIOLIN.......................(M. Willy Kaye).......................................
- QUADRILLES..........................."Ireland,"...............................Dr. Mark.
- SONG..............................."The Low Back'd Car,"......................S. Lover.
- GRAND SOLO VIOLIN......(Mr. J. Osborne Sturge.)..................................
- SELECTIONS FROM "LURLINE"..Wallace.
- SONG. ...."Limerick Races."..
- GRAND SOLO TROMBONE, "Cujus Animam" from Rossini's "Stabat Mater."
- GALOP......................"Hunting at Sandringham,"...............Dr. Mark.

PART 2.

- OVERTURE........................"La Gazza Ladra,"..........................Rossini.
- DUETT................................"All's Well,"..............................Braham.
- GRAND SOLO VIOLIN......(Mr. J. Osborne Sturge.)..................................
- SONG..........................."The Bold Soldier Boy."..................................
- SELECTIONS of Irish, English, Scotch, Welsh, German, and American Melodies...Arranged by Dr. Mark.
- SONG AND CHORUS......"Pretty Little Polly Perkins,"..............H. Clifton.
- GALOP................................"Erin go Bragh,"..........................Dr. Mark.
- To conclude with "Now Pray we for Ould Ireland" & the "National Anthem."

Selections of "Martha," "Fra Diavolo," and other popular Operas, will be introduced as a change, together with all the popular music of the day.

The performances are also intended to illustrate Dr. Mark's original and effective system of Musical Education, copies of which may be had direct of Dr. Mark, or his agents.

EXTRACT FROM THE UNANIMOUS OPINION OF THE PRESS.

"We have great pleasure to invite the attention of our readers to Dr. Mark's Entertainment. A gentleman who has done so much to raise the musical standard amongst the rising generation of this country, and has secured to himself, by his praiseworthy exertions to establish a College of Music for poor little children, the universal esteem of all classes of society, and the title of 'Children's Friend'—is deserving of every encouragement and support, especially on this occasion when he is about giving a series of Concerts in aid of a national Establishment so full of benefits to the country. This institution, which is about to be erected, is intended to admit poor children from all parts of the country, who will be clothed, educated, both generally and musically, and after their fifteenth year, either finished in their education as musical performers or professors and teachers of music, all free of expense. The great want of such an institution has been long and severely felt; we quote Dr. Mark's own words when we state, 'that there is an abundance of musical talent in the country, which only requires the fostering hand to promote its growth.' The desire for social and domestic education becomes stronger every day; and it cannot be denied that music is a most powerful element to aid in realising this desirable object, especially when inculcated in the young minds and blended with useful and general education as Dr. Mark's scheme embraces. Dr. Mark's indefatigable and valuable services which he has rendered to this country by educating and maintaining hundreds of boys gratuitously, and by practically illustrating its results in travelling about the country to rouse and emulate the rising generation, have fully proved to the public the great value and necessity of these institutions. Dr. Mark is, therefore justly entitled to every praise and credit, which should bespeak at all times for him that support he so justly merits. But we feel great pleasure in drawing especial attention to his present visit, feeling convinced that we encourage the right thing, and the right man in the right place. Some estimate may be formed of Dr. Mark's labours by appending an interesting extract from the last annual report—that 'during the past seventeen years Dr. Mark has been engaged in prosecuting his mission, he has given no less than 8,889 Concerts, 5,250 Lectures; has had the honour to play before Her Majesty and the Royal Family several times, also before 4,945,781 children, 4,145,989 adults, played the National Anthem 9,282 times, travelled 206,600 miles, expended £115,000, and independent of £25,000 of his own resources; he has established a Royal College of Music, and several Conservatoires of Music, organised a number of Juvenile Bands, and upwards of 5,500 Private and Class Pupils have been taught upon his system, many of them being educated and maintained free of expense.'"

127 and 127A
Although the possession of a piano is supposed to have been a Victorian status symbol, it did not become common until the latter half of the nineteenth century. The Great Exhibition of 1851 provided the necessary impetus and saw the culmination of many years of countless adjustments and refinements of the piano mechanism, but prior to this pianos were uncommon in the smaller provincial towns. This letter to the printer, from Topliff, which accompanied the poster confirms this view.

Dec. 1st, '44

Dear Sir,
If you can't get a Piano we cannot have the Performance. I am at a loss to know why Mr. Johnson refuses his Piano, as every care was taken of it on the last occasion. There are none to be hired at Stockton. I am obliged to a private individual—it is the same here—Miss Carlen being kind enough to lend hers—I would have one from Sunderland, but there is not time to know whether it is disengaged, previous to your Printing the bills—if you get an instrument an answer to the Town House, Stockton will oblige,
Yours R. Topliff

127 shows the whole poster. 127A is a detail of the programme on that bill.

127A

THE PROGRAMME.

Part First.

Introductory Observations.

Old Melody—"Let us be Merry."

Fragment of an ancient Ballad,—"Early One Morning."

Recitative and Air,

"Friend of the Brave"—Calcott.

Air on the Musical Glasses,

"Within a Mile of Edinburgh Town."

Local Song—"The Pitman's Courtship."

Arne's Aria—"Where the Bee sucks,"—from the Tempest.

Rondo (Piano-Forte)

"Till the Tide comes in," and "Go to the Kye,"

From the Melodies of the Tyne and Wear.

Local Song—"As Me and maw Marrow."

Air—"Maids, get up and bake your Pies,"

Harmonized from the "Melodies of the Tyne and the Wear."

Buffo Song—"Wanted a Governess."

AN INTERVAL.

Part Second.

Ballad—"The [Mis]letoe Bough."

Sunderland Ditty. "Spottee."

Fantasia (Piano-forte), in which will be introduced the "Keel row," from "The Melodies," &c.

Local Song—"Little Pee Dee."

Original Song in *As you like it*, (from Pills to purge Melancholy, 1590,)

"Under the Greenwood Tree."

Manuscript Song—"The Sailor Boy's Dream."

Irish Melody on the Musical Glasses,

"Robin Adair."

Snatches of Local Songs, Sunderland Cries, Sword Dancers, and Kitty Bo Bo.

The Gem of the North—"Up the Raw."

AN INTERVAL.

Part Third.

Cumberland Ballad—"Geordie Gill."

The Pit Boy's Song......Topliff.

Cumberland Ballad—"My Mother was takin' her Nuin's Rest."

Song—"The Old English Gentleman."

Scotch Air (Musical Glasses) "Auld Langsyne."

Song—"The Weshin' Day,"

By the Author of *The Pitman's Pay*.

Duet—"The Keel Row"—From "The Melodies," &c.

Finale—Buffo Song—

"Forensic Oratory, or Hooks and Eyes,"

A curious Law Case.

Doors open at Half-past Seven, Entertainment to commence at Eight o'Clock.

127

TOPLIFF'S

LOCAL

MERRY NIGHT.

THEATRE ROYAL,

NEWCASTLE-UPON-TYNE.

Mr. TOPLIFF has the Honour to announce to his Friends and the Public, that he has taken the THEATRE ROYAL, NEWCASTLE-UPON-TYNE,

FOR ONE NIGHT ONLY,

And will give his Popular

MUSICAL

ENTERTAINMENT

INCLUDING

Local and other Songs, Duets, and Performances on the Piano-forte, and his much admired

MUSICAL GLASSES,

ON

THURSDAY, NOV. 21st, 1844.

IN THE COURSE OF THE EVENING HE WILL INTRODUCE

"The Pitman's Courtship," "As Me and Maw Marrow," "Spottee," "Little Pee Dee," "The Weshin' Day," "Up the Raw," "The Keel Row," &c. &c. &c.

THE PROGRAMME.

Part First.

Introductory Observations.

Old Melody—"Let us be Merry."

Fragment of an ancient Ballad,—"Early One Morning."

Recitative and Air,

"Friend of the Brave"—Calcott.

Air on the Musical Glasses,

"Within a Mile of Edinburgh Town."

Local Song—"The Pitman's Courtship."

Arne's Aria—"Where the Bee sucks,"—from the Tempest.

Rondo (Piano-Forte)

"Till the Tide comes in," and "Go to the Kye,"

From the Melodies of the Tyne and Wear.

Local Song—"As Me and maw Marrow."

Air—"Maids, get up and bake your Pies,"

Harmonized from the "Melodies of the Tyne and the Wear."

Buffo Song—"Wanted a Governess."

AN INTERVAL.

Part Second.

Ballad—"The [Mis]letoe Bough."

Sunderland Ditty. "Spottee."

Fantasia (Piano-forte), in which will be introduced the "Keel row," from "The Melodies," &c.

Local Song—"Little Pee Dee."

Original Song in *As you like it*, (from Pills to purge Melancholy, 1590,)

"Under the Greenwood Tree."

Manuscript Song—"The Sailor Boy's Dream."

Irish Melody on the Musical Glasses,

"Robin Adair."

Snatches of Local Songs, Sunderland Cries, Sword Dancers, and Kitty Bo Bo.

The Gem of the North—"Up the Raw."

AN INTERVAL.

Part Third.

Cumberland Ballad—"Geordie Gill."

The Pit Boy's Song......Topliff.

Cumberland Ballad—"My Mother was takin' her Nuin's Rest."

Song—"The Old English Gentleman."

Scotch Air (Musical Glasses) "Auld Langsyne."

Song—"The Weshin' Day,"

By the Author of *The Pitman's Pay*.

Duet—"The Keel Row"—From "The Melodies," &c.

Finale—Buffo Song—

"Forensic Oratory, or Hooks and Eyes,"

A curious Law Case.

Doors open at Half-past Seven, Entertainment to commence at Eight o'Clock.

Dress Boxes, 2s.; Upper Boxes, 1s. 6d.; Pit, 1s.; Gallery, 6d.

Tickets to be had at the principal Music Shops, and of Mr. Carey, at the Box Office of the Theatre, where Seats may be secured from Twelve till Three o'Clock on the Day of the Concert; also of Messrs. Shield and Turner, Booksellers, Grey-Street, from Three till Six o'Clock.

Newcastle-upon-Tyne: Printed at the Journal Office, 19, Grey-Street, by John Hernaman.

128
Such shows are not very popular today except in places such as a sideshow at Blackpool or Southend but our Victorian forefathers were not quite so thin-skinned as we are, and anyhow, before the days of the Welfare State such an unfortunate person had to earn his living in some sort of fashion, and this was as good as any.

129
In the early part of the nineteenth century many devices were perfected for making a large range of notes possible on brass instruments. A famous brass band conductor of Victorian times wrote 'instruments made by the Sax family rapidly became favourites with the public for their tune and equality and also with the players—for their ease in blowing and simple fingering. The latter quality was an inestimable boon, for most of the members of this class of band were drawn from the weekly wage earning classes and their hands, horned and often malformed, were well served in these instruments.'

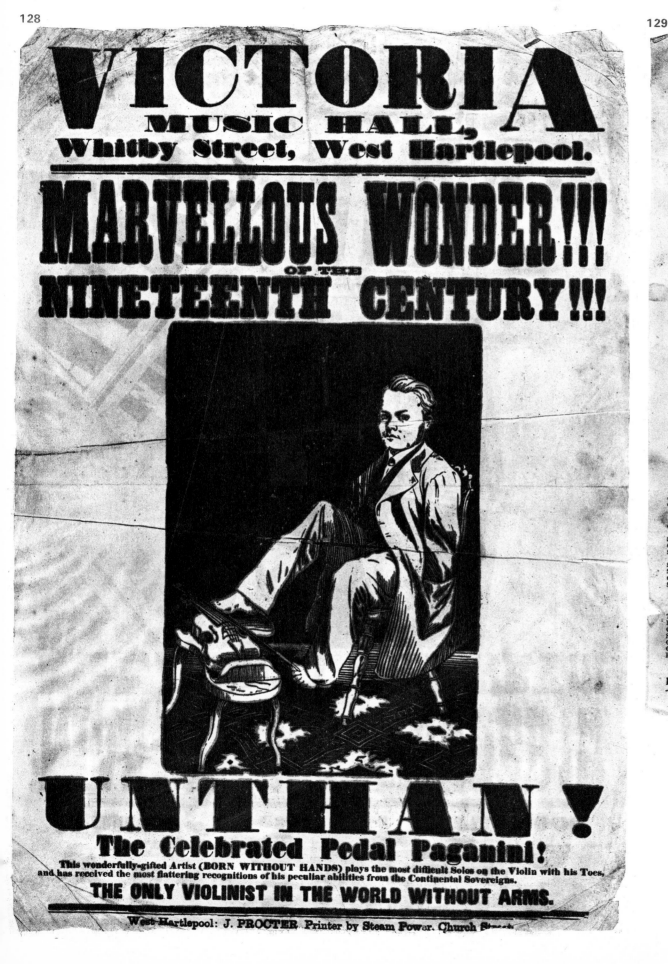

128

VICTORIA
MUSIC HALL,
Whitby Street, West Hartlepool.
MARVELLOUS WONDER!!!
OF THE
NINETEENTH CENTURY!!!
UNTHAN!
The Celebrated Pedal Paganini!
This wonderfully-gifted Artist (BORN WITHOUT HANDS) plays the most difficult Solos on the Violin with his Toes, and has received the most flattering recognitions of his peculiar abilities from the Continental Sovereigns.
THE ONLY VIOLINIST IN THE WORLD WITHOUT ARMS.
West Hartlepool: J. PROCTER, Printer by Steam Power, Church St

129

ATHENÆUM,
WEST HARTLEPOOL.
THURSDAY EVENING, SEPTEMBER 1, 1853.
GRAND
CONCERT,
BY THE
DISTINS
THE ORIGINAL PERFORMERS ON THE
SAX-HORNS.

The Messrs. DISTIN will perform on their improved Sax-Horns, in addition to their Operatic Selections, their much admired
"CUCKOO GALOP,"
And a new Selection from "LA SOMNAMBULA." Mr. DISTIN, Sen., will introduce his celebrated Trumpet Solo, "The Soldier Tired."

VOCALISTS:—
MRS. THEODORE DISTIN,
And Messrs. DISTIN.
PIANO-FORTE, HERR WOLFSOHN.

PROGRAMME—PART I.

Grand Quartett, from the Opera of "Nino" Sax-Horns	Messrs. Distin, accompanied by Herr Wolfsohn ... Bellini.
Song—"When the Swallows"	Mrs. Theodore Distin ... Abit.
Glee—"How Merrily we live"	Mr. and Messrs. Distin ... Fate.
Solo—"All is Lost,"—"La Somnambula"—Sax Horn, Tenor	Mr. Theodore Distin ... Bellini.
Solo—Pianoforte	Herr Wolfsohn ... Rossellen.
Song—"Non Piu Andrai"	Mr. T. Distin ... Mozart.
Glee—"Hark! 'tis the Indian Drum"	Mrs. and Messrs. Distin ... Sir H. R. Bishop
Solo, Trumpet—"The Soldier Tired"	Mr. Distin, senior ... Dr. Arne.

AN INTERVAL OF TEN MINUTES.

PART II.

Trio—"Quanto in quest' alma, "Sax Horns"	Messrs. Distin ... Rossini.
Duetto Buffo—"The Singing Lesson"	Mr. and Mrs. Theordore Distin ... Barnet.
Grand Concerted Piece, Sax-Horns	Messrs. Distin ... Beethoven.
Song—"Primroses deck the bank's green side"	Mrs. T. Distin ... T. Linley.
Galop—"The Cuckoo," Sax-Horns	Messrs. Distin ... Arranged by T. Distin.
Glee—"Oh! happy pair"	Mrs. and Messrs. Distin ... Shiel.
Finale—"God Save the Queen"	Messrs. Distin.

Doors open at Half-past Seven; Concert to commence

Reserved Seats, 2s. 6d.; Back

J. PROCTER, Printer, High Street Hartlepool, and Victoria Terrace W

CONCERT POSTPONED

IN CONSEQUENCE OF THE TOWN HALL BEING ENGAGED FOR PUBLIC BUSINESS ON THE NIGHTS ADVERTISED.

MR. H. WALKER

Begs to announce to the Public, that the TWO

ENTERTAINMENTS

Will take place in the above Hall, on the Evenings of

Friday & Saturday, March 19 & 20,

WHEN HE WILL INTRODUCE HIS

ROCK HARMONICON

OR MUSICAL STONES,

Sing a variety of Comic and Sentimental Songs, with Harp Accompaniment. Also, exhibit a beautiful Selection of

DIORAMIC SCENERY!!!

To conclude with the Laughable Effects of the

PHANTASCOPE

TO COMMENCE AT EIGHT O'CLOCK.

Reserved Seats, 1s.; Front Seats, 6d.; Back Seats, 3d.

From the Office of J. PROCTER, High Street, Hartlepool, and Victoria Terrace, West Hartlepool.

130
Mr. Walker does not beat about the bush. He tells us the facts and announces his future plans, but what he has to offer seems meagre fare. The Rock Harmonicon was a sort of primitive xylophone, and there were plenty of people who could sing comic and sentimental songs, and dioramic scenery was nothing new and not likely to produce an audience. But he has something out of the ordinary with his phantascope. Was it a sort of distorting mirror which provided the 'laughable effects'?

131
This is the sort of popular family entertainment Dickens refers to in 'The Uncommercial Traveller', as being presented at a provincial Mechanics' Institute No one ever thought of presenting a programme of songs to delight the audience without creating an artificial and tenuous link between them. This programme is entitled the 'Rose, Shamrock & Thistle' but somehow Italy and America are included in the performance. The programme of anecdotes makes very amusing reading and no typographer could ask for a greater profusion of typefaces.

132
Ned Corvan was no stranger to Hartlepool as this letter of his to John Procter reveals:
Fairless Arms, South Shields

Dear Sir,
I am glad to hear you are enjoying good health a friend of mine informed so. I like to hear your name as it recalls the memory of the past when I ran from home with the strolling players. Poor old Billy, I have written an entertainment of his life and death and were I to give it in Hartlepool I am confident I should meet with success.

What delightful song titles!

131

MR.

CHAS. COTTON'S

NEW VOCAL

ENTERTAINMENT,

ENTITLED THE

Rose, Shamrock, & Thistle;

OR, A PEEP AT

ENGLAND, IRELAND, & SCOTLAND.

INTRODUCING

ENGLISH, IRISH, SCOTCH,

WITH INCIDENTAL ITALIAN AND AMERICAN SONGS,

INTERSPERSED WITH

ORIGINAL, AMUSING, AND CURIOUS ANECDOTES.

PROGRAMME—Part I.

Introduction—An evening party—The unity of the Rose, Shamrock, and Thistle—Comparisons—Strange arguments.

IRISH SONG . . . . . "Terence's Farewell to Kathleen."
(Written and Composed by the Right Hon. Lady Dufferin.)

Arrangements for a month's tour—First trip to Clifton—Description of a few passengers—An evening at the Victoria Hotel.

ITALIAN ARIA . . . . . . "Infelice e tuo credevi." . . . . *Verdi.*

An Italian exile and patriot, who possesses a strong attachment for his country—Reminiscences of Italy, and description of the Lake of Como.

OLD SONG . . . . "The Friar of Orders Grey."

Crossing from Bristol to Cork—A returned Crimean hero belonging to the Connaught Rangers, who gives an amusing description of camp life, its pleasures, glories, and privations.

IRISH SONG . . . . "Molly Bawn." . . . . *S. Lover.*

The effects of sea travelling—Arrival at Cork—Visit to Killarney—Kerry o'Leary's artificial wake—A ride from Killarney to Talbert—Irish flattery with heaps of blessings.

IRISH SONG . . . . "The Low Backed Car," . . . . *S. Lover.*

AN INTERVAL OF TEN MINUTES.

Part II.

A trip up the Shannon to Limerick—Unceremonious visit of an American who gives an amusing description of down South.

NEGRO MELODY . . . . . "The Old Folks at Home."
(As Sung by Miss Greenfield, the Black Swan, in two distinct voices.)

Journey from Limerick to Dublin—A stage-struck he[illegible]—Ready wit of an Irish carman—Strange doings at the Theatre Royal, Dublin.

SCOTCH SONG . . . . . . "Gang nae mair a roving."

Crossing to Liverpool—A gentleman troubled with a short memory—Arrival at Westmorland—The lakes, fishermen, and their customs.

NEW SONG (MS.) . . . . . "Fare thee well, but not for ever." . . . . *J. Blewett.*
(The last production of this talented Composer, and presented by him to Mr. Charles Cotton.)

Strange legends in connexion with Cumberland—A remarkable incident at Gretna Green—Arrival at the beautiful city of Edinburgh—The historian on Arthur's Seat.

JACOBITE SONG . . . . "Charlie's Coming." . . . . . . *Crawshaw Johnson.*

The return to London—Concluding remarks, introducing

THE "LAND OF ST. PATRICK," "AULD LANG SYNE," AND "RULE, BRITANNIA."

MRS. CHARLES COTTON WILL PRESIDE AT THE PIANOFORTE.

132

TOWN HALL, HARTLEPOOL

On Wednesday, Dec. 19, 1855

GRAND ORIGINAL TYNESIDE ENTERTAINMENT!

Under Distinguished Patronage.

MR. E. CORVAN

THE CELEBRATED TYNESIDE POET, VOCALIST, & JESTER,

Will have the honor of appearing, FOR THE FIRST TIME IN HARTLEPOOL, in the above HUMOUROUS ENTERTAINMENT, assisted by

MR. J. H. SPIERS,

The Popular Irish Comedian.

PROGRAMME.—PART FIRST.

Bonny Coaly Tyne—The Keelmen in difficulties—MARROWS, am gaun ti leave ye.

Original Song, "Asstrally's Goold Fields," Mr. Corvan.

Tommy Carr's Letter—The Unfortunate Pe de—a Taste for the Drama—Recollections of

Billy Purvis

Song, Original, "Billy's Deeth," Mr. CORVAN.

Imitations of Performers—THE BUNDLE—A make-up for a Highland Chief—Song, Original,

"Snook, the Artist,"

Introducing a correct Portrait of Old Billy—The Russian Emperor, &c.—Musical Ideas—A Word about the Pea Straw.

Violin Solo, "Nannie, wilt thou gang wi' me," "We Sailed from the Downs."

This will conclude the First Part of Mr. CORVAN'S Entertainment.

GRAND SCOTCH & IRISH ENTERTAINMENT

Mr. J. H. SPIERS, the Popular Eccentric Comedian.

PART SECOND.

Mr. E. CORVAN.—The Tyneside Factory Lass—Carlin Sunday—Cuckoo Jack—Grappling for Perpetual Motion.

Song, "Am Sweet Siventeen," Mr. CORVAN.

With Inimitable Sketches of Tyneside Life—The Moosecathers, or Hairy Gobs—with a Short Lecture.

Song Original, "Hairy Gobs," Mr. CORVAN. Grand Dialogue Song, Mr. CORVAN.—CAT GUT JIM—the Street Minstrel, in which Mr. C. will introduce the following Solos, &c.:—"Far upon the Sea,"' "Annie Lawrie," "Auld Robin Gray," "Exile of Erin," "Imitation of the Bagpipes," &c.

ADMITTANCE.—FRONT SEATS, 1s,; BACK SEATS, 6d.

Doors open at Seven o'clock, to commence at Half-past.

J. PROCTER, Printer, High Street, Hartlepool, and Church Street, West Hartlepool.

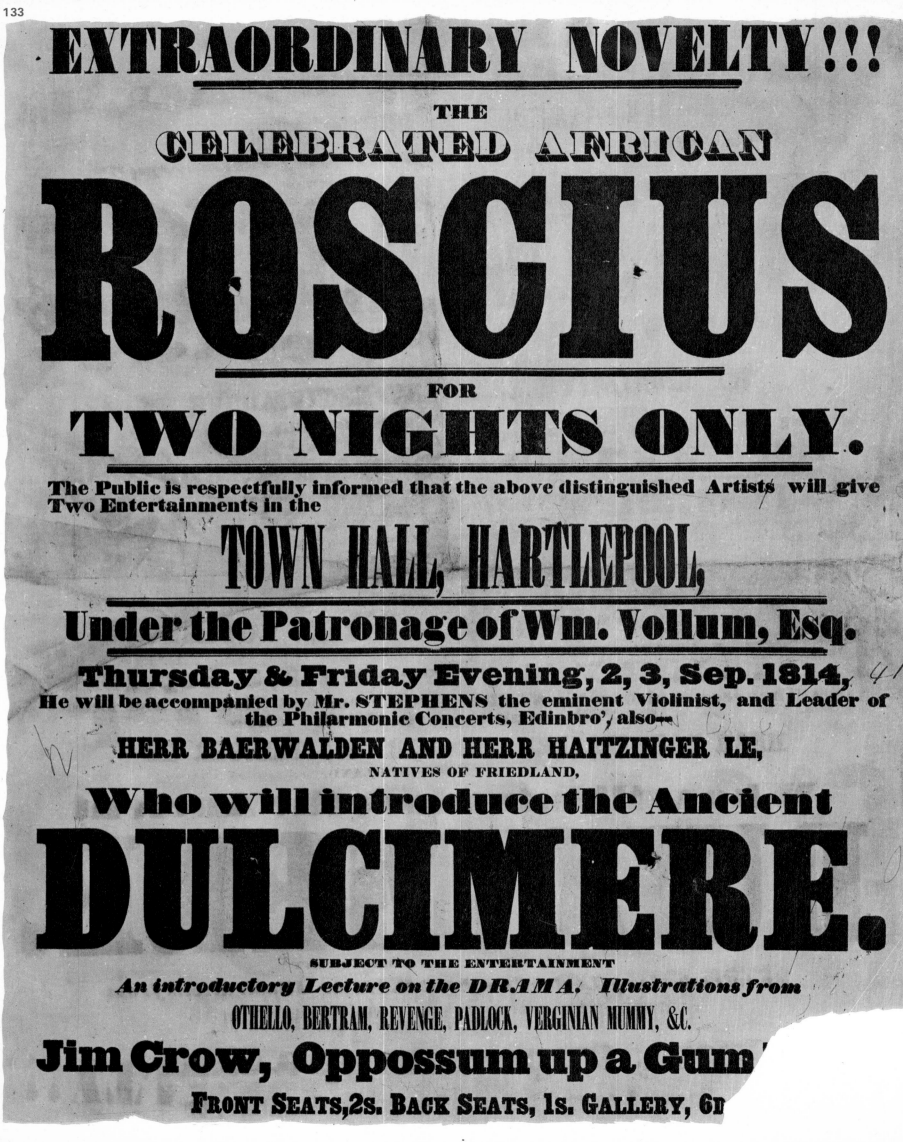

EXTRAORDINARY NOVELTY!!!

THE

CELEBRATED AFRICAN

ROSCIUS

FOR

TWO NIGHTS ONLY.

The Public is respectfully informed that the above distinguished Artists will give Two Entertainments in the

TOWN HALL, HARTLEPOOL,

Under the Patronage of Wm. Vollum, Esq.

Thursday & Friday Evening, 2, 3, Sep. 1814,

He will be accompanied by Mr. STEPHENS the eminent Violinist, and Leader of the Philarmonic Concerts, Edinbro', also—

HERR BAERWALDEN AND HERR HAITZINGER LE,

NATIVES OF FRIEDLAND,

Who will introduce the Ancient

DULCIMERE.

SUBJECT TO THE ENTERTAINMENT

An introductory Lecture on the DRAMA. Illustrations from

OTHELLO, BERTRAM, REVENGE, PADLOCK, VERGINIAN MUMMY, &C.

Jim Crow, Oppossum up a Gum

FRONT SEATS, 2S. BACK SEATS, 1S. GALLERY, 6D

133
In spite of his awe-inspiring title this gentleman signed his letter I. F. Aldridge when he wrote giving details of the number of bills he desired Procter to 'knock off' as he elegantly put it. Nor was that all he wanted, for he went on 'perhaps you would procure me a sitting room and a couple of bed rooms. I will only want them for about three days and usually pay at the rate of 15 or 16 shillings per week'.

134
The Bearnais Artistes rely on their national costume and choral singing to bring in the crowds. No doubt they did well, for the love of choral music is a long-standing tradition in the North of England and the costume adds that little bit of 'improving information' which, together with their national songs, would make it acceptable to the most strait-laced Victorian.

135
The Steel Band might sound very modern but it is, nevertheless, one of the many curious ways of making music that Victorians amused themselves with a hundred years ago. Another bill in this selection presents Musical Glasses and on others we find Musical Haybands, which were probably a primitive form of xylophone. A museum in the Lake District houses some of the stones used in this or a similar Rock Band.

134

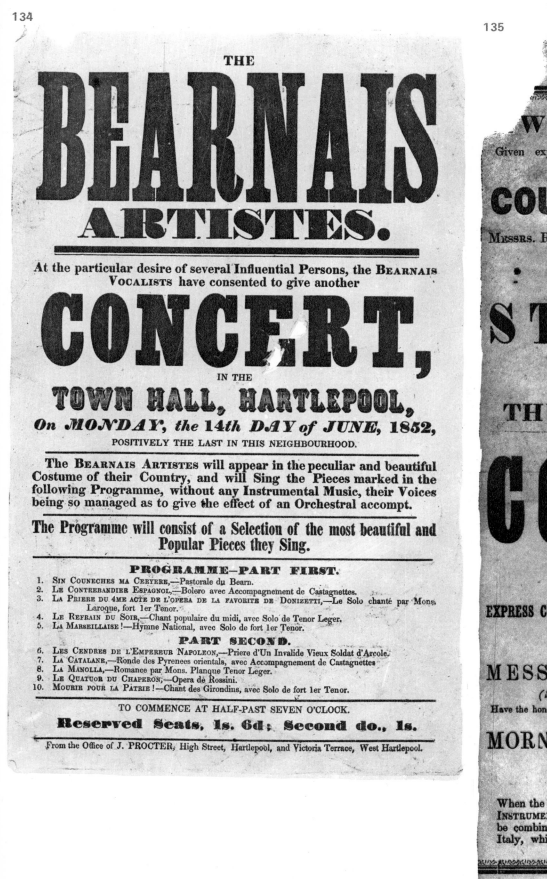

THE

BEARNAIS

ARTISTES.

At the particular desire of several Influential Persons, the Bearnais Vocalists have consented to give another

CONCERT,

IN THE

TOWN HALL, HARTLEPOOL,

On MONDAY, the 14th DAY of JUNE, 1852,

POSITIVELY THE LAST IN THIS NEIGHBOURHOOD.

The Bearnais Artistes will appear in the peculiar and beautiful Costume of their Country, and will Sing the Pieces marked in the following Programme, without any Instrumental Music, their Voices being so managed as to give the effect of an Orchestral accompt.

The Programme will consist of a Selection of the most beautiful and Popular Pieces they Sing.

PROGRAMME—PART FIRST.

1. Sin Couneches ma Ceryere,—Pastorale du Bearn.
2. Le Contrebandier Espagnol,—Bolero avec Accompagnement de Castagnettes.
3. La Priere du 4me acte de l'opera de la favorite de Donizetti,—Le Solo chanté par Mons. Laroque, fort 1er Tenor.
4. Le Refrain du Soir,—Chant populaire du midi, avec Solo de Tenor Leger.
5. La Marseillaise !—Hymne National, avec Solo de fort 1er Tenor.

PART SECOND.

6. Les Cendres de l'Empereur Napoleon,—Priere d'Un Invalide Vieux Soldat d'Arcole.
7. La Catalane,—Ronde des Pyrenees orientals, avec Accompagnement de Castagnettes
8. La Manolla,—Romance par Mons. Planque Tenor Leger.
9. Le Quatuor du Chaperon,—Opera de Rossini.
10. Mourir pour la Patrie !—Chant des Girondins, avec Solo de fort 1er Tenor.

TO COMMENCE AT HALF-PAST SEVEN O'CLOCK.

Reserved Seats, 1s. 6d; Second do., 1s.

From the Office of J. PROCTER, High Street, Hartlepool, and Victoria Terrace, West Hartlepool.

135

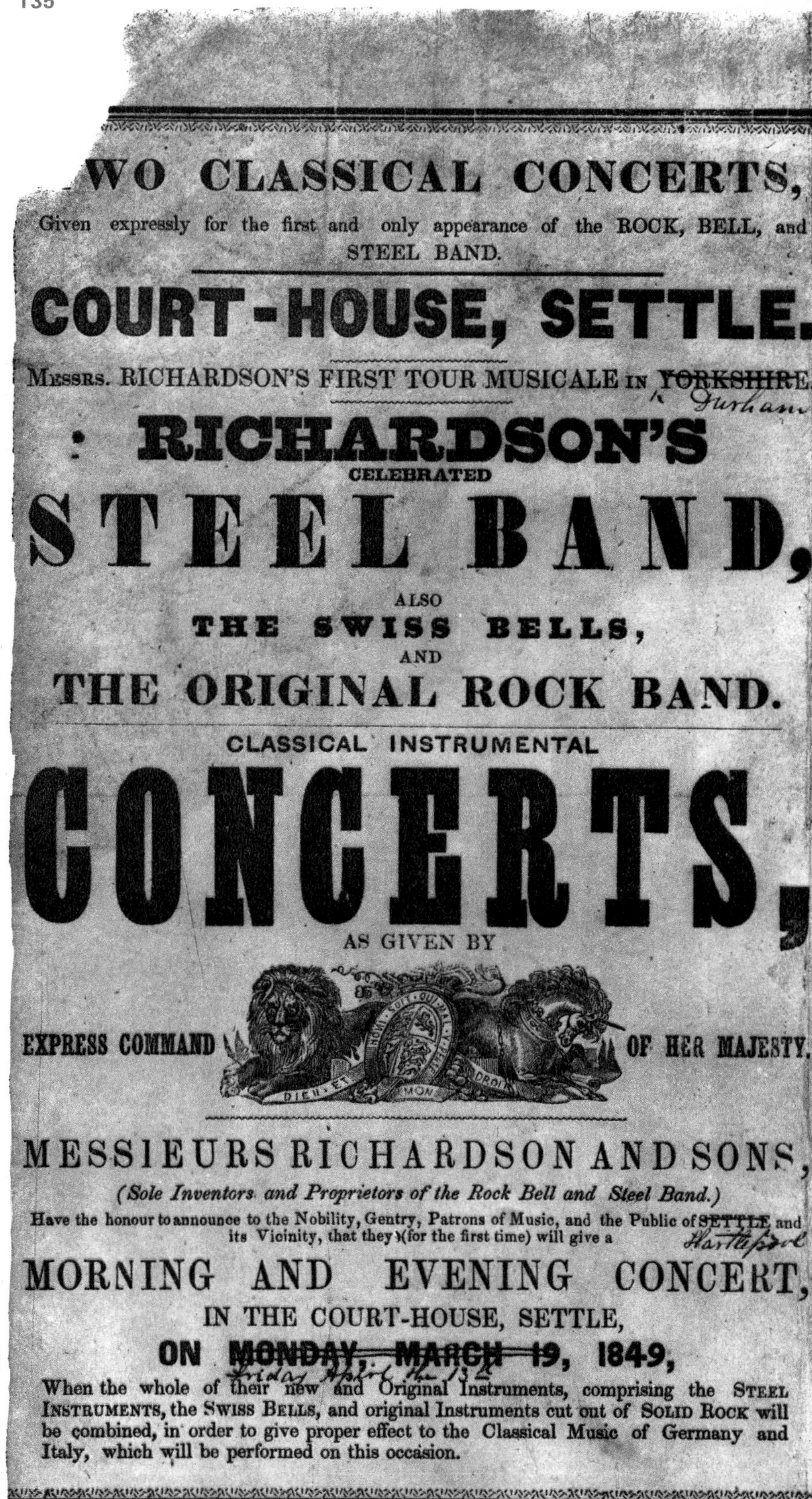

BY PERMISSION
TOWN HALL, HARTLEPOOL.

HERR SOMMER

In consequence of the satisfaction given Last Night, HERR SOMMER is induced to give a SECOND

CONCERT
This Evening,

26TH NOVEMBER, 1852.

PROGRAMME.

PART I.

1—BAND—OVERTURE—William Tell .... ROSSINI
2—SOLO—Cornet-a-Piston—Variations—Tyrolese Air —by Herr Kessler.................... KESSLER
3—BAND—"Peasant Polka" .... KESSLER
4—BALLAD—"Smiling Faces," by Miss Norman, Piano-Forte Accompaniment .... GLOVER
5—STORM SONNATTA—Piano-Forte, by Master Hilton .... STEIBELT
6—BAND—(by desire)—"Wellington March," to be performed in Honour of the Great Duke.... HASSÉ
7—FANTASIA—From the Opera "Il Puritani," for the Sommerophone Baritone, by Herr Sommer.. SOMMER
8—BAND—Tiger and Amazon Galop .... BÜLLER

PART II.

1—BAND—Farewell to the Exhibition—as performed by command, of her Majesty the Queen .... SOMMER
2—SONG—"Molly Bawn," by Miss Norman....... LOVER
3—BAND—Waltz—"Dew Drop" .... CHAS. D'ALBERT
4—"The Exiles Lament," for the Sommerophone Alto, by Herr Sommer .... ROCH ALBERT
5—BAND—The Echo Polka—(by desire).......... SOMMER
6—SCOTCH BALLAD—"Bonnie Dundee," by Miss Norman .... NELSON
7—BAND—OVERTURE—"Zampa" .... HEROLD
8—FINALE—"GOD SAVE THE QUEEN," by Isabella Wilson, and the whole Company.

ADMISSION—Front Seats, 2s.; Back Seats, 1s.

Doors open at Half-past Seven, to commence at Eight precisely.

136
Herr Sommer did not always give satisfaction. A letter from Staley Bridge to John Procter asks 'Would you be kind enough to tell me what the dates of the Concerts were that Herr Sommer's Band gave at Hartlepool and Stockton I believe he gave two at Hartlepool and one at Stockton and you printed the bills. My reason for wishing to know the dates is because, like most of the travelling gentry, he forgot to pay people when he engaged them and as he is at present at the Belle Vue Gardens, Manchester I want to present him with my bill for playing at Three Concerts for him.
Edw. Hilton, Organist and Choirmaster, All Saints, Manchester.'

137
Mr. Loder seems to have made Sunderland the centre of his agency, if it may be so called. He was a friend of Mr. Friend who arranged matters for the Distin family and for a Mr. Phillips. It may be that he was simply good-hearted but his correspondence certainly reveals him as a muddler.

138
This is another example of private enterprise, such as we have already encountered with Mr. Smith's Music Saloon and Billy Purvis's players. It is a strictly musical programme, however, and, if the names of some of the celebrated German performers seem rather too foreign, there is no denying the irresistible attraction of the 'Ancient Dulcimero'.

139
From Von Hartman's correspondence he appears to have done very well, but it is to be hoped that John Procter remembered the warning he received from Harrison Penney and did not trust him 'one ½d'

137

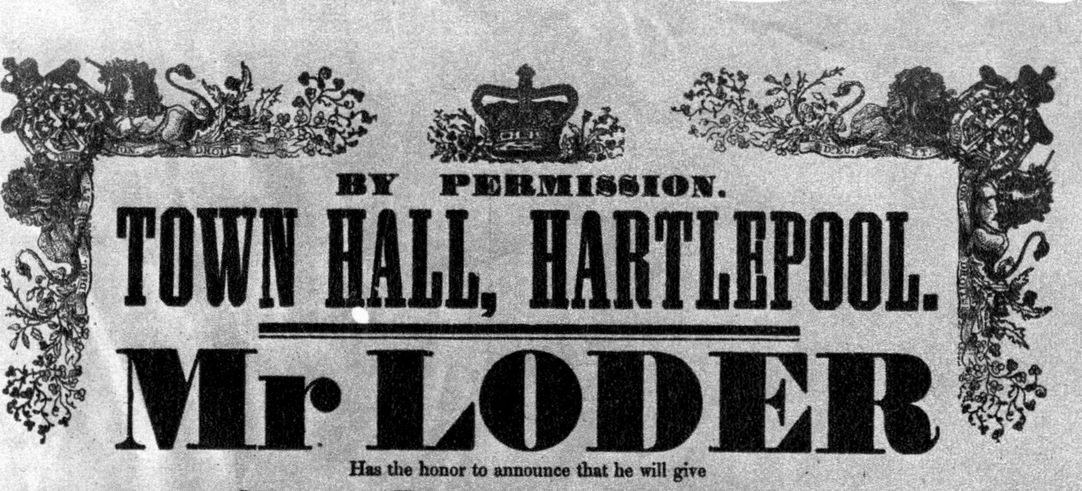

BY PERMISSION.

TOWN HALL, HARTLEPOOL.

Mr LODER

Has the honor to announce that he will give

A GRAND CONCERT

On Thursday Evening, April 7th, 1853,

IN THE ABOVE HALL.

VOCAL PERFORMERS:—

Miss ANNE LODER, from the Exeter Hall Concerts, London, Mr. DODDS, Mr. LODER, and the POPULAR BARYTONE, Mr. R. FERRY.

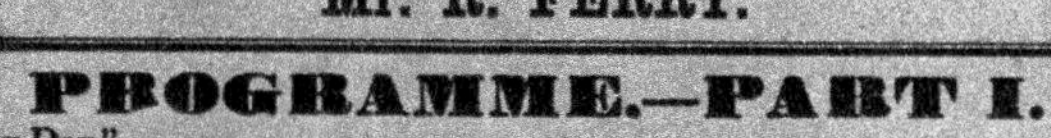

PROGRAMME.—PART I.

GLEE—"May Day" .... MULLER
SONG—"Merry Sunshine" .... Miss Loder .... GLOVER
TRIO—"O Happy Fair" .... SHIELD
SONG—"British Anchor" .... Mr. Ferry .... LODER
DUET—"Merry Month of May" .... Miss Loder and Mr. Dodds .... MULLER
SONG—"You'll Remember Me" .... Mr. Dodds .... BALFE
GLEE—"May Day" .... MULLER
SONG—"Kathleen Mavourneen" .... Miss Loder .... CROUCH
SONG—"Three Ages" .... Mr. Ferry .... LODER
TRIO—"Hail Smiling Morn" .... SPOFFORTH

PART II.

GLEE—"Peace to the Souls" .... CALCOTT
SONG—"I'm thine" .... Miss Loder .... BENEDICTS
DUET—"What are the Wild Waves" .... Miss Loder and Mr. Ferry ....
SONG—"Last Rose of Summer" .... Mr Dodds .... IRISH
TRIO—"Blow Gentle Gales" .... BISHOP
SONG—"The Stout Nor'wester" .... Mr. Ferry .... LODER
SONG .... Miss Loder .... BALFE
GLEE—"Mynheer Vandunck" .... BISHOP
SONG—"She Shines before Me" .... Mr. Ferry .... MACFARREN

FINALE—"GOD SAVE THE QUEEN."

PIANO-FORTE:—MR. LODER.

ADMISSION:—FRONT SEATS, 1s. 6d.; BACK SEATS, 1s.

TICKETS TO BE HAD OF MR. J. PROCTER, BOOKSELLER.

Doors open at Half-past Seven, to commence at Eight o'clock.

J. PROCTER, Printer, High Street, Hartlepool, and Victoria Terrace, West Hartlepool.

138

GRAND MUSICAL ENTERTAINMENT.

MR. J. R. STEPHENS

From the Orchestre, Italian Opera House, London, And formerly Leader of the Philharmonic Concerts, EDINBURGH, and now Violinist to the AFRICAN ROSCIUS,

Begs respectfully to announce to the Gentry and Public of Seaton, that he will give a

CONCERT,

OR GRAND MUSICAL MELANGE,

In Corner's Large Room, 7 Stars Inn, Seaton Carew, On Saturday Evening Sep 4th, 1841, When he will be assisted in the Vocal Department, by

MRS. STEPHENS.

J. R. S. has succeeded in engaging for the Occasion the celebrated

HERR BAERWALDEN, AND HERR HAITZINGER LE, Who will introduce the

Ancient Dulcimero.

The Execution and Effects produced on this Instrument by these extraordinary Artistes, excited the Admiration of her most Gracious Majesty QUEEN VICTORIA, before whom they had the Honour of Performing at Buckingham Palace.

PROGRAMME.—PART I.

VIOLIN SOLO, Opera 40, "*Mayseder*," with Piano and Dulcimero accompaniments .... Mr. Stephans
SONG, "*Happy Land*" .... Mrs Stephans
OVERTURE, "*La Caravan*" .... Herr Baerwaden and Haitzinger Le
VIOLIN SOLO, "*Overture to Lodoiska*" (in which will be introduced his imitation of the French Fiddle &c.) .... Mr Stephens
STRAUS'S ROSA WALZER, (Dulcimero, Violin, & Violoncello) .... Herr Baerwalden, Haitzinger Le, J. R. Stephens and J. P. Jewson
SONG, "*O! Give me but my Arab Steed*," .... Mrs. Stephens
IMITATION OF SCOTTISH BAGPIPES .... Mr. Stephens
BALL RAKETAN WALTZ, (Dulcimero, Violin & Violoncello) Herr B., H. Lee, Stephens & Jewson

PART.—II.

OVERTURE, "*Tancredi*" (Dulcimero, Violin, and Violoncello) Herr B., H. Lee, Stephens and Jewson
SONG, "*Rosy tints of Evening*" .... Mrs Stephens
SOLO, Hibernian Tema "*Rory O'More*" with Variations .... Herr Baerwalden
GRAND FANTASIA, from "*Mayebeer's Opera les Huguenotes*" .... Herr B. accompanied by H. Le Stephens and Jewson
VIOLIN SOLO, *Rhodes Air*, with variations, (Piano accompaniment) .... Mr. Stephens
LIGHT OE OTHER DAYS, (with variations) .... Herr B. and H. Le
FANTASIA COMIQUE, "Grandmama" .... Mr. Stephens
SONG .... Mrs. Stephens
FINALE.... "*GOD SAVE THE QUEEN*" Herr B., H. Lee, Stephens and Jewson.

MR JEWSON, WILL PRESIDE AT THE PIANO FORTE.

Doors open at half-past 7. To commence at 8.

Tickets of Admission 2s. 6d. Children, half-price.

J PROCTER, PRINTER, HIGH STREET, HARTLEPOOL.

139

BY PERMISSION.

TOWN HALL, HARTLEPOOL.

Great Musical Attraction.

VON HARTMAN,

THE UNRIVALLED PERFORMER ON THE ONE-STRINGED VIOLIN.

Miss Hartman & Miss E. Hartman,

VOCALISTS,

(Whose Performances have met with unbounded applause througout the United Kingdom,) most respectfully announce their intention of giving

TWO EVENING CONCERTS

On Monday & Tuesday Evenings, March 8th & 9th, 1847.

Piano-forte or Spanish Guitar, Miss Hartman.

MONDAY EVENING.

PART I.

DUET.—"Come dwell with me," Misses C. and E. Hartman *Hodson*
GRAND SCENA, (from Sonnambula) "As I view these scenes so charming," Miss E. Hartman .... *Bellini*
DE BERIOT'S 6th Grand FANTASIA, (Violin) Von Hartman *De Beriot*
SONG.—"My Beautiful Rhine" Miss Hartman .... *Rosse*
SONG.—"Bid me discourse," Miss E. Hartman ...... *Sir H. Bishop*
VIOLIN SOLO,—"The Light of other Days," (Balfe's celebrated Air) and Irish Melody, on one string (the fourth), with variations on the four strings, arranged to be performed by Von Hartman *A la Paganini*
DUET,—"Come o'er the moonlit Sea," Misses Hartman ...*Devereux*
SONG,—Comin' through the Rye," Miss E. Hartman .... *Burnett*
GRAND FANTASIA,—(Violin) "Au claire de la lune," with brilliant variations, Von Hartman .... *Ghys*
SONG,—"I wish he would decide," Miss E. Hartman .... *Wilson*
DUET,—"The Keel Row," Misses Hartman .... *Watson*

PART II.

DUET,—"Hear me Norma," Misses Hartman .... *Bellini*
SONG,—(from the Bohemian Girl) "I dreamt that I dwelt in Marble Halls," Miss Hartman .... *Balfe*
VIOLIN SOLO,—An original Theme of Signor Paganini, entirely on one string, (the fourth) with splendid variations, after which, "Speed the Plough" with variations, on 4 strings, Von Hartman *A la Paganini*
RECITATIVE & AIR,—"O Patria tu che accendi," and "Di tanti Palpiti," Miss E. Hartman .... *Rossini*
VIOLIN SOLO,—(*De Beriot's seventh*) introducing the "Last Rose of Summer," *entirely on one string*, (the third) Von Hartman *De Beriot*
SONG,—"I'm owre young to marry yet," Miss E. Hartman.
VIOLIN SOLO,—Irish national Melody, "My lodging is on the cold ground," *on one string*, (the fourth in harmonics) and "Norah Creina," with variations on the four strings, Von Hartman *A la Paganini*
BALLED,—"The fine Young English Lady, one of the present time," Miss E. Hartman .... *Parday*
FINALE,—"RULE BRITANNIA," VERSES AND CHORUS.

TUESDAY EVENING.

PART I.

DUET,—"Ye Banks and Braes o' Bonny Doon," Misses C. and E. Hartman .... *Burns*
SONG.—"Pretty Star of the Night," Miss E. Hartman ... *Mrs Waylet*
BRILLIANT VARIATIONS on a favourite Air, from L'Elisir d'Amour, Violin, Von Hartman .... *Thirlwall*
GRAND SCENA, (from Sonnambula) "Do not mingle," Miss E. Hartman .... *Bellini*
THE POLKA SONG,—Miss Hartman .... *Jullien*
VIOLIN SOLO,—"Robin Adair," and Scotch Melody "Auld Lang Syne, *on one string*, (the fourth in harmonics) with variations on four strings, Von Hartman
DUET,—"The Ties of Friendship," from the new opera of "The Crusaders," Misses Hartman .... *Benedict*
GRAND RONDO,—(Violin) "Le Petit Tambour," Von Hartman *Mayseder*
SONG,—"The Woodland Call," Miss E. Hartman
DUET,—"Mighty Jove" from the Opera "Barber of Seville" Misses Hartman .... *Rossini*

PART II.

THE BRIGAND'S DUET, from Auber's New Opera, "The Crown Jewels," Misses Hartman .... *Auber*
SONG,—"The Merry Swiss Maid," Miss Hartman .... *A. Lee*
VIOLIN SOLO,—"Signor Paganini's Celebrated Prayer," from "Mosé in Egitto, and "Non piu Mesta," entirely on the one-stringed Violin, Von Hartman .... *a la Paganini*
DUET,—"Oh what will a' the lads do?" Misses Hartman *Sir H. Bishop*
SONG,—"Mamma wont let me marry yet," Miss E. Hartman *Westrop*
CONCERTO,—(Violin) Viotti's Celebrated in A. major, Von Hartman
SONG,—"I leave you to guess," Miss E. Hartman
VIOLIN SOLO,—"Oh! as we never mention her," and "St. Patrick's Day," *on one string* (the fourth) with variations on four strings, Von Hartman
FINALE,—"GOD SAVE THE QUEEN," VERSE & CHORUS

No Admittance Fees received at the Door; all respectable Persons having Free Entrance.

At the close of the first part of the Concert, a Collection in Silver will be made for the benefit of the Performers.

Doors open at Half-past Seven o'clock, the Performance to commence at Eight and conclude at Ten.

Printed by J. PROCTER, High Street, Hartlepool.

140 and 141

It seems to have been the acceptable practice for the bills of concerts and musical programmes to be of a more delicate design than those for theatrical productions. The printer has taken immense care to produce an artistic bill in each case, using variations in the size of letters, and subtle spacing, to get the effect he desires.

The African Roscius of the Theatres Royal, Drury Lane and Covent Garden posed a problem for he included an enormous amount of information which cannot possibly be digested at a casual glance. The important information, however, was readily discernable, and that is the mark of a skilful printer. The list of distinguished patrons is the only part of the poster produced here. This practice of featuring the nobility and other important persons, before whom the entertainer had performed, on playbills and posters was characteristic of many Victorian performers.

140

TOWN HALL,

HARTLEPOOL.

ONE NIGHT.

MR. BRAHAM

Has the honour to announce to the nobility, gentry, and inhabitants of Hartlepool and its vicinity, that he will give a

GRAND CONCERT,

ON

ON THURSDAY EVENING, OCT. 10th, 1844,

On whic[illegible]casion he will introduce his sons and pupils,

MR. CHARLES BRAHAM

AND

MR. HAMILTON BRAHAM.

MR. BRAHAM WILL SING

THE SEA FIGHT, DEEPER AND DEEPER STILL, MOLLY BAWN, THE BETTER LAND

WILLIAM TELL, THE BAY OF BISCAY, ETC.,

And with his sons, several

POPULAR DUETS AND GLEES.

PART I.

Air—On the cold shores *(Bellini)* .... Mr. C. Braham.
Song—The Sea Fight—Stand to your guns *(Carter)* .... Mr. Braham.
Song—Sun of Freedom *(Bellini)* .... Mr. H. Braham.
Witches' Glee—When shall we three meet again.. *(King)* Mr. Braham, Mr. C. Braham, and Mr. H. Braham.
Song—A man's a man for a' that *(Burns)* .... Mr. Braham.
Serenade from Don Pasquale—Oh, Summer night, so sweetly bright *(Donizette)* .... Mr. C. Braham.
Irish Song—Molly Bawn *(Lover)* .... Mr. Braham.
Duet—Voglio dire lo Stupendo. From L'Elisir d'Amore *(Donizetti)* .... Mr. Braham and Mr. H. Braham.
Song—William Tell *(Braham)* .... Mr. Braham.

PART II.

Glee—The wind whistles cold. From the Opera of Guy Mannering *(Bishop)* .... Mr. Braham, Mr. C. Braham, and Mr. H. Braham.
Grand Scena from the Oratoria of Jeptha *(Handel)*
Recit.—Deeper and deeper still .... } Mr. Braham.
Air—Waft her, angels .... }
Song—My heart with love is beating *(Shield)* .... Mr. C. Braham.
Song—Rage, thou angry storm *(Benedict)* .... Mr. H. Braham.
Duet—Oh, Albion *(Braham)* .... Mr. Braham and Mr. C. Braham.
Song—(By desire) The better land (*Nelson*) .... Mr. Braham.
Song—The Wanderer (*Schubert*) .... Mr. H. Braham.
Duet—The Brothers (*Knight*) .... Mr. C. Braham and Mr. H. Braham.
Song—While the lads of the village (*Dibdin*) .... Mr. C. Braham.
Song—The Bay of Biscay (*Braham*) .... Mr. Braham.

Tickets—Front Seats, 3s 6d; Back Seats, 2s—to be had of Mr. PROCTER, Bookseller.

TO COMMENCE AT EIGHT O'CLOCK.

Printed at the office of JOHN PROCTER, Union Place, High Street, Hartlepool.

141

His Royal Highness the Duke of Sussex
His Royal Highness the Duke of Gloucester
Their Graces the Duke & Duchess of St. Albans
His Grace the Duke of Rutland
Their Graces the Duke and Duchess de Roviego
His Excellency Prince Esterhazy, Austrian Ambassador to the British Court
His Grace the Duke of Wellington
Her Grace the Duchess of Cannizarro
Their Graces the Duke & Duchess of Leinster
The Most Noble the Marquis of Anglesea
The Marquis and Marchioness of Wellesley
Right Hon. Lord Brougham and Vaux
The Duke and Duchess of Cambridge
Princess Augusta of Cambridge
Prince George of Cambridge
Marquis of Lansdowne
Col. Piper and Officers, 38th Regiment
Miss L. E. Landon
Major Magennis and Officers, 87th Regiment
Col. Clarke and Officers, 76th Regiment
John J. Bigger, Esq. Sovereign, Dundalk
Rev. John Herbert, Rector, Killarney
The Marquis of Kildare
His Grace the Archbishop of Tuam
Right Rev. Dr. Kyle, Bishop of Cork
Marquis of Granby
The Right Hon. Earl and Countess of Glengall
The Ladies Butler
The Earl and Countess Kenmare
The Earl and Countess Camperdown
The Earl of Wilton
The Earl and Countess Listewell
Lord and Lady Headley
The Earl and Countess of Charleville
Lord Arthur Lennox
Lord George Fitzgerald
Lord George Lennox
Capt. Hemans and Officers, 78th Depot
Lord Dundas
Lord Petre
The Hon. Stuart & Lady Emmeline Wortley
Col. Cairncross and Officers, 68th Regiment
Col. Badcock and Officers, 15th Hussars
Major and Lady Elizabeth Wathen
Doctor Valpy
Mrs. Hemans
Col. Stisted and Officers, 3rd Dragoons
Sir Robert and Lady Bateson, Londonderry
Sir William de Bathe
Sir C. and Lady Morgan
William Denny, Esq. High Provost, Tralee
Right Hon. Viscount Lorton
Lord and Lady Downs
Col. Campbell and Officers, 95th Regiment
Col. Paty and Officers, 94th Regiment
General Sir H. and Lady Vivian
Sir Walter Scott, Bart.
Major General Sir E. Blackney

7

SEE
WITH
WONDER AND
DELIGHT
THE GREAT AMERICAN BANJOIST.
PATRONISED
BY

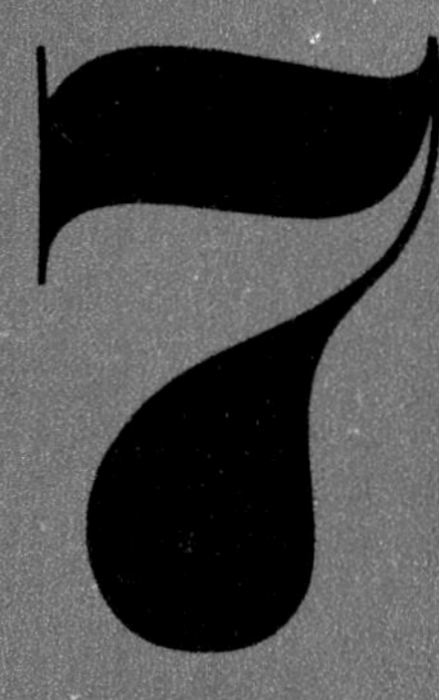

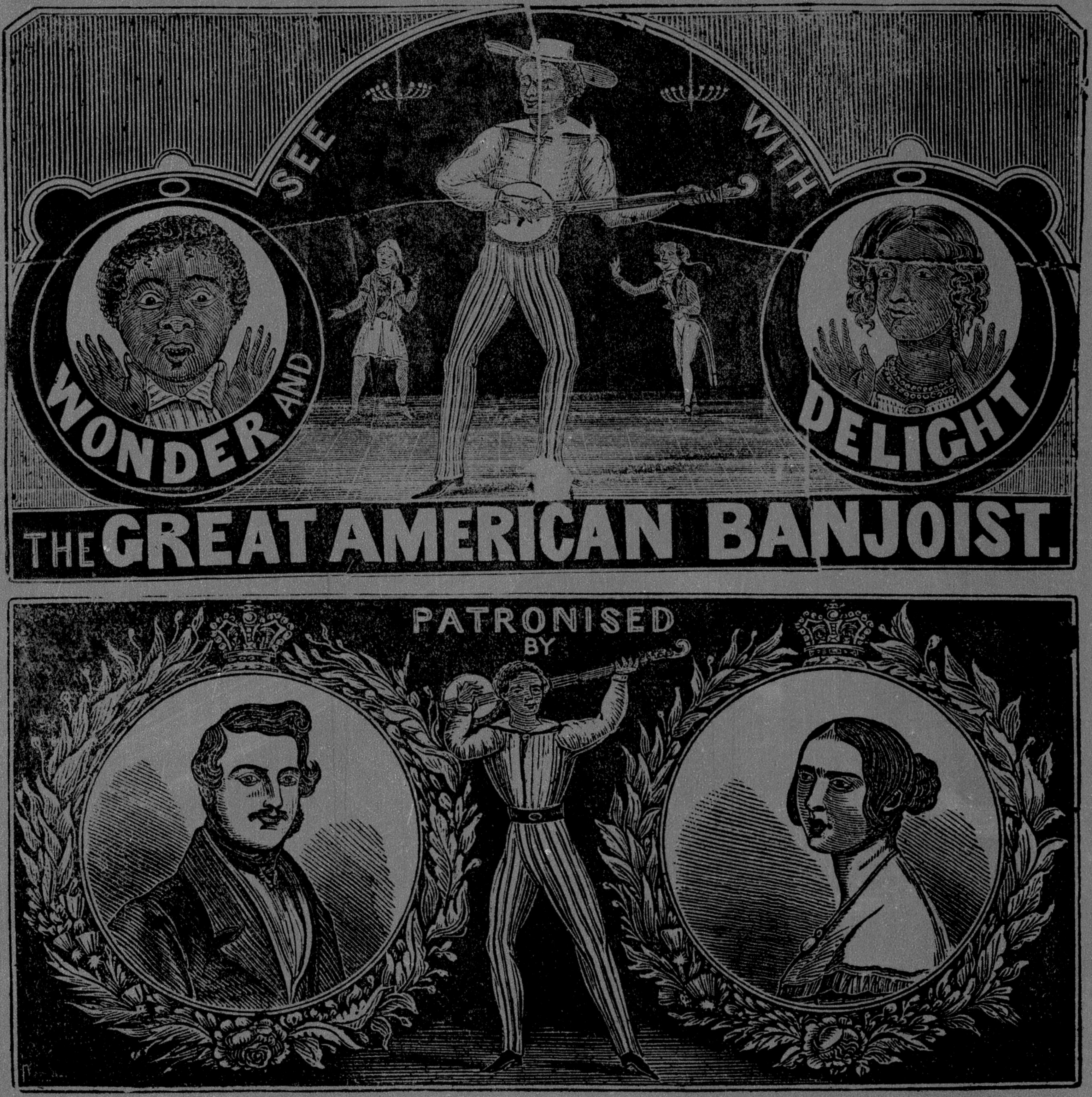

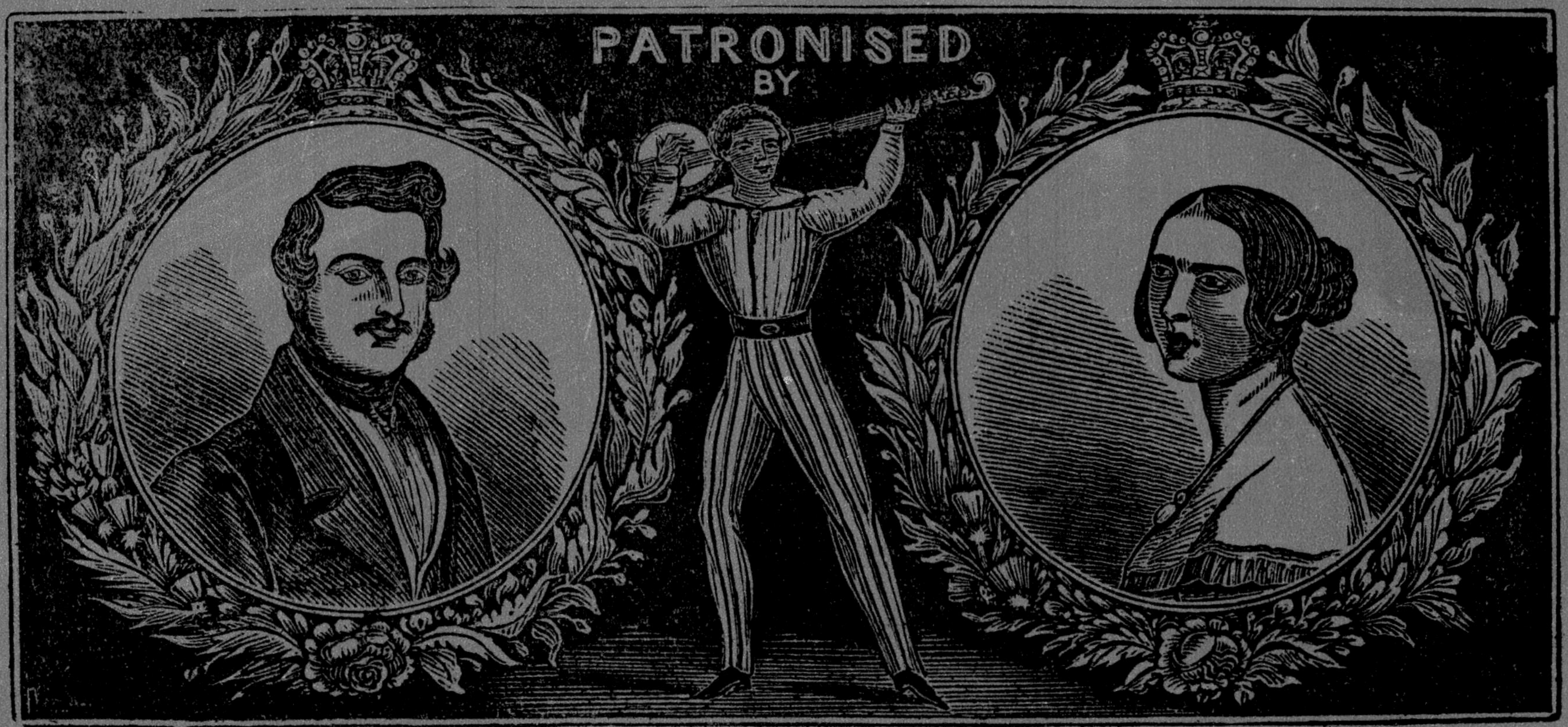

The nigger minstrels were a sensation when they first came to England around the middle of the century. Negroes themselves were no novelty to Englishmen for no fashionable lady of the eighteenth century would have been seen out of doors without a little negro boy as a page. The whole essence of the original minstrel show was that it was a masquerade in which white men daubed with burnt cork pretended to be stupid and ignorant negroes for the amusement of white audiences.

The nigger minstrel idea was conceived by Thomas D. Rice, a young actor of New York, after a summer season in Louisville in 1828. In the stable-yard of a man named Crow, just a few yards from the theatre, an old, decrepit slave was employed who used to amuse himself by rocking backwards and forwards on his heels whilst he crooned doggerel verses. As was usual at that time, he had taken his master's name, and so called himself Jim Crow. The chorus he sang at the end of every verse, whilst he shuffled round in a weird dance, was as follows:

'First on de heel tap, den on de toe.
Eb'ry time I wheel about, I jump. Jim Crow.
Wheel about, an' turn about, an' do jest so,
An' eb'ry time I wheel about, I jump. Jim Crow.'

Rice was fascinated with the old negro's tune and fitted his own words to it. Then one night, when there was an awkward gap in the programme at the theatre, he borrowed the old darkie's clothes and character and made his appearance on the stage. The audience went frantic with delight and he was recalled again and again. From that night in 1828, for the rest of his life, he was known as 'Jim Crow' Rice.

In 1833 he added to the act by dumping a blackened boy out of a sack on to the stage whose main role was to imitate Rice's dancing and act as his foil.

He came to England in 1836 and performed 'Jim Crow' and 'Sich a gettin' upstairs' at the Adelphi and other theatres and was an enormous success. Such was his success that within two years his imitators were appearing in every public house and theatre up and down the country. Every second-rate provincial actor did a 'Jump, Jim Crow' act.

But it was E. P. Christy who originated the style which became standard practice amongst negro minstrels. His show consisted of three parts. When the curtain rose the minstrels were to be seen standing in a semi-circle with a white faced 'Mr. Interlocutor' in the centre. He it was who said 'Gentlemen, be seated' and became the foil for the wise-cracks and badinage of the two end-men, Mr. Bones and Mr. Tambo. There were riddles and conundrums and comic and sentimental songs until it was time for the full chorus and grand walk-around. The second part was known as the 'olio', a mixture of dances, songs, music, and stump speeches. This concluded with a Hoe-down dance which was accompanied by rhythmic hand clapping and singing. Then came the third part, the after-pieces, which like the old theatre programmes, consisted of farces, comic opera, and burlesque.

It was for Christy that Stephen Foster wrote his well-known negro and sentimental songs. The original Christy Minstrels appeared in New York in 1846, but another company which performed as minstrels with blackened faces travelled from Boston to London in the same year and opened at the St. James' Theatre as 'The Ethiopian Serenaders'. They were five in number and so successful that they were commanded to appear before Queen Victoria.

They had imitators by the score. Until about 1880 the country was inundated by 'Original Christy Minstrels' 'Court Minstrels', 'Ohio Minstrels', 'Southern Christy Minstrels', and 'Buckley's Minstrels'. There were also 'The Only Original Christy Minstrels', the 'Mohawk Minstrels', the 'Queen's Minstrels', and the OICM (the 'Original Illustrated Christy Minstrels') who appeared complete with scenery.

Those were the days of the American Civil War and 'Uncle Tom's Cabin' which appeared in 1852 and was dramatised, together with Harriet Beecher Stowe's second anti-slavery novel, 'Dred, or the Dismal Swamp'. The plight of the negro slave was of much public concern. At Athenaeums and Mechanics' Institutes throughout England negroes made a good living recounting their alleged experiences as slaves and their thrilling escapes to freedom.

The Minstrels presented a more pleasant picture and audiences who arrived to show their sympathy for the negro stayed to enjoy the performance as entertainment and went away demanding more. The comic songs, the break-down dances, the haunting refrains and the sentimental spirituals were a sensational discovery and it took the Victorians years to get over it.

They flocked to see these professional companies but went away determined to emulate them. Men who under ordinary circumstances would never have been bold enough to appear on a stage took advantage of the black-faced anonymity of the coon, and the fellowship of the chorus, and banded themselves into Nigger Minstrel troupes. Every Sunday School, Club, Institute, and Volunteer Regiment in the land seemed to have its own minstrels who performed at every charitable function at which they were invited to appear.

They provided innocent fun but they did misrepresent the negro. He was shown as shiftless, stupid, lazy, dishonest, improvident and loud-mouthed, but he was also shown as peaceable, happy, and lovable. It is doubtful, to say the least, whether any member of the audience would be naive enough to believe that real negroes behaved like those they had seen on the stage.

The minstrels still remain with us, of course, a form of entertainment as stereotyped as Harlequin and Columbine used to be in the early Victorian pantomimes.

142
In an age of experiment when every conceivable instrument was tried, the Victorians must have been delighted to hear the banjo for the first time. 1846 is the year in which the Christy Minstrels first appeared and it is obvious from the poster that the later routine of the standard minstrel show has not yet been developed. The poster itself is more highly pictorial than the average bill which advertised shows and has an authentic and pleasing quaintness.

143
From the many posters which John Procter printed it is obvious that Mr. Gray and his son emulated the original 'Jim Crow' Rice, but they appear to be in strange company. Harpists and violinists were unusual companions for negro slaves but such a combination would not have upset the performers or the audience.

142

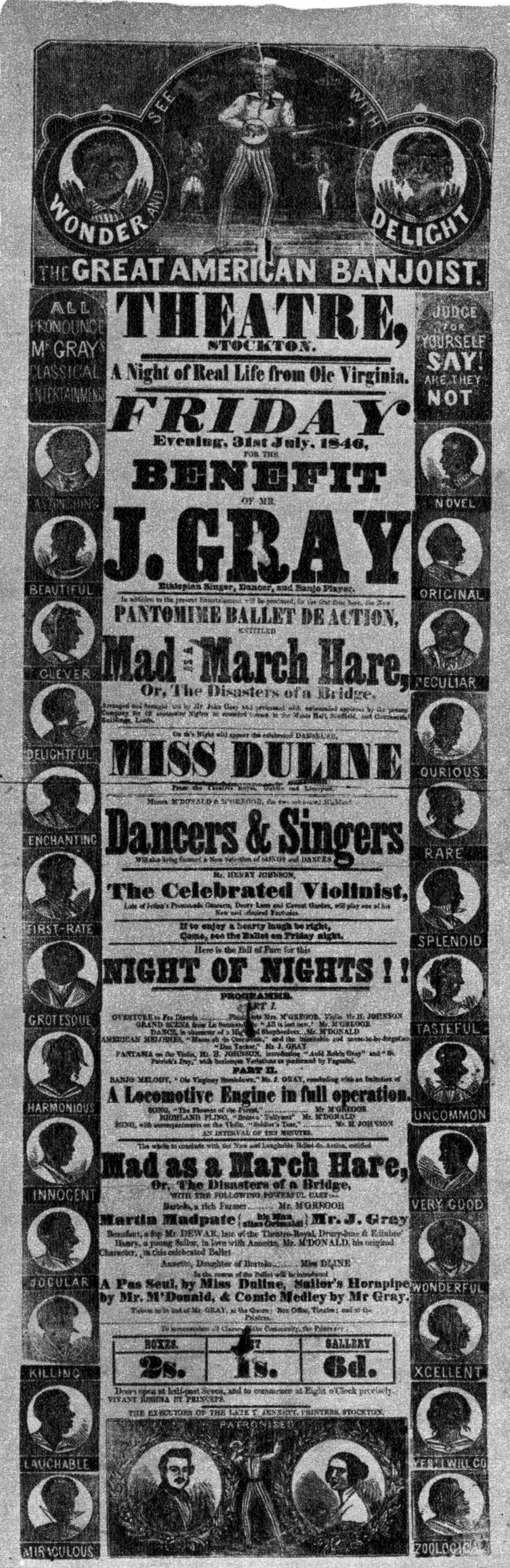

143

GRAND MUSICAL OLIO!

OR CONCERT AND BALL,

IN

THE TOWN HALL, HARTLEPOOL,

On THURSDAY, April 20.

The Entertainments will be of an entirely Novel description, and each Performer in their various departments Challenge England for Equal.

Mr. JOHN GRAY

The Great Virginian Banjo Melodist,

And only correct delineator of a Life of SLAVERY IN NORTH AMERICA, the Vicissitudes of the Mississippi Raftsman, the Wild Chanting of the Negro Crossing the Alleghany Mountains; together with the Fascinating and Fantastic Evolutions in the Lousiana Cane Breaks, render it the acme of Life in the Southern States.

MASTER GRAY,

The Bone Castanet Performer;

Alphonso Bowmer,

The Celebrated Harpist, from Her Majesty's Concerts;

MR. T. C. OWDEN,

The Violinist, Leader of the various Concerts at the Hanover Square Rooms.

The whole in conjunction with that highly-talented Artiste, Mr.

ARTHUR NELSON,

The Merry Musical Momus,

Whom for Versatility of Talent has no Rival. Mr. N. will first introduce that wonderfully natural Instrument, the

ROCK HARMONICON,

Producing the most delightful sounds and exquisite Harmony from

Solid Lumps of Stone.

After which, Mr. N. will introduce

THE XILO CORDION.

An instrument composed of Solid Pieces of Common Wood, and laid upon Plats of Straw, beat with Two Hammers, and from this simple material will produce Powerful Music. In another part of the Entertainment, Mr. N. will perform upon his

MONSTER DULCIMER!!!

Which was presented to him by Mr. Chickering, of Boston, in the United States, in the presence of the President of America! At the conclusion of this, the audience will say they are spending an Evening with Nelson, during which time he will introduce his Side-splitting TABLE TALK, consisting of Electioneering Speeches, Lectures upon Phrenology, Mesmerism, Cold Water Cures, History of England, Love, Folly, a Theatrical Career, Political Quirks, &c., &c., too numerous to mention, in fact it will be a Banquet of Wit. The whole to conclude with

The Railroad Overture, or North Carolina Crash.

PRICES OF ADMISSION:—

FRONT SEATS, 2s. 6d.; SECOND SEATS, 1s.; BACK SEATS, 6d.

Programmes of the Entertainment will be given on entering the Room. Seats may be taken from 2 to 4 o'Clock.

To commence at Half-past Seven o'Clock. No Half-price.

Persons taking a Front Seat Ticket will be admitted Free to the Ball, otherwise an extra charge of 1s.

TICKETS to be had of Mr GREY, Wheat Sheaf Inn, and of Mr PROCTER, Printer.

J. PROCTER, Printer, Union Place, High Street, Hartlepool.

144, 144A and 144B
An unknown mid-Victorian minstrel troupe appears at a provincial theatre. Was it as good as it declares? Show business being what it is, we must leave the question unanswered.

144

VICTORIA
CONCERT HALL,
WHITBY STREET, WEST HARTLEPOOL.
PROPRIETOR MR W. H. WRIGHT.
EXTRAORDINARY ATTRACTION
☞ The best Company ever known in West Hartlepool.
ON FRIDAY, September 3rd, 1869
BEING FOR THE
FAREWELL BENEFIT
OF
DWIGHT'S
MARYLAND MINSTRELS

Upon which occasion, the following Talented Artistes will appear.
For this Night only and last time this Season, Mr. and Mrs.
WAT MELTON!
Duettists and Dancers, have kindly consented to introduce their
WONDERFUL BOX TRICK!
Which caused such a Great
SENSATION!
On Saturday Last. Upon this occasion Mrs MELTON, will defy any Gentleman to tie her in the Sack and Box so that she cannot extricate herself in given time.
Also for this Night only Miss
GILFORD MAYNE!
Serio-Comic and Sentimental Vocalist.
MISS MARION FITZ-WILLIAMS
Queen of Serio-Comic Vocalists.
Mr. Dave Hilton!!!
The Popular Baritone.
HERR DEANI
The Celebrated Clown Pantomimist and Greatest Contortionist in the World.
THE SISTER & BROTHER ALBERT.
THE BROTHER & SISTER EDMUNDS.
HARRY DWIGHT'S
MARYLAND MINSTRELS
The "Original," and only acknowledged Male and Female Ethiopian Troupe ever organized in this or any other country, comprising the following Talented STAR ARTISTES :—
MRS. H. C. DWIGHT
Mdlle. JULIE!
Mr Tony Harris
Mr Carl Zita
MDLLE. CELIA
COMICAL YOUNG ZIPO,
MR. HARRY DWIGHT!
Upon which occasion they will introduce their Celebrated
ANVIL CHORUS!
With Steel Anvil Accompaniments, and their Highly-trained Troupe of Performing
Jerusalem Ponies!
They will also appear as the
SEVEN GREAT GIBBLE GOBBLES!
☞ Look out, & Don't Forget Friday, Sept. 3rd, 1869. Come Early.
In consequence of the Great Length of the Programme, the doors will open half-an-hour previous to the usual time.
PRICES AS USUAL.
West Hartlepool: J. PROCTER, Printer and Lithographer by Steam Power.

144A

HARRY DWIGHT'S
MARYLAND MINSTRELS
The "Original," and only acknowledged Male and Female Ethiopian Troupe ever organized in this or any other country, comprising the following Talented STAR ARTISTES :—

MRS.
H. C. DWIGHT
The Pure Soprano, Vocalist and Instrumentalist, &c.

Mdlle. JULIE!
Mezzo Soprano, and "Star of the Terpsechorean Art."

Mr Tony Harris
Comedian, Dancer, Bones and Tambourine Performer.

Mr Carl Zita
Vocalist and Dancer.

COMIC MAGICAL WITTY JOCULAR MERRY MUSICAL FUNNY AND FREE

MDLLE. CELIA
The Melodious Contralto, and principal Solo Vocalist of the Troupe.

COMICAL
YOUNG ZIPO,
The quickest, most active, and most Comical Darkey extant.

MR. HARRY
DWIGHT!
"The Original Emperor of the Darkies," Instrumentalist, Vocalist, Comedian and Dancer.

Upon which occasion they will introduce their Celebrated
ANVIL CHORUS!
With Steel Anvil Accompaniments, and their Highly-trained Troupe of Performing
Jerusalem Ponies!
They will also appear as the
SEVEN GREAT GIBBLE GOBBLES!
☞ Look out, & Don't Forget Friday, Sept. 3rd, 1869. Come Early.
In consequence of the Great Length of the Programme, the doors will open half-an-hour previous to the usual time.
PRICES AS USUAL.
West Hartlepool: J. PROCTER, Printer and Lithographer by Steam Power.

144B

DWIGHT'S
MARYLAND MINSTRELS

Upon which occasion, the following Talented Artistes will appear.

145 and 145A
There were many who exploited the new American entertainment known as 'Jim Crow' before it became well-known to the audiences in provincial towns. The title or sobriquet of 'Yankee' seems to have been adopted by any 'down-at-heels' entertainer who sought to take advantage of the new craze. A Yankee Cooke and a Yankee Brown also appeared in Hartlepool.

146
Another Victorian minstrel group.

147
The extract from the bill shows the programme which is divided into three parts, but these do not appear to conform to the traditional show.

148 (overleaf)
Yet another group of Ethiopian Serenaders and the perennial list of distinguished persons.

145

SMITH'S ROYAL MUSIC SALOON.
UNDER THE SOLE MANAGEMENT OF MR. J. BILLINGS.
ENGAGEMENT OF
Yankee Brooks

Performer on the BANJO, ACCORDION, BONES, &C., &C.,
ALSO,
MISS KATE MARTIN
From the ALBERT ROOMS, Liverpool, and
Miss Bloomfield,
FROM THE ROYAL CASINO, MANCHESTER.

Mr. B. begs most respectfully to inform his friends, the public, and the
LOVERS of HARMONY
That the high estimation in which this popular and well conducted Establishment has been held by the public, and the unanimous and enthusiastic approbation that greeted the performances of the several Artistes who have already appeared, together with an anxious desire to retain the reputation of this
PALACE OF MOMUS,
He has been induced to spare no expense in adding to the comfort and amusement of his visitors, by engaging several new and
Talented Performers!
Who will appear successively; and he hopes to receive a repetition of former favours, which will encourage him to renewed and increasing exertions to satisfy the public taste. The previous productions having been successful, it is with pride that the attention of the supporters of
INTELLECTUAL AMUSEMENTS,
Is called to the fact, that the talent which will appear during the Season, will surpass, with their new and effective performance, all previous efforts; and it is confidently hoped that a rapid succession of Novelties will ensure that share of the public's patronage, it will ever be his study to merit and acknowledge. The following names will at once prove that this Establishment can now boast of having
The Best Company out of London!

On Monday Evening, August 12,
MR. BROOKS,
THE CELEBRATED DELINEATOR OF NEGRO LIFE.
Will make his First Appearance in Hartlepool.

The fame of BROOKS has through Europe spread,
He is the Nigger and he goes a-head!
His darkie Songs—his new and varied styles—
Have gained applause throught the British Isles:
Let all then hear him—if they want a treat—
His personations are in truth complete;

His Dances, too, require a short allusion—
They are given nightly and in great profusion—
At once then seize the present chance and trace
The oddities of all the Negro Race!
With favorite Banjo before Lords and Dukes
Go and see the inimitable Nigger, BROOKS!

Miss Bloomfield,
The much admired and pleasing little Ballad Singer, from the Royal Casino, Manchester:
Mr. WILKIE will still continue to sing his favourite Sentimental & Nautical Songs.
MRS. HOWELL,
The Favourite Danseuse,
From the Theatre Royal York, Leeds, Hull, &c., where she has, by her graceful and spirited Performances, created an immense impression, to which the repeated shouts of approval which hailed her upon each appearance loudly testify.
MR. J. BILLINGS
The most humourous Comic Singer of the Day,
Whose Whimsicalities and numerous Hits have been the constant theme of admiration with every laughter-loving son of Momus, will on each evening amuse the Audience with his Funny Jokes, Quaint Sayings, Laughable Songs, &c.
MRS. SINCLAIR, SENTIMENTAL SINGER. MR. SINCLAIR, VIOLINIST.
Miss KATE MARTIN,
The celebrated Characteristic Singer,
From the Albert Rooms, Liverpool, will make her first appearance, on Monday, August 26.
Engagements are also pending with Mr. and Mrs. COLLINETTI, the Celebrated Comic Duett Singers, of which due Notice will be given.
The charges for Refreshments are so priced as to meet the public at large. A variety of Amusements will take place each Evening, so as to form a Rational Entertainment, blended with good Humour, Fun, and Frolic.
ADMISSION FREE!
Entertainments to commence at SEVEN o'Clock.
PROPRIETOR, Mr. SMITH—MANAGER, Mr. BILLINGS.

From the Office of J. PROCTER, Printer, High Street, Hartlepool.

145A

On Monday Evening, August 12,
MR. BROOKS,
THE CELEBRATED DELINEATOR OF NEGRO LIFE.
Will make his First Appearance in Hartlepool.

The fame of BROOKS has through Europe spread,
He is the Nigger and he goes a-head!
His darkie Songs—his new and varied styles—
Have gained applause throught the British Isles:
Let all then hear him—if they want a treat—
His personations are in truth complete;

His Dances, too, require a short allusion—
They are given nightly and in great profusion—
At once then seize the present chance and trace
The oddities of all the Negro Race!
With favorite Banjo before Lords and Dukes
Go and see the inimitable Nigger, BROOKS!

146

THE NORTHERN MINSTRELS.—On Monday, the so-called Northern Minstrels, gave a Concert in the Town Hall, Hartlepool, before a numerous and highly-respectable company, illustrative of Negro Life. The programme, included some of the most beautiful and popular Negro Melodies, and were rendered with a degree of taste and feeling which justifies us in pronouncing "The Northern Minstrels" to be the best of the kind we have heard for some time past, and certainly very superior to the half dozen that endeavoured to pass themselves off at this town a month ago as the "real original Serenaders." The Castanet and Tambourine playing was thoroughly artistic, and altogether the performances merited the frequent plaudits that were bestowed upon them.—*Stockton and Hartlepool Mercury, March 8th*, 1856.

CONCERT.—On Monday last, the Northern Minstrels gave a Concert of Vocal and Instrumental Music, in the Town Hall. The audience was small, but it did not seem to damp the hearts of the performers, as they gave every satisfaction to their hearers, and surpassed by far, every company of the same description that has visited this town.—*Hartlepool Free Press, March 8th*, 1856.

147

PROGRAMME.

PART I.

OPENING OVERTURE, ... FULL BAND
GLEE & CHORUS—"Come, Darkies, Sing," .... COMPANY
SONG—"Uncle Ned," .... COON
——— "Walk Jaw Bone," .... WHITE
——— "Dandy Jim," .... BROOKS
——— "Lucy Long," .... WHITE
——— "Ginger Blue," .... COON
——— "De Pride ob New Orleans," .... WHITE
——— "Ole Dan Tucker," .... BROOKS

PART II.

OVERTURE, (Polka) .... BAND
SONG—"Dinah Clare," .... WHITE
——— "A Life in Ole Virginny," .... COON
——— "Walk into de Parlour," .... WHITE
——— "Missus Tucker,—Ole Dan's Wife .... BROOKS
DUET, Violin and Bones, ... Messrs. COON & GLEN
SONG—"Ober de Mountain," .... WHITE
DUET, Stop dat Knocking, ... Messrs. COON & GLEN

PART III.

OVERTURE, (Breakdown) .... BAND
DUET, Who's dat knocking at de Door, ... Messrs. WHITE & KING
SONG—"De Ole Jaw Bone," .... COON
——— "Ole Joe," .... WHITE
——— "A Nigger's description of a Voyage from Ole Virginny to Hartlepool," .... BROOKS
——— "De Ole Grey Goose & Gander," .... WHITE
——— "Ole Virginny am de Place Boys," .... COON
GLEE—"Good Bye John," .... COMPANY

PUBLIC ROOMS, RIPON

UNDER THE SPECIAL PATRONAGE
OF

HENRY RUSSELL

THE CELEBRATED AMERICAN VOCALIST,

THE NEW ORLEANS ETHIOPIAN

SERENADERS

MESSRS. SANFORD, BURKE, OLE BULL, JUN. RAINER, AND SWAINE,

(FROM AMERICA),

Who have had the honour of appearing before Her Most Gracious Majesty, His Royal Highness Prince Albert,

Her Majesty the Queen Dowager
Their Royal Highnesses the Duke and Duchess of Cambridge
Her Royal Highness the Duchess of Gloucester
Marquis Provenzali, and Countess Dietrichstein
Count A. Patocki, the Belgian Minister, and Madame Van-de-Weyer
The Wurtemberg Minister
Baron Koller
The Sweedish Charge d' Affaires, and the Baroness de Cetto
The French Minister, and Countess de Jarnac

The Duke of Wellington
The Duke of Rutland
The Duke of Richmond
The Duke of Norfolk
The Duke of Northumberland
The Duke of Beaufort
The Duke of Somerset
The Duke of Grafton
The Duke of Sutherland
The Duke of Cleveland
The Duke of Atholl
The Duke of Devonshire

The Duchess of Buccleugh
The Duchess of Inverness
The Duchess of Buckingham
The Duchess of Grafton
The Duchess of Cleveland
The Duchess of Bedford
The Marquis and Marchioness of Ormonde
The Earl and Countess of Zetland
Lord and Lady John Russel
Sir Robert and Lady Peel, &c., &c., &c.

WILL GIVE THEIR

INIMITABLE ENTERTAINMENT,

ILLUSTRATIVE OF NEGRO LIFE AND CHARACTER,

ON FRIDAY, JULY 16th, 1847,

AT THE PUBLIC ROOMS, LOW SKELLGATE.

The following Letter has been received by the Serenaders from the celebrated Vocalist HENRY RUSSELL.

14, Park Place Villas, Maida Hill West, London.

Gentlemen,

Although personally opposed to any imitation of the Negro Character, yet from the very great talent evinced in your personification of the Negroes of the United states, and the excellent harmonies of your arrangements of many of the Melodies you sing, it affords me great pleasure in recommending you to the notice of the Musical Public.

I am, Gentlemen, yours truly,

HENRY RUSSELL.

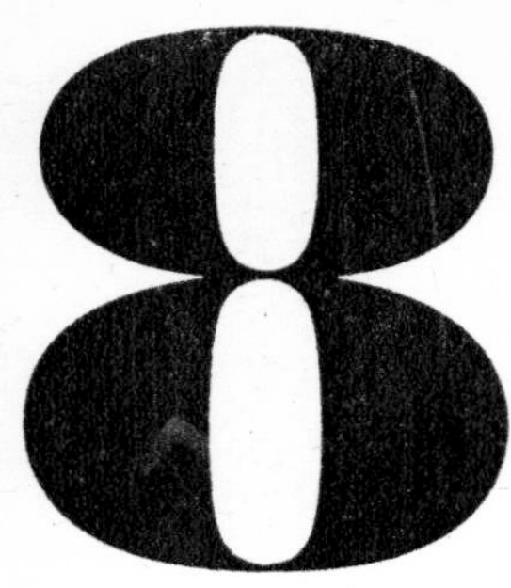

Educational Entertainment

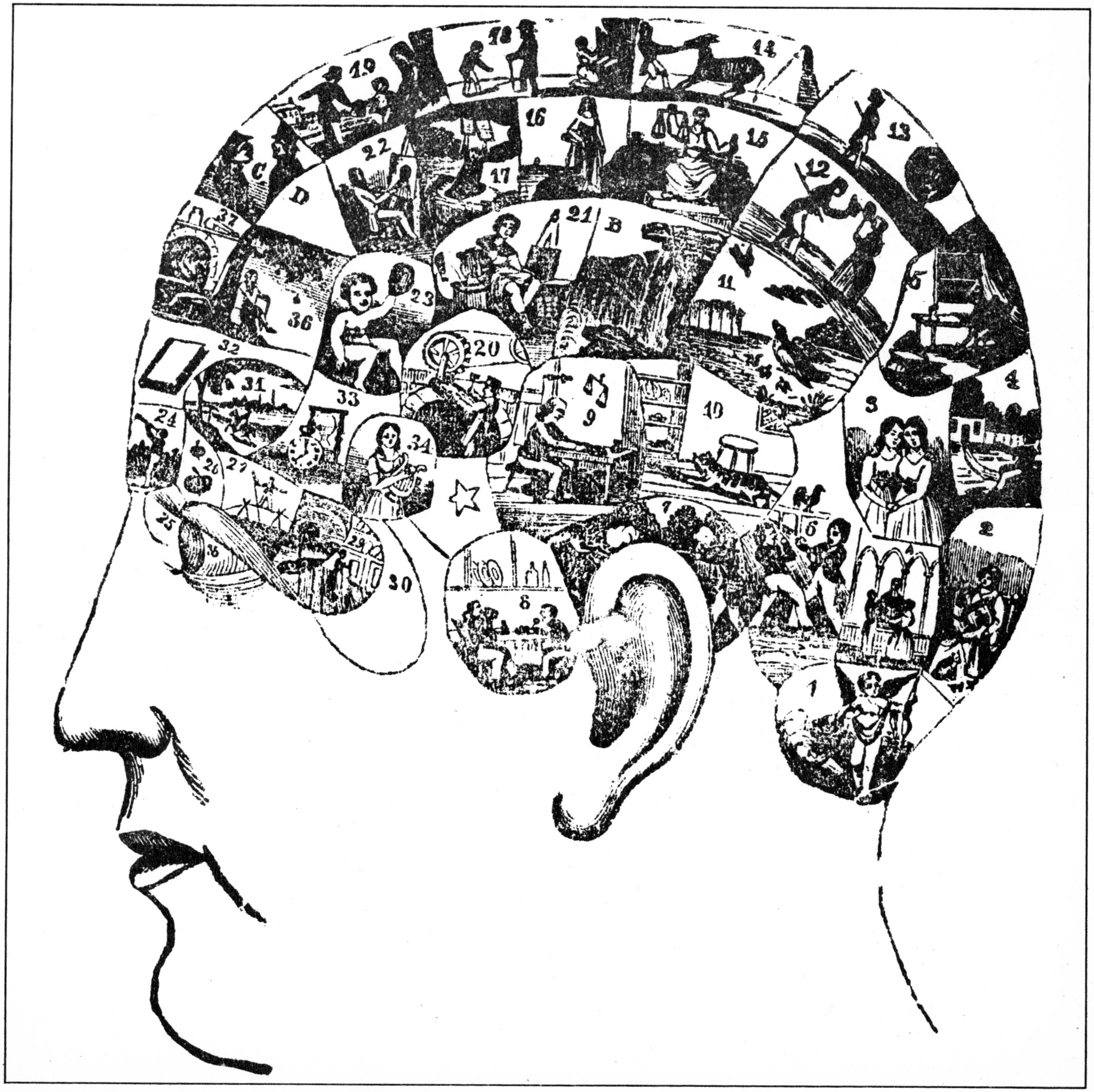

The Industrial Revolution that had wrought such sweeping changes in England since its inception around the middle of the 18th century, and which had continued into the 1830s, gathered even greater momentum during the early parts of the Victorian era. For the first time man seemed to appreciate the broad implications of the new sources of energy and power. The emergence of new and better means of communication, and of the railways in particular, played a crucial part. Railway transport was quick, cheap, safe and convenient. Steamships were no longer at the mercy of the wind; places once seemingly remote were brought within easy reach of merchants and travellers.

The French Revolution had shaken the foundations of the old society, set in its ways and composed in its ideas. There was a fresh approach to be made to all of the old problems and the prospect of a Brave New World to excite thinkers and dreamers. For the first time an intellectual movement existed among the working classes, and cheap pamphlets were published, aimed at the small tradesman and artisan, the mill worker and miner, advocating radical reform. Weekly papers appeared in all the leading industrial towns and found a ready sale. The new towns were full of people who had changed their homes and familiar surroundings and were engaged in new occupations. Such people felt the strain of change. Many of their neighbours were not only strangers but alien in background, religion, and race. Small wonder that there was discontent and a desire for improvement. In the popular phrase of the time, they desired to 'better themselves'.

Among all the theories and systems for public advancement which were advocated one idea dominated the rest to such an extent that it was never questioned; the belief that the remedy for all discontent lay in the full implementation of the Industrial Revolution. It offered the poor man the chance to 'get on', for diligence and industry, enterprise and intelligence, would reap a rich reward. Commercial success became the measure of a man's worth, and freedom to make the most of oneself in competition with others the most important of all human rights. Mechanics' Institutes were established to disseminate scientific knowledge and increase the workman's efficiency. There seemed to be no limits to the possibilities of further discoveries in science and mechanics with the enthusiastic assistance of informed artisans. But the sad truth was that many of the workmen lacked elementary book-learning and the Institutes found themselves struggling with classes in the Three Rs instead of enjoying lectures on scientific principles. Popular lecturing was a new thing and not many were good at it. It was said in 1849 that 'A man must have a very happy talent for lecturing if he succeeds in making scientific lectures popular.' The sad result of over-ambitious programmes was that the working man stayed away from the Institute designed for him and his vacant place was taken by the clerk and the craftsman and, later still, by the business and professional man.

Nevertheless the desire for knowledge was genuine enough and numbers of working men banded themselves together to meet regularly in the evening to endeavour to improve themselves by mutual intercourse. The Ten Hours Act of 1847 and subsequent related changes gave people additional leisure time and by 1849 there was a large increase in the number of these unofficial classes. Lectures of a scientific nature could be a success if given by the right sort of man, as has already been pointed out, and the case of Mr. Richardson, whose startling poster is to be seen on the opposite page, was cited as an example of the best sort of itinerant lecturer.

He was a self-educated teacher who, since 1835, had travelled as a peripatetic lecturer on science to the scattered northern villages where 'the toiling mining population of Durham and Northumberland proceed over the hills in rain, sleet, and frost, that they may learn the great truths which civilisation has made manifest.' There is a solid foundation of fact behind this high-sounding phrase as a syllabus of his course of four lecturures makes clear. Part is reproduced in a subsequent poster. Although lacking in oral finesse he knew his facts, conducted his experiments with dexterity and skill, and never failed to interest and instruct his audience. Let us meet him as he negotiates with John Procter.

Rawtenstall, near Bury, Lancs.
Oct. 21st, 1852

Dear Sir,
I have no doubt you will recollect me Lecturing at Hartlepool some years ago in the Town Hall. I have to lecture at Northallerton next week on the Monday, Tuesday, Thursday, and Friday. I lectured at all the towns a year ago up to Stockton on Tees. I am thinking of coming to Hartlepool the week after I have done at Northallerton. I recollect last time I was in Hartlepool I had the use of the Town Hall for the cleaning expenses. Can you enquire about the matter for me and drop me a line by return of post? I shall get home tomorrow and remain there till Sunday night when I shall leave for Leeds to be ready to travel by the first train from there to Northallerton. I am thinking of going my old ground over again in the good old County of Durham – Hartlepool, Thornley, perhaps Sedgefield, Durham, etc. etc. If you can arrange for me in the Court House I can forward the wood cut and form of bill on Monday next from Northallerton.

Enclosed you will find a Syllabus on how the Lectures are managed by me, please write by return of post and tell me what you think about my visit once more through the County of Durham. My own residence is High Field, Southowram, near Halifax, after Sunday morning next Golden Lion Inn, Northallerton
Yours most truly,
Wm. Richardson

We may have to take other people's word about Mr. Richardson's skill as a lecturer but there is no doubt from his letters that he knew how to organise his affairs.

Not all lecturers talked about Science. Vincent, the orator, was a very popular visitor. There were many who thought that noble thoughts, nobly uttered, uplifted and inspired men, and there were those who combined instruction with entertainment by exhibiting the subjects of their experiments with laughing gas, mesmerism, and hypnotism to the amusement of their friends. Many of the Victorians seemed to spend their leisure time in telling or hearing some new thing. Little seemed to bore them as this selection of posters confirms.

149

THORNLEY SCHOOL ROOM.

"O ye Lightnings, that glance with forked fury from the angry gloom."

PHILOSOPHICAL LECTURES

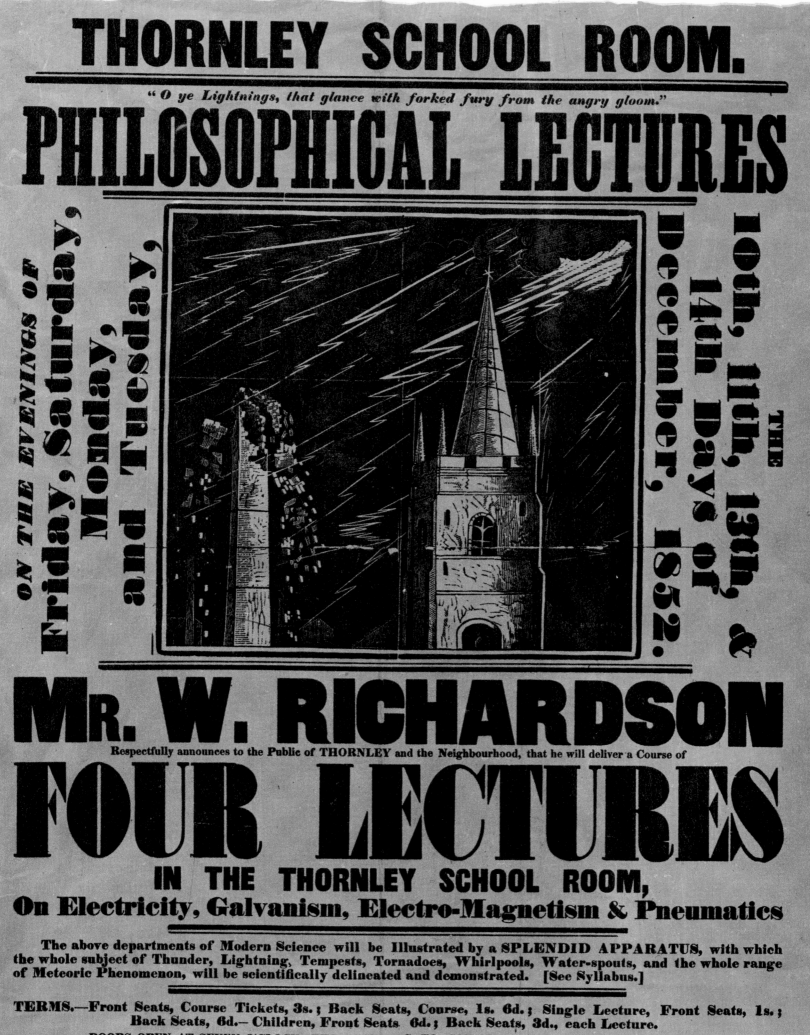

ON THE EVENINGS OF
Friday, Saturday,
Monday,
and Tuesday,

THE
10th, 11th, 13th, &
14th Days of
December, 1852.

MR. W. RICHARDSON

Respectfully announces to the Public of THORNLEY and the Neighbourhood, that he will deliver a Course of

FOUR LECTURES

IN THE THORNLEY SCHOOL ROOM,

On Electricity, Galvanism, Electro-Magnetism & Pneumatics

The above departments of Modern Science will be Illustrated by a SPLENDID APPARATUS, with which the whole subject of Thunder, Lightning, Tempests, Tornadoes, Whirlpools, Water-spouts, and the whole range of Meteoric Phenomenon, will be scientifically delineated and demonstrated. [See Syllabus.]

TERMS.—Front Seats, Course Tickets, 3s.; Back Seats, Course, 1s. 6d.; Single Lecture, Front Seats, 1s.; Back Seats, 6d.— Children, Front Seats 6d.; Back Seats, 3d., each Lecture.

DOORS OPEN AT SEVEN O'CLOCK, THE LECTURES TO COMMENCE AT HALF-PAST PRECISELY.

From the Office of J. PROCTER, High Street, Hartlepool, and Victoria Terrace, West Hartlepool.

149 (page 123)
Here we have one of the arresting bills of the lecturer on science who was admired all over the North. The block from which the startling illustration was printed was his own and forwarded to the printer to be used on his bills. In 1852 he spoke of making another lecture tour in 'good old County Durham' and here we see him at Thornley, among the colliers he so enthralled that they would tramp through any sort of weather to hear him.

150
Mrs. Kneebon was the wife of the Free Church minister and proposes to open a school in her own house. The fees are very moderate but how extraordinary that she has not made it clear that her school is for little girls. This must be inferred from her pledge to improve her charges in the 'Substantials of Female Education'.

151
The synopsis of Mr. Richardson's last lecture of a 4-day course on 'Electricity & Pneumatics' held in October 1842.

152
It is difficult to see the connection between mesmerism and phrenology but presumably Mr. Brownless would find one, and thus provide his audience with the opportunity of hearing about both.

153
This is a hybrid performance combining something of the educational lecture with that of a typical panorama and using a panorama of the heavens as its centre piece. It is interesting to note that Mr. Henry, F.S.A., would be appearing in Newcastle in four days time.

150

EDUCATION.

M. J. KNEEBON

BEGS TO INTIMATE TO HER FRIENDS AND THE PUBLIC, THAT SHE WILL

OPEN A SCHOOL,

ON MONDAY, JANUARY 12th 1857,

At No. 17, Northgate Street, Hartlepool,

And she pledges her utmost efforts to improve the Children of her charge, in Morals, Manners, and the Substantials of Female Education.

TERMS.

Reading, Spelling, Knitting, and Plain Needle Work, per Quarter.............. 6s.

Writing, Arithmetic, Grammar, Geography, History, Drawing, and Fancy Needlework, per Quarter .... 9s.

N. B. Morning Attendance, during Winter, from 9 to 12, and Afternoon, from 1 to 4 o'clock; during Summer, from 9 to 12, and from 2 to 5 o'clock.

151

LECTURE 3—~~THURSDAY~~—PNEUMATICS.

That the Air is a Fluid. Its materiality demonstrated by a resistance it opposes to various bodies in motion. The Air Pump; its construction and action explained. Weight and pressure on the Earth's surface demonstrated by exhausted Receivers. Magdeberg Hemispheres, and other highly interesting experiments. The variable Densities of the Atmosphere. Torricellian Experiment. Principle of a Suction Pump explained and illustrated by an elegant Working Model of that useful domestic machine. The Syphon. The absurdity of Suction shown as vaguely used to explain the cause of various effects arising from Atmospheric Pressure.

LECTURE 4—~~FRIDAY~~—PNEUMATICS.

152

PHRENO-MESMERISM.

The Inhabitants of HARTLEPOOL are respectfully informed, that a

MEETING

ON THE ABOVE SUBJECT, WILL BE HELD

In Mr. Bell's School Room, Darlington Street, On Monday Evening 11th September, 1843,

TO COMMENCE AT EIGHT AND CLOSE AT TEN;

When Mr. T. BROWNLESS will give a History of the Science, and the Conduct of its Opponents; the Impetus it has given to the Study of Phrenology; its use as a Curative Agent; also the Conditions to be observed in its Practice.

☞ The Lecture will be illustrated by one of the most interesting Female Mesmeric Subjects in the Kingdom

Admittance, 6d. each—Reserved Seats, 1s.

J. PROCTER, PRINTER, &c., UNION PLACE, WEST-END HIGH STREET, HARTLEPOOL.

153

This Night

THURSDAY, Nov. 4th, 1847.

DEMONSTRATIONS OF THE

HEAVENS AND THE EARTH!

TOWN HALL, HARTLEPOOL, TO COMMENCE AT EIGHT O'CLOCK.

The Exhibition will be given in the Theatre Royal, Newcastle, on Monday Night, the 8th of November.

MR. HENRY, F. S. A.,

Has the honour to announce his intention of giving a Popular Exposition of the Science of ASTRONOMY, illustrated by a

MAGNIFICENT PANORAMA

OF THE

HEAVENS!

Comprising more than 7,000 Comets, Nebulæ, and other objects of

UNIVERSAL STELLAR CREATION,

WITH SPLENDID PAINTINGS OF THE

EARTH!!

ZODIACS, AND CONSTELLATIONS,

And assisted by valuable Astronomical instruments, including the immense

PLANETARIUM

Showing, at one view, all the Planets in actual motion, by

MACHINERY,

AND OCCUPYING A SPACE OF MORE THAN 200 FEET.

This Instrument is of a most costly and splendid description, being on a scale of Magnitude and Magnificence never before attempted in England. To the spectator, the Sun and Planets, the accuracy of their motions, with the changing of the Moon from the first to the last Quarter, and their appearances as though they were suspended in space, produce one of the grandest illustrations of the Heavens that can be conceived; conveying to the youthful mind a more correct notion of the

SOLAR SYSTEM

THAN YEARS OF STUDY.

SCENE 1.—An Exquisite Painting, showing an Astronomical View of all the Constellations, Stars, and Nebulæ of the Northern Hemisphere.
SUBJECT.—The Fixed Stars—the Planets—the Constellations.
SCENE 2.—A Magnificent View of the Earth, 45 feet in circumference, apparently suspended in space, surrounded with its Atmosphere and Clouds.
SUBJECT.—The Earth's Shape—its Size, how ascertained—its Distance from the Sun—its Velocity, &c.
SCENE 3.—A Splendid Geometrical Projection of the Earth.
SUBJECT.—The Measurement of Planetary Distances.
SCENE 4.—An Exquisitely-finished Drawing of the Modern Zodiac, showing the Earth's Position in the Ecliptic, at various Seasons of the Year.
SUBJECT.—The Cause of the Seasons—Winter, Summer, Spring, and Autumn.
SCENE 5.—Highly-finished Drawing of the Hindoo Zodiac, taken from the Hindoo Pantheon, with remarks.
SCENE 6.—Sculpture-like Painting of the celebrated Denderah Zodiac, taken from the Temple of Isis, in Egypt, and supposed to be Antediluvian; copied, by permission of French Government, from the original, now in the King's Museum at Paris.

Scene 7.—Moveable Astronomical Instrument for showing the Cause of Eclipses.

The Machinery will be combined with Dioramic effect, producing an exact representation of an Eclipse. The Scene represents the venerable Ruins of St. Mary's Abbey, York, at midnight, and from that hour till the Moon reaches the highest point in the horizon, the various effects of light are brought to view—the lingering darkness gradually disappears—the Clouds change both in form and colour—the enchanting Ruins melt into light—the ivy leaves sparkle with a silvery brightness—the Moon gradually becomes eclipsed—all the gradations of light and shade are observable without there being the slightest perception in what manner these changes are produced.

Scene 8.—The Magnificent and Unrivalled Planetarium, with the Panorama of the Heavens.

In this splendid View of the Solar System, the motions of the Planets, both primary and secondary, may be seen at one glance. MERCURY, VENUS, the EARTH, and MOON, with the continual variation of its Phases from the first to the last quarter—MARS, JUPITER, and its four Moons, SATURN, its Rings and seven Moons, as also HERSCHELL and its six Moons; conveying to the spectator the most sublime view of the beautiful precision and harmony of the Celestial Spheres that is possible to conceive.

The last new discovered Planet by Le Verrier, is added to the Machinery of the Planetarium, and will be seen revolving in its orbit, the distance of which from the Sun is 3,200,000,000 miles, and the size of which is computed to be more than 48 times larger than the Earth.

SCENE 9.—A Telescopic View of the Moon as seen through Lord Rosse's immense Telescope, within the last three months. This

MAP OF THE MOON

Is the most correct ever taken, and is 30 feet in circumference.——After the conclusion of the Astronomical Entertainment, a variety of

DISSOLVING ILLUSTRATIONS

OF THE MOST REMARKABLE PLACES IN

THE WORLD

BEING FORTY IN NUMBER,

AND 4,000 SQUARE FEET OF ILLUMINATED SCENERY,

Including VIEWS of PALESTINE, INTERIORS of CASTLES, RUINS of REMARKABLE ABBEYS, LANDSCAPES, ALPINE PASSES, GLACIERS, AVALANCHES, VOLCANOES, ICEBERGS, WATERFALLS, and FORESTS, will be exhibited.

PROGRAMME AS FOLLOWS:—

VIEWS OF PALESTINE.—Pool of Siloam.—Lake of Gennesereth, by Moonlight.—Village of Bethany, with the Tomb of Lazarus and the Dead Sea.—Mount Tabor and the River Kishon.—Church of the Holy Sepulchre and Mosque of Omar.—Tomb of Absalom—Valley of Jehoshaphat.—Crypt of the Holy Sepulchre.—View of Jerusalem from the Mount of Olives.—Interior of the Church of the Nativity at Jerusalem.—VIEWS OF ENGLAND.—Interior of St. Paul's Cathedral, London.—Cloister's of Fountains Abbey, Yorkshire.—Tower of London, from the Thames.—Bideford Bridge.—Ruins of Whitby Abbey.—Thames Tunnel.—Ruins of Netley Abbey, by moonlight.—IRELAND.—Cavern in Giant's Causeway.—Ruins of Abbey Dermot.—Lake of Killarney.—WALES.—Ruins of Tintern Abbey.—Vale Crucis Abbey, near Llangollen.—Neath Abbey.—River Wye.—INDIA.—The Taj Mahal, at Agra, from the River Jumna.—The Sacred Shrines at Dwarka.—SYRIA.—Pilgrims at Antioch.—Falls of Cydnus, near Tarsus.—GERMANY.—Tomb of Maximilian I, at Inspruck.—The Giesbach Cascade.—SCOTLAND.—Ruins of Holyrood Palace, by Moonlight.—AMERICA.—Charlestown, on the Mississippi.—FRANCE.—Hospital of invalids, at Paris.—Smuggler's Cave, by Moonlight.—SWITZERLAND.—The Castle of Chillon.—Lake of Geneva.—Swiss Cottage and Water Mill.—NAPLES.—Eruption of Mount Vesuvius, with the City and Bay.—FLANDERS.—An Old Convent at Bruges.—CHINA.—Capture of the Bogue Forts.—Capture of the Batteries on the Woo Sung River.—POLAR REGIONS.—View of the Grand Icebergs, by Captain Ross. And alternating with the

CHROMATROPE

PRODUCING AN UNIQUE AND BRILLIANT DISPLAY OF

CHINESE FIREWORKS.

Admission—Front Seats, 2s.—Second Class Seats, 1s.—Schools & Children admitted at 1s. each to the Front Seats only.

The whole of the above extensive Scenery will be exhibited in ONE *Night, although the entertainments usually occupy Two Nights.*

Doors open at Half-past Seven, and the Exhibition to commence at Eight precisely, and terminate at a Quarter to Ten.

An interval of Ten Minutes between the Celestial Scenery and the Views.

A FAMILY TICKET to admit Three Adults to the Front Seats, 5s. each, may be had of Mr. PROCTER, High Street; or of Mr. HENRY, at the King's Head Hotel, Hartlepool.

J. PROCTER, PRINTER, UNION PLACE, HIGH STREET, HARTLEPOOL.

154
The respect which Henry Vincent was accorded, irrespective of the subject he chose to speak on, is reflected in the names of the eminent citizens who have consented to preside at the lectures. Yet who would patronise such topics today? Each synopsis seems an echo of the still-born speech of Toad of Toad Hall.

155
To the Victorians phrenology was as scientific as electricity and mechanics. They saw its uses if properly applied and hoped with its aid to place education and character training into an organised system.

154

HARTLEPOOL MECHANICS' INSTITUTE.

The Inhabitants of Hartlepool, West Hartlepool, and Vicinity, are respectfully informed that the Committee of this Institution have arranged with

HENRY VINCENT, ESQ.,

THE WELL-KNOWN POPULAR ORATOR, TO DELIVER

FOUR ORATIONS

IN THE

TEMPERANCE HALL, HARTLEPOOL,

ON THE EVENINGS OF

Thursday and Friday, the 24th & 25th of April, and on Thursday and Friday, the 1st & 2nd of May, 1862.

ON THE FOLLOWING INTERESTING AND ENTERTAINING TOPICS.

LECTURE 1.—THURSDAY, APRIL 24th,

The American Revolution, its Causes and Consequences.

Social and Political weakness and strength of the United States—The Slave Institution, and its action.—The Abolitionists—The Compromise Parties—The Free Soil Party—Intrigues of the South to master the Federal Government—Lincoln's Election to the Presidency—Insurrection of the South; will the North win? and will Slavery die? —Influence of the movement upon the commercial and financial condition of England.

LECTURE 2.—FRIDAY, APRIL 25th,

JOHN MILTON.

JOHN MILTON, The Man, The Scholar, The Poet, The Patriot. The Active Man, The Prose Writer, The Puritan, The Republican, The Political Prophet, The Prodigy of his own age, and the glory of all time.

LECTURE 3.—THURSDAY, MAY 1st.

Daily Life and Duty in Hard Lessons from People we run against. Illusions of Young People. The World all Sunshine. Influence of Smooth Words, Fine Dress, and Rich Men's Feasts! Importance of Early Discipline in Morals and Mind. Weak Props. "Rich Relations." People who make Promises. Flatterers. Well-wishers. Sneaks. Over-polite People. Blunt People. "People who can't help it." "People who would if they could." "People who wouldn't if they could." The True Heroism of Life—how best Realised. Activity and Energy, Self-reliance, Intelligence—the great qualities from which Great Lives spring.

LECTURE 4.—FRIDAY, MAY 2nd.

A[illegible]y passages from the Constitutional History of English Parliaments.

A few pages from the Constitutional History of English Parliaments. The Ancient British, Roman, Saxon, Danish, and Norman Eras. Liberty overthrown by the Arms of Feudalism, but gradually restored by the Industry and Intelligence of the People. Influence of the Reformation and Puritanism upon our Liberties. Progress of the Representative Power to the days of Queen Victoria. The Dangers that now threaten it. England the upholder of Representative Institutions.

THE FOLLOWING GENTLEMEN WILL PRESIDE AT THE LECTURES:—

On Thursday Evening, April 24th, the WORSHIPFUL THE MAYOR, (WM. GRAY, Esq.,) President of the Institute, On Friday Evening, April 25th, GEORGE JAFFREY, Esq., Vice-president. On Thursday Evening, May 1st, WILLIAM EALES, Esq., J. P. On Friday Evening, May 2nd, GEORGE BLUMER, Esq.

ADMISSION.—To the Course—Reserved Seats, 5s.; Front Seats, 3s.; Back Seats, 1s. Single Lecture—Reserved Seats, 1s. 6d.; Front Seats, 1s.; Back Seats, 6d. Tickets to be had of the Committee, of the Secretary, and of Mr. J. PROCTER, Bookseller, where a Plan of the Lecture Hall may be seen, and Reserved Seats, secured.

As the proceeds of these Lectures will be solely applied to the Improvement of the Library of the Institute, the Committee confidently hope to secure a large attendance of all interested in the Progress and Welfare of Mechanics' Institutes.

Doors open at Half-past 7. Chair to be taken at 8 o'clock precisely.

☞ Entrance to the Reserved Seats Fronting Lumley Square.

J. HINDMARSH, HON. SEC.

J. PROCTER, Printer and Lithographer, Southgate, Hartlepool.

155

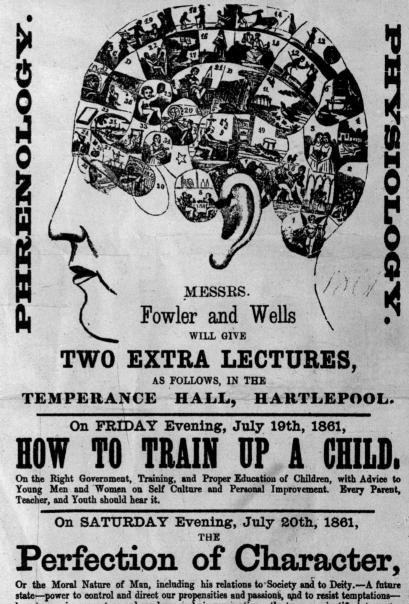

TWO EXTRA LECTURES

[No study can compare with that of MAN, either in magnitude or practical utility. It teaches us OURSELVES, our fellow men, our duties, and our capabilities. Phrenology puts the finger of ABSOLUTE knowledge on the whole cycle of human interest—material, social, intellectual, and moral,—every good, and its increase; every evil, and its remedy. Man's morals may be improved, his vices suppressed, his virtues developed, and Phrenology shows how. Should it not therefore, command your first attention.

PHRENOLOGY.

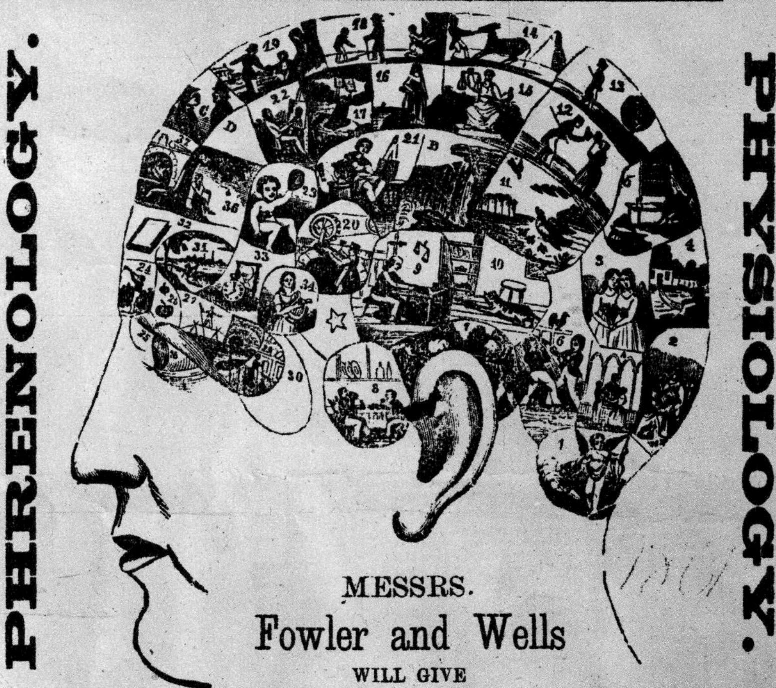

PHYSIOLOGY.

MESSRS.
Fowler and Wells
WILL GIVE

TWO EXTRA LECTURES,

AS FOLLOWS, IN THE

TEMPERANCE HALL, HARTLEPOOL.

On FRIDAY Evening, July 19th, 1861,

HOW TO TRAIN UP A CHILD.

On the Right Government, Training, and Proper Education of Children, with Advice to Young Men and Women on Self Culture and Personal Improvement. Every Parent, Teacher, and Youth should hear it.

On SATURDAY Evening, July 20th, 1861,

THE

Perfection of Character,

Or the Moral Nature of Man, including his relations to Society and to Deity.—A future state—power to control and direct our propensities and passions, and to resist temptations—how to acquire respect, moral prudence and circumspection—the true or scientific interpretation of FAITH, HOPE, and CHARITY.

Tickets—Front Seats, 1s.; Second do., 6d.; Back do., 3d.

Doors open at Half-past Seven, to commence at Eight. Each Lecture to close with Public Examinations.

☞ PRIVATE EXAMINATIONS. ☜

Professional Delineations, with Charts and full written Description of Character, and advice in regard to "WHAT TO DO," or the most appropriate occupations and pursuits in life; Faults, how to correct them; Health, how to secure and retain it; the Management of Children; Self-improvement, Marriage, &c., given during the day in private reception rooms of the Temperance Hall. Persons desiring the services of Messrs. FOWLER & WELLS, should call early, as their stay in Hartle[illegible] terminates soon, and another opportunity may not occur.

156
We are more than halfway through the reign of Victoria and new wonders keep appearing. There are still plenty of panoramas making the rounds, but here we have a magic lantern entertainment which may disappoint some of the audience. Are the slides of splendid views painted by celebrated artists, or are they what they say, splendid views of celebrated artistes? There isn't much doubt which it will be, even if the gentleman prefers to remain anonymous.

157
Professor Chadwick's poster is clearly an attempt to 'blind people with science' for he calls mesmerism electrobiology. Part of his programme illustrates a Victorian characteristic, that of delighting in the discomfort or misfortune of others. The volunteers who 'will be deprived of the Power of Speech, Hearing and Sight', who will 'believe themselves to be the Duke of Wellington, Nelson, Napoleon . . . , who will be Made Drunk on Cold Water' will certainly succeed in arousing the sadistic emotions of the audience.

156

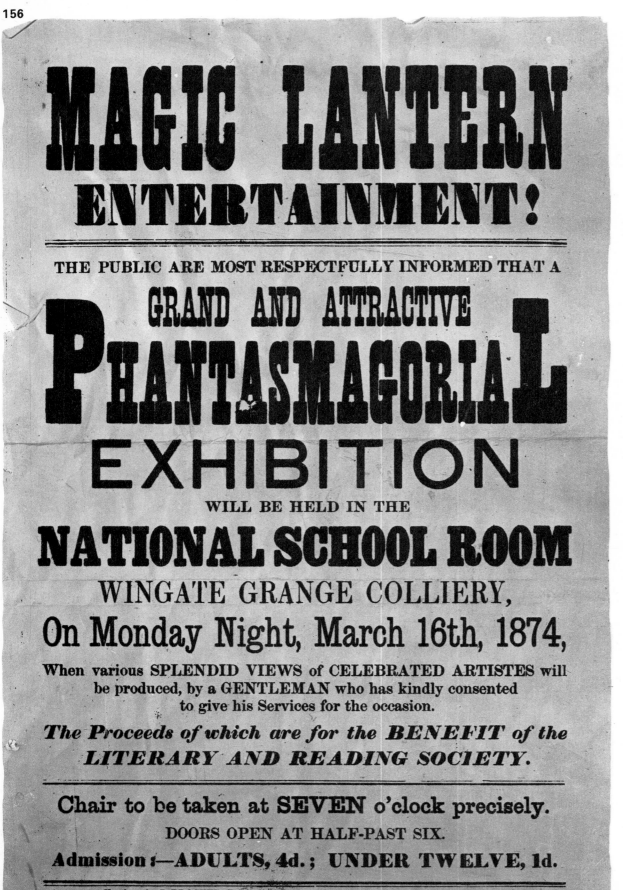

MAGIC LANTERN

ENTERTAINMENT!

THE PUBLIC ARE MOST RESPECTFULLY INFORMED THAT A

GRAND AND ATTRACTIVE

PHANTASMAGORIAL

EXHIBITION

WILL BE HELD IN THE

NATIONAL SCHOOL ROOM

WINGATE GRANGE COLLIERY,

On Monday Night, March 16th, 1874,

When various SPLENDID VIEWS of CELEBRATED ARTISTES will be produced, by a GENTLEMAN who has kindly consented to give his Services for the occasion.

The Proceeds of which are for the BENEFIT of the LITERARY AND READING SOCIETY.

Chair to be taken at SEVEN o'clock precisely.

DOORS OPEN AT HALF-PAST SIX.

Admission:—ADULTS, 4d.; UNDER TWELVE, 1d.

Hartlepool: J. PROCTER, Printer and Lithographer by Steam Power, Southgate. 21,668.

157

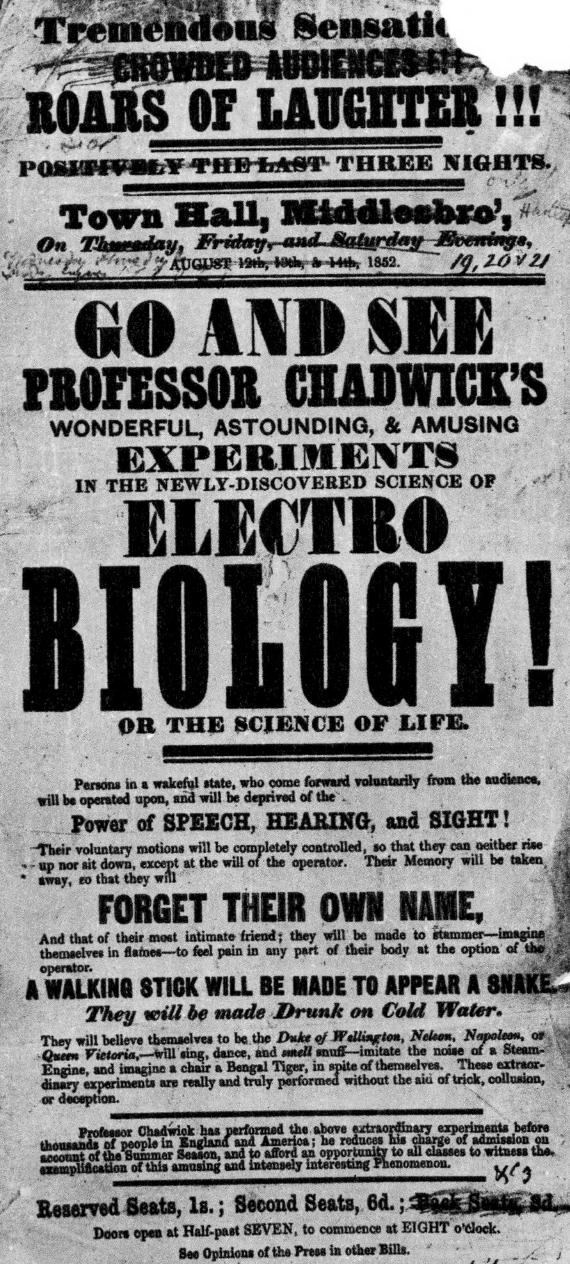

158
Victorian Education in a nutshell. There is no doubt that this subject exercised the minds of many earnest and God-fearing men but it was not often that the object of this laudable project was put as bluntly as it is here.

159
It may suprise some to know that Mormon missionaries were at work in England well over a hundred years ago, and that their richest harvest was achieved in the industrial North. In an age when religion was a great bone of contention, especially with regard to education, it is not surprising to find public lectures for and against particular creeds. Note that this particular lecture is to be delivered in the open air, probably because neither the Colliery management nor the Church would lend a room for the purpose.

160
A refugee was a rare phenomenon to the Victorians and one to be listened to with respect and sympathy. The great Liberal tradition caused men to cherish the victims of Continental tyranny. The 1848 Revolutions ended five years previously yet Capt. Kastner is still able to give an account of his thrilling escape and sell pamphlets to a sympathetic crowd.

158

A Black Native of Kentucky, one of the United States of America.

The Lecturer will give a Short History of his Life, bearing testimony to the authenticity of Mrs. B. Stowe's Statements.

Mr. WATSON is well known to the Rev. CANON HEY, of York, and the Rev. H. T. CATTLEY, of Hull, who also aided him with means to enable him to prosecute his Studies at King's College, London.

In Canada alone, there are 80,000 Persons of Colour, chiefly Fugitives, in a most deplorable condition as to Education; and in other British Colonies, there are many thousands of Coloured People, whose Education is totally neglected.

As the whole of the Coloured People require Education to make them useful subjects of the Crown, many influential advocates of this object are fully persuaded, that, should the opportnnity be afforded them to obtain Education, they would not only make clever Mechanics, Manufacturers, Agriculturalists, &c., but useful Physicians, if trained up to medical skill; and they would also be the means of civilising their sable brethren in the interior of Africa. If the Coloured Subjects in the British Colonies were Educated, they would volunteer to search, not only the African Coast, but the Interior of their Ancestors' Land

159

TRUTH IS MIGHTY, AND WILL PREVAIL.

"A just man is equal in all his ways."

NOTICE.

A

LECTURE

WILL BE DELIVERED IN THE OPEN AIR,

CASTLE EDEN COLLIERY,

On Sunday Evening, Sept. 16th, 1855, by

ELDER SAMUEL HARGRAVES,

In reply to a Lecture delivered by Mr. J. W. NEESHAM, on Saturday Evening, the 8th inst., entitled,

Apparition of Angels, the Origin of Mormonism; or the Question, was JOSEPH SMITH a True or False Prophet.

Hour of Meeting, FIVE o'clock, p.m. (weather permitting.)

HEAR, AND THEN JUDGE.

From the Office of J. PROCTER, Printer and Lithographer, Hartlepool and West Hartlepool.

160

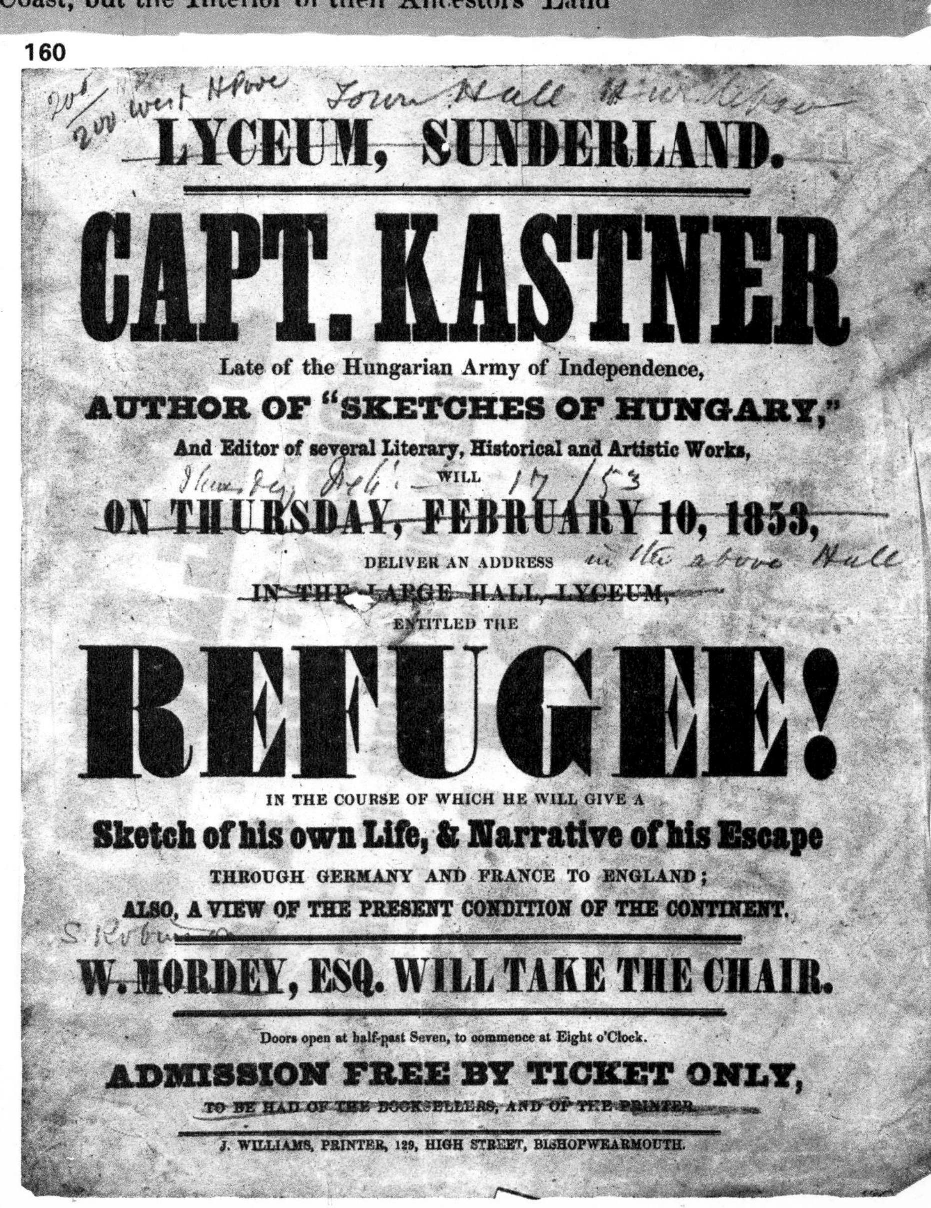

~~LYCEUM, SUNDERLAND.~~

CAPT. KASTNER

Late of the Hungarian Army of Independence,

AUTHOR OF "SKETCHES OF HUNGARY,"

And Editor of several Literary, Historical and Artistic Works,

WILL

~~ON THURSDAY, FEBRUARY 10, 1853,~~

DELIVER AN ADDRESS

~~IN THE LARGE HALL, LYCEUM,~~

ENTITLED THE

REFUGEE!

IN THE COURSE OF WHICH HE WILL GIVE A

Sketch of his own Life, & Narrative of his Escape

THROUGH GERMANY AND FRANCE TO ENGLAND;

ALSO, A VIEW OF THE PRESENT CONDITION OF THE CONTINENT.

W. MORDEY, ESQ. WILL TAKE THE CHAIR.

Doors open at half-past Seven, to commence at Eight o'Clock.

ADMISSION FREE BY TICKET ONLY,

~~TO BE HAD OF THE BOOKSELLERS, AND OF THE PRINTER.~~

J. WILLIAMS, PRINTER, 129, HIGH STREET, BISHOPWEARMOUTH.

161A, 161B, 161C and 161D
The wonders of science were not meant to be coldly observed in the clinical atmosphere of the laboratory but to be admired and relished by an awe-struck crowd. To many of us the latest scientific discoveries are quite beyond our comprehension and few non-specialists attempt to learn the language of modern scientists. The Victorians had yet to reach even that baffling stage. To them the wonders of Nature were just waiting to be revealed before their eager eyes. These extracts from four posters reveal something of the amazing variety of topics on which a Victorian could feast.

161A

GALVANISM;

THE CHROMATIC FIRE CLOUD,

In which Waves of richest coloured Flames roll and flash in gorgeous Magnificence on the Ceiling;

The effects of the

INTOXICATING GAS.

161B

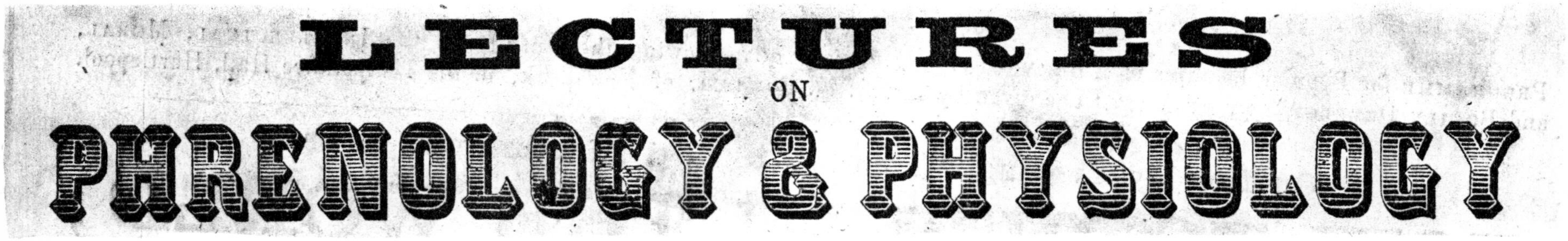

LECTURES

ON

PHRENOLOGY & PHYSIOLOGY

161C

A Course of Eight Lectures

ON THE SUBLIME AND INTERESTING

SCIENCE OF ASTRONOMY,

IN THE

~~LARGE ROOM, BINKS'S HOTEL.~~ Town Hall

161D

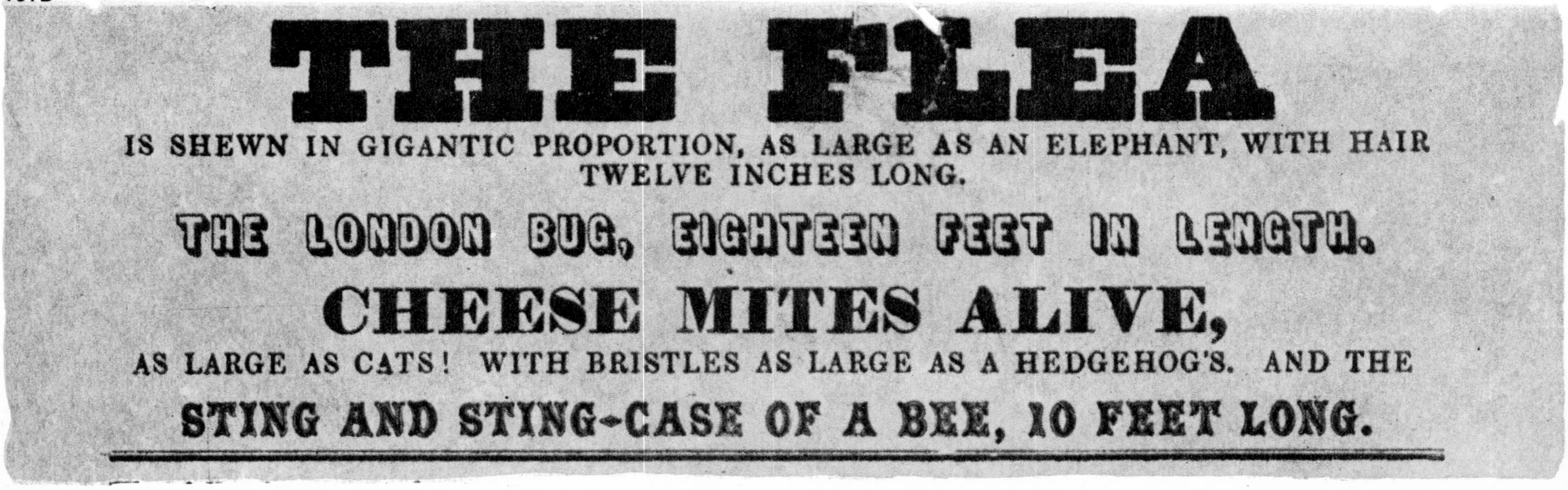

THE FLEA

IS SHEWN IN GIGANTIC PROPORTION, AS LARGE AS AN ELEPHANT, WITH HAIR TWELVE INCHES LONG.

THE LONDON BUG, EIGHTEEN FEET IN LENGTH.

CHEESE MITES ALIVE,

AS LARGE AS CATS! WITH BRISTLES AS LARGE AS A HEDGEHOG'S. AND THE

STING AND STING-CASE OF A BEE, 10 FEET LONG.

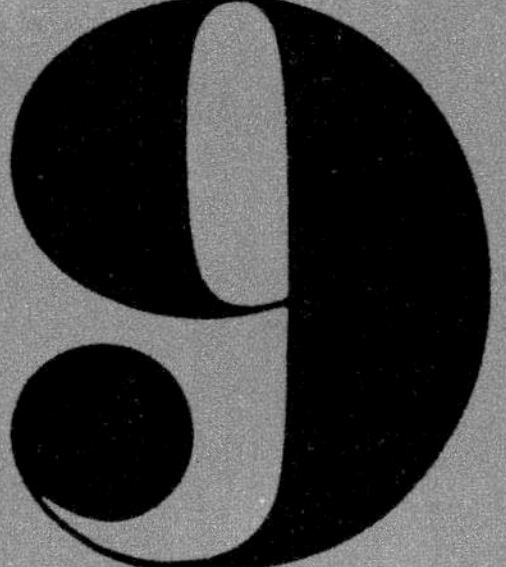

Excursions and Trading

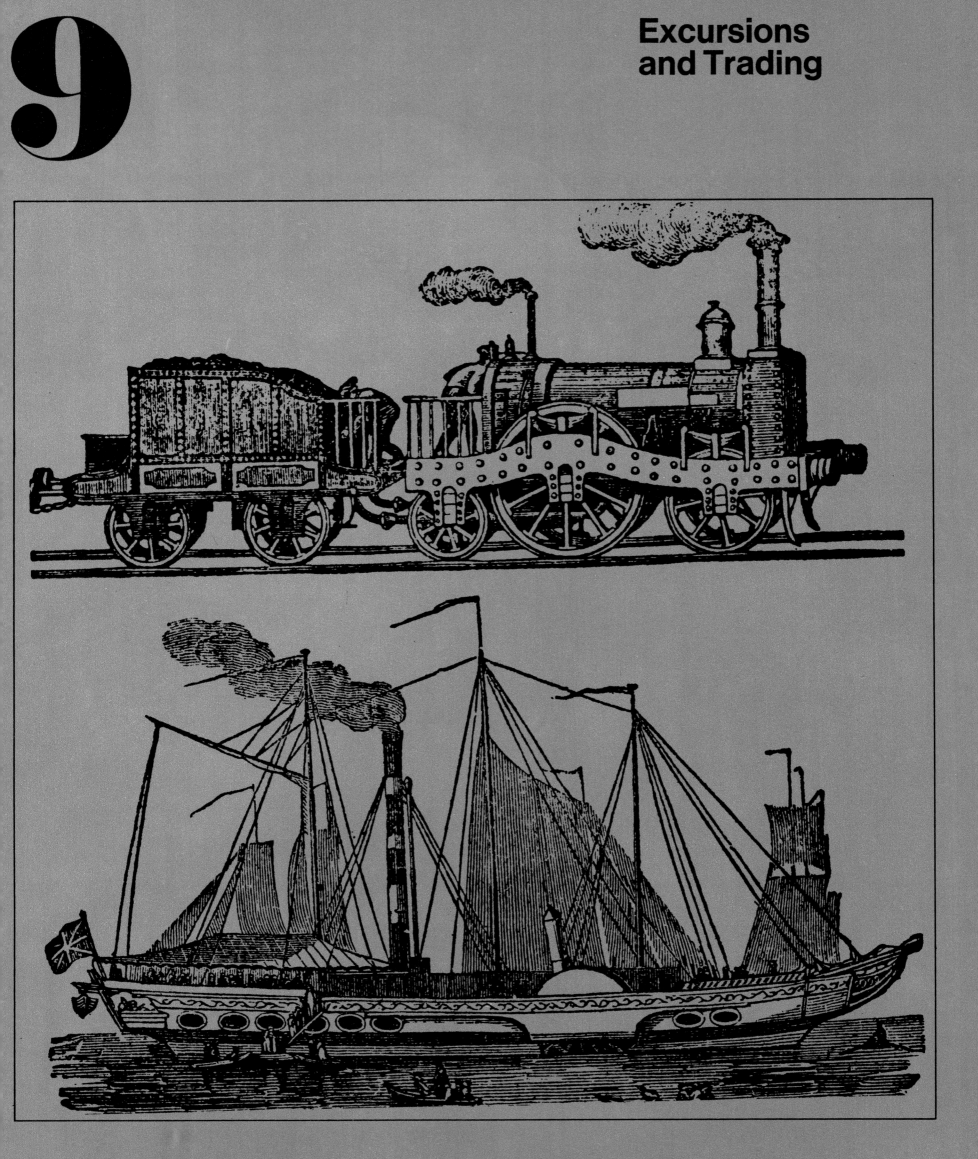

From the submergence of Roman Britain in the fifth century until the emergence of the stage-coach in the eighteenth, the roads of Britain were bad. They were neglected because the upkeep of the highway became the responsibility of the parish through which it passed, and although the law required every parishioner to do six days unpaid work annually on the roads where and when the parish surveyor of the highways demanded it, he was a citizen too, a reluctant farmer elected into the job, and it pleased everyone if he had few demands to make. In the eighteenth century a scheme was devised for providing better roads by levying tolls at bars or pikes placed across the highway on posts and with this money the turnpike roads were properly designed and maintained. The system was not universal for it had to be operated by a turnpike trust with statutory powers granted by Parliament. So, at the beginning of Victoria's reign, the roads of Britain were an assortment of a few good turnpikes, usually main roads, and many bad parish roads.

But another form of transport, was the ship, in common use on the coast and on navigable rivers and canals. These small craft could be accommodated in tiny ports and were used to carry the parcels and passengers we now send by rail, road or air. The Yarm and Cleveland Shipping Company began a regular service between that small town on the River Tees and London in 1813, and the Tees and Thames Steam Navigation Company started the first paddle steamer service in 1831. A state cabin to London cost 27 shillings and 6 pence but it was possible to travel steerage for 14 shillings. Passengers were taken on shorter trips, too. The regular fare from Hartlepool to Middlesbrough was 6 pence, and to Stockton 9 pence which compared very favourably with the coach price of 2 shillings and 6 pence. The Mullet and Wasp sailed regularly every week between Hartlepool and Newcastle.

In 1850 the following extensive facilities for transit by sea were advertised at Whitby and the same sort of opportunity was available at most British ports.

The water-transit for goods and passengers, by numerous trading vessels, takes place weekly to Middlesbrough, Hartlepool, Stockton, Sunderland, Newcastle, Hull, and London.

The present Traders from Toppin's Wharf, London, are: The London, Capt. Thos. Postgate; The Pickering, Capt. James Girdwood; and the Whitby, Capt. Robt. Kilvington; Mr. Mathew Wright, Agent.

From Chamberlain's Wharf: the Astraea, Capt. Wm. Sanderson; the Dispatch, Capt. John Newton; and the Enterprize, Capt. Robt. Sanderson, Mr. Edward Dale, Agent.

The Steanshalh, Capt. C. Swallow, plies between Newcastle and Whitby, calling off Sunderland and Shields every Friday, remaining at Hartlepool one day each voyage; her power of engine is thirty-six, and her tonnage forty-five, exclusive of engine room. Cabin fare, to Hartlepool 2/-, Deck, 1/6 and vice versa. The Neptune, Capt. Thompson, plies between Newcastle and Hull during the summer months with Passengers, calling at Whitby on Wednesdays and Saturdays, weekly.'

These services were as much a part of daily life as equivalent services are today and they were used extensively. Miss Burdon, a gentlewoman of Castle Eden, wrote to John Procter in 1840 'Miss Burdon was much obliged to Mr. Procter for the message about the Packet to Whitby, but she was desirous of knowing if it could take a carriage, as she has to send one to Whitby, and she wished to know if it could be put on board safely at Hartlepool and could be also landed at Whitby, She wished to know, too, what the charge for carriage would be, and what is the Fare for Passengers, and also, if the Packet returns to Hartlepool the same days, and how long it usually is on the Passage. She supposed it leaves Hartlepool a little before high tide. The time when she wanted to send the Carriage was on Friday week.'

The answer was that the charge for the carriage was 20 shillings, the fare 1 shilling and 6 pence, and the time taken, about three hours.

It cost 2 shillings to send a box or parcel from London to Hartlepool by sea. The service was cheap, regular, and efficient. A parcel was more likely to be mislaid on the railway than it was on board ship and, in fact, until the present century, local tradesmen in the North of England had their London parcels sent by sea.

Naturally on the East coast the emphasis of overseas trade was with Germany and the Baltic countries and a steamer could be taken to Hamburg any Wednesday or Saturday. The usual fare was 40 shillings return, first class but, occasionally, excursion tickets could be obtained for as little as 15 shillings.

During Victoria's reign the rapid spread of the railways resulted in the more remote parts of Europe being linked and opened up the undeveloped regions of the West. But the railway systems of early Victorian times were vastly different to those in existence today. Most of the early railways were built to carry coal and there was little revenue from the conveyance of other goods before 1840. For instance in 1839 such revenue was only 8 per cent of the income of the Stockton and Darlington Railway. Its goods traffic for the first nine years was in the hands of private carriers, for the first railways followed the example of the turnpike roads. The company provided the railroad and the carriers were free to use their own engines and wagons on payment of the appropriate toll. Many railways employed horses to pull their wagons instead of engines; steam power was not used on the Whitby and Pickering or the Durham and Sunderland Railways prior to 1841

The companies perpetuated the old stage-coach traditions. To this day we have 'Guards' on our trains and the passengers travel in 'Coaches'. Indeed, until 1834 many of the old stage-coaches were being converted into railway coaches by the simple process of substituting flanged wheels for road wheels. The stations were makeshift affairs. Originally Hartlepool Station was the poop of an old Dutch galliot stranded on dry land. Its cabins housed the Booking Clerk and the Station Master. Booking Clerks still have employment but little of the paperwork that a Victorian clerk suffered, such as having to number the paper tickets and fill in the date of issue, the time of departure, and perhaps the destination. Gradually the small companies were swallowed up by the larger ones and by 1870 the North Eastern Railway had become the great organisation it remained for another fifty years.

162
The printer's block which provides such a striking feature of this poster came from the stock supplied by the old established firm of William Davison of Alnwick (Alnwick is an ancient Northumbrian town 32 miles north-west of Newcastle). Except for the smoke-stack the ship bears an uncanny resemblance to a large Chinese junk, probably because the line of the hull is obscured by the canvas awning on the poop-deck.

163
To this very day the captain of the first ship to sail up the St. Lawrence Seaway each spring receives a silver-topped walking stick or some similar memento to mark the occasion.

162

PLEASURE TRIP

FOR THE BENEFIT OF THE

WIDOW & ORPHAN'S FUND

IN CONNECTION WITH THE INDEPENDENT ORDER OF ODD FELLOWS, M. U.,
ST. HILDA'S LODGE, HARTLEPOOL.

THE PUBLIC ARE RESPECTFULLY INFORMED THAT THE

FAST STEAM
SAILING BOAT,

GLEANER

WILL LEAVE THE
Corporation Quay, STOCKTON, at ¾ before 6, and MIDDLESBRO' at ¼ past 6,
Returning the same Evening,

On Thursday Morning, Aug. 29,

FOR

SHIELDS

Calling at SUNDERLAND, in going and returning.

FARES THERE & BACK.
STOCKTON & MIDDLESBRO' TO SUNDERLAND & SHIELDS, 1s. 6d.

On this occasion parties wishing to witness the

QUEEN

Pass over the High Level Bridge, at Newcastle,
On her route into Scotland, will have an opportunity of doing so, as the Boat will start precisely at the time advertised.

The Committee have much pleasure in calling the attention of the Brethren of the Order and the Public generally to the above Trip, and beg to assure them that this being their first Trip, nothing shall be wanting on their part to secure the comfort and accomodation of all on board.

AN EXCELLENT QUADRILLE BAND WILL BE ON BOARD.

AUGUST 22nd, 1850.

From the Office of J. PROCTER, High Street, Hartlepool.

163

Notice to Shippers.

First Spring Ship
FROM

HARTLEPOOL

FOR

QUEBEC,

Having the principal part of her Cargo engaged,
WILL CLEAR ON THE 28th MARCH,
THE FINE FAST-SAILING FIRST CLASS BRIG,

RICHMOND LASS

OF HARTLEPOOL, CAPT. JOHN LISK,
BURTHEN 500 TONS,

Possessing excellent accommodation for Cabin and Steerage Passengers, presents an excellent opportunity for persons wishing to Emigrate to British America.

☞ As the number of Passengers will be limited to 50, every attention as to Comfort will be attended to.

FOR FREIGHT & PASSAGE, APPLY TO

GILLIES, HUTTON & Co.
BROKERS, HARTLEPOOL.

Hartlepool, 1st March, 1841.

FROM J. PROCTER'S, OFFICE, HARTLEPOOL.

164
Any event provided an excuse for a boat trip. The Races were a great attraction and many of the bills on Procter's files were for such events. Others, which lack of space prevents us from including, were for trips to see the Queen crossing the High Level Bridge at Newcastle, engineers moving Sunderland Lighthouse to a new site, and the jet workers unearthing a fossil at Whitby. (Jet is a black lignite-like mineral mined since Bronze Age times and used for making beads, etc.).

165
It is perhaps unkind to display this bill with its corrected misprint but it does provide a clue to the colloquialisms expressed by the workmen.

166
It is doubtful if this is a genuine advertisement for a steamboat trip. Lord Harry Vane and Captain Bowes were both conservative candidates in the South Durham elections.

167
This magnificent poster is of great historical significance for it indicates the widening horizon of Victorian trade and the greater interest in travel for its own sake. The ports of England's east coast naturally looked towards the Continent for trade and the promoters of the new port of West Hartlepool encouraged the merchants of Prussia and other Baltic countries to bring their business to them. This company developed into the West Hartlepool Steam Navigation Company which still flourishes, although it no longer offers 15/– return trips to Hamburg!

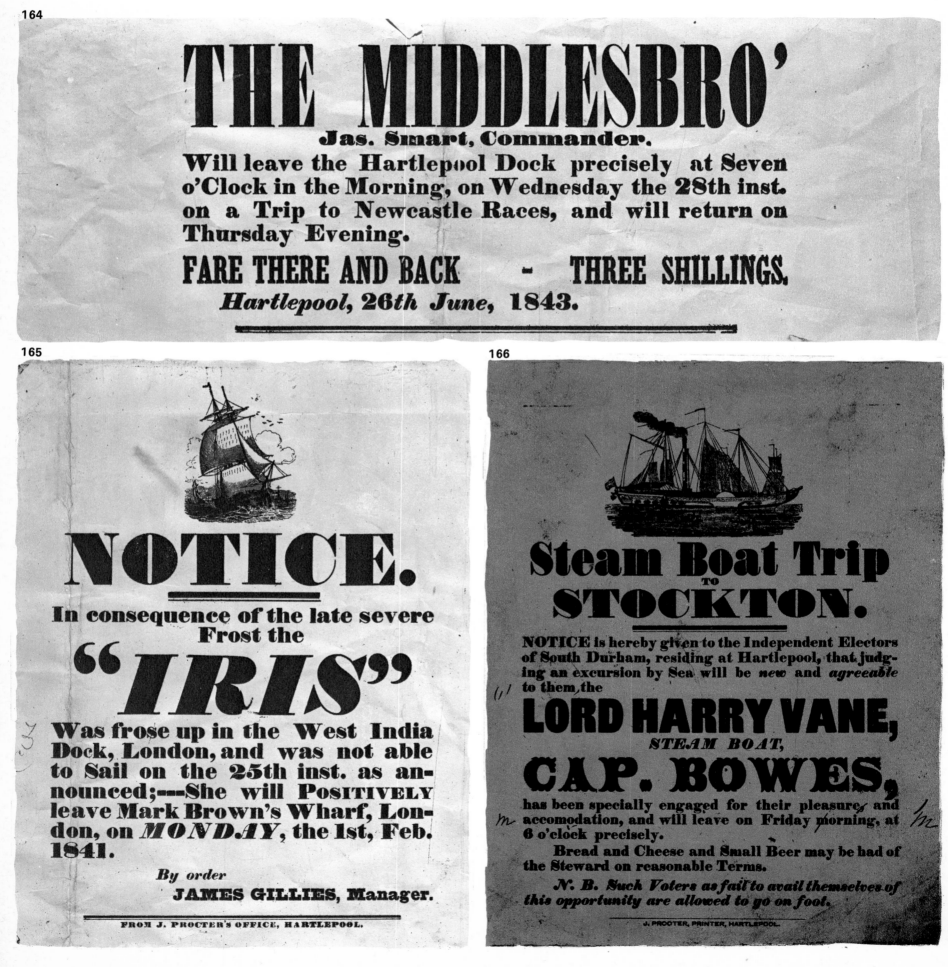

164

THE MIDDLESBRO'

Jas. Smart, Commander.

Will leave the Hartlepool Dock precisely at Seven o'Clock in the Morning, on Wednesday the 28th inst. on a Trip to Newcastle Races, and will return on Thursday Evening.

FARE THERE AND BACK - THREE SHILLINGS.

Hartlepool, 26th June, 1843.

165

NOTICE.

In consequence of the late severe Frost the

"*IRIS*"

Was frose up in the West India Dock, London, and was not able to Sail on the 25th inst. as announced;---She will POSITIVELY leave Mark Brown's Wharf, London, on *MONDAY*, the 1st, Feb. 1841.

By order

JAMES GILLIES, Manager.

FROM J. PROCTER'S OFFICE, HARTLEPOOL.

166

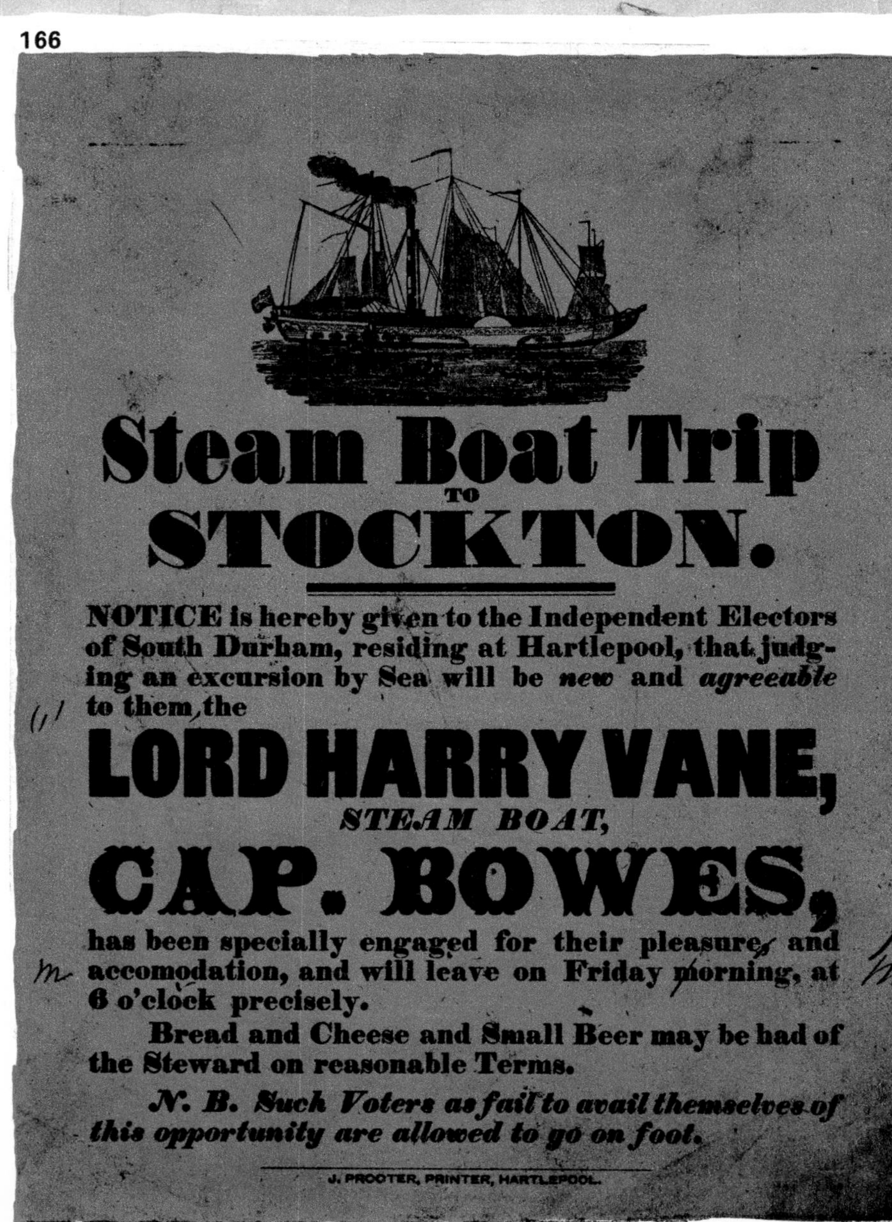

Steam Boat Trip
TO
STOCKTON.

NOTICE is hereby given to the Independent Electors of South Durham, residing at Hartlepool, that judging an excursion by Sea will be *new* and *agreeable* to them, the

LORD HARRY VANE,

STEAM BOAT,

CAP. BOWES,

has been specially engaged for their pleasure, and accomodation, and will leave on Friday morning, at 6 o'clock precisely.

Bread and Cheese and Small Beer may be had of the Steward on reasonable Terms.

N. B. Such Voters as fail to avail themselves of this opportunity are allowed to go on foot.

J. PROCTER, PRINTER, HARTLEPOOL.

167

CHEAP TRIP

FROM

WEST HARTLEPOOL

TO

HAMBURG.

THE LARGE

AND POWERFUL

PADDLE STEAMER,

'SHANNON,'

540 TONS REGISTER, AND 240 HORSE POWER,

(WILLIAM WRAIGHT COMMANDER,)

Will leave West Hartlepool for Hamburg, on MONDAY, AUGUST 22nd, at SIX, p.m.; and Hamburg for West Hartlepool, on MONDAY, AUGUST 29th.

This Powerful and Splendid Steamer is authorised by the Government Inspectors to carry 500 Passengers; she has a Magnificent Saloon and Dining Room, a Spacious Poop Quarter Deck, and her Private Cabins, Sleeping Berths, and general arrangements, are replete with comfort and elegance.

To the Tourist, the Commercial Community, and the Valetudinarian, the present affords an apportunity of Visiting some of the principal Capitals and Watering Places in Europe, which for Cheapness and Comfort, has seldom, if ever been offered to the Public.

FARES, THERE AND BACK:—

Saloon and After Cabin - - - - - - - - -	35s.
Fore Cabin - - - - - - - - - -	25s.
Deck - - - - - - - - - - -	15s.

Private Cabins for Families, containing Four Berths and every accommodation, (each) £8 8s.

STEWARDS FEES INCLUDED.

Passengers can, at their own option, return by this Vessel, either on Monday, August 29th, or on Monday, September 12th.

Wines and Provisions of the best Quality to be had on Board, on reasonable Terms.

For further Particulars apply to

M. PEARSE  & CO.,

West Hartlepool, August 12th, 1853.

WEST HARTLEPOOL.

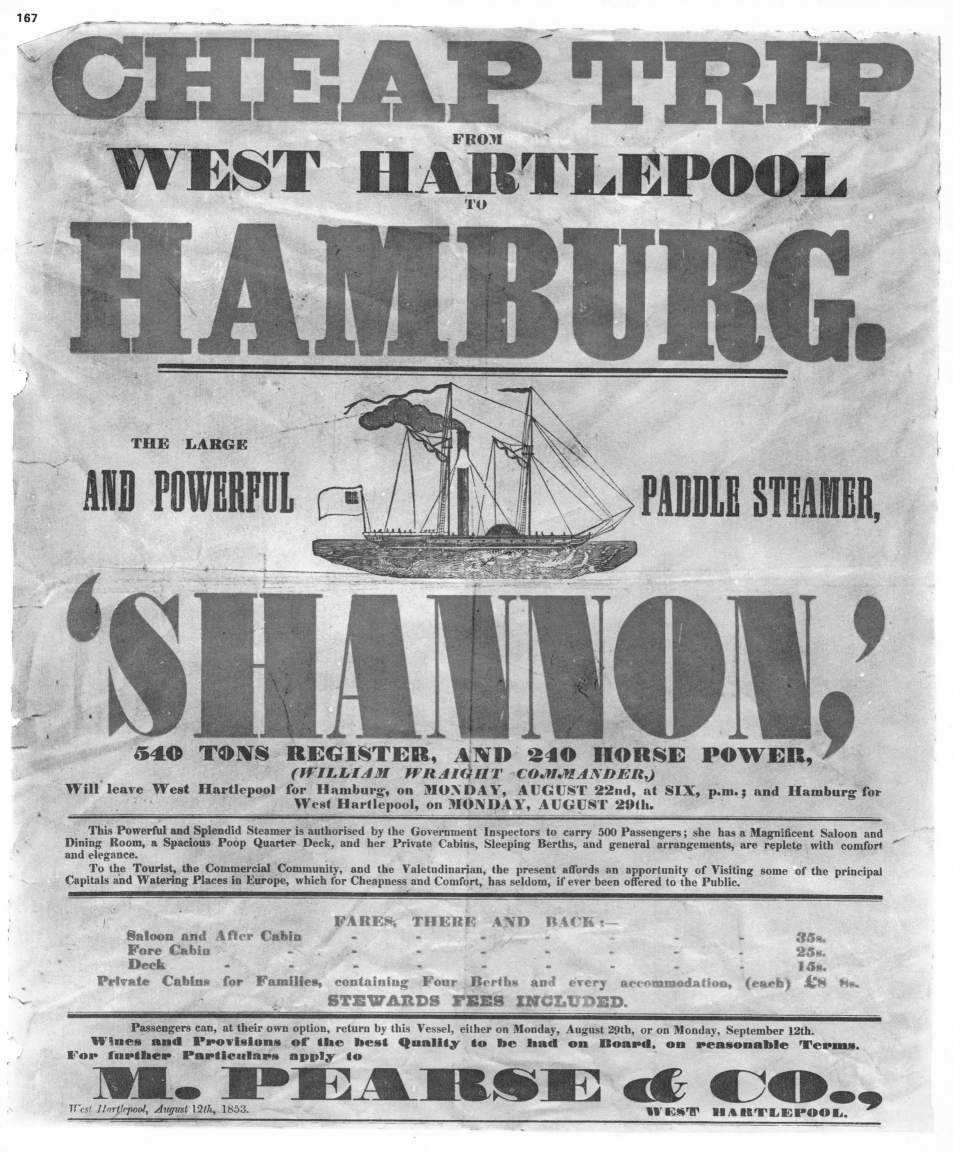

168
It must be remembered that Middlesbro' and Hartlepool were rival towns. The first house in Middlesbro' was built in 1830, previously there had been one farm house on the site of the future town. In the case of Hartlepool the resurrection of the decayed fishing village did not come until 1832 and by 1840, because of its easier access from the sea, it had eclipsed Middlesbro' as a coal exporting town. But in 1850 the Cleveland ore was exploited for the first time and Middlesbro' blossomed into a great iron-producing centre and left Hartlepool behind.

169
A trip across Tees Bay and beneath the towering cliffs of the Cleveland Hills was a favourite Victorian excursion. Many of the Hartlepool residents hailed from the old port of Whitby and the day out was an opportunity to meet friends and relations at a very small cost. Unfortunately, for the last fifty years, it has not been possible for anyone to share their enjoyment by making a similar voyage.

170
A small pocket card of the West Hartlepool and Hamburg Company which became the West Hartlepool Steam Navigation Company of the present day.

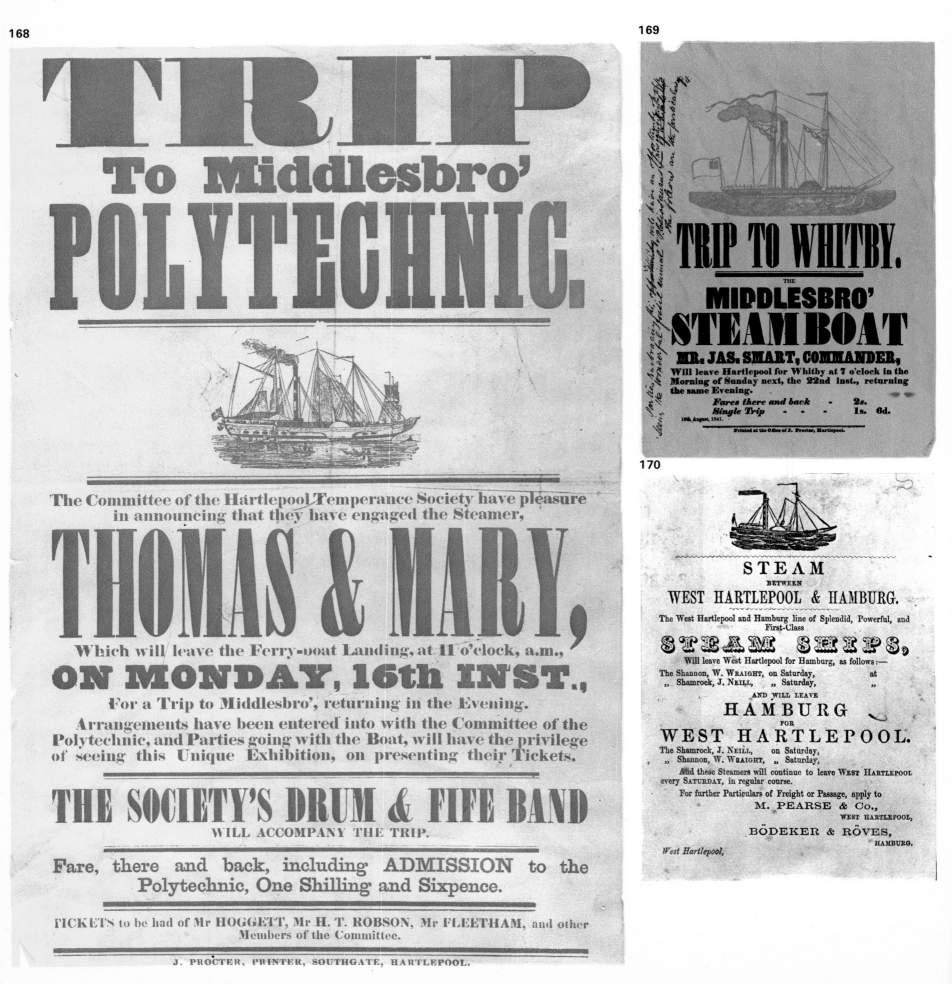

168

TRIP
To Middlesbro'
POLYTECHNIC.

The Committee of the Hartlepool Temperance Society have pleasure in announcing that they have engaged the Steamer,

THOMAS & MARY,

Which will leave the Ferry-boat Landing, at 11 o'clock, a.m.,

ON MONDAY, 16th INST.,

For a Trip to Middlesbro', returning in the Evening.

Arrangements have been entered into with the Committee of the Polytechnic, and Parties going with the Boat, will have the privilege of seeing this Unique Exhibition, on presenting their Tickets.

THE SOCIETY'S DRUM & FIFE BAND
WILL ACCOMPANY THE TRIP.

Fare, there and back, including ADMISSION to the Polytechnic, One Shilling and Sixpence.

TICKETS to be had of Mr HOGGETT, Mr H. T. ROBSON, Mr FLEETHAM, and other Members of the Committee.

J. PROCTER, PRINTER, SOUTHGATE, HARTLEPOOL.

169

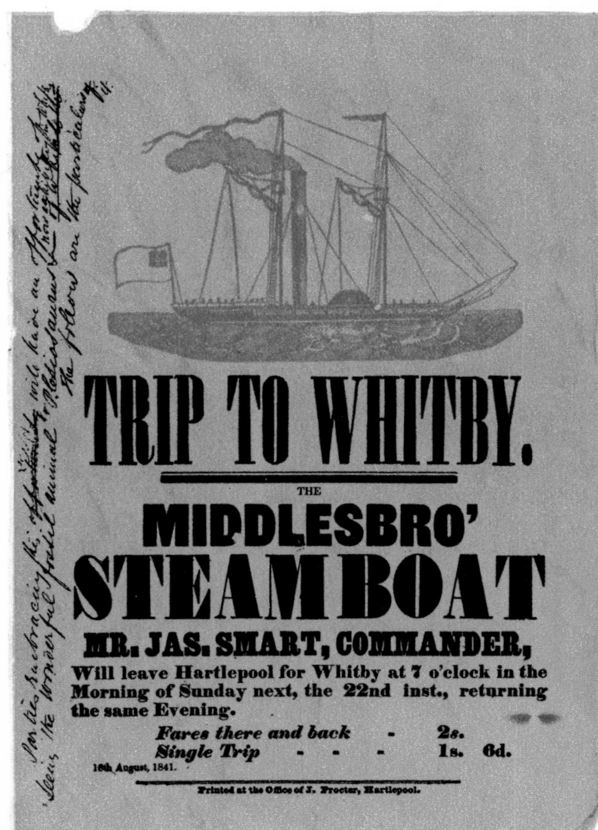

TRIP TO WHITBY.
THE
MIDDLESBRO'
STEAMBOAT
MR. JAS. SMART, COMMANDER,
Will leave Hartlepool for Whitby at 7 o'clock in the Morning of Sunday next, the 22nd inst., returning the same Evening.

Fares there and back - 2s.
Single Trip - - - 1s. 6d.

18th August, 1841.

Printed at the Office of J. Procter, Hartlepool.

170

STEAM
BETWEEN
WEST HARTLEPOOL & HAMBURG.

The West Hartlepool and Hamburg line of Splendid, Powerful, and First-Class

STEAM SHIPS,

Will leave West Hartlepool for Hamburg, as follows:—

The Shannon, W. WRAIGHT, on Saturday, at
„ Shamrock, J. NEILL, „ Saturday, „

AND WILL LEAVE
HAMBURG
FOR
WEST HARTLEPOOL.

The Shamrock, J. NEILL, on Saturday,
„ Shannon, W. WRAIGHT, „ Saturday,

And these Steamers will continue to leave WEST HARTLEPOOL every SATURDAY, in regular course.

For further Particulars of Freight or Passage, apply to
M. PEARSE & Co.,
WEST HARTLEPOOL,
BÖDEKER & RÖVES,
HAMBURG.

West Hartlepool,

171 and 172

Victorians derived considerable pleasure in achieving a worthwhile result whatever the task. Work of a slovenly kind was unacceptable. They kept account books in superb copper plate writing and even their colliery certificates, showing the number of tons of coal shipped from the port, were things of beauty. Copper engravings were expensive but this was justified in the notable certificate produced.

There were six main types of decoration. If the colliery was owned by a noble person then his coat of arms could be included, as with the certificates of the Londonderry and Lord Howden Collieries. Some companies, such as that of Castle Eden (171), were satisfied with an engraving of the colliery itself, although Abbey Wallsend used one of Durham Cathedral. Alternatively the railway engine which drew the train down to the port, the chalder wagon which carried the coal, or the ship which brought it to London were also used. The port from which it was shipped sometimes was featured; Hartlepool and West Hartlepool appear on some certificates, for example.

Such engravings form a much neglected branch of Victorian art.

171

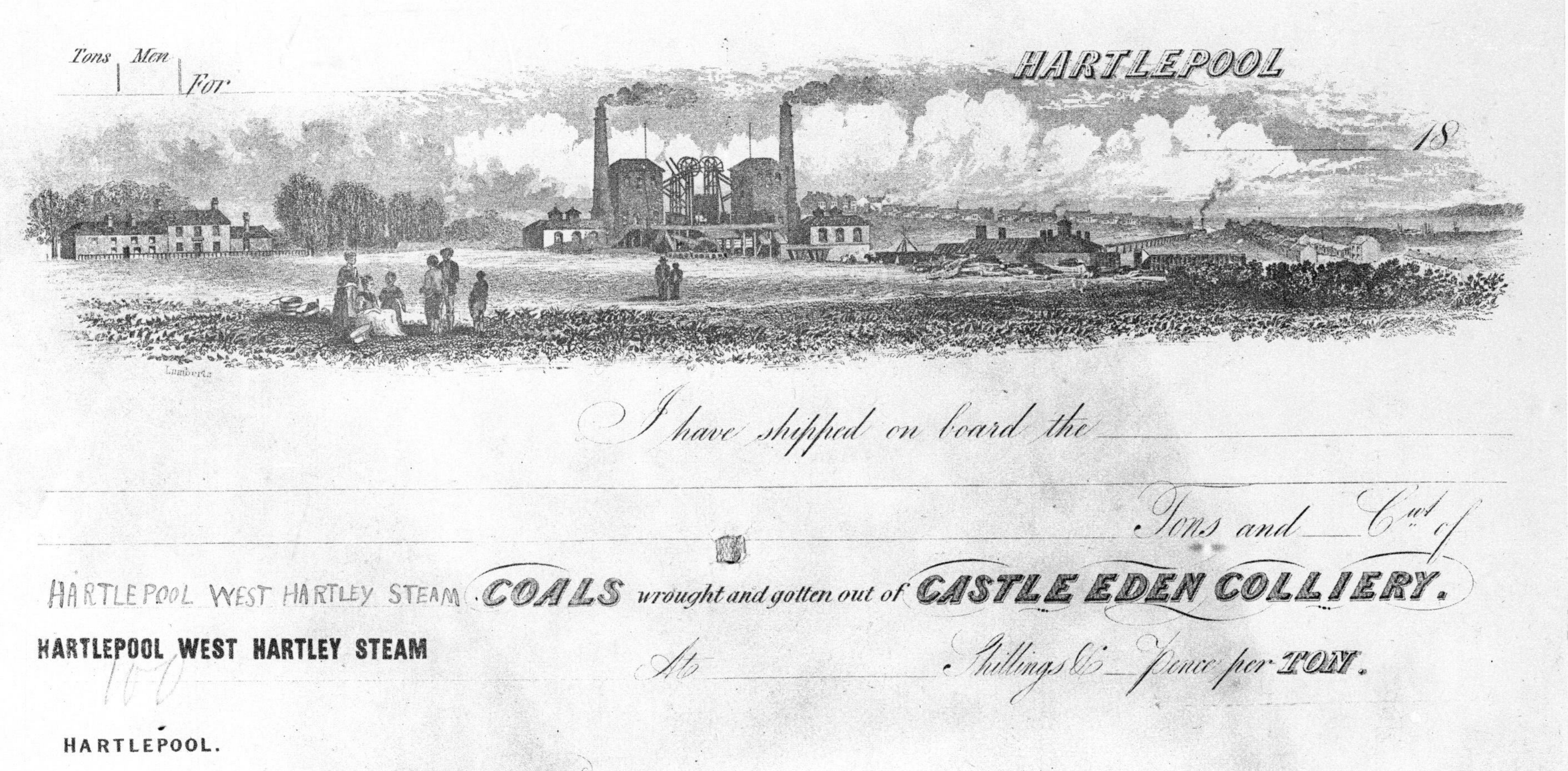

Tons | Men | For

HARTLEPOOL

18

I have shipped on board the

Tons and Cwt of

HARTLEPOOL WEST HARTLEY STEAM COALS wrought and gotten out of CASTLE EDEN COLLIERY.

HARTLEPOOL WEST HARTLEY STEAM

100

At Shillings & Pence per TON.

HARTLEPOOL.

172

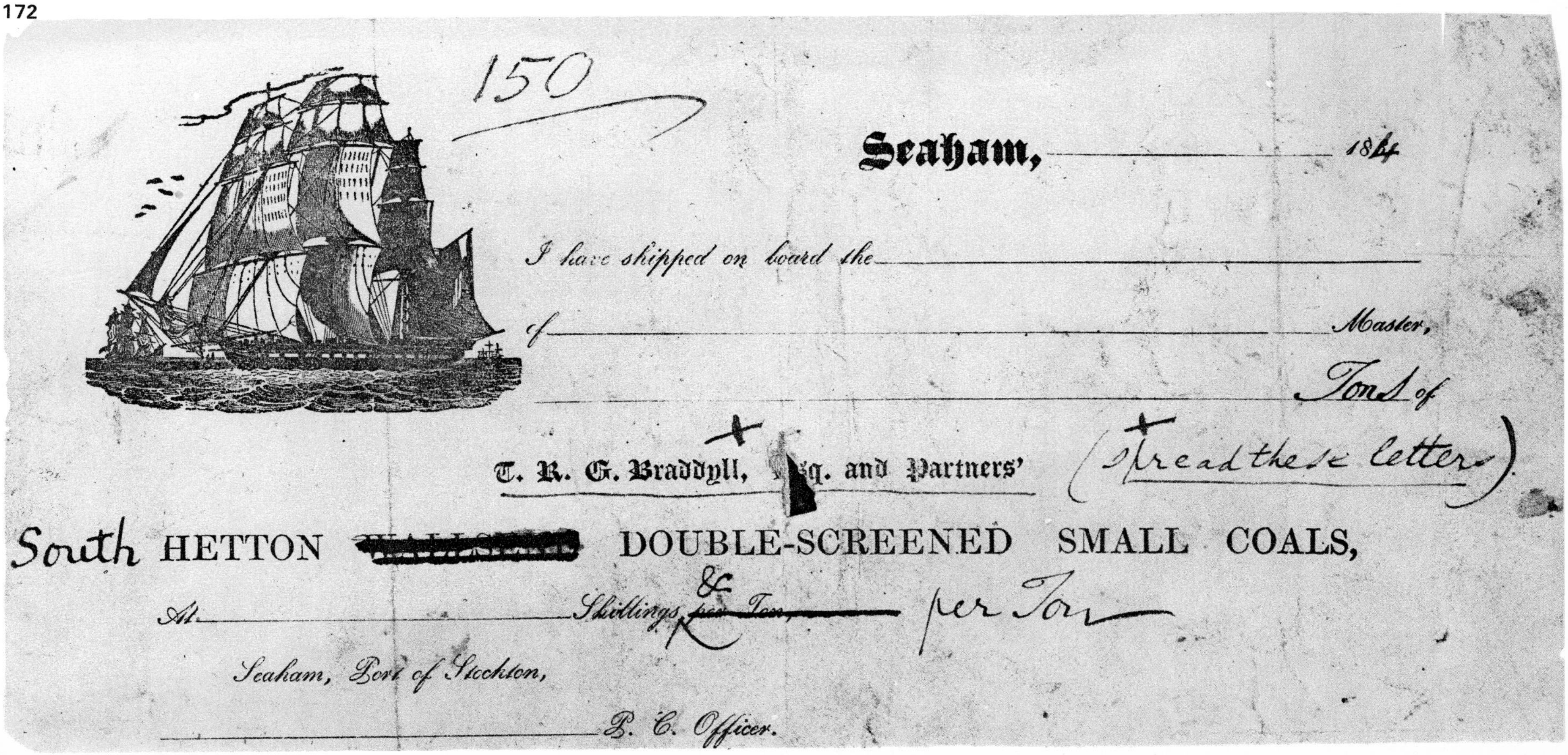

150

Seaham, 184

I have shipped on board the

of Master,

Tons of

T. R. G. Braddyll, Esq. and Partners' (spread these letters)

South HETTON ~~WALLSEND~~ DOUBLE-SCREENED SMALL COALS,

At Shillings & ~~per Ton,~~ per Ton

Seaham, Port of Stockton,

P. C. Officer.

173

THE RED OMNIBUS.

G. ADAMSON,

Commercial Hotel,

NORTHGATE, HARTLEPOOL,

Returns his sincere thanks to his Friends and the Public for the liberal support he has received since commencing in the above line, and respectfully informs them that he continues to run his

RED OMNIBUS

To and from the **WEST HARTLEPOOL RAILWAY STATION,** meeting every Train during the day, at the following reduced prices,

4d. Inside, 3d. Outside,

Calling at Mrs. HUMBLE'S, the Cleveland Hotel, Northgate, or any part of the Town, if required.

Hack Horses, Phæton, Gigs, and Cars Let out on Hire, on the most reasonable Terms.

Hartlepool, 8th March, 1849.

173
The Red Omnibus was a link between the rival towns of Hartlepool and West Hartlepool. Such was the antagonism between them that from 1845 to 1862 there was no rail link, and Mr. Adamson's omnibus was brought into service.

174
'I have today returned from my sea-voyage from that infernal and ever to be detested place London from which I gained nothing; but from the sea voyage I gained as much health and vigour as would almost enable me to leap on the Town Hall turn a somerset on the top and come down again in perfect safety to the astonishment of all beholders. We had a comfortable passage down, 28 passengers and very pleasant company . . .
Such was the letter received from one obviously satisfied passenger!
This bill is of great interest in that it illustrates the extraordinary number of ports of call where parcels and such like would be delivered or accepted.
The conditions of carriage are not so dissimilar from those stated nowadays.

175
'Lime or Lemon Juice, Sugar and Vinegar, are to be served out to the Crew, whenever they shall have been consuming Salt Provisions for Ten Days.'
This regulation was the result of Captain Cook's voyages in which he avoided scurvy amongst his crew. It led to British ships being called 'lime-juicers' and to the nickname of 'limey'.

176
An early railway ticket printed on paper and copied from tickets of the Durham and Sunderland Railways. The printer had obligingly left on the spike file the ticket from which he copied.

174

Beal's Wharf, Southwark.

THE STOCKTON and LONDON SHIPPING COMPANY's VESSELS sail every SATURDAY, *from BEAL's WHARF,* LONDON, *to C. MARTIN's WHARF,* STOCKTON; *and from thence to* LONDON, *also, every* SATURDAY, *wind and weather permitting.*

Atkinson & Co., Printers, 10, Charterhouse-square.

The Fast-Sailing New Schooners.

The DARLINGTON, Capt. Robert Tate
RICHMOND, Capt George Hepinstall
BARNARD-CASTLE, Capt John Farmer
The AUCKLAND, Capt. John Burdon
THIRSK, Capt. Nicholas Rippon
NORTHALLERTON, Capt. George Gaudie

FOR

STOCKTON,

THE BARNARD-CASTLE,

JOHN FARMER, *Master*.

*** The last day of taking in goods is Saturday.

Takes in Goods and Passengers for the following Places.

Ambleside
Aycliffe
Askrigg
Appleby
Ayton, Ask
Aldborough
Branspeth
Billingham
Brompton
Barnard-Castle
Bedale, Barton
Bishopton
Bishop-Auckland
Brough, Bowes
Borrowby
Colgarth
Cockerton
Cotherston
Cleasby
Carlton
Coxhoe
Cornforth
Commondale
Crakehall
Cross-lane
Castle-Eden
Carthorp
Castleton
Catterick
Crathorne
Churchborough
Cockfield
Darlington
Durham
Egglestone
Egglescliffe
Fishburn
Gunnerside
Gilling
Gayles
Guisbrough
Gainford
Hart, Hawes
Hur[illegible]
Haughton
Hartlepool
Hutton-Rudby
Kingsm[illegible]burn
Kendal
Kirby-Stephen
Kirkleatham
Keswick
Kilvington
Leyburn
Lofthouse
Middleton-Tyas
Middleton in Teesdale
Masham
Middleham
Morland
Newby-Wisk
Northallerton
Norton
Osmotherley
Ormsby
Potto, Pickhill
Penrith
Piersbridge
Ravenstonedale
Raby
Reeth
Ripon
Richmond
Redcar
Sedgefield
Skelton
Staindrop
Stockton
Stokesley
Saithes
Shap
Sedburgh
Swainby
Southchurch
Summerhouse
Trimdon
Temple-Sowerby
Topcliffe
Thirsk
Tanfield
Upleatham
Wolviston
West-Layton
East-Layton
West-Auckland
Wynyard
Worsal, Yarm

And all places adjacent, in Yorkshire, Durham, Westmoreland, and Cumberland, contiguous to the River Tees.
The Master, or Wharfinger, to be spoken with at the said Wharf, or on the Irish Walk in 'Change hours.

Goods for the above-mentioned and adjacent places are not received at, nor shipped from, this Wharf, but on the conditions following: that is to say, that the Wharfingers will not be accountable (or engage to forward them by any particular vessel named in the receipt given), either for loss by fire, river navigation, lighterage, high tides, vermin, leakage and wastage, act of God, the Queen's enemies, or loss occasioned by imperfect directions, marks, or packing; neither will any advice be given of the shipment of goods which may have been left out of former vessels.

☞ Please to send the particulars of what the packages contain, and Wharf charges.

All goods shipped by this vessel will be considered as general Liens, and subject not only to the money due for the freight of such particular goods, but also to the general balance due from the respective owners to the owner of the said vessels. Not accountable for loss by fire. The receipts given to be in force only twelve months.
No goods received after dark.

1842. **GRIFFIN & HILLHOUSE, Wharfingers.**

May 31st s. d.
No. of Packages One. Received Wharfage 1/-
Sailed 5th May

175

SCALE
FOR
VICTUALLING MERCHANT VESSELS AT SEA,
(WHEN SAILING IN THE FOREIGN TRADE)
RECOMMENDED BY THE
COMMITTEE OF THE GENERAL SHIPOWNERS' SOCIETY.

FOR EACH MAN FOR FOURTEEN DAYS.

DAYS OF THE WEEK.	Bread.	Salted. Beef.	Salted. Pork.	Flour.	Rice.	Peas.	Tea.	Sugar.	Mustard.	Water.	Per Act of Parliament. Vinegar.	Per Act of Parliament. Lemon or Lime Juice.	Per Act of Parliament. Sugar for Lime Juice.
		lb.	lb.	lb.	lb	pt.	oz.	lb.	oz.	qt.	pt	oz.	oz.
Sunday	As much as they can eat without waste.	1¼	—	½	One pound per week.	—	¼	¾	To be considered as an extra, and issued at the discretion of the Master.	3	½	½	½
Monday		—	1¼	—		¼	¼	—		3	—	½	½
Tuesday		1¼	—	—		—	¼	—		3	—	½	½
Wednesday		—	1¼	—		¼	¼	—		3	—	½	½
Thursday		1¼	—	½		—	¼	—		3	—	½	½
Friday		—	1¼	—		¼	¼	—		3	—	½	½
Saturday		1¼	—	½		—	¼	—		3	—	½	½
Sunday		—	1¼	—		¼	¼	¾		3	½	½	½
Monday		1¼	—	½		—	¼	—		3	—	½	½
Tuesday		—	1¼	—		¼	¼	—		3	—	½	½
Wednesday		1¼	—	½		—	¼	—		3	—	½	½
Thursday		—	1¼	—		¼	¼	—		3	—	½	½
Friday		1¼	—	½		—	¼	—		3	—	½	½
Saturday		—	1¼	—		¼	¼	—		3	—	½	½
Totals for 14 days		8¾	8¾	3	2	1¾	3½	1½		42	1	7	7

SUBSTITUTES.

1 oz of Coffee or Cocoa or Chocolate, may be substituted for ¼ oz of Tea.
Molasses, for Sugar; the quantity to be one-half more.
1 lb Potatoes or Yams to be considered equal to ¼ lb. Flour or Rice, or ¼ pint of Peas.
When FRESH MEAT be issued, the proportion to be 2 lbs. per man per day, in lieu of Salt Meat, Flour, Rice, and Peas.
The allowance of Small Stores being considered as an equivalent for Spirits, Spirits are only to be issued under particular circumstances at the discretion of the Master.

By the *Merchant Seaman's Act* (7 and 8 Vict. c. 112, s. 18):—
"Lime or Lemon Juice, Sugar, and Vinegar, are to be served out to the Crew, whenever they shall have been consuming Salt Provisions for *Ten Days*. The Lime or Lemon Juice and Sugar daily, after the rate of half an ounce of each per day, and the Vinegar weekly, at the rate of half a pint per week to each person so long as the consumption of Salt Provisions be continued."

By order of the Committee,
NATHL. W. SYMONDS, Secretary.

72, Cornhill, Dec., 1844.

Printed and Sold by J. PROCTER, High Street, Hartlepool.

176

Hartlepool Railway.

No.

18

Paid

Please to keep this ticket in hand until asked for by the conductor.

177 and 178
These specifications are a logical sequel to the practice of allowing different companies to use their own rolling stock. The railway company, after a series of mishaps, was forced to require a minimum standard for engines and trucks.

179
Many a modern railway enthusiast would give anything to have been on this excursion for it ventured in to the territory of companies long since dead. It began at Gateshead on the line of the York, Newcastle, and Berwick Railway and before it had gone thirty miles it had crossed the lines of the West Hartlepool Railway, the Stockton and Darlington Railway, and the Clarence Railway. At Northallerton it crossed the Leeds Northern Railway, and at either Leeds or York it entered on to the York and North Midland line.

177

The Soles

If made of good English Oak, to be not less than 6½ inches deep by 6 inches thick, or if made of any other Timber to be not less than 7½ inches by 6½ inches.

Bottom Sheths

To be made of good English Oak, two of which in each Wagon, to be 6½ inches by 4 inches, and other two to be 9 inches by 4 inches; the height of the underside of the Soles to be 1 foot 8 inches above the level of the tops of the Rails of the Railway.

Centre Bars

To be of Forged Iron 3½ inches broad by 1¼ inch thick from the outer end to beyond the bolt-hole at the first Sheth, and 3½ inches broad by 1 inch thick the remainder of their length.

Coupling or Centre Chains

To be made of 1 inch round Iron, with Shackels made of 1¼ inch round Iron, and the Centre pins or bolts to be 1¼ inch diameter from the shoulder to the bottom-end. The Chains to be of such length as that when they are stretched tight the sole-ends of the Wagons so connected shall be 6 inches distant.

Protecting or Side Chains

To be made of ⅝ths of an inch round Iron, and of such length as to admit the sole-ends of the Wagons connected by them to be 9 inches apart when the Chains are stretched tight.

178

Each Engine and Tender to be coupled by a dragbar and two side chains; the dragbar to be of the best scrap Iron and to contain not less than five square inches in its cross section, and the side chains to be made of not less than five-eighths-of-an-inch best cable Iron, and when either the Engine or Tender is to be coupled to Wagons the connection to be by a centre chain of one inch best cable Iron and two side chains of five-eighths Iron of the same quality.

Every Engine to be provided with a screen in the smokebox or cap upon the chimney of not more than three-eighths-of-an-inch in the wash, and so connected to the smokebox or chimney as to prevent the escape of cinders larger than will pass through the washes of the cap or screen. No chimney to exceed thirteen feet in height from the top of the rails of the Railway to the top of the cap upon the chimney.

No Engine to be used upon the Railway unless capable of taking 20 empty coal wagons from the Staiths at the Docks to the foot of the selfacting planes in less than 20 minutes, or 24 wagons in 24 minutes, nor to come upon the Railway after it shall be so much worn, broken, or decayed, as to endanger the persons or property of parties who may use the Railway, or be in anyway connected therewith.

179

GRAND EXCURSION

FOR 3 OR 8 DAYS, TO

LEEDS, LIVERPOOL, BLACKPOOL, AND FLEETWOOD.

NEXT WEDNESDAY Morning, AUGUST 14, 1850,

A CHEAP TRAIN

Will start from GATESHEAD STATION at SEVEN o'Clock,

Calling at all the Stations, between and at the following Towns:

NEWCASTLE, NORTH AND SOUTH SHIELDS, SUNDERDAND, DURHAM, AND HARTLEPOOL,

At the following extraordinary Low Fares, there and back:

FARES TO LEEDS, LIVERPOOL, BLACKPOOL, OR FLEETWOOD, AND BACK.

	1st Class,	2nd Class,	3rd Class,
FROM NEWCASTLE & ALL THE TOWNS & STATIONS AS FAR AS SHINCLIFFE AND HARTLEPOOL - -	10 s.	11 s.	14 s.
FROM FERRY HILL AND OTHER STATIONS AND DARLINGTON - - - - - - - - -	9 s.	10s.	13 s.

FARES TO LEEDS AND BACK.

	1st Class,	2nd Class,	3rd Class,
From NEWCASTLE and all the Towns and Stations as far as SHINCLIFFE and HARTLEPOOL - -	5 s.	6 s.	7 s.
FROM FERRY HILL AND OTHER STATIONS AND DARLINGTON - - - - - - - - - - - -	4 s.	5 s.	6 s.

Tickets may be had at all the Stations on the Line and Branches.

Small Bills with full particulars may be seen at the Railway Stations, in the Shop Windows, and one will be given to each Passenger after the Train has started, which will serve as a guide during the Journey. The Manager will go with the Trip to Liverpool, and will be glad to give all the information possible.

THOMAS CLAPHAM.

From the Office of J. Procter, Printer, High Street Hartlepool.

180A

This is a simple sailing notice which must have been displayed on hoardings along London's river every time the 'Iris' berthed there. The date and the name of the master are left blank; they would be filled in as required.

180B

The exquisite blocks of an early train make this timetable a work of art.

180C

John Brown could not have known how imminent was his eclipse for in December 1840 the Stockton and Hartlepool Railway was opened.

180D

There are a number of breweries which have at one time or another been accused of selling water, but it is rare to find one which advertises the fact. The explanation is a simple one. Hartlepool stands on a limestone headland and at certain stages of the tide the town wells became brackish. There was no piped water but the brewery was fortunate in having a spring of fresh water. Ships in the harbour were only too pleased to pay for salt-free water with which to fill their water barrels.

180E

These Rules and Regulations were compiled by John Fowler, Junior, as he used to sign himself, the engineer of the Stockton and Hartlepool Railway. He was a young man and this was his first executive post. He ruled his department with a rod of iron though he grew more tolerant in later years when he became Sir John Fowler, celebrated for designing the first Forth Bridge.

180A

180B

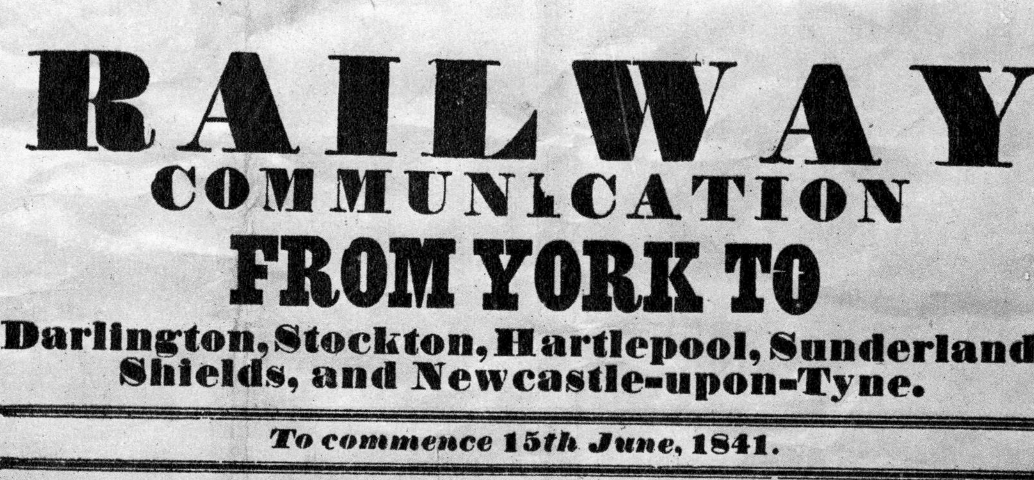

LONDON to YORK.	YORK to DARLINGTON.	DARLINGTON to STOCKTON.	STOCKTON to HARTLEPOOL.	HARTLEPOOL to SUNDERLAND	SUNDERLAND to NEWCASTLE and SHIELDS.	NEWCASTLE to CARLISLE,
H. M	H. M.	H M.	H. M.	H. M.	H. M.	H. M.
.. ..	.. ..	.. ..	.. ..	.. ..	.. ..	a. m. 5 30
.. ..	.. ..	.. ..	.. ..	.. ..	.. ..	9 —

180C

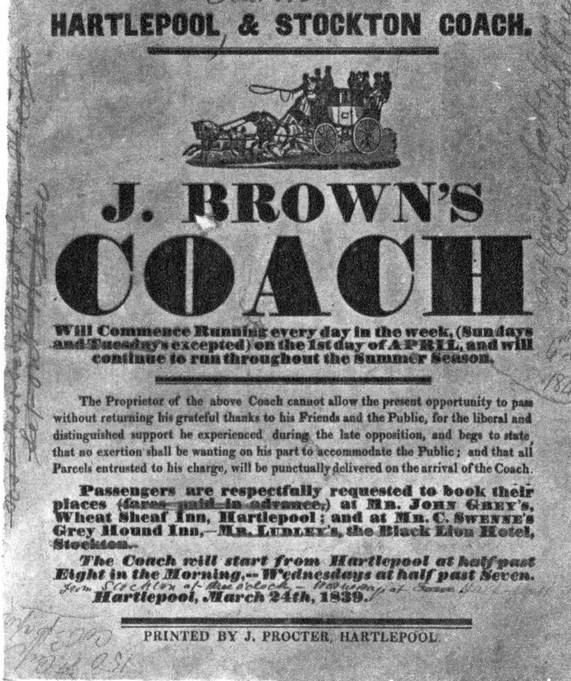

180D

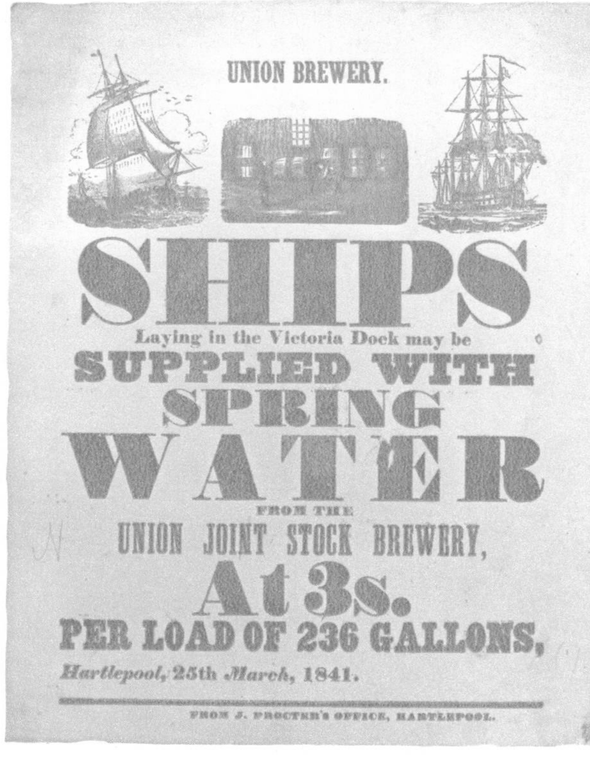

180E

REGULATIONS TO BE OBSERVED

BY THE

ENGINEMEN WORKING THE COAL ENGINES

UPON THE

Stockton & Hartlepool Railway

s. d.

On the Engines coming upon the Stockton and Hartlepool Railway, the Men in charge of the same to be under the Orders of the Superintendent, who will give them such instructions as are necessary for conducting the traffic on the Railway, and to be subject to the undermentioned Fines for any Breach of the following Rules :—

1. For any wilful delay in going upwards or downwards on the Railway, or Stopping at any beer house on the line - - - - 2 6
2. For not slacking the speed of the Engine when taking the Sidings or Crossings at the Switches 2 6
3. For propelling the Engine with a loaded train in the day time at a greater speed than 8 miles per hour, or at night than 7 miles per hour. The same regulation to apply to empty wagons - - - - - - 2 6
4. For neglecting to have fire Lamps to the Engine, and last Wagon of the Train at night
   For the first Offence - - - 2 6
   For the second Offence - - 5 0
   And to be dismissed for the third

181
This time-table is surely a perfect specimen of Victoriana. Who else but a Victorian would contrive such a border for a subject so banal?

182
The block at the head of the bill shows a coach but no engine for the very good reason that it would be pulled not by an engine but by a horse. It was a private venture of Mr. Humble's for which he would pay toll to the railway company.

183
The Pride of Hartlepool. A young apprentice must have spent a good deal of his time setting out this exercise in typography. It is regrettable that he left no name for our enlightenment.

184
Another delightful pictorial heading to a timetable for us to admire. Only the top half of the poster is reproduced here but further similar details were included for the journey between Stockton and Darlington, Sunderland and Hartlepool, and Port Clarence and Billingham Station.

181

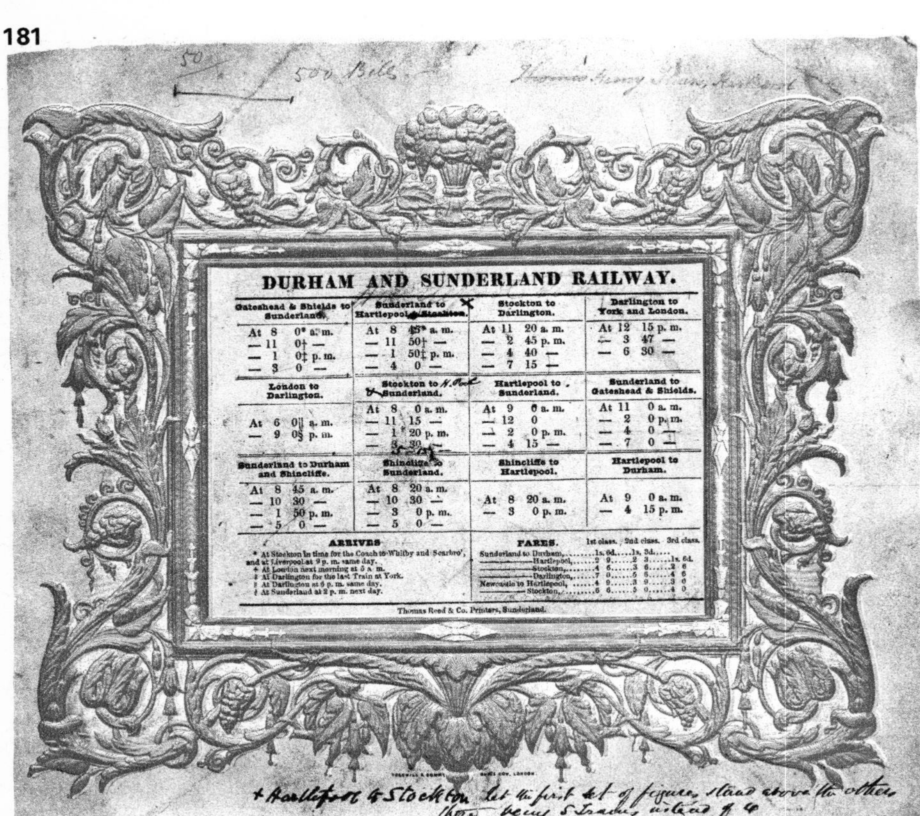

DURHAM AND SUNDERLAND RAILWAY.

Gateshead & Shields to Sunderland.	Sunderland to Hartlepool & Stockton.	Stockton to Darlington.	Darlington to York and London.
At 8 0* a. m. — 11 0† — — 1 0‡ p. m. — 3 0 —	At 8 45* a. m. — 11 50† — — 1 50‡ p. m. — 4 0 —	At 11 20 a. m. — 2 45 p. m. — 4 40 — — 7 15 —	At 12 15 p. m. — 3 47 — — 6 30 —
London to Darlington.	**Stockton to Sunderland.**	**Hartlepool to Sunderland.**	**Sunderland to Gateshead & Shields.**
At 6 0‖ a. m. — 9 0§ p. m.	At 8 0 a. m. — 11 15 — — 1 20 p. m. — 3 30 —	At 9 0 a. m. — 12 0 — 2 0 p. m. — 4 15 —	At 11 0 a. m. — 2 0 p. m. — 4 0 — — 7 0 —
Sunderland to Durham and Shincliffe.	**Shincliffe to Sunderland.**	**Shincliffe to Hartlepool.**	**Hartlepool to Durham.**
At 8 45 a. m. — 10 30 — — 1 50 p. m. — 5 0 —	At 8 20 a. m. — 10 30 — — 3 0 p. m. — 5 0 —	At 8 20 a. m. — 3 0 p. m.	At 9 0 a. m. — 4 15 p. m.

ARRIVES

* At Stockton in time for the Coach to Whitby and Scarbro', and at Liverpool at 9 p. m. same day.
† At London next morning at 5 a. m.
‡ At Darlington for the last Train at York.
‖ At Darlington at 6 p. m. same day.
§ At Sunderland at 2 p. m. next day.

FARES.	1st class.	2nd class.	3rd class.
Sunderland to Durham	1s. 6d.	1s. 3d.	
—— Hartlepool	2 9	2 3	1s. 6d.
—— Stockton	4 6	3 6	2 6
—— Darlington	7 0	5 6	4 6
Newcastle to Hartlepool	4 9	3 9	3 0
—— Stockton	6 6	5 0	4 0

Thomas Reed & Co. Printers, Sunderland.

183

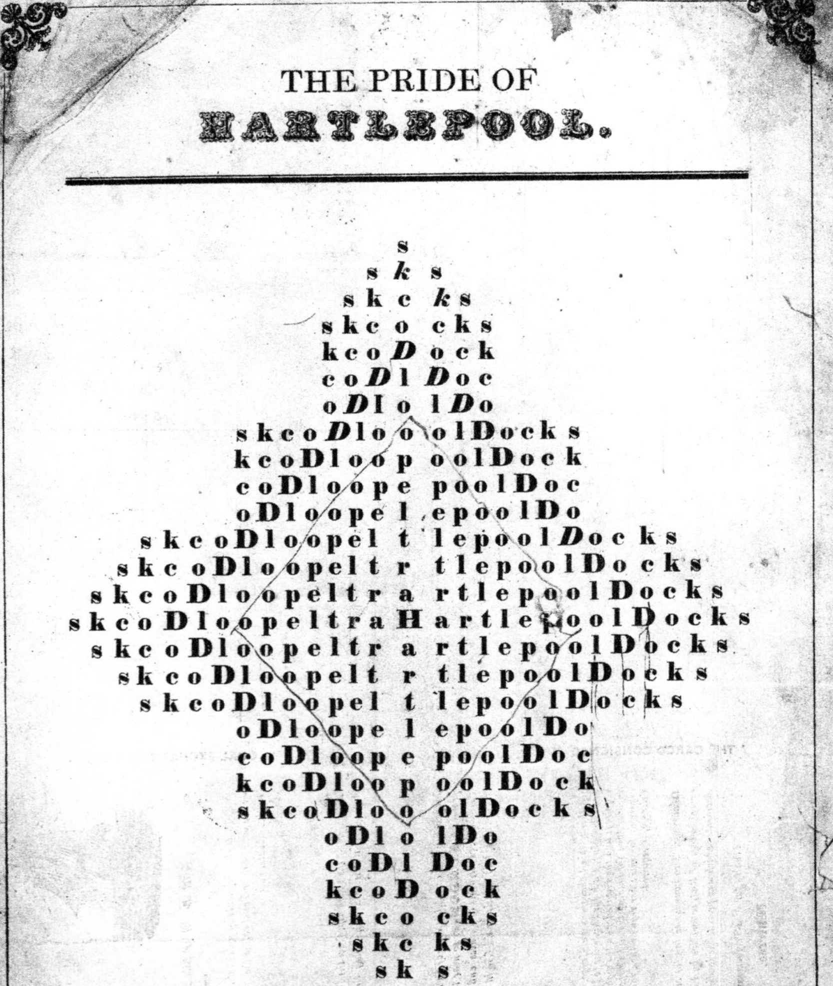

THE PRIDE OF

HARTLEPOOL.

s
s k s
s k c k s
s k c o c k s
k c o D o c k
c o D l D o c
o D l o l D o
s k c o D l o o l D o c k s
k c o D l o o p o o l D o c k
c o D l o o p e p o o l D o c
o D l o o p e l e p o o l D o
s k c o D l o o p e l t l e p o o l D o c k s
s k c o D l o o p e l t r t l e p o o l D o c k s
s k c o D l o o p e l t r a r t l e p o o l D o c k s
s k c o D l o o p e l t r a H a r t l e p o o l D o c k s
s k c o D l o o p e l t r a r t l e p o o l D o c k s
s k c o D l o o p e l t r t l e p o o l D o c k s
s k c o D l o o p e l t l e p o o l D o c k s
o D l o o p e l e p o o l D o
c o D l o o p e p o o l D o c
k c o D l o o p o o l D o c k
s k c o D l o o l D o c k s
o D l o l D o
c o D l D o c
k c o D o c k
s k c o c k s
s k c k s
s k s
s

182

RAILWAY
COACH
FROM
HARTLEPOOL TO HASWELL.

R. HUMBLE,

Respectfully informs the Public that his Railway Coach will commence running between the above places on

SUNDAY FIRST.

The Coach will leave Hartlepool at 8 o'clock in the Morning, and return at 11,—at 4 o'clock in the Afternoon from Hartlepool and from Haswell at 6 o'clock in the Evening.

Cleveland Arms, March 20, 1841.

J. PROCTER, PRINTER, HARTLEPOOL.

184

STOCKTON & HARTLEPOOL RAILWAY.

Stockton to Hartlepool.			Hartlepool to Stockton.		
First Trip ..		8 o'Clock.	First Trip ..	at	9 o'Clock.
Second do. ..	at half-past	10 do.	Second do.	at quarter-past	11 do.
Third do. ..	at	3 do.	Third do. ..	at	4 do.
Fourth do. ..	at	5 do.	Fourth do. ..	at	6 do.

The 8, half-past 10, and 3 o'Clock Trains leave STOCKTON on the arrival of the Stockton and Darlington Trains.

An Omnibus is in readiness to convey Passengers between the Stockton and Hartlepool Railway Station, and the Stockton and Darlington Railway Station:—

10

Butcher, Baker and Candlestick Maker

The probable initial reaction today of most readers of Victorian shop advertisements is to gasp at the prices and compare them with present ones, but a moment's thought will bring to mind the very great difference between Victorian rates of pay and our own and the balance is redressed. One's general impression gained from such advertisements and bills is that the most noticeable difference is one of attitude. The Victorian shopkeeper was a member of a profession, he was punctilious in his relations with his customers and always most anxious to please. His customers expected willing service of him and showed no hesitation in expressing their dissatisfaction if they thought he was at fault. John Procter seems to have been a most efficient and helpful tradesman and therefore he prospered in his business. The famous colliery manager and engineer William Armstrong once wrote to him concerning Evenwood Colliery

'The owners were anxious to have their forms all done at Stockton but I informed them that under my tuition my Bookseller had acquired considerable celebrity in this department of his trade, particularly in dispatch; that in skill and neatness he had no equal, and only one superior, (his brother at Durham) and acting under my advice they entrusted you with the order.'

Willie Armstrong may have been pulling Procter's leg a little but Procter generally gave satisfaction, except for the case of the letter from the irascible Mr. Thomas Richardson, owner of the Hartlepool Iron Works. He was a 'character' and his comments should be treated with caution.

'Messrs. Richardson and Sons not wishing to deprive Mr. Procter of his rare and curious assortment of envelopes beg to return them to him and will be most happy to wait till Mr. Procter has leisure to order a stock of more modern date of manufacture and better calculated for business purposes. The Antique specimens are returned forthwith. Copy of Order sent Monday afternoon

500 envelopes with deep black edging, viz 250 large 250 small

Received: – small envelopes with deep black edging, large envelopes with deep black edging, about 200 mongrels exceedingly small with extremely minute black edging

N.B. Required to make above agree with the order sent.'

The language of commerce was more formal and decorous than it is today and letters were couched in most courteous terms. The wholesaler was deferential to the retailer, but woe betide the unfortunate merchant who couldn't pay his bills, for then the wholesaler was very forthright in his dunning letters. Commercial travellers visited periodically and also acted as the collectors of their firms' accounts. The wholesaler sent a letter printed in most elegant style warning the shopkeeper of his approach and asking for the favour of a further order, at the same time giving a statement of account and requesting that anything outstanding should be paid to the traveller.

This added responsibility sometimes gave commercial gentlemen an inflated sense of their own importance. A hundred years ago the gentleman from London was often regarded with awe and treated with deference at the inn which he made his headquarters whilst he toured the district. The story is told of one such pompous gentleman who was staying at the King's Head in Barnard Castle and made himself offensive to a Quaker quietly reading his newspaper beside the fire. He pulled out a bundle of banknotes and proceeded to dilate on the joys of rich living and the pleasures that wealth could bring. He suggested that the Quaker's frugal life and sober attire would soon be discarded if he became rich and that it was a case of 'sour grapes'. The Quaker leisuredly pulled out a £5 note and said, 'Match thy money with mine and show that it means as little to thee as it does to me.' And with that he threw his note into the fire. The commercial traveller was non-plussed, but, not willing to be out-faced, took a similar note from his bundle and did likewise. Thereupon the Quaker took out another note and repeated the performance. The red-faced traveller jumped up, mumbling something about not being willing to chaffer with mad-men, and rushed out of the room, whereupon all the locals had a good laugh for the Quaker was Jonathan Backhouse who owned the Darlington Bank and issued his own banknotes.

There is little to find if we seek for changes in shops. Indeed many survive showing little outward change, but there were some tradesmen we do not encounter today. Each provincial town had it 'cowkeepers' who supplied their customers with fresh milk; an honest cowkeeper was greatly valued by his customers. A number of itinerant workers moved from place to place practising their trade. Many older readers will certainly remember the knife and scissors grinder who wheeled his strange contraption from street to street creating an aurora borealis in miniature with his sparks. Some watch and clock repairers visited a country village periodically and were undoubtedly highly welcome. There were also tailors who travelled round making up the customer's own material into the garments he desired in return for board and lodging and 18 pence a day. This way of making a living was so popular among free tailors that they coined a special phrase for it known as 'flogging the cat.' Painters produced silhouettes and 'likenesses' at prices ranging from 2 shillings and 6 pence to 1 guinea. They usually lodged at the local inn and exhibited specimens of their talent staying until the supply of clients was exhausted. Many of the small, delicate portraits printed on card, which are still treasured by families, are examples of the work of the itinerant painter.

In seaports the opportunity often arose of purchasing a chance cargo which a venturesome captain might have brought instead of coming in ballast. The enterprising shopkeeper would print bills advertising such products as cider from the West of England, potatoes from Scotland or apples or furniture from Germany. In some cases the siting of special industries can be traced to such an origin. For instance, clay pipe makers have existed on the North-east coast for three hundred years and it is probable that the trade flourished there because the pipeclay could be procured free from the ballast dumped by west country ships.

The ordinary tradesman did not venture from his shop but drapers and milliners in quite small towns thought little of visiting London to obtain the latest fashions for their customers.

There is little to say about the articles for sale in the shops. Naturally there are changes and in those we find our pleasure, for it is often in the ordinary commonplaces of life that the changes become most apparent.

185
This appears to have been a mixed cargo that a speculative captain has brought rather late in the season, probably with the Christmas trade in mind. He is quoting old country measures rather than the pounds and ounces of the grocer.

186
Most probably a speculative venture on the part of a West country captain who had taken a few barrels on board instead of sailing in ballast. Whether the North country customers took kindly to it is doubtful but some of the colliers were Cornishmen who would most probably have relished it.

187
A rather ornate and tastefully designed price list issued by one of Hartlepool's leading grocers. The ladies of the time would have been most interested in the item in larger print for tinned fruit was still rather a novelty. Although the principle of canning was not new—it had been used since early in the century for foodstuffs for the armed forces and explorers—it had taken the housewife a long time to realise its advantages.

188
The prices may seem very low but so was the average wage, and Champagne was still something of a luxury.

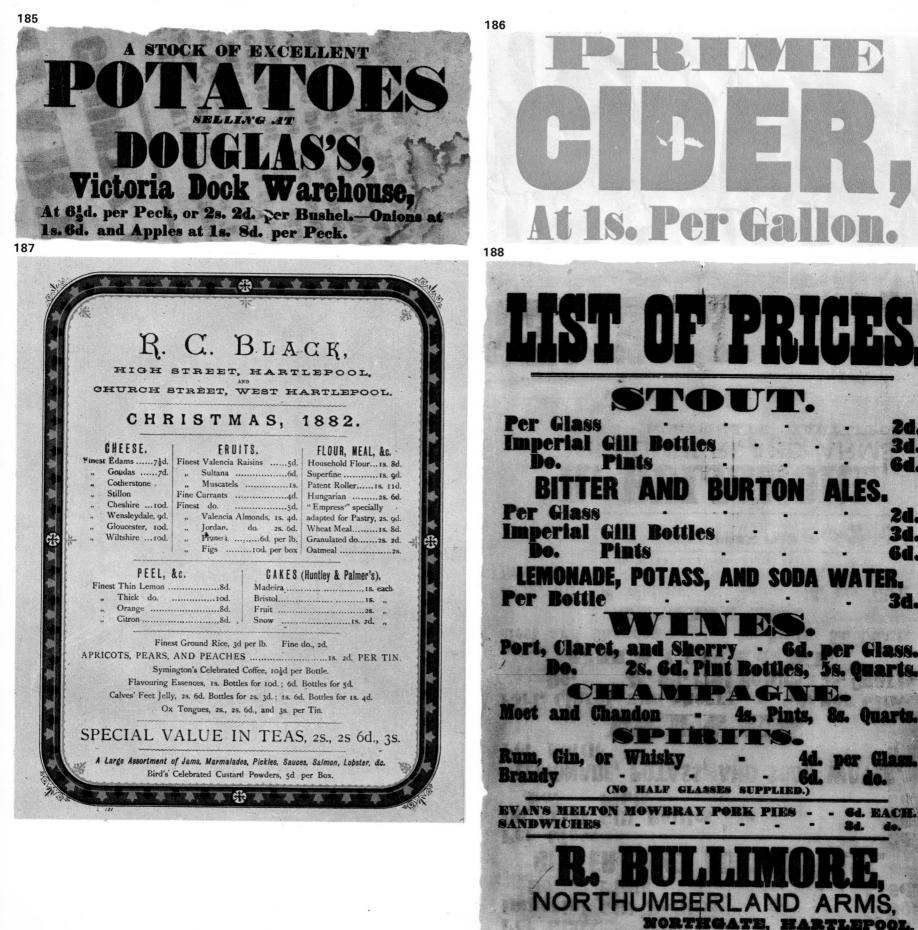

185

A STOCK OF EXCELLENT
POTATOES
SELLING AT
DOUGLAS'S,
Victoria Dock Warehouse,
At 6½d. per Peck, or 2s. 2d. per Bushel.—Onions at 1s. 6d. and Apples at 1s. 8d. per Peck.

186

PRIME
CIDER,
At 1s. Per Gallon.

187

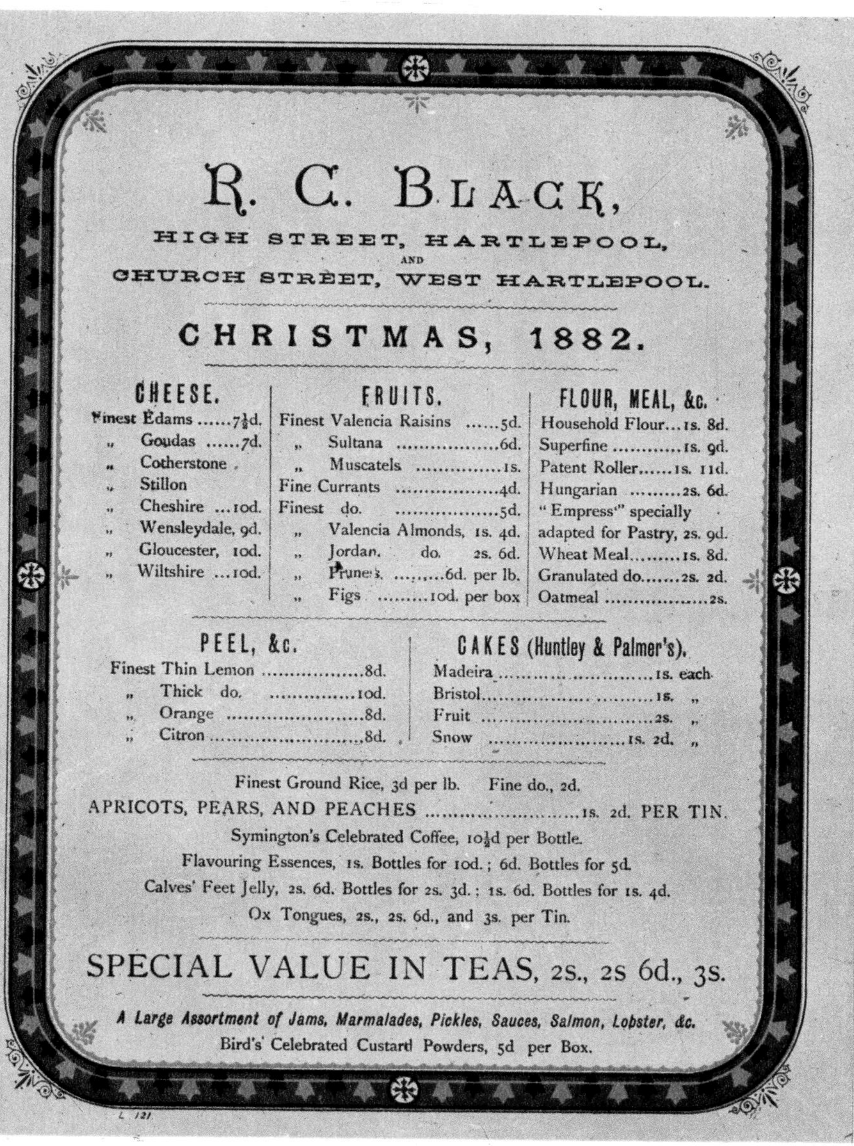

R. C. BLACK,
HIGH STREET, HARTLEPOOL,
AND
CHURCH STREET, WEST HARTLEPOOL.

CHRISTMAS, 1882.

CHEESE.	FRUITS.	FLOUR, MEAL, &c.
Finest Edams ......7½d.	Finest Valencia Raisins ......5d.	Household Flour...1s. 8d.
„ Goudas ......7d.	„ Sultana ....6d.	Superfine ....1s. 9d.
„ Cotherstone	„ Muscatels ....1s.	Patent Roller......1s. 11d.
„ Stillon	Fine Currants ....4d.	Hungarian ....2s. 6d.
„ Cheshire ...10d.	Finest do. ....5d.	"Empress" specially
„ Wensleydale, 9d.	„ Valencia Almonds, 1s. 4d.	adapted for Pastry, 2s. 9d.
„ Gloucester, 10d.	„ Jordan do. 2s. 6d.	Wheat Meal.........1s. 8d.
„ Wiltshire ...10d.	„ Prunes ....6d. per lb.	Granulated do.......2s. 2d.
	„ Figs ....10d. per box	Oatmeal ....2s.

PEEL, &c.	CAKES (Huntley & Palmer's).
Finest Thin Lemon ....8d.	Madeira ....1s. each
„ Thick do. ....10d.	Bristol..................................1s. „
„ Orange ....8d.	Fruit ....2s. „
„ Citron ....8d.	Snow ....1s. 2d. „

Finest Ground Rice, 3d per lb. Fine do., 2d.
APRICOTS, PEARS, AND PEACHES ....1s. 2d. PER TIN.
Symington's Celebrated Coffee, 10½d per Bottle.
Flavouring Essences, 1s. Bottles for 10d.; 6d. Bottles for 5d.
Calves' Feet Jelly, 2s. 6d. Bottles for 2s. 3d.; 1s. 6d. Bottles for 1s. 4d.
Ox Tongues, 2s., 2s. 6d., and 3s. per Tin.

SPECIAL VALUE IN TEAS, 2s., 2s 6d., 3s.

A Large Assortment of Jams, Marmalades, Pickles, Sauces, Salmon, Lobster, &c.
Bird's' Celebrated Custard Powders, 5d per Box.

188

LIST OF PRICES.

STOUT.
Per Glass - - - - 2d.
Imperial Gill Bottles - - 3d.
Do. Pints - - - 6d.

BITTER AND BURTON ALES.
Per Glass - - - - 2d.
Imperial Gill Bottles - - 3d.
Do. Pints - - - 6d.

LEMONADE, POTASS, AND SODA WATER.
Per Bottle - - - - 3d.

WINES.
Port, Claret, and Sherry - 6d. per Glass.
Do. 2s. 6d. Pint Bottles, 5s. Quarts.

CHAMPAGNE.
Moet and Chandon - 4s. Pints, 8s. Quarts.

SPIRITS.
Rum, Gin, or Whisky - 4d. per Glass.
Brandy - - - 6d. do.
(NO HALF GLASSES SUPPLIED.)

EVAN'S MELTON MOWBRAY PORK PIES - - 6d. EACH.
SANDWICHES - - - - - - 3d. do.

R. BULLIMORE,
NORTHUMBERLAND ARMS,
NORTHGATE, HARTLEPOOL.

189
Mr. Scotson was an old established grocer. The billhead gives a true picture of his shop in the High Street and no doubt the carriage and costumes are typical of the time. It will be noted that Huntley and Palmer's Biscuits and Crosse and Blackwell's Pickles were celebrated even a hundred years ago.

190
The Victorians were most particular about their teas. Notice the prices and the variety offered. Gunpowder and Hyson were very popular green teas: people anxious to make an impression aired their knowledge of teas in the same way that we might talk about wines. The fresh tea delivered each season brought high prices, hence the advent of the tea clipper.

191
A somewhat curious question which was probably related to a popular local conundrum of the time.

192
Here is William Gray's shop in Victoria Street. A young man of 26 when he signed this bill, fifty years later he was knighted by Queen Victoria for his services to British shipbuilding.

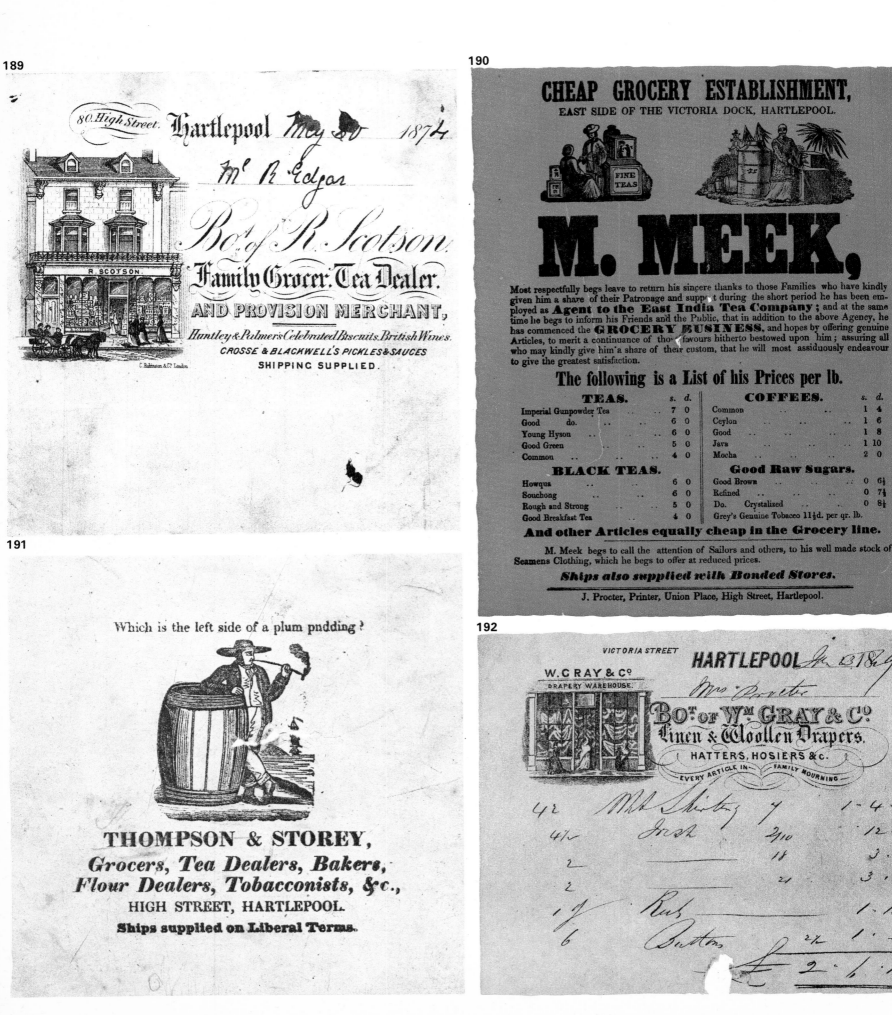

189

80 High Street. Hartlepool May 30 1874
Mr R Edgar
Bot. of R. Scotson.
Family Grocer, Tea Dealer.
AND PROVISION MERCHANT,
Huntley & Palmer's Celebrated Biscuits. British Wines.
CROSSE & BLACKWELL'S PICKLES & SAUCES
SHIPPING SUPPLIED.

190

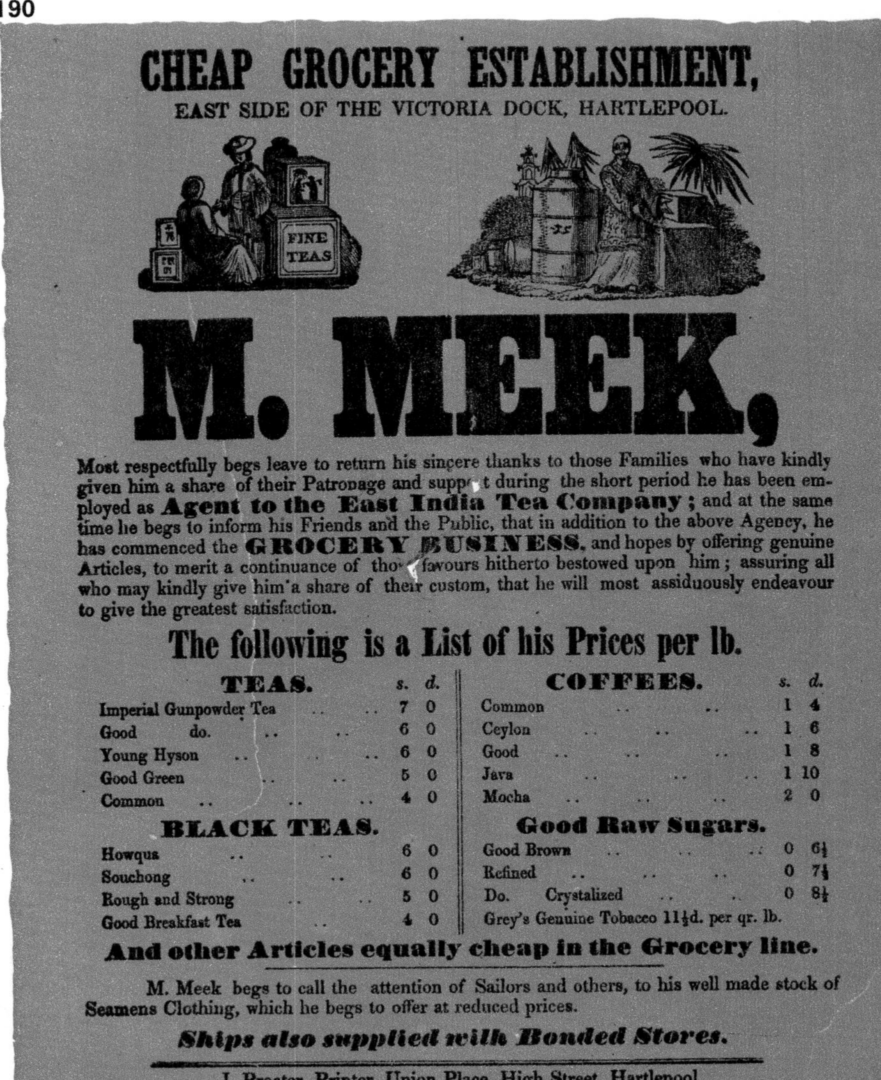

CHEAP GROCERY ESTABLISHMENT,

EAST SIDE OF THE VICTORIA DOCK, HARTLEPOOL.

M. MEEK,

Most respectfully begs leave to return his sincere thanks to those Families who have kindly given him a share of their Patronage and support during the short period he has been employed as **Agent to the East India Tea Company;** and at the same time he begs to inform his Friends and the Public, that in addition to the above Agency, he has commenced the **GROCERY BUSINESS**, and hopes by offering genuine Articles, to merit a continuance of those favours hitherto bestowed upon him; assuring all who may kindly give him a share of their custom, that he will most assiduously endeavour to give the greatest satisfaction.

The following is a List of his Prices per lb.

TEAS.	s.	d.	COFFEES.	s.	d.
Imperial Gunpowder Tea	7	0	Common	1	4
Good do.	6	0	Ceylon	1	6
Young Hyson	6	0	Good	1	8
Good Green	5	0	Java	1	10
Common	4	0	Mocha	2	0
BLACK TEAS.			**Good Raw Sugars.**		
Howqua	6	0	Good Brown	0	6½
Souchong	6	0	Refined	0	7½
Rough and Strong	5	0	Do. Crystalized	0	8½
Good Breakfast Tea	4	0	Grey's Genuine Tobacco 11½d. per qr. lb.		

And other Articles equally cheap in the Grocery line.

M. Meek begs to call the attention of Sailors and others, to his well made stock of Seamens Clothing, which he begs to offer at reduced prices.

Ships also supplied with Bonded Stores.

J. Procter, Printer, Union Place, High Street, Hartlepool.

191

Which is the left side of a plum pudding?

THOMPSON & STOREY,
Grocers, Tea Dealers, Bakers, Flour Dealers, Tobacconists, &c.,
HIGH STREET, HARTLEPOOL.
Ships supplied on Liberal Terms.

192

VICTORIA STREET HARTLEPOOL
W. GRAY & Co DRAPERY WAREHOUSE.
Mrs Procter
Bot. of Wm. GRAY & Co.
Linen & Woollen Drapers.
HATTERS, HOSIERS &c.
EVERY ARTICLE IN FAMILY MOURNING

42	Shirting	7	1 - 4 - 6
4½	Irish	2/10	12 - 9
2		18	3 - 0
2		21	3 - 6
1½			1 - 10
6	Buttons	2½	1 - 3
		£	2 - 1 - 10

193
A typical butcher's billhead of the time. All seaports had a great number of butchers because with no means of refrigeration fresh meat had to be obtained as frequently as possible. The establishments clustered on the main roads to the docks.

194
Mr. Smith cannot resist illustrating the latest achievements of modern engineering science on his trade card. The extraordinary instrument on the right is a household pump still popular in the North of England. Before piped water was easily available every household had its well and the pump was used for drawing up the water from it.

195
Another versatile but much more successful chemist. William Davison printed books, produced inks and cattle medicines, and travelled the North Country with his wares. He prospered in the days when the provinces were self-supporting.

196
It would seem that Mr. Paddon sold most things. He was willing to look after both man and beast concocting mixtures to suit either: his skill extended to dentistry, bleeding and cupping. A veritable 'Jack of all trades', he was probably master of none for he was bankrupt two years later.

197
This is an eighteenth century billhead still used in the nineteenth century. This is not unusual because the provinces were often slow to follow the current fashion. If something appealed to a tradesman he would not discard it lightly.

198
Mr. Stokell, the Chymist of Sedgefield, was not the mass murderer his advertisement might lead us to believe. Strange as it may seem, hydrocyanic acid, or prussic acid, as it is more generally known, taken in very diluted form, does relieve coughing. Such a medicine was still sold well into the present century.

193

194

195

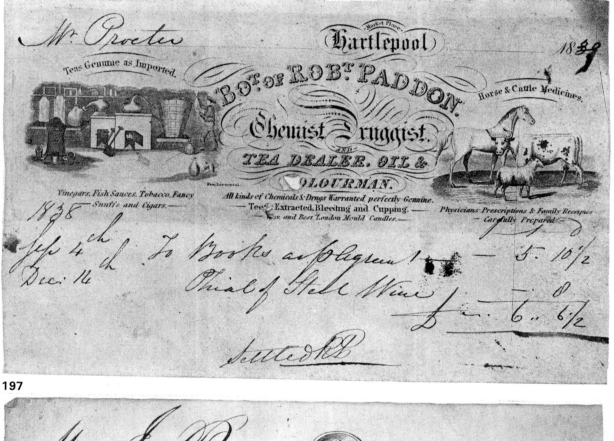

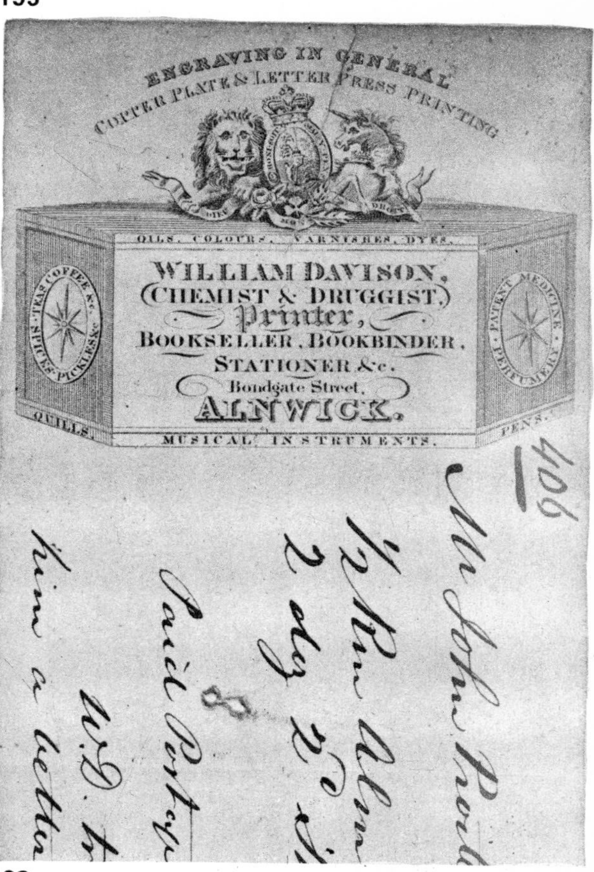

196

Market Place
Hartlepool
Teas Genuine as Imported.
Bot. of ROBt. PADDON.
Chemist & Druggist,
AND
TEA DEALER, OIL &
COLOURMAN.
Horse & Cattle Medicines.
Vinegars, Fish Sauces, Tobacco, Fancy Snuffs and Cigars.
All kinds of Chemicals & Drugs Warranted perfectly Genuine.
Teeth Extracted, Bleeding and Cupping.
Wax and Best London Mould Candles.
Physicians Prescriptions & Family Receipes Carefully Prepared.

197

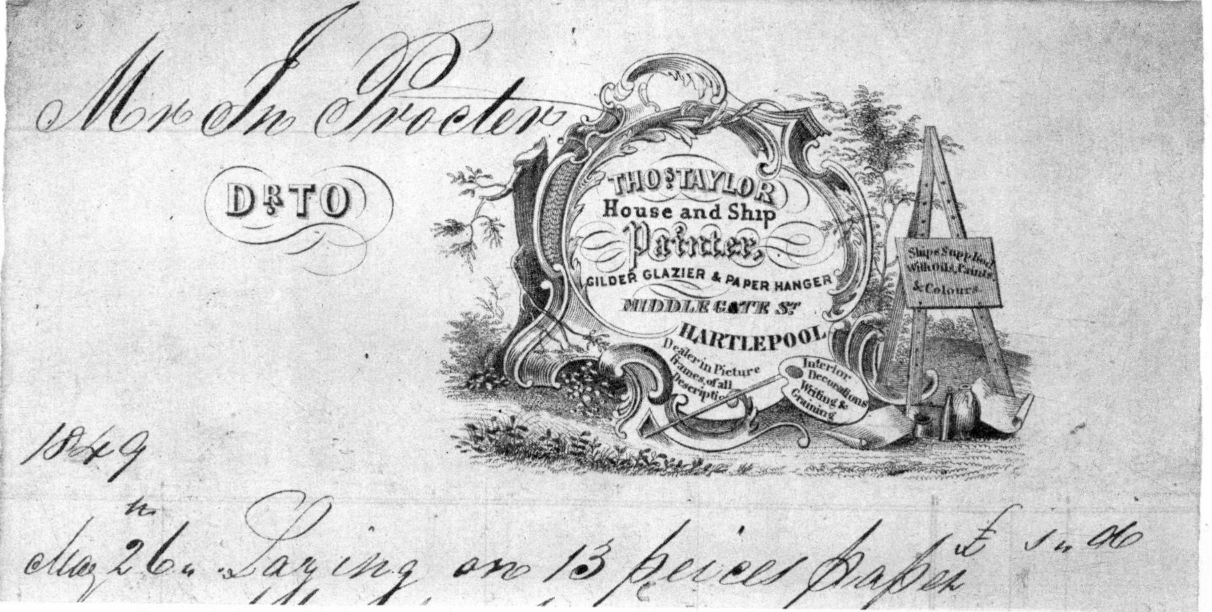

198

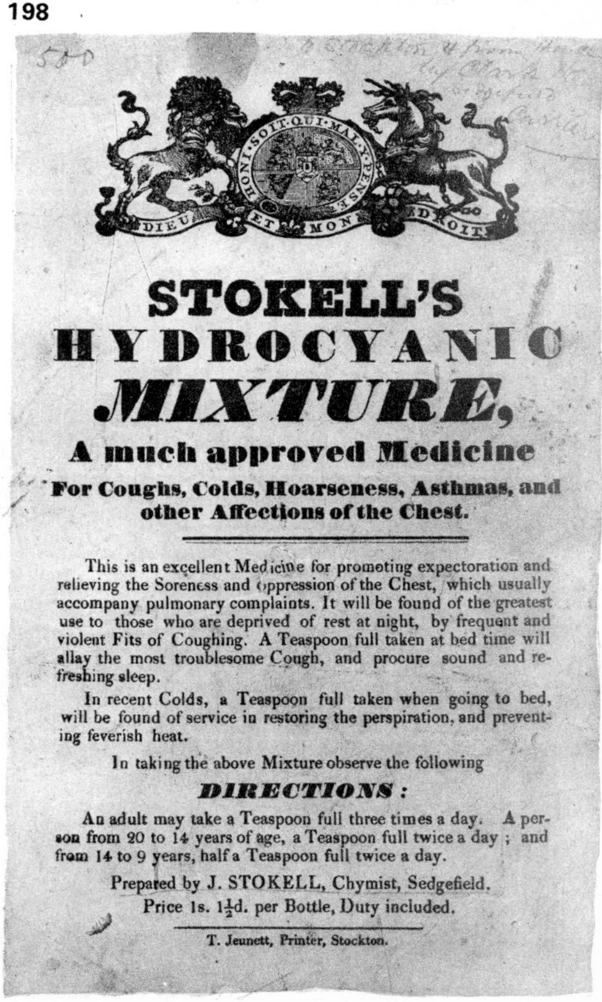

199, 200, 201 and 202
Before there was a local newspaper these were typical of the sale bills which a local tradesman would have printed and posted around. That of R. France is a fine example of a bill whose type has been well selected to give emphasis to the important items. The style is almost certainly around 1840.
It makes an interesting comparison with that of A. Nathan. They are quite obviously the products of two different printing offices. On no occasion did John Procter ever use the quaint nautical block which has such an eighteenth century flavour.
The dignified bill of Thomas Barkhouse, restrained both in design and language, is typical of the local printing styles of the first half of the nineteenth century.
199, part of which is reproduced here, advertises the goods of John Hawkridge, a tailor and clothier who became well-known in West Hartlepool. Until very recently a house there had an inscribed stone let into its facade which read
This is the house that Jack built.

203
Mr. Kaim claims to be able to do what other contemporary photographers still found impossible.

204
The Victorian era was the golden age of the patent medicine man. The crowding together of ignorant folk into insanitary and unsavoury tenements brought a recurrence of the great epidemics which had terrified our mediaeval ancestors. Any mixture which claimed to prevent, alleviate, or cure cholera could not fail to be a best seller. Other ailments had their own appropriate remedies.

199

Item	£	s	d	Item	£	s	d	Item	£	s	d
Boy's Flushing Suit.........	0	18	0	Moleskin Trousers, from ...	0	3	6	Short Suit best Saxony Wool	3	3	0
Men's Flushing Suit.........	1	2	0	Mole Printed ditto	0	4	0	Long Suit of Black	2	10	0
Pilot Cloth Suit	1	18	0	Pilot Coats, from 17s. to ...	2	0	0	Ditto, best Quality	3	15	0
Superfine ditto	2	4	0	Short Suit of Men's Fine ...	1	15	0	Splendid Satin Vest	0	5	0
First-rate ditto, warranted	2	8	0	Ditto, prime quality	2	7	0	Figured Silk Velvet, 12s. to	0	14	0
Best made ditto..............	2	12	0	Ditto, extra super............	2	12	0	Brown Flushing Trousers...	0	6	9
Best Beaver made............	2	14	0	Ditto, rich quality	2	18	0	White Mole Suit	0	16	0
Blouses, from	0	5	0	Ck. Woollen Coat 17s. 6d. to	1	1	0	Vests, from	0	1	6
Prime Paris Hat	0	6	0	Prime Tweed do. 16s. 6d. to	0	18	6	Drab Dvnshr. cloth Trousers	0	17	6
Jenny Lind Jackets, from...	0	14	0	Blue Witney Watch Coat ...	2	0	0				

200

Clothing! Clothing!!

SELLING OFF CHEAP!

A. NATHAN

Respectfully informs his Friends and the public generally that he has determined to clear out a large portion of his valuable Stock of

CLOTHING, WOOLLEN CLOTHS, &c.,

Comprising Broad and Narrow WOOLLEN CLOTHS, in Doeskins, Tweeds, Bedford Woollen Cords, Beavers, Witneys, Pilots, Cotton Cords; Self, Drab, Black, Brown and Fancy Moleskins; Russell Cords, and Cobourgs in all Colours. Blue, Red, Check and Fancy Flannels; White and Grey Kerseys, Sagathys, Twills and Swans' Downs; Velvet and Velveteens; Rugs, Sheets, Blankets, White and Grey Calicoes &c,

Ready-made Clothing,

to suit all Classes, selling considerably under cost price.
A Large Assortment of BOYS' and YOUTHS' CLOTHING, Good Serviceable Boys' Suits, at 10s, worth 13s 6d. Youths' Suits, of Superior Quality, at 13s, 18s, 22s, all under cost price.
A very large Stock of Wool, Striped, Fancy, and White Shirts, all at cost Price. Good Striped Shirts at 2s 4d, and 2s 6d, and 3s.
Men's Duck JACKETS, Good Quality, at 2s 6d, worth 3s.

HATS AND CAPS,

Comprising all the Newest Styles, will be cleared out at an Immense Sacrifice, Yankee Hat, 2s 9d, worth 3s 6d; Finest quality, 3s 6d, worth 5s. MILLITARY CAPS a[illegible], 10½d, and 12d. An Immense Stock of Seamen's and Mechanics' CLOTHING, all reduced in price in order to clear out the stock.

OBSERVE:

34, HIGH-STREET,

Hosiery and Haberdashery of every description remarkably cheap

HARTLEPOOL.

~~Printed at the Hartlepool "Free Press" Office.~~

201

Selling OFF,

A LARGE AND VALUABLE STOCK OF LINEN & WOOLLEN

DRAPERY,

HABERDASHERY, HOSIERY,
HATS, CAPS, &c.,
AT THE SHOP OF R.

France,

High Street, HARTLEPOOL,
who is about leaving the place in a few Weeks.
Purchasers will find this a favourable opportunity, as the whole of the Stock will be offered from
10 to 20 per cent. below the regular selling prices, which will be found, on inspection, to be no PUFF.

R. F. In returning his sincere thanks to his Friends and the Public for past favours, begs to call their attention to his

STOCK OF PRINTS;

London printed Cambrics, at 3d. yard, worth 6d. do. 6d. worth 9d. do. the best Styles in the Trade 9d. regularly sold from 14d. to 16d.

Woollen Cloths

of every Colour and Quality, at a **REDUCTION** of **20 PER CENT.**
An extensive Stock of Waterproof **HATS,** from **3s. 3d.** upwards, and every other Article in the Trade will be offered equally low.

N. B. The

HOUSE & SHOP

TO LET (with or without the SHOP FIXTURES) and may be entered upon at May-day next.

J. PROCTER, PRINTER, HIGH-STREET, HARTLEPOOL.

202

THOMAS BARKHOUSE,

(FROM LONDON),

TAILOR,

Habit, Dress, & Pelisse Maker,

No. 5. George Street, South Terrace,

Respectfully informs the Inhabitants of Hartlepool and its vicinity, that he intends to carry on the above business in all its branches; and having been in practice for himself seven years, he hopes by steadiness and strict attention to merit a share of their patronage and support.

Hartlepool, 7th November, 1838.

PRINTED BY J. PROCTER, HARTLEPOOL.

205
Another glimpse of a world long since disappeared. In the age of the motor-car we can compare the virtues of different grades of petrol and motor oil, but how many of us today are even aware that there were these medicines for horses, and that the same chemist sold another eight different varieties of ball? See also no. 195.

206
William Heron's verse—part only is reproduced here—speaks for itself.

207
Part of the bill of a travelling pedlar who has opened a Dutch Fair in the town to attract customers and sell them his shoddy wares.

208
Mr. Hardy was a very energetic man if he was really able to carry out the Monday tour which he specifies. Such a journey of 25 miles was formidable in those days without allowing for time spent in sweeping chimneys or providing his other services.

209
In a rapidly expanding shipbuilding town such as Hartlepool a sawmill was almost certain of abundant custom, hence the reason for this list. The anonymity of this particular trader suggests that his was the only sawmill in Hartlepool at that time. The prices cannot be compared with those for similar work today because the nature of the work was quite different. One point of comparison however, is the charge for labour, 6d. per hour in 1839, with a present basic rate of 7/2½d.

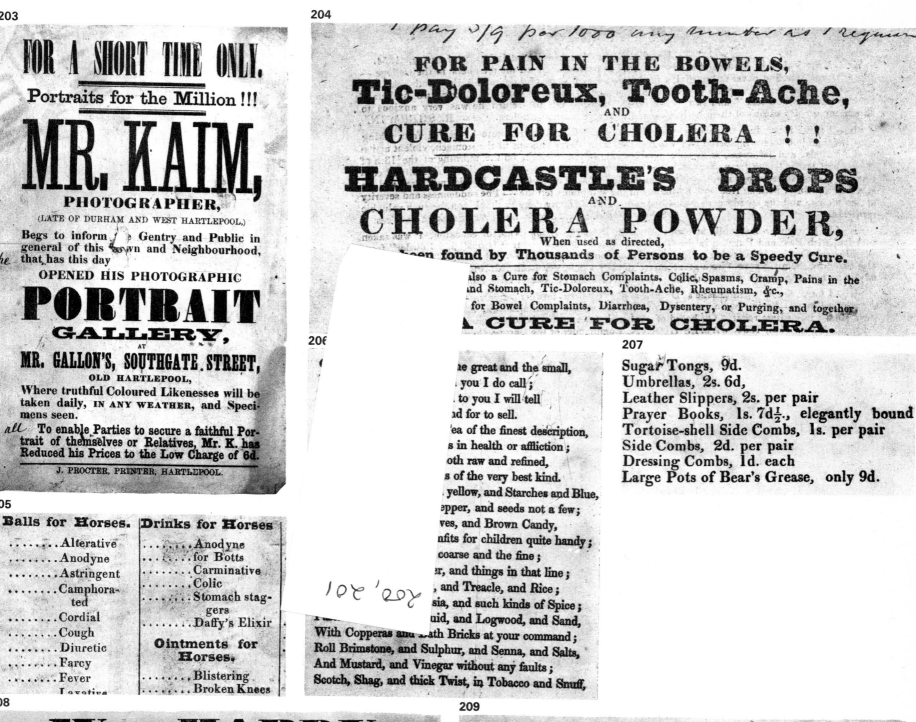

203

FOR A SHORT TIME ONLY.

Portraits for the Million !!!

MR. KAIM,

PHOTOGRAPHER,

(LATE OF DURHAM AND WEST HARTLEPOOL,)

Begs to inform [the] Gentry and Public in general of this [town] and Neighbourhood, that has this day OPENED HIS PHOTOGRAPHIC

PORTRAIT GALLERY,

AT

MR. GALLON'S, SOUTHGATE STREET, OLD HARTLEPOOL,

Where truthful Coloured Likenesses will be taken daily, IN ANY WEATHER, and Specimens seen.

To enable Parties to secure a faithful Portrait of themselves or Relatives, Mr. K. has Reduced his Prices to the Low Charge of 6d.

J. PROCTER, PRINTER, HARTLEPOOL.

204

FOR PAIN IN THE BOWELS,

Tic-Doloreux, Tooth-Ache,

AND

CURE FOR CHOLERA ! !

HARDCASTLE'S DROPS

AND

CHOLERA POWDER,

When used as directed,

[have] been found by Thousands of Persons to be a Speedy Cure.

[...] also a Cure for Stomach Complaints, Colic, Spasms, Cramp, Pains in the [...]nd Stomach, Tic-Doloreux, Tooth-Ache, Rheumatism, &c.,

[...] for Bowel Complaints, Diarrhœa, Dysentery, or Purging, and together

[...] A CURE FOR CHOLERA.

206

[...]e great and the small,
[...] you I do call;
[...] to you I will tell
[...]d for to sell.
[...]ea of the finest description,
[...]s in health or affliction;
[...]oth raw and refined,
[...]s of the very best kind.
[...] yellow, and Starches and Blue,
[...]epper, and seeds not a few;
[...]ves, and Brown Candy,
[...]nfits for children quite handy;
[...] coarse and the fine;
[...]r, and things in that line;
[...], and Treacle, and Rice;
[...]sia, and such kinds of Spice;
[...]uid, and Logwood, and Sand,
With Copperas an[d] [B]ath Bricks at your command;
Roll Brimstone, and Sulphur, and Senna, and Salts,
And Mustard, and Vinegar without any faults;
Scotch, Shag, and thick Twist, in Tobacco and Snuff,

207

Sugar Tongs, 9d.
Umbrellas, 2s. 6d,
Leather Slippers, 2s. per pair
Prayer Books, 1s. 7d½., elegantly bound
Tortoise-shell Side Combs, 1s. per pair
Side Combs, 2d. per pair
Dressing Combs, 1d. each
Large Pots of Bear's Grease, only 9d.

205

Balls for Horses.	Drinks for Horses
........Alterative	........Anodyne
........Anodyne	........for Botts
........Astringent	........Carminative
........Camphorated	........Colic
........Cordial	........Stomach staggers
........Cough	........Daffy's Elixir
........Diuretic	**Ointments for Horses.**
........Farcy	........Blistering
........Fever	........Broken Knees

208

Wm. HARDY,

CHIMNEY SWEEP,

Smoke Jack Cleaner and Fire Extinguisher,

Begs to inform the inhabitants of Hartlepool and its neighbourhood, that he now resides in Chapman Street, immediately behind Mrs. Lovett's, Bread and Biscuit Baker, and he hopes by using his best endeavours in giving satisfaction to his employers, to meet with public support.

GOOD CLOTHS PROVIDED FOR UPPER ROOMS.

W. H. will attend the following places the first Monday in every Month, viz:— Stranton, Seaton, Wolviston, Billingham, Norton and Castle Eden. Hartlepool, December 12th, 1842.

209

A LIST OF THE

PRICES OF SAWING

AT HARTLEPOOL,

FEBRUARY, 1839.

	s.	d.
All American Pine under 12 inches cut into boards at per 100 - - - - - -	2	9
All above 12 inches 1*d*. per inch per 100 extra		
All Scantlings out of Timber do.	3	0
All Memel and Red Pine under 12 inches cut into boards do. - - - -	3	0
Above 12 inches 1*d*. per inch per 100 extra		
Scantlings out of Memel and Red Pine do.	3	0
Scotch Fir do. - - - - - -	3	0
Larch do. - - - - - - -	3	9

210
Most of the examples in this miscellany are typical of the kind of bill which a housewife would see on the hoardings or find pushed through her letter-box. The exception is the price list of the Black Boy Coal Company which was sent out to its customers (part is reproduced here). In spite of the difference in wages, the prices still seem incredible.

211
William Jones was an itinerant craftsman—note the blank space on his bill, to be filled in with his temporary address. The old flint-lock was evidently still in use since he advertised 'Guns altered from Flints to Percussions . . .

212
One often complains about the low standard of some of the popular periodicals but they compare favourably with those of the Victorians. The Last Dying Confession broadsheets of the eighteenth century did not disappear until the middle of the nineteenth. Even then they survived in another, more sophisticated form as this advertisement shows.

213
Bone-setters have always been esteemed in the North of England and their numbers have declined only since the National Health Service came into being. There are still many old people who consider them more skilled in their particular speciality than the ordinary medical practitioner!

214
A sale of tropical birds is a rather unusual item.

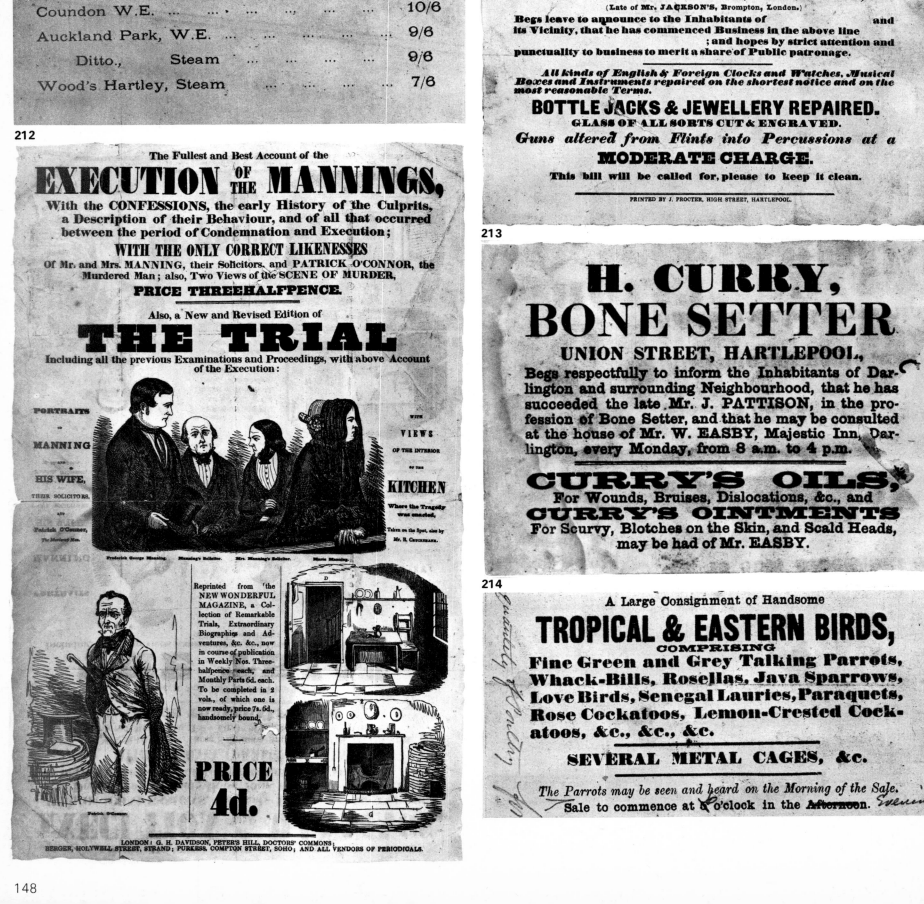

210

	Per Ton.
Tees W.E.	11/-
Coundon W.E.	10/6
Auckland Park, W.E.	9/6
Ditto., Steam	9/6
Wood's Hartley, Steam	7/6

211

WILLIAM JONES
CLOCK & WATCH MAKER, ENGRAVER, &c.
(Late of Mr. JACKSON'S, Brompton, London.)
Begs leave to announce to the Inhabitants of and its Vicinity, that he has commenced Business in the above line ; and hopes by strict attention and punctuality to business to merit a share of Public patronage.

All kinds of English & Foreign Clocks and Watches, Musical Boxes and Instruments repaired on the shortest notice and on the most reasonable Terms.

BOTTLE JACKS & JEWELLERY REPAIRED.
GLASS OF ALL SORTS CUT & ENGRAVED.
Guns altered from Flints into Percussions at a
MODERATE CHARGE.
This bill will be called for, please to keep it clean.

PRINTED BY J. PROCTER, HIGH STREET, HARTLEPOOL.

212

The Fullest and Best Account of the
EXECUTION OF THE MANNINGS,
With the CONFESSIONS, the early History of the Culprits, a Description of their Behaviour, and of all that occurred between the period of Condemnation and Execution;
WITH THE ONLY CORRECT LIKENESSES
Of Mr. and Mrs. MANNING, their Solicitors, and PATRICK O'CONNOR, the Murdered Man; also, Two Views of the SCENE OF MURDER,
PRICE THREEHALFPENCE.

Also, a New and Revised Edition of
THE TRIAL
Including all the previous Examinations and Proceedings, with above Account of the Execution:

PORTRAITS OF MANNING AND HIS WIFE, THEIR SOLICITORS, AND Patrick O'Conner, The Murdered Man.

WITH VIEWS OF THE INTERIOR OF THE KITCHEN Where the Tragedy was enacted, Taken on the Spot, also by Mr. R. Cruikshank.

Reprinted from the NEW WONDERFUL MAGAZINE, a Collection of Remarkable Trials, Extraordinary Biographies and Adventures, &c. &c., now in course of publication in Weekly Nos. Threehalfpence each, and Monthly Parts 6d. each. To be completed in 2 vols., of which one is now ready, price 7s. 6d., handsomely bound.

PRICE
4d.

LONDON: G. H. DAVIDSON, PETER'S HILL, DOCTORS' COMMONS; BERGER, HOLYWELL STREET, STRAND; PURKESS, COMPTON STREET, SOHO; AND ALL VENDORS OF PERIODICALS.

213

H. CURRY,
BONE SETTER
UNION STREET, HARTLEPOOL,
Begs respectfully to inform the Inhabitants of Darlington and surrounding Neighbourhood, that he has succeeded the late Mr. J. PATTISON, in the profession of Bone Setter, and that he may be consulted at the house of Mr. W. EASBY, Majestic Inn, Darlington, every Monday, from 8 a.m. to 4 p.m.

CURRY'S OILS,
For Wounds, Bruises, Dislocations, &c., and
CURRY'S OINTMENTS
For Scurvy, Blotches on the Skin, and Scald Heads, may be had of Mr. EASBY.

214

A Large Consignment of Handsome
TROPICAL & EASTERN BIRDS,
COMPRISING
Fine Green and Grey Talking Parrots, Whack-Bills, Rosellas, Java Sparrows, Love Birds, Senegal Lauries, Paraquets, Rose Cockatoos, Lemon-Crested Cockatoos, &c., &c., &c.
SEVERAL METAL CAGES, &c.

The Parrots may be seen and heard on the Morning of the Sale.
Sale to commence at ~~2~~ o'clock in the ~~Afternoon~~. Evening

11

Be Warned and Informed

FELONS
NOTICE
ABSCONDED
MAD DOG

At the beginning of Queen Victoria's reign most public services were carried out by various individuals in the community, either as private acts of charity and goodwill or because they had been elected into the office by their fellow parishioners. The Parish Constable saw that the few regulations laid down by the Justices of the Peace were observed and called on his neighbours to help him out if the need arose. The whole parish helped to put out fires, and perhaps the shoemaker or dame taught the children the elements of reading and writing in return for a few coppers. In most small towns and villages the poor and needy and the sick and aged were relieved by a neighbourly concern for their welfare, and a system of outdoor relief.

The first break with this centuries-old system came with the Poor Law Amendment Act of 1834 which grouped parishes into unions under Boards of Guardians and attempted to stop all outdoor relief and confine all paupers to the workhouse. This met with determined opposition, especially in the industrial North of England. The working classes believed that the new poor law was a law to punish poverty and many northern communities persisted in giving outdoor relief. Indignation was widespread. Charles Dickens satirised the new Boards of Guardians and their workhouses in 1838 in 'Oliver Twist'.

With the change in social conditions brought about by the growth of the industrial towns new problems emerged. The strangers with no urban roots were probably responsible for a good deal of the pilfering and wanton damage committed in the surrounding districts; and the riotous, disorderly, and drunken assemblies of truculent navvies could not be dispersed by aged Parish Constables. Throughout England substantial citizens banded themselves together into Associations for the Prosecution of Felons in which, for a modest fee, they obtained the real security of having their names published as members of an association which would prosecute vigorously whoever committed any trespass, robbery, or damage on the property or persons of those on its books, and pay a substantial reward to those who assisted in securing the malefactors.

A great deal was still left to private enterprise and so there were many occasions for appeal to the public. These were sometimes made by announcements in the newspapers but, as these were expensive and only appeared weekly, it was more usual to have urgent and more parochial announcements 'called' by the Town Crier or printed on posters and displayed on gateposts and fences where they could be read by passers by. Public meetings were often called in this way to discuss methods of raising funds to succour the victims of calamities. There were a number of mining disasters and, on the coast, there were frequent wrecks; the bereaved families were relieved by public subscription.

The Victorians were practical and charitable and adept at organising soup kitchens and friendly societies to help improvident families. They were also sentimental and who would deny them the luxury of indulging the softer side of their nature if they were prepared to pay for it out of their own pockets? Drinking fountains with carved spouts and surmounted by whimsical or pious inscriptions were not exactly a necessity for the weary wayfarer but they added to the pleasure of a country stroll.

Nowadays, when cremation is popular there are many who have no memorial. This was a situation of which no good Victorian could bear to think. The tattoo marks traditionally linked with the sailor were originally designed to serve a practical purpose. In the event of his death by drowning they provided an additional means of identifying the body and, when the corpse was unrecognisable because of the battering it had received from the rocks or the length of time it had been in the water, these marks often remained.

A deeprooted and earnest desire existed among the fisher folk to recover the bodies of their dead and to give them a decent burial. In most coastal churchyards rest the bones of mariners washed up by the sea, unknown by name to those who worship in the church.

At election times the hoardings must have presented fascinating reading material, for candidates and their opponents wrote and published things about each other which today no printer could be coaxed to set up in type. Much of the material was amusing and ingenious in the way in which it was presented to the public. Lists of candidates would be made out as racehorses with highly libellous pedigrees, or entered on a playbill as dramatis personae. Some bills are so amusing that they bring their authenticity into doubt. The 'Special Notice' on page 153 is a case in point. We can scarcely imagine the Victorians having such a sense of humour and yet this notice was posted on the wall in a public house in the 1870s. The notices about cholera and mad dogs must have been quite terrifying. Not since the Great Plague of London had there been any major epidemics, but in the crowded insanitary slums of the industrial towns with inadequate drains and polluted wells there arose the same conditions as in the London of Charles II and with similar dire results. Fortunately the increased medical knowledge gained in the intervening centuries, and prompt measures taken by the authorities, prevented anything quite as disastrous as happened in 1666 but it was a long time before the ignorant population could be persuaded that the closing of their wells and the provision of taps was anything other than a cunning way of bolstering up the profits of water companies.

Many and various are the occasional announcements to be found on Victorian hoardings. Those reproduced here represent but a very small proportion of the ones available, bills which must have provided amusement and sorrow for many a literate workman and a readymade opportunity of learning to read for illiterates anxious to improve themselves.

215
Such pitiful notices were only too common in the days of the collier brigs, and a self-respecting family would leave no stone unturned nor spare any expense to recover the body of a dear one lost at sea. Even if the body was not recovered the full details of his loss, with the name of his ship, would be inscribed on the family headstone as his memorial.

216
A notice which we find very amusing today but which local innkeepers would have taken more seriously.

217
The Surveyors of the Highways warn vagrants to get out of the town. It is rather amusing to note the way in which they seek to avoid the censure of their friends and neighbours over the small matter of the threat to prosecute those who left carts in the streets, by adding to the announcement 'By order of the General Vestry.'

218
This notice of the impudent theft of the official notice boards reflects the period of anarchy through which Hartlepool was passing at this time. The old Corporation was a corrupt one and had been suppressed in 1834 leaving the town with no controlling civic authority. In 1837 the parish council, or the Vestry, is in control. This reward is offered by two of its late officials.

219
The sting in this apparently normal advertisement for a missing man lies in its tail. Unless the Victorians were very different from us the casual addition that the man 'is insane' is hardly likely to encourage people to go looking for him.

215

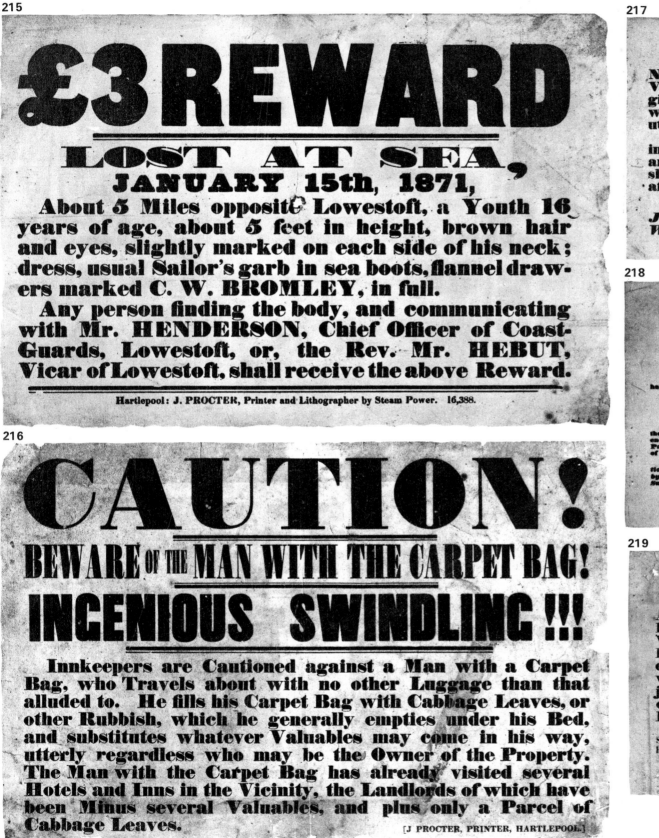

£3 REWARD

LOST AT SEA,

JANUARY 15th, 1871,

About 5 Miles opposite Lowestoft, a Youth 16 years of age, about 5 feet in height, brown hair and eyes, slightly marked on each side of his neck; dress, usual Sailor's garb in sea boots, flannel drawers marked C. W. BROMLEY, in full.

Any person finding the body, and communicating with Mr. HENDERSON, Chief Officer of Coast-Guards, Lowestoft, or, the Rev. Mr. HEBUT, Vicar of Lowestoft, shall receive the above Reward.

Hartlepool: J. PROCTER, Printer and Lithographer by Steam Power. 16,388.

216

CAUTION!

BEWARE OF THE MAN WITH THE CARPET BAG!

INGENIOUS SWINDLING!!!

Innkeepers are Cautioned against a Man with a Carpet Bag, who Travels about with no other Luggage than that alluded to. He fills his Carpet Bag with Cabbage Leaves, or other Rubbish, which he generally empties under his Bed, and substitutes whatever Valuables may come in his way, utterly regardless who may be the Owner of the Property. The Man with the Carpet Bag has already visited several Hotels and Inns in the Vicinity, the Landlords of which have been Minus several Valuables, and plus only a Parcel of Cabbage Leaves.

[J PROCTER, PRINTER, HARTLEPOOL.]

217

VAGRANTS.

Notice is hereby given, that all Vagrants found Strolling or Begging in the Township of Hartlepool will be prosecuted according to the utmost rigor of the Law.

And all Persons leaving Carts in the Streets, or committing Nuisances in any part of the said Township, will likewise be prosecuted after this notice.

By order of the General Vestry.

Johnson Worthy,
William Sotheran, } *Surveyors.*

Hartlepool, June 13th 1837.

From the Office of J. PROCTER, High Street, Hartlepool.

218

FIVE SHILLINGS
REWARD.

Whereas some malicious and evil designed Person or Persons, have feloniously taken taken down and carried away, TWO LARGE

Boards,

the one placed upon the Town Hall, and the other placed upon the end of the Free School; and upon which an abstract of an Act of Parliament was painted to prevent nuisances &c. in the Township of Hartlepool.

Whoever will give such information as may lead to the conviction of the offender or offenders, shall, receive the above reward by applying to Mr. Robt. Humble, or, Mr. R. Watson, late Surveyors of the Highways for Hartlepool.

November 3rd, 1837.

J. PROCTER, PRINTER, HARTLEPOOL.

219

WHEREAS

A Sailor of the name of Jargen Kroger, left or strayed away, on Wednesday the 13th ult. from the Danish Vessel, Persina of Blankenese; he is about 40 years of age, walks slow, was dressed in a blue jacket, fustian trousers and waistcoat, scotch cap, cannot speak English and is insane.

Whoever finds him, and will bring him to Mr. Johnson, Seaham, or Mr. Sharp, Solicitor, Hartlepool, will be most handsomely rewarded for their trouble.

Seaham, 15th June, 1838.

From the Office of J. PROCTER, Hartlepool.

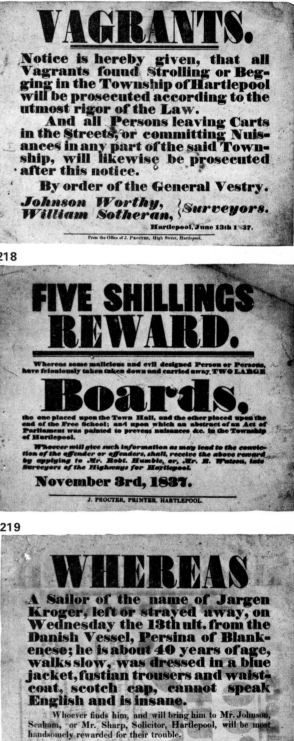

220
A typical reward notice of the period.

221 and 222
Here we see mediaeval and modern methods of obtaining justice side by side. It was said in 1816 that a court-baron and a court-leet were held twice a year in Hartlepool by the recorder, who was the steward of the borough. The grand jury presented all offences contrary to good order, and to the statutes and ordinances of the corporation. The court-leet took cognisance of all debts under 40 shillings and was of great advantage to the inhabitants who would otherwise have had to seek justice at Stockton or Durham. These manorial courts were concerned with the daily life and work of small communities, and breaches of the peace. At the court-leet ale-tasters, pounders, grass-men and inspectors of weights and measures were appointed. Men still accepted the principle of social obligation and service in these offices was compulsory and unpaid. The function of the jury was to declare the custom of the manor. In 1843 this court-leet was really an archaic survival of mediaeval days for its functions could be just as easily carried out by the Parish Vestry. The associations for the prosecution of felons have been described on page 150.

223
Another typical notice issued by the Surveyors of Highways.

224
It seems incredible that in a town like Hartlepool, situated on a peninsula of limestone where almost all the wells were so brackish that people went miles for sweet water, it took twenty years for them to secure an adequate supply of piped water (after the railway had come to the town).

220

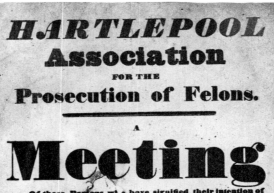

£2.
REWARD.
STOLEN
From a Dwelling House at Middleton, near Hartlepool, late on Monday Night or early on Tuesday Morning last, a small
Gold Watch
And Gold Chain, with a scrolled engine-turned Case, Silver Dial, and Horizontal Skeleton movement. The Gold Chain forms a square, with a slide containing a small Garnet Stone;—the shape of a hand, in gold, is fixed on it so as to attach the Guard to the Watch.

Whoever will bring the above to Mr. Humphreys, Watch Maker, Hartlepool, shall receive a Reward of Two Pounds.

Middleton, 28th Dec., 1842.

J. Procter, Printer, Hartlepool.

221

HARTLEPOOL
Association
FOR THE
Prosecution of Felons.
A
Meeting
Of those Persons who have signified their intention of uniting themselves into an ASSOCIATION FOR THE PROSECUTION OF FELONS, will be held in the TOWN HALL, on *Tuesday the 28th day of June*, at half past six in the Evening, to form Rules for its regulation; and it is particularly requested, that as many will attend as can make it convenient.

N. B. Such as feel disposed, but have not yet signified their intention of becoming Members of this Association, may still have an opportunity of doing so, by entering their names on the Signature-list, which lies at the Office of Mr. Procter, Bookseller, Hartlepool, before Tuesday Evening.

Hartlepool, June 25th, 1836.

From the Office of J. Procter, Hartlepool.

222

BOROUGH
OF
HARTLEPOOL
NOTICE IS HEREBY GIVEN,
That the COURT LEET with view of Frank Pledge, and Court Baron for the Borough of Hartlepool in the Bishoprick of Durham, will be holden and kept in the TOWN HALL in Hartlepool aforesaid, before Henry Stapylton, Esq., Barrister-at-Law, Steward of the said Courts (or his Deputy in his absence) on MONDAY, the 8th day of May next, at 11 o'clock in the Forenoon. All Resiants, Inhabitants, and other persons within the said Borough who owe suit and service to the said Courts respectively, are required to be and appear at the time and place aforesaid, then and there to do and perform their said suit and service.

BY ORDER,
THOMAS. BELK,
TOWN CLERK.

N. B. Summonses for the recovery of debts under Forty Shillings may be had at the Town Clerk's Office, until Thursday the 4th day of May next, inclusive.

Hartlepool, April 20th, 1843.

J. PROCTER, PRINTER, UNION PLACE, HARTLEPOOL.

223

HIGHWAYS.
WHEREAS,
Divers parts of the Streets and Highways in this Township have been broken up and injured. This is to give notice, that any parties who shall in future break up the said Street and Roads, without leave from the Surveyors, will be prosecuted with the utmost Rigour of the Law.

MATTHEW PEACOCK
THOMAS BIRD } SURVEYORS.

Hartlepool, 24th July, 1840.

FROM J. PROCTER'S OFFICE, HARTLEPOOL.

224

BEWARE!!
Beware of the clap-trap about cheap Gas and Water; the Borough has not gone to the expense of obtaining a New Charter to save half-a-crown a year in Gas and Water.

Beware OF THE LARGE HOLDERS OF PROPERTY, if you want to see how they will carry out the Health of Towns Act, go and ask the unfortunates who live in their houses, what they lay out in a year to make them fit for human beings to live in; and also, how much they have expended on the Streets and Drains.

BEWARE
OF SLAUGHTER HOUSES, DUNG-HILLS, and CESSPOOLS; Men connected with them WILL NOT DO!!!

Hartlepool, Dec. 14th, 1850.

From the Office of J. PROCTER, Printer, High Street, Hartlepool.

225
The first of Sir Robert Peel's new force established by his Police Bill of 1829 appeared in blue tailcoats and top-hats in September of that year. The municipal boroughs followed suit as the years passed but in county and rural districts it was not until 1856 that the establishment of a police force was no longer left to the discretion of the local Justices but became compulsory.

226
The army was not very popular for many years after the Napoleonic Wars. Until the Crimean War and the Indian Mutiny the ordinary citizen had little reason to consider an army necessary.

227
In most cases the mariners were both pilots and fishermen and most of the families were so intermarried that there would be few at the meeting who had not lost someone in the storm.

228
This poster is so amusing that one almost doubts its authenticity, yet it was posted on a public house wall in Hartlepool in the 1870s.

229
Although a local newspaper had existed since 1855 the Bellman or Town Crier still served a useful purpose among the illiterate workers.

225

TO THE
TAILORS & DRAPERS
OF HARTLEPOOL.

The Watch Committee of the Borough of Hartlepool
HEREBY GIVE NOTICE,
That they will, until Six, p. m., on the 23rd day of January instant, receive
TENDERS
For supplying the Constables of the said Borough with FROCK COATS, TROUSERS, CAPES, and HATS.

Samples may be seen at the Police Station; and further Information had of CHIEF CONSTABLE WATERS.

Tenders, marked "CONSTABLES' CLOTHING," to be sent to
Thomas Belk,
TOWN CLERK.
Town Clerk's Office, Hartlepool,
January 15th, 1858.

HARTLEPOOL: J. PROCTER, PRINTER, SOUTHGATE STREET.

226

V R
BOUNTY,
SIX POUNDS!!
Young Men from 18 to 35 Years of Age, 5 feet 4 inches high, and upwards, are invited to
VOLUNTEER
FOR THE
NORTH DURHAM
OR 43 REGIMENT OF
MILITIA
COMMANDED BY
THE RIGHT HON. THE EARL VANE.
They will Receive, in addition to Her Majesty's Bounty of Six Pounds, their Daily Pay, Rations, and Clothing.

Application to be made to the Recruiting Officer, at the King's Head Hotel, Hartlepool.
GOD SAVE THE QUEEN.

From the Office of J. PROCTER, Printer and Lithographer, Hartlepool and West Hartlepool.

227

A
PUBLIC
MEETING
WILL BE HELD IN THE
TOWN HALL,
ON
Tuesday Evening, at 7 o'clock,
To consider the best Means of supporting the Widows and their Families who lost their Husbands in the last Gale.
The Pilots and Fishermen, are particularly requested to attend.
THOMAS ROWELL,
MAYOR.
February 18th, 1843.

Printed at the Office of J. Procter, Hartlepool.

228

SPECIAL
NOTICE.

A man is specially engaged and kept in the back yard to do all the shouting, cursing and swearing, that is required in this establishment.

A dog is also kept to do all the barking.

Our fighting man or chucker-out has won 75 prize-fights, and is a splendid shot with a revolver.

An undertaker calls here every morning for orders.

C. B.

229

BOROUGH OF HARTLEPOOL.
NOTICE.
The Corporation are prepared to receive Applications and Tenders for the Office of
BELLMAN OR TOWN CRIER.
Sealed Tenders, addressed to the Town Clerk, stating the Amount that will be given per annum, to be sent in not later than 7, p.m., on the 17th inst., when the Applicants are requested to appear in person.

BOROUGH BUILDINGS,
14th February, 1870.
THOMAS BELK,
TOWN CLERK.

Hartlepool: J. PROCTER, Printer and Lithographer by Steam Power. 14,6/78.

230, 231, 232 and 232A
The local politics of Hartlepool were more confused in the early days of Victoria's reign than at any other time in its history. The ancient borough which received its charter from King John in 1201 fell into abeyance through neglect in 1834 and for six years the town was in a state of anarchy. Those years, unfortunately, were ones in which the town was expanding rapidly and the citizens petitioned for a new charter in order to obtain some sort of law and order. A new charter was granted in September, 1841, but great disappointment was felt because it was a simple renewal of the Elizabethan Charter and not one on the lines of the Municipal Act whereby the councillors would be freely elected. Public feeling was such that in 1850 another charter was applied for and it was granted in 1851. But the bitterness of the struggle was not forgotten and election notices were more than usually hard-hitting.

230

1874.

MUNICIPAL ELECTION.

NO. 2.

ELECTORS,

"An Old Elector" has called your attention to the forthcoming Election, and has described, in his view, the qualifications of the Four Candidates soliciting your suffrages. And in doing so, introduces,

FIRST.—Mr. Robert Walker, *"as a cautious spender of public money,"* with a recommendation that, as *MAYOR*, *"He has upheld the dignity and importance of this Ancient Borough."* He forgets, however, to tell you that Mr. Walker has been so cautious a spender of our money, that, as Mayor by his own Casting Vote, he gave to himself a Salary of £50 for the year of his Mayoralty, and also, that he was one of the parties who so well managed ("without fagging") the finances, as to incur a debt of about £3,000, the effect of which we have been and are now feeling in the *increased rates we pay.— "Do you not feel this?"*

SECOND.—Mr. W. J. Sivewright is described to be *"as well known as the Church Clock,"* who, with his active little body, always trotted incessantly in the interests of the Ratepayers. I need not call your attention to the fact, that the Town Clock is rarely correct, and cannot be relied upon as a true and satisfactory worker. Mr. Sivewright is also now engaged trotting about all day at West Hartlepool; and I would also like to ask An Old Elector what good he did when he was in the Council before? An Old Elector's views must be judged by his comparisons.

THIRD.—Mr. W. Bainbridge, described as not having any modesty, *did not a second time* ask our Votes until Mr. Sivewright, who was considerably below him on the Poll on the 2nd instant (notwithstanding HIS modesty), also again solicited our Votes. Mr. Bainbridge has, however, the modesty not to tell us that, by his business ability and attention, he has been able to invest in the Borough large sums of money in the purchase of property, and owns, in our midst, more property than any of the other Candidates before you; and whether supported by "Good Templars," "Publicans," or the general body of Ratepayers, his interest in the Borough is sufficient as a guarantee that he at any rate WILL NOT INCREASE OUR RATES.

FOURTH, AND LASTLY.—"Old Elector" has called attention very properly to the fact that we are sufficiently Hors(l)ey'd already. It will be for your consideration whether you will jockey the Hors(l)eys any more by voting for a mere *Boy*.

Fellow-Electors!—After a due consideration,

PLUMP FOR BAINBRIDGE!

Yours respectfully,

ANOTHER ELECTOR.

Hartlepool: J. PROCTER, Printer and Lithographer by Steam Power. 22,676.

231

ELECTORS OF HARTLEPOOL.

To the Rescue. Deliver your Borough from the hands of a Drunken and incompetent Council.

Think of at least three Honourable Gentlemen who had gone in with cringing promises of Economy, Diligence, &c., &c., being drunk at one time, and another filled to repletion, and oblivious of the external world.

Think of men pandering to the cry of a false Economy, till the Corporation is struck fast for funds; and when you are run upwards of £1,000 in Debt, and your Credit damaged, a deputation is sent off to beg the loan of £150 to pay Interest; it is for you to say when the misrule of the Borough shall cease, when drunken rows in the Town HALL shall end, when the paltry dribbling expenditure of your money, which gives you almost nothing in return, shall give place to an enlightened and comprehensive Economy, which, while careful of the true Interests of the Borough, shall give you Value for the Money you contribute to the Taxes of the Town.

In the approaching Election, beware of Men who come to you with the Address of a mean hireling, full of empty and unmeaning promises.

Value and support manly Independence; look carefully to the previous character of the Candidates, for Honesty, Truth, Sobriety, and Intelligence.

Good character is the best guarantee, that you will be faithfully served, and well Represented in the Council of the Borough.

True Men are now before you, Among such are STEPHEN ROBINSON, and WILLIAM GRAY, Rally round them, give them your support on the day of Election, Return them as your Representatives.

Slumbering Electors, "Awake, arise, or be for ever fallen."

I am, Gentlemen,

Yours faithfully,

Anglo-Saxon.

Hartlepool, Oct. 27, 1857.

J. PROCTER, PRINTER, HIGH ST

232

might not be done at first; but, remember, if you are once committed to this Measure, there are no means by which you can again have them in your own charge. If, therefore, a few years shewed an enormous increase in the Cost of the Police, you would have no remedy. Now, you can appoint, dismiss, reduce the Salary, or do any other thing you please with your Police,—then, you could do nothing. Look at France and Austria, to see how this sort of thing works. Would you like our Country to be like these? Remember the State Trials of thirty years ago;—see what an important part Government Spies played then, and decidedly that you will not have it so now! You happily have the remedy in your own hands. You have Four Men to send to the Council on Tuesday, who will be in time to Vote on Wednesday Night. Vote for no man who will not pledge himself to Oppose the obnoxious Measure. Attend the Meeting on Wednesday—mark the men who wish to make a change—and, as soon as you have an opportunity, turn them out.

232A

An attempt is going to be made in the Council on Wednesday Night, to take from you the Management of your Police, and to convert them into Government Spies, by incorporating them with the County Constabulary. When this Police Bill was before Parliament, you expressed in an unmistakable manner your abhorrence of the Measure, by the unanimous Vote at a Public Meeting. The Council also expressed themselves very strongly by sending a Deputation to London, to oppose the Bill. Now a Cuckoo-cry of Economy is got up; and your Liberty is to be wrested from you, with no means of again recovering it. Did you expect, when you sent these men to the Council, that they would confess their inability to manage the Police?—For this is what is meant by the cry of economy,—that our Council cannot do the work as well as Major White. But if they are unable to do this, is that any reason why they should hand over the management of the Police to some one else. No; let them confess their inability, and give place to better men. The Watch Committee have very full powers; and, if any faults are to be found with the Police Force at present, the blame rests with them, and the remedy is in their own hands. The money that is spent in Clothing, &c., for the Police, is now spent in the Town. Would it be so if Major

233
In earlier days it had been usual to make the matter clear to everybody by heading such notices 'Mad Dog'. It is doubtful whether this new title would have the same salutary effect.

234
The 'fearful havoc', which the Mayor refers to, was the death of 57 inhabitants in 1832 out of a total population of 1,400. It is unfortunate that notices of this sort did little to clear up the filthy mess and in 1849 the town again paid the penalty of neglect. The population had increased to 9,000 and 161 people died of cholera. It is notable that in four small streets which were cul-de-sacs, 61 of the deaths occurred, six times as many as the average for the other streets in the town.

235
It was only natural that people who failed to keep abreast of the wonders of modern science should find themselves confused about the exact purpose to which water closets could be put. They had to be instructed in their use and warned of the penalties of their abuse.

233

NOTICE!

WHEREAS,

HYDROPHOBIA

Has appeared in this Borough, and Death has resulted from the Bite of a Dog: AND WHEREAS, several Dogs are stated to have been Bitten, and many others are constantly Wandering about the Streets, apparently without any Owners, to the Danger and Annoyance of Passengers therein:

NOTICE IS HEREBY GIVEN

That all Dogs found in the Streets, without Owners, will be Taken Charge of by the Police; and, unless such Dogs are Claimed within Forty-eight Hours after Capture, they will be Destroyed.

Owners of Missing Dogs should apply at the Police Station.

GEORGE MOORE,

Hartlepool, July 15th, 1870. **MAYOR.**

Hartlepool: J. PROCTER, Printer and Lithographer by Steam Power, Southgate. 15,445.

234

NOTICE.

THOS. ROWELL, ESQ.,

MAYOR OF HARTLEPOOL,

Having, with a regard to the health of the inhabitants and to guard against the attacks of that dreadful disease, the Cholera, (which caused such fearful havoc here a few years ago, and which there is too much reason to suppose is again fast approaching our shores) surveyed the various streets, lanes, and yards, in this borough, and having found vast accumulations of filth and impurities of every description therein, hereby recommends the removal of the same forthwith to a distancee from the town; and he further solicits the inhabitants generally to co-operate with him in his exertions to promote cleanliness, and to have every source of contagion removed; bearing in mind the old proverb, that "to be forewarned is to be forearmed".

The Mayor will be glad to receive any communication from parties who have reason to complain, and it will be received confidentially. The police have received instructions from the Mayor to report, daily, any nuisance which may be found in the borough.

Hartlepool, May 30th, 1846.

Printed by J. PROCTER, Hartlepool.

235

CAUTION

All Tenants of Houses who have had Water Closets supplied, are hereby informed, that if any House Refuse, or other substance, be thrown into the Water Closets, proceedings will be taken against all who so offend, under the powers of the Local Board: and a

REWARD OF ONE POUND

will be paid, by the Owners of the Property, to any one who will give such Information as may lead to the Conviction of the Offender or Offenders.

BY ORDER OF

F. G. MORRIS,

Hartlepool, November, 1857. Surveyor to the Local Board.

HARTLEPOOL: J. PROCTER, PRINTER, HIGH STREET.

236
Most people were aware of the value of vaccination and this advertisement shows that the Board of Guardians was anxious to help the public and carry out a service not often associated with the rulers of the workhouse.

237
It must be remembered that at this time Hartlepool had no one in authority: the Corporation was in abeyance and no one assumed responsibility. This bill is an attempt to get the support of the inhabitants for an occasion of public rejoicing. For those readers to whom the phrase 'relieve the wants of the destitute' sounds horribly Dickensian, it should be added in fairness to the hospitable soul responsible for this poster that he proposed on part of the bill not reproduced here to 'regale the poor of this parish with meat, plum pudding, and ale'

238
Inhabitants of the North of England are notorious for their unembellished language and even as recently as twenty years ago a similar building in West Hartlepool was still known to the man in the street as the Dead House, although it always appeared in official reports as the Public Mortuary. It was used most frequently for those unfortunate enough to be killed on the railway or found drowned.

236

STOCKTON UNION.

GRATUITOUS

VACCINATION

It is requested that Parents of Children, and all other Persons, will TAKE NOTICE of the provisions made by the Act of the 3rd and 4th years of the reign of Queen Victoria, for THE EXTENSION OF VACCINATION WITH THE COW POX, and THE PREVENTION OF THE SPREAD OF SMALL POX; which latter Disease, chiefly in consequence of the want of due care, and the proceedings of ignorant individuals, has occasioned annually not only the DEATHS OF MANY THOUSAND PERSONS IN ENGLAND AND WALES, but has entailed Suffering and Permanent Disfigurement, and occasionally Loss of Sight, to a much larger number of Persons who have been attacked by the Disease, but have escaped Death.

Cow Pox is merely a mild form of Small Pox: VACCINATION WITH THE COW POX IS PERFECTLY FREE FROM DANGER, and either prevents or mitigates an attack of Small Pox. In nearly all the instances in which Small Pox has attacked Persons who have been Vaccinated, the Vaccination has been imperfectly performed, or the attack of Small Pox has been in a very mitigated Form, nearly free from Danger of Disfigurement or Danger to Life. By Vaccination being made universal, Small Pox would be entirely banished from the Country: to secure the benefits of Vaccination, it should be performed, and its progress watched, by a Medical Man.

For the Extension of Vaccination it is provided, under the authority of the Act, that the following duly authorized Medical Practitioners are appointed to Vaccinate Persons resident in this Union, without charge to such Persons:—

Names of the Medical Practioners who are the Public Vaccinators.	*Their Residences.*	*Days and Hours of Attendance for performing Vaccination thereat.*

237

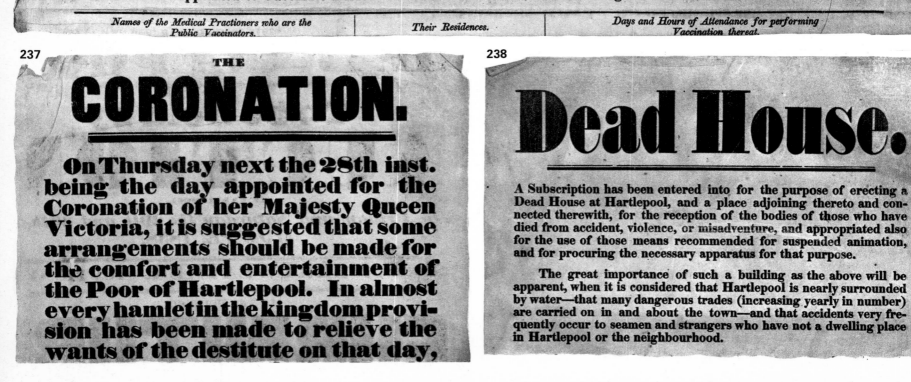

THE

CORONATION.

On Thursday next the 28th inst. being the day appointed for the Coronation of her Majesty Queen Victoria, it is suggested that some arrangements should be made for the comfort and entertainment of the Poor of Hartlepool. In almost every hamlet in the kingdom provision has been made to relieve the wants of the destitute on that day,

238

Dead House.

A Subscription has been entered into for the purpose of erecting a Dead House at Hartlepool, and a place adjoining thereto and connected therewith, for the reception of the bodies of those who have died from accident, violence, or misadventure, and appropriated also for the use of those means recommended for suspended animation, and for procuring the necessary apparatus for that purpose.

The great importance of such a building as the above will be apparent, when it is considered that Hartlepool is nearly surrounded by water—that many dangerous trades (increasing yearly in number) are carried on in and about the town—and that accidents very frequently occur to seamen and strangers who have not a dwelling place in Hartlepool or the neighbourhood.

12 Dead and Buried

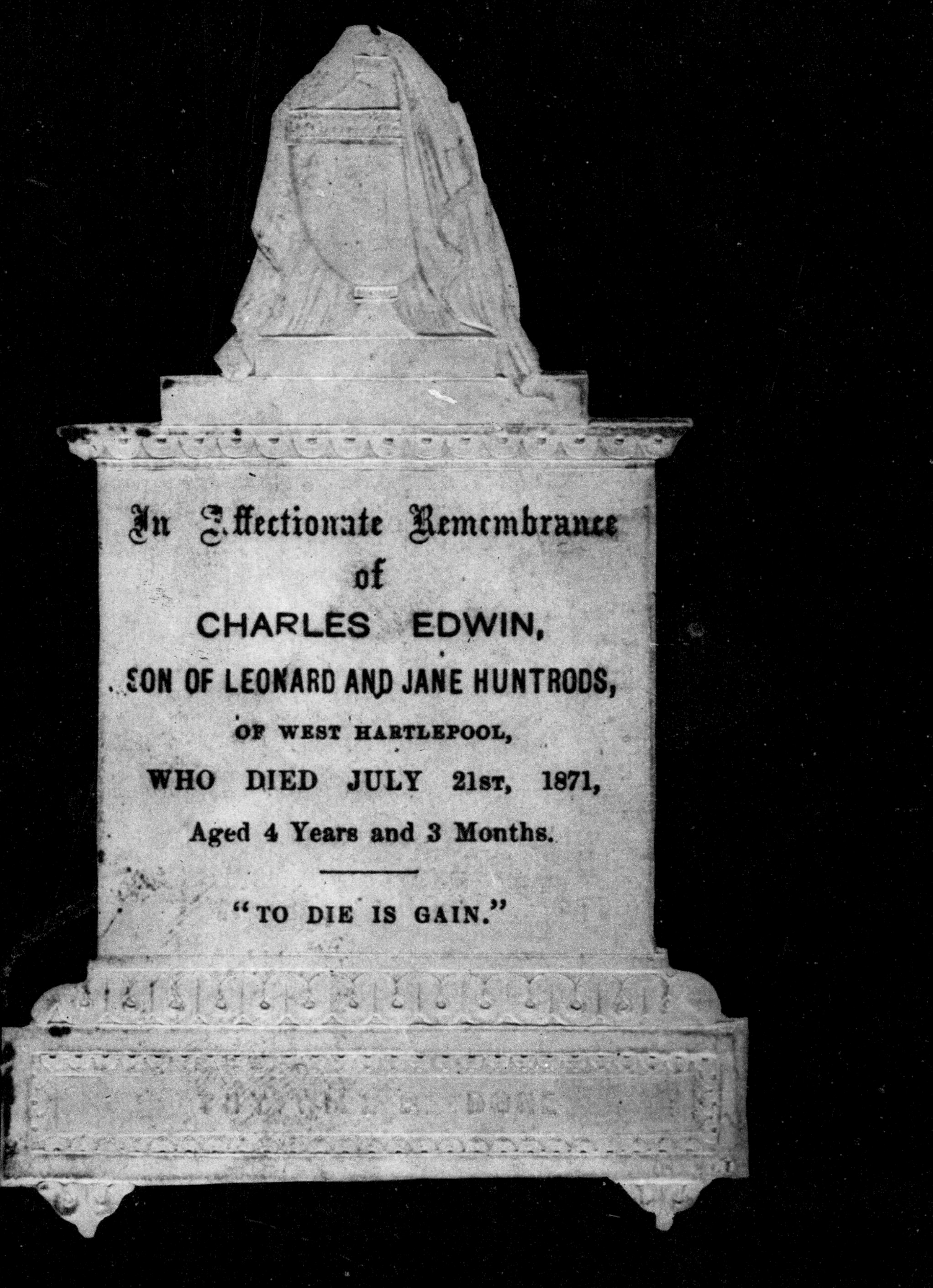

In Affectionate Remembrance
of
CHARLES EDWIN,
SON OF LEONARD AND JANE HUNTRODS,
OF WEST HARTLEPOOL,
WHO DIED JULY 21st, 1871,
Aged 4 Years and 3 Months.
"TO DIE IS GAIN."

The Victorians are often censured for taking what appears to be a morbid pleasure in the panoply of death. This judgement may be unjust and appearances may be deceptive. Mistaken ideas may have been formed because their lives were surrounded by the conventional emblems of bereavement—widow's weeds, black-edged visiting cards, note paper and envelopes, memorial cards, and extravagant obsequies.
The fashions and habits of the upper classes have notoriously been copied by the lower classes after a lapse of time. The funerals of the aristocracy of the late seventeenth century, and more especially those of the eighteenth century, were occasions of great ostentation with displays of funeral hatchments, torchlight processions, escorts of mutes, and gifts of mourning rings, scarves and gloves. The middle classes of the nineteenth century who continued this fashion in a minor form were only aping their 'betters' of a previous generation.
Moreover, the Victorian Age was the first in which a large proportion of the babies born survived infancy. Victorian families were large and therefore death was commonplace. Funerals were the most likely occasions at which all the members of the family would make a most determined effort to be present to pay their last respects. They came from far and near and some of the journeys must have taken many hours. It was imperative, therefore, that they should be provided with a substantial meal. Those who boasted that they had 'buried him with ham' were proud of the fact that they had performed a necessary duty well. Ostentation had no part in it. As the meal invariably took place after the funeral, and often many of those present had not seen each other for some time, they took advantage of the

239

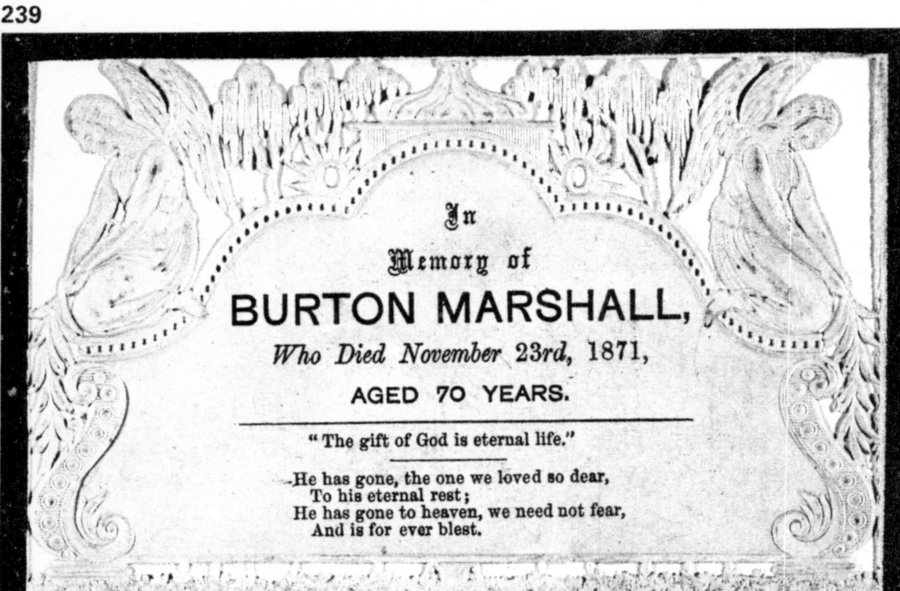

In Memory of
BURTON MARSHALL,
Who Died November 23rd, 1871,
AGED 70 YEARS.

"The gift of God is eternal life."

He has gone, the one we loved so dear,
To his eternal rest;
He has gone to heaven, we need not fear,
And is for ever blest.

242

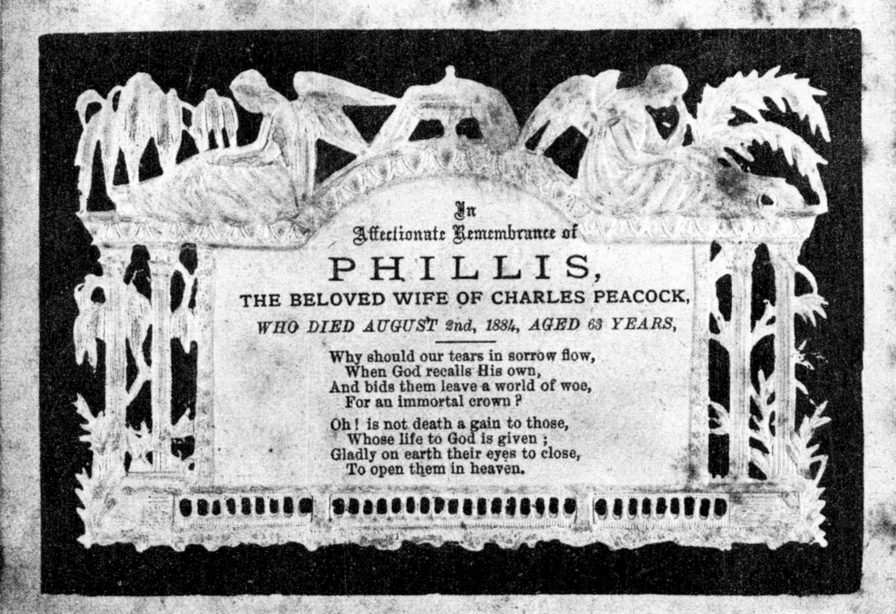

In Affectionate Remembrance of
PHILLIS,
THE BELOVED WIFE OF CHARLES PEACOCK,
WHO DIED AUGUST 2nd, 1884, AGED 63 YEARS,

Why should our tears in sorrow flow,
When God recalls His own,
And bids them leave a world of woe,
For an immortal crown?

Oh! is not death a gain to those,
Whose life to God is given;
Gladly on earth their eyes to close,
To open them in heaven.

240

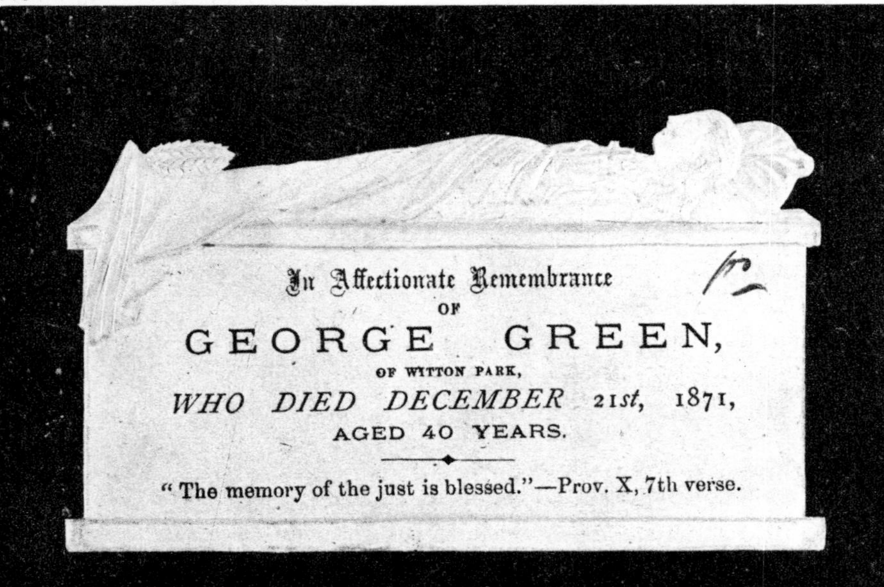

In Affectionate Remembrance
OF
GEORGE GREEN,
OF WITTON PARK,
WHO DIED DECEMBER 21st, 1871,
AGED 40 YEARS.

"The memory of the just is blessed."—Prov. X, 7th verse.

241

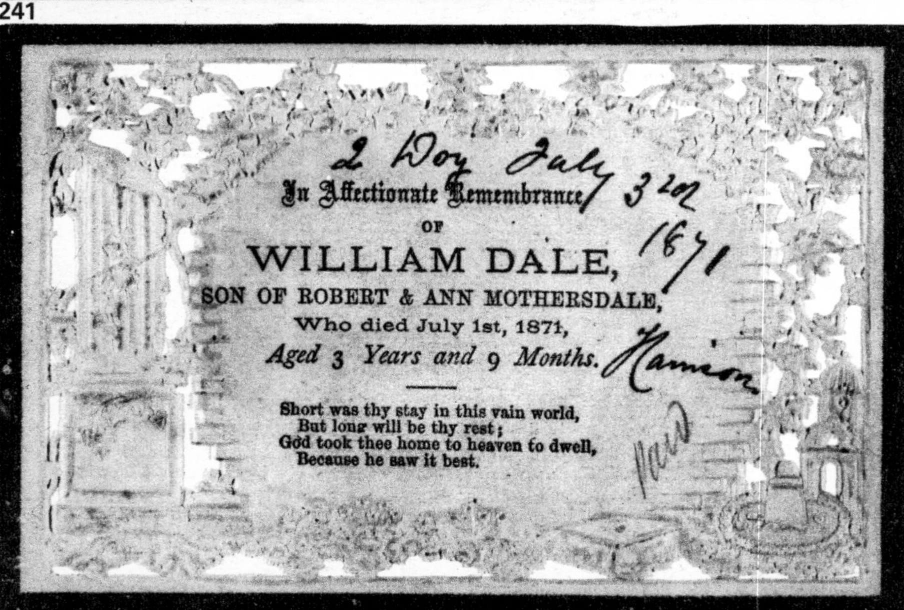

2 Doy July 3 2d
In Affectionate Remembrance
OF
WILLIAM DALE,
SON OF ROBERT & ANN MOTHERSDALE,
Who died July 1st, 1871,
Aged 3 Years and 9 Months.
1871
Harrison

Short was thy stay in this vain world,
But long will be thy rest;
God took thee home to heaven to dwell,
Because he saw it best.

243

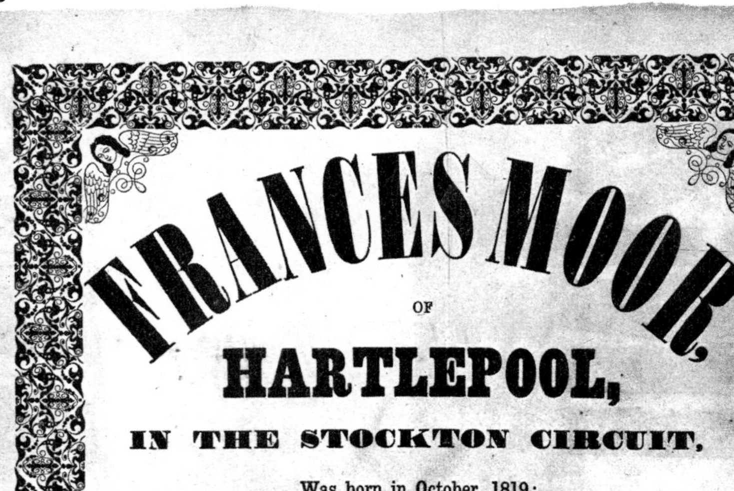

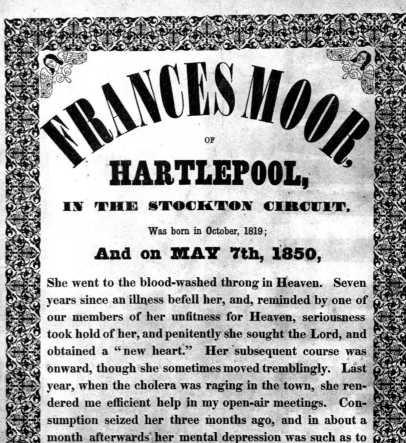

FRANCES MOOR,
OF
HARTLEPOOL,
IN THE STOCKTON CIRCUIT,
Was born in October, 1819;
And on MAY 7th, 1850,

She went to the blood-washed throng in Heaven. Seven years since an illness befell her, and, reminded by one of our members of her unfitness for Heaven, seriousness took hold of her, and penitently she sought the Lord, and obtained a "new heart." Her subsequent course was onward, though she sometimes moved tremblingly. Last year, when the cholera was raging in the town, she rendered me efficient help in my open-air meetings. Consumption seized her three months ago, and in about a month afterwards her mental depression was such as to inspire all her friends with sorrowful sympathy on her behalf. My soul was much bowed down on her account; but, to my surprise and joy, when I entered her room about a fortnight before her death, she exclaimed, "Heaven's my home!" Her future experience was quite satisfactory. As she neared the eternal world she said, "I see my way clearly. Come, Jesus! I am ready;" and with that assurance she departed.

opportunity to exchange family news and express delight or sorrow depending on each other's circumstances. No wonder that to outsiders it often appeared a festive occasion.

The early death of the Prince Consort and the deep and long-continued mourning of the Widow of Windsor set the seal of approval on long and extravagantly displayed periods of mourning. Black and purple gowns and bonnets, with accessories and jewellery of similar hues, became the mode, and Whitby jet, worked into beads, bracelets, and brooches had a long period of popularity. It was an age which delighted in keepsakes and it was not thought barbaric to have a tress of hair cut from the head of the dear departed and cunningly woven or spun into a watch chain.

The newly-acquired literacy and even the discoveries of science were employed to extend the methods by which the memory of the dead could be preserved. Large and sumptuously bound family bibles appeared complete with brightly decorated inserts in which to inscribe the births, marriages, and deaths of the family. It was considered most proper for photograpns of the family headstones to be framed and hung on the walls of the home. The early Victorian memorial cards with their cut-out and embossed figures of angels and funeral monuments and mourning widows are a pleasant form of commercial art sufficiently archaic to have that special sort of charm which will no doubt sooner or later cause them to be seized by collectors who now seem scarcely aware of their existence. Verses such as 243 and 244 were frequently written and printed, full of false sentiment and mawkish emotion. They are probably the most unlikeable products of the Victorian era.

244

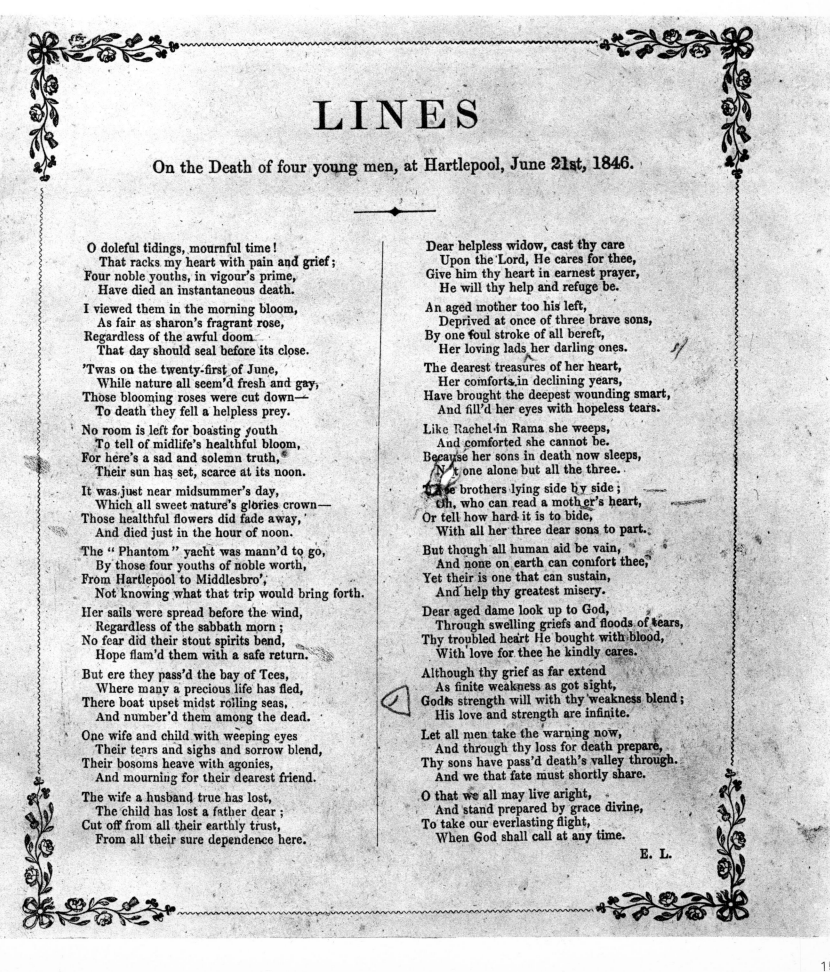

LINES

On the Death of four young men, at Hartlepool, June 21st, 1846.

O doleful tidings, mournful time!
That racks my heart with pain and grief;
Four noble youths, in vigour's prime,
Have died an instantaneous death.

I viewed them in the morning bloom,
As fair as sharon's fragrant rose,
Regardless of the awful doom
That day should seal before its close.

'Twas on the twenty-first of June,
While nature all seem'd fresh and gay,
Those blooming roses were cut down—
To death they fell a helpless prey.

No room is left for boasting youth
To tell of midlife's healthful bloom,
For here's a sad and solemn truth,
Their sun has set, scarce at its noon.

It was just near midsummer's day,
Which all sweet nature's glories crown—
Those healthful flowers did fade away,
And died just in the hour of noon.

The "Phantom" yacht was mann'd to go,
By those four youths of noble worth,
From Hartlepool to Middlesbro',
Not knowing what that trip would bring forth.

Her sails were spread before the wind,
Regardless of the sabbath morn;
No fear did their stout spirits bend,
Hope flam'd them with a safe return.

But ere they pass'd the bay of Tees,
Where many a precious life has fled,
There boat upset midst rolling seas,
And number'd them among the dead.

One wife and child with weeping eyes
Their tears and sighs and sorrow blend,
Their bosoms heave with agonies,
And mourning for their dearest friend.

The wife a husband true has lost,
The child has lost a father dear;
Cut off from all their earthly trust,
From all their sure dependence here.

Dear helpless widow, cast thy care
Upon the Lord, He cares for thee,
Give him thy heart in earnest prayer,
He will thy help and refuge be.

An aged mother too his left,
Deprived at once of three brave sons,
By one foul stroke of all bereft,
Her loving lads her darling ones.

The dearest treasures of her heart,
Her comforts in declining years,
Have brought the deepest wounding smart,
And fill'd her eyes with hopeless tears.

Like Rachel in Rama she weeps,
And comforted she cannot be.
Because her sons in death now sleeps,
Not one alone but all the three.

These brothers lying side by side;
Oh, who can read a mother's heart,
Or tell how hard it is to bide,
With all her three dear sons to part.

But though all human aid be vain,
And none on earth can comfort thee,
Yet their is one that can sustain,
And help thy greatest misery.

Dear aged dame look up to God,
Through swelling griefs and floods of tears,
Thy troubled heart He bought with blood,
With love for thee he kindly cares.

Although thy grief as far extend
As finite weakness as got sight,
God's strength will with thy weakness blend;
His love and strength are infinite.

Let all men take the warning now,
And through thy loss for death prepare,
Thy sons have pass'd death's valley through,
And we that fate must shortly share.

O that we all may live aright,
And stand prepared by grace divine,
To take our everlasting flight,
When God shall call at any time.

E. L.

Index

References to illustrations are indicated by italics

7/5063 44408 PR4244